Getting Started with Taipy

The definitive guide to creating production-ready
Python applications for data professionals

Eric Narro

‹packt›

Getting Started with Taipy

Portfolio Director: Sunith Shetty

Relationship Lead: Nilesh Kowadkar

Project Manager: Shashank Desai

Content Engineer: Gowri Rekha

Technical Editor: Seemanjay Ameriya

Copy Editor: Safis Editing

Indexer: Rekha Nair

Proofreader: Gowri Rekha

Production Designer: Nilesh Mohite

Growth Lead: Merlyn M Shelley

First published: September 2025
Production reference: 1170925

Published by Packt Publishing Ltd.
Grosvenor House
11 St Paul's Square
Birmingham
B3 1RB, UK.

ISBN 978-1-83620-381-0

www.packtpub.com

I'd like to dedicate this book to the people I love most:

Poppy, my awesome wife; my parents, Ilde and Josiane, who did their best; and Adrian, my amazing brother.

A heartfelt thank you to the team at Packt. It was a long adventure, but I truly enjoyed working with you: Paridhi, Gowri, Nilesh, Shambhavi, and everyone I didn't get a chance to meet.

Special thanks to Alvaro, Aurélien, and Laurent for your valuable reviews; to all the team at Taipy for answering my questions when I had them; and to Irv, Zac, and the team at Les Mousquetaires for letting me interview them.

Finally, thanks to the group in Bergerac: I wouldn't be who I am today without you.

– Eric Narro

Contributors

About the author

Eric Narro is a data analyst and Python enthusiast with experience in both insurance and agriculture. His journey began in the wine industry, where the absence of digital tools led him to explore solutions using QGIS and Python. This practical need awoke in him a deeper interest in programming, which he pursued through structured learning (several MOOCs, and one year of remote university studies in computer science). Along the way, he developed several applied projects that helped him build the skills and confidence to successfully transition into the tech industry.

In 2022, he discovered Taipy, fell in love with its concept, and quickly became an active contributor. He has written several Medium articles on Taipy's main components, and frequently uses Taipy to develop prototypes, dashboards, chatbots, and other specialized apps.

About the reviewers

Laurent Berder is a data scientist at ORUS, with 10 years of experience in the field of data science applied to various industries (automotive, maritime trade, manufacturing, and airline), as well as a previous life of 10 years as a human resources officer. He is now bringing his expertise to a satellite building and operating company in order to uncover a wealth of knowledge from hyperspectral images through the development of specialized domain-specific models.

Alvaro Fernandez is a developer specializing in backend systems, IoT, and software architecture, with over 10 years of experience delivering innovative solutions for clients including Sephora, L'Oréal, Nestlé, and Nissan, among others. Passionate about building intelligent and interactive systems, he is currently focused on developing autonomous IoT solutions controlled by AI agents. He is the creator of DOMIoT.org (Document Object Model for IoT), an open framework that leverages the HTML and JavaScript DOM to build interactive physical systems, with applications such as connected homes, security systems, and logistics solutions. Alvaro also founded Codidactic.com, a platform that teaches children programming and robotics through play, and has authored several educational workbooks and games.

Aurélien Amblard is a data science and AI engineer with 17 years of experience in analytics, data engineering, and governance. He specializes in data warehousing, BI, and applied AI, helping organizations transform decision support systems. At PRO BTP, he led a multidisciplinary team for five years, overseeing ELT, dashboards, and GDPR compliance. Previously, he spent over 10 years at Allianz across multiple roles—controlling, marketing, sales, and head of data innovation and governance for a P&C department—demonstrating versatility while building specific data marts and delivering data science initiatives in accordance with business objectives. Aurélien focuses on bridging business priorities with robust data architectures, strengthening governance, and scaling AI/analytics for measurable business outcomes. His commitment to continuous learning underpins a pragmatic, ethical approach to delivering resilient, value-driven data solutions.

Table of Contents

Part 1: Understanding Taipy and Its Components

1

2

Creating User Interfaces with Taipy   25

3

Connecting to Data Sources with Data Nodes   57

4

Orchestrating Taipy Applications   73

5

Managing Scenarios with Taipy   91

6

Deploying Your Taipy Applications   109

Part 2: Building Real-World Applications with Taipy

7

Taipy for Finance: Sales Forecasting and BI Reports   125

8

Taipy for Logistics: Creating Supply Chain Management Apps   147

9

Taipy for Urban Planning: Creating a Satellite Image App   171

10

Building an LLM Chatbot with Taipy   203

Part 3: Advanced Taipy: Building Efficient and Complex Apps

11

12

13

Creating Real-Time Apps with Taipy   271

14

Embedding Iframes in Taipy Applications   289

15

Exploring Taipy Designer (Enterprise Version)   303

Preface

Taipy is an open source Python library that allows users to build data applications and bring them to production environments. As an application builder, it offers a simple API to create dashboards, machine learning applications, chatbots, and many other types of applications.

What sets Taipy apart from other libraries is all the abstractions it brings to make your apps production-ready. For instance, the state management creates new user sessions, by default, for each new app connection, making it suitable for collaboration by design. It also brings abstractions to control the behavior of the page and its elements (you can activate and deactivate parts or the whole page, based on specific events), or to handle long-running callbacks without needing to manually handle async Python or threads.

On top of these abstractions, Taipy also brings Scenario Management capabilities that allow AB testing and scenario comparison, two common tasks in enterprise and BI environments. This book covers this concept extensively.

Finally, as Taipy is a Flask-based application builder, you can deploy it as any other Flask application in production environments.

This book has three distinct parts. First, we present the basic components of Taipy, from the main visual elements to how to set up complete Scenario Management pipelines and scenario comparison; this part also covers how to deploy your applications. In the next four chapters, we create more realistic applications of different types, such as time series analysis, optimization, and geographical or chatbot apps; the goal of this part is to give you use case ideas while helping you master the basic concepts and introducing advanced ones. The third and last part of the book focuses on advanced concepts and use cases to make the applications more efficient, or to use Taipy with edge cases, such as IoT components, or to handle large volumes of data.

Who this book is for

This book is for data analysts, data scientists, and BI experts who need to build complete data applications using Python. If your scripts and models aren't being used, Taipy helps you integrate them into applications for end users quickly and easily.

Whether you are creating prototypes, proofs of concept, or robust, scalable systems, Taipy can help you. This book will also be valuable for developers and engineers who want to streamline their data workflows without relying on a stack other than Python.

What this book covers

Chapter 1, Discovering Taipy, gives a broad overview of Taipy and its main components. This chapter guides you through installing Taipy and creating your first minimal applications.

Chapter 2, Creating User Interfaces with Taipy, shows you how to create a GUI with Taipy. You'll be able to create basic applications with Taipy thanks to this chapter alone!

Chapter 3, Connecting to Data Sources with Data Nodes, shows you how to use Data Nodes. Data Nodes provide an abstraction to connect with your data (inputs, outputs, and intermediate steps). They are important components of Scenario Management pipelines, but you can also use them alone.

Chapter 4, Orchestrating Taipy Applications, shows you how to create and orchestrate Scenario Management pipelines with Taipy. You'll learn how to configure and link Data Nodes and tasks together to create scenarios.

Chapter 5, Managing Scenarios with Taipy, explains how to use the scenarios and compare them to each other using a classic machine learning example.

Chapter 6, Deploying Your Taipy Applications, explains how to deploy Taipy applications in a variety of contexts, such as Linux-based servers, a cloud service (Google Cloud), and Docker containers.

Chapter 7, Taipy for Finance: Sales Forecasting and BI Reports, guides you through the steps to create a complete forecasting application. This example invites you to consider factors beyond Taipy's API that will contribute to your app's success (such as data modeling or how to choose your data sources). This example will also show you how to put time series models and comparison tools in the hands of final users.

Chapter 8, Taipy for Logistics: Creating Supply Chain Management Apps, illustrates the use of Taipy with optimization models. This guided tutorial shows how to use Taipy to set parameters and constraints to create optimal scenarios and compare the outcomes based on the assumptions.

Chapter 9, Taipy for Urban Planning: Creating a Satellite Image App, shows how to use Taipy with external compute servers (in this case, the European Space Agency) and how to compare scenarios based on satellite image data.

Chapter 10, Building an LLM Chatbot with Taipy, explains how to use Taipy to create a chatbot. You'll discover the chat visual element and ways to interact with LLMs from different UI components.

Chapter 11, Improving the Performance of Taipy Applications, shows methods and components you can use to make your applications run faster. We also cover components to use to run long-running callbacks to make your apps run smoothly.

Chapter 12, Handling Large Data in Taipy Applications, discusses how to use tools to handle large amounts of data with Taipy, including Spark or Dask. This chapter also shows you some options from Taipy charts that help you visualize large amounts of data effectively.

Chapter 13, Creating Real-Time Apps with Taipy, shows how to set up long-running callbacks to poll data, or even to stream it. This chapter shows how Taipy can adapt to different data acquisition and data update techniques, from batch updates for reporting to near-real-time and real-time applications for IoT or any real-time monitoring needs.

Chapter 14, Embedding Iframes in Taipy Applications, explains how to embed iframes in your Taipy applications. The use of iframes allows simple integrations (such as PDF documents or YouTube videos), but it also allows you to integrate Python libraries that output HTML components (such as Folium), and even to create your own custom JavaScript-based components.

Chapter 15, Exploring Taipy Designer (Enterprise Version), discusses Taipy Enterprise, the business subscription offer from Taipy. This chapter shows how to use Taipy Designer, a no-code component of Taipy Enterprise that allows users to create drag-and-drop UIs.

Chapter 16, Who Uses Taipy?, introduces you to three Taipy users. You'll discover projects that made it into production, and you'll see what users value the most when using Taipy.

To get the most out of this book

Taipy is a Python library designed for teams that manipulate data using Python to take their models, algorithms, and visual representations, and turn them into web applications that run in production environments for multiple users. Therefore, the only strong prerequisite is to know how to use Python.

Having some general knowledge of web development can certainly help, since Taipy apps can be styled using CSS (although this isn't strictly necessary). *Chapter 6* assumes some knowledge of Linux systems, the cloud, and Docker, since it discusses deployment strategies. Some chapters use specialized libraries to create more realistic examples, but the book and the GitHub repo provide examples and comments to understand them.

Download the example code files

The code bundle for the book is hosted on GitHub at `https://github.com/PacktPublishing/Getting-Started-with-Taipy`.

We also have other code bundles from our rich catalog of books and videos available at `https://github.com/PacktPublishing`. Check them out!

Conventions used

There are a number of text conventions used throughout this book.

`CodeInText`: Indicates code words in text, database table names, folder names, filenames, file extensions, pathnames, dummy URLs, user input, and X/Twitter handles. For example: "A `Gui` object with a `run` method and some key settings."

A block of code is set as follows:

```
with tgb.Page() as hello_earth_python:
    tgb.text("# Hello Earth!", mode="md")
```

When we wish to draw your attention to a particular part of a code block, the relevant lines or items are set in bold:

```
import taipy as tp
from taipy import Config, Orchestrator
```

Any command-line input or output is written as follows:

```
$ pip install taipy
```

Bold: Indicates a new term, an important word, or words that you see on the screen. For instance, words in menus or dialog boxes appear in the text like this. For example: "To change the element's properties, click **Graphical Properties** in the right pane."

> Warnings or important notes appear like this.

Get in touch

Feedback from our readers is always welcome.

General feedback: If you have questions about any aspect of this book or have any general feedback, please email us at customercare@packt.com and mention the book's title in the subject of your message.

Errata: Although we have taken every care to ensure the accuracy of our content, mistakes do happen. If you have found a mistake in this book, we would be grateful if you could report this to us. Please visit http://www.packt.com/submit-errata, click **Submit Errata**, and fill in the form.

Piracy: If you come across any illegal copies of our works in any form on the internet, we would be grateful if you would provide us with the location address or website name. Please contact us at copyright@packt.com with a link to the material.

If you are interested in becoming an author: If there is a topic that you have expertise in and you are interested in either writing or contributing to a book, please visit http://authors.packt.com/.

Your Book Comes with Exclusive Perks - Here's How to Unlock Them

Unlock this book's exclusive benefits now	**UNLOCK NOW**
Scan this QR code or go to `packtpub.com/unlock`, then search this book by name. Ensure it's the correct edition.	
Note: Keep your purchase invoice ready before you start.	

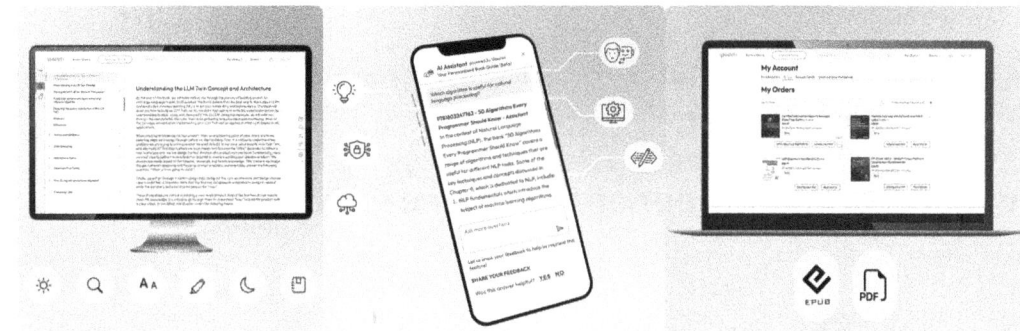

Enhanced reading experience with our Next-gen Reader:

Multi-device progress sync: Learn from any device with seamless progress sync.

Highlighting and notetaking: Turn your reading into lasting knowledge.

Bookmarking: Revisit your most important learnings anytime.

Dark mode: Focus with minimal eye strain by switching to dark or sepia mode.

Learn smarter using our AI assistant (Beta):

Summarize it: Summarize key sections or an entire chapter.

AI code explainers: In the next-gen Packt Reader, click the **Explain** button above each code block for AI-powered code explanations.

Note: The AI assistant is part of next-gen Packt Reader and is still in beta.

Learn anytime, anywhere:

Access your content offline with DRM-free PDF and ePub versions—compatible with your favorite e-readers.

Unlock Your Book's Exclusive Benefits

Your copy of this book comes with the following exclusive benefits:

Next-gen Packt Reader

AI assistant (beta)

DRM-free PDF/ePub downloads

Use the following guide to unlock them if you haven't already. The process takes just a few minutes and needs to be done only once.

How to unlock these benefits in three easy steps

Step 1

Keep your purchase invoice for this book ready, as you'll need it in *Step 3*. If you received a physical invoice, scan it on your phone and have it ready as either a PDF, JPG, or PNG.

For more help on finding your invoice, visit `https://www.packtpub.com/unlock-benefits/help`.

> **Note:**
> Did you buy this book directly from Packt? You don't need an invoice. After completing Step 2, you can jump straight to your exclusive content.

Step 2

Scan this QR code or go to `packtpub.com/unlock`.

On the page that opens (which will look similar to Figure 1 if you're on desktop), search for this book by name. Make sure you select the correct edition.

<packt>   Q Search...   Subscription   🛒   👤

Explore Products   Best Sellers   New Releases   Books   Videos   Audiobooks   Learning Hub   Newsletter Hub   Free Learning

Discover and unlock your book's exclusive benefits

Bought a Packt book? Your purchase may come with free bonus benefits designed to maximise your learning. Discover and unlock them here

Discover Benefits   Sign Up/In   Upload Invoice

Need Help?

✦ 1. Discover your book's exclusive benefits   ∧

Q Search by title or ISBN

CONTINUE TO STEP 2

👥 2. Login or sign up for free   ∨

☁ 3. Upload your invoice and unlock   ∨

Figure 1: Packt unlock landing page on desktop

Step 3

Sign in to your Packt account or create a new one for free. Once you're logged in, upload your invoice. It can be in PDF, PNG, or JPG format and must be no larger than 10 MB. Follow the rest of the instructions on the screen to complete the process.

Need help?

If you get stuck and need help, visit `https://www.packtpub.com/unlock-benefits/help` for a detailed FAQ on how to find your invoices and more. The following QR code will take you to the help page directly:

Note:

If you are still facing issues, reach out to `customercare@packt.com.`

Share Your Thoughts

Once you've read *Getting Started with Taipy*, we'd love to hear your thoughts! Scan the QR code below to go straight to the Amazon review page for this book and share your feedback.

`https://packt.link/r/1836203810`

Your review is important to us and the tech community and will help us make sure we're delivering excellent quality content.

Part 1:
Understanding Taipy
and Its Components

In the first part of this book, you'll gain a broad understanding of Taipy's core com-ponents. We'll start with the visual elements used to build user interfaces, then move on to the backend aspects of Scenario Management, and finally, explore how to deploy Taipy applications. By the end of this part, you'll be able to create and de-ploy complete Taipy applications.

This part of the book includes the following chapters:

- *Chapter 1, Discovering Taipy*
- *Chapter 2, Creating User Interfaces with Taipy*
- *Chapter 3, Connecting to Data Sources with Data Nodes*
- *Chapter 4, Orchestrating Taipy Applications*
- *Chapter 5, Managing Scenarios with Taipy*
- *Chapter 6, Deploying Your Taipy Applications*

1

Discovering Taipy

Taipy is an open-source Python library that allows anyone working with data (data scientists, data and **business intelligence** (**BI**) analysts, etc....) to create complete data applications. A complete data application is a tool that handles every step of data work—from collection to analysis—in one place, so users can easily manage data and generate insights. Data professionals use the Python ecosystem to build models, conduct analysis, and generate visualizations. Taipy solves the last-mile problem: deploying these solutions into production environments.

In this chapter, you'll discover Taipy's main uses and the reasoning behind the library's creation. Then, you'll install Taipy and some development tools to start your journey. Together, we will create our first application using two types of syntax allowed by Taipy: the Markdown API and the Python API (our book focuses on the latter). Finally, you'll learn how to use the **Taipy CLI**, a tool for initializing your projects and helping you use some Taipy components.

In this chapter, you'll learn about the following topics:

- Meeting Taipy: a data application library
- The main components of Taipy
- Installing Taipy and creating your setup
- Creating your first Taipy application
- Using the Taipy CLI
- Why is Taipy different?

Technical requirements

You can find all the code provided in this chapter in the GitHub repository for this book at `https://github.com/PacktPublishing/Getting-Started-with-Taipy/tree/main/chapter_01`.

To install Taipy, you need at least Python version 3.9. We recommend working with newer versions such as 3.11 or 3.12.

Meeting Taipy – a data application library

Taipy is an open-source Python library created by Avaiga, a company founded by Vincent Gosselin and Albert Antoine. Both Vincent and Albert transitioned from Java to Python as they saw it become the most relevant language in data-related operations (data analysis, data science, and even data engineering).

Indeed, Python offers a convenient way for data professionals to test and experiment with models, analyze data, create interesting visuals, and interact with data in enterprise structures (retrieving from databases, inserting into databases, carrying out data transformations, and so on). Here are some popular Python libraries for these tasks:

- **Machine learning (ML)**: scikit-learn, spaCy, and **Natural Language Toolkit (NLTK)**
- **Data manipulation**: NumPy, pandas, Polars, and PySpark (Spark API for Python)
- **Data visualization**: Plotly, Matplotlib, Altair, Seaborn, and Bokeh
- **Artificial intelligence (AI)**: Python APIs for almost all **large language models (LLMs)**, LangChain, TensorFlow, and PyTorch
- **Others**: NetworkX, SciPy, and GeoPandas

The ecosystem around Python also contributes to the success of the language among data professionals. Jupyter notebooks (and other similar products) offer a convenient way for analysts to test models and explore data. The combination of Markdown and code is a great way to explain the logic behind a process. These notebooks are easy to run and install on servers for team collaboration.

The missing link in the Python data landscape

This rich ecosystem for data manipulation and handling contrasts with the lack of tools for delivering insights in production environments, in the form of complete data applications.

A data application is a program that lets data and industry professionals analyze or visualize data through a **graphical user interface (GUI)**. End users don't mind the exact code that is generating the visuals or running the models. Instead, they want to understand what products are generating more revenue, predict supply needs so they don't run out of stock, compare providers to reduce costs or carbon emissions, detect fraudulent users to comply with regulations, or know more about how their customers use their products.

Taipy is a pure Python application builder, which makes it easy to learn for all data professionals who already use Python. Taipy applications are also production-ready; they run on production servers, handle large amounts of data, and multiple users can interact with them at the same time. In other words, Taipy fills the gap between data professionals and end users.

Some application examples

Here are some examples of applications that you can create with Taipy:

- **Dashboards** to visualize your data and track **key performance indicators** (**KPIs**), charts, maps, and more. Help decision-makers and business analysts understand the company's current status.

- **Predictive ML applications**, such as fraud detection apps, sales forecasting for retail operations, or energy consumption forecasting to control costs.

- **Image classification applications**, such as detecting crop diseases or nutrient deficiencies in agriculture or performing medical image analysis for disease detection.

- **Real-time data processing applications**, such as displaying and analyzing data from an external device like a camera for face detection or a specific measuring instrument. This makes Taipy useful for research or innovation projects as well.

- **LLM chatbots** for customer support, data analysis, task assistance, and documentation. Connect your chatbots to your preferred LLMs or use an in-house, local, quantized model. Use any part of your LLM stack, including RAG and vector databases. Taipy provides an excellent interface for your chatbot.

It's also worth noting that you don't always have to use all the power of Taipy: you can create *small useful applications*, such as unit converters and all sorts of calculators. These can be great for education purposes or a wide range of small professional operations (calculating gravity centers in a plane, calculating fertilizer requirements based on composition, surface, and crop needs, etc.).

Whatever your industry is, Taipy can help your decision-makers and analysts to make informed, effective decisions.

The main components of Taipy

As a project, Taipy is primarily a Python library, but it also includes other significant components:

- Taipy Studio, the **Visual Studio Code** (**VS Code**) extension.

- Taipy CLI, a **command-line interface** (**CLI**). It's also coded in Python, and you install it with the other components when you install Taipy with `pip`. Technically, it's part of the Python library, but you won't use it as such.

The project has a free and **open-source software** (**OSS**) part, and an Enterprise Edition, with a paid subscription. **Taipy Enterprise** has its own classes, but we won't be covering those in this book (we might discuss them briefly when appropriate). An exception to this is **Taipy Designer**, a drag-and-drop application builder that you can test for free; we talk about it in *Chapter 15*.

As an OSS library, Taipy has two main sublibraries:

- A GUI generation component (the `taipy.gui` sublibrary)
- Taipy for Scenario Management (`Orchestrator()`, `Cycle()`, and `Config()` classes)

The following diagram shows the main components of Taipy, as a project:

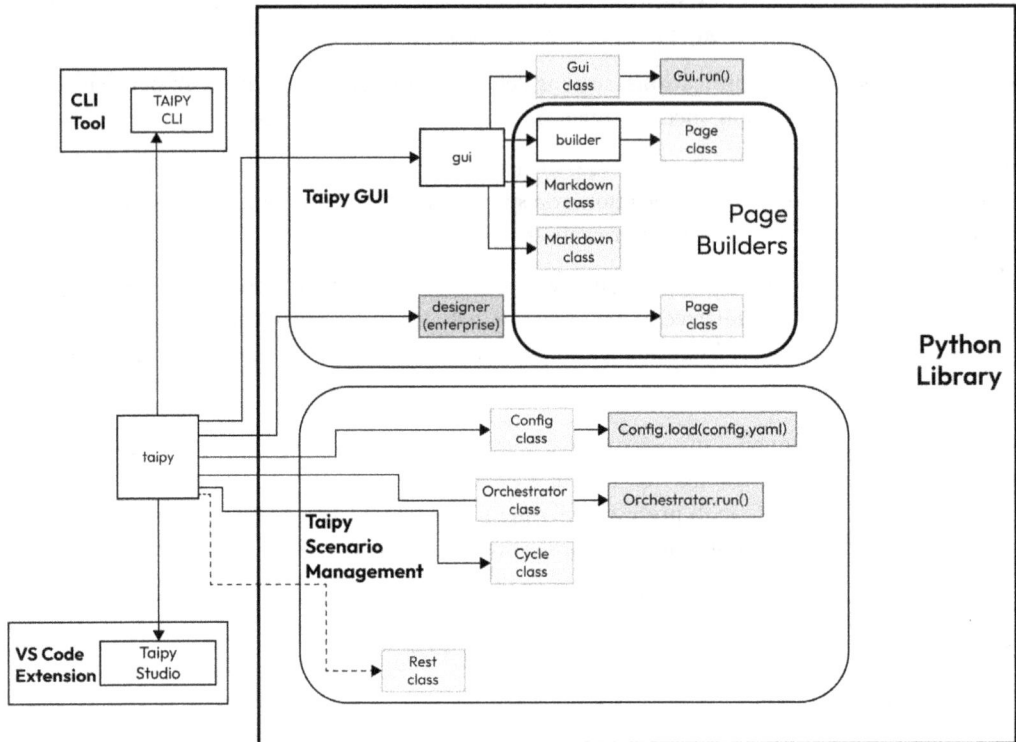

Figure 1.1 – Taipy's main components

Figure 1.2 shows the main Python classes (in yellow) and the most important functions (in blue). The Taipy GUI is the frontend component and offers four APIs to build apps. Taipy Scenario Management is the backend and offers a clean declarative way to orchestrate your pipelines, as well as specific methods to define scenarios and to schedule your applications.

Taipy for GUI

The GUI component of Taipy is the major one. With this sublibrary, you can create all kinds of data applications; we cover all this in detail in *Chapter 2*. Here are some things you can do with it:

- Add controllers such as buttons, gliders, or input forms

- Link them to Python variables and make those variables change as the user interacts through the GUI
- Change the style of your application to make it more appealing or add your corporate style
- Arrange the elements in columns, create multiple-page applications, and add visual elements such as charts or maps

Taipy for GUI has a main class, named `Gui`, which you need to import to create your applications, like this:

```
from taipy.gui import Gui
```

The `Gui` class has a Python method called `run` that you call to run the application. The way to call the method is by passing a `page` (or `pages`) argument to the `Gui` class itself. We will explain this in depth in *Chapter 2*, but here is how the statement looks:

```
Gui(page=your_page).run()
```

💡 **Quick tip**: Enhance your coding experience with the **AI Code Explainer** and **Quick Copy** features. Open this book in the next-gen Packt Reader. Click the **Copy** button (**1**) to quickly copy code into your coding environment, or click the **Explain** button (**2**) to get the AI assistant to explain a block of code to you.

```
function calculate(a, b) {
  return {sum: a + b};
};
```
Copy   Explain
  1   2

🔒 **The next-gen Packt Reader** is included for free with the purchase of this book. Scan the QR code OR go to `packtpub.com/unlock`, then use the search bar to find this book by name. Double-check the edition shown to make sure you get the right one.

The `page` argument can take five types of data:

- Text as Python strings (`str`)
- An element from a Taipy Gui class called `gui.builder`

- An element from a Taipy Gui class called `gui.Markdown`

- An element from a Taipy Gui class called `gui.Html`

- An element from a Taipy Designer class called `designer`

The reason behind this is that you can create Taipy applications in four main ways:

- With a special Markdown templating syntax, you can pass this type of text string (the `str` type) as an argument directly to the `Page` element. You can also use a specific Markdown class to create your page!

- With an HTML template syntax. You won't be using it in this book.

- The Taipy application builder provides a set of Python functions for building apps. Taipy incorporated this application builder in version 3, and it's the one you'll be using in this book.

- Using Taipy Designer, a drag-and-drop tool. This is an Enterprise (paid) feature. You have access to a one-month free trial, and we'll cover this in *Chapter 15* of the book.

Taipy Scenario Management

Taipy Scenario Management is the backend part of Taipy applications. You can create complete applications without it, but it offers a convenient and declarative way to abstract the data inputs, outputs, and function calls of your application, through configuration files.

This way of creating pipelines makes it easy to switch your application from a *test* environment to a *production* environment. For example, if you retrieve your data from a test database, you will just need to change the name of the database in the configuration file when you switch to production, without touching any code.

You can achieve the following with Taipy Scenario Management:

- **Data integration**: Connect to any data source and keep track of its changes using the same API for each data source

- **Task orchestration**: Orchestrate tasks in Taipy; use your data to generate all the content for your applications

- **Define scenarios**: Track your data and KPIs over time

- **What-if analysis**: Change the input parameters of your tasks to create different solutions and scenarios

You can choose two ways to configure your pipeline with Taipy. You can use TOML files (a human-readable configuration file format); when you use Taipy Studio, you create a **directed acyclic graph (DAG)**, a visual representation of your data workflow with a UI, and it creates a TOML file. You can also use a Python API to configure your pipelines.

On top of these, Taipy Scenario Management also offers methods to orchestrate your data. This is one of the features that makes Taipy different and suited for production environments, where you want your applications to live, using updated data and with minimal manual intervention.

Another advantage of Scenario Management is that you can declare and configure scenarios and link them to your GUI app. This way, end users can test and compare different possible scenarios.

Taipy Scenario Management configuration

Taipy comes with a `Config` class that inherits from the Taipy library directly. You can import it using the following:

```
from taipy import Config
```

`Config` itself offers two ways to define your configurations:

- With a Python API.
- Using a TOML configuration file. Taipy Studio interprets this configuration file and lets you visualize and edit the pipelines.

Taipy Cycle

The `Cycle` class is somewhat advanced, but it's easy to use since it has few components. This part of Taipy allows you to schedule your tasks by selecting when your occurrences start and finish, as well as the frequency (e.g., once a week, once a month, etc.). We'll cover this in depth in Chapter 5.

Now that you know how the project's structure works, let's code!

Installing Taipy and creating your setup

Before installing Taipy to create new projects, as with any other Python library, you can create a virtual environment. You can create isolated Python environments for each project with virtual environments, preventing dependency conflicts. This makes your projects more organized and reproducible. You can also create environments for collaboration, so several users use the same versions of the libraries, and you can also reproduce your virtual environment to ensure proper deployment of your applications (with a `requirements.txt` file). Here's a way to create a virtual environment:

```
$ python -m venv name-of-your-environment
```

Then, activate it with the following command:

```
$ .\name-of-your-environment\Scripts\activate
```

For macOS and Linux, use the following:

```
$ source name-of-your-environment/bin/activate
```

If you use Conda, you can create it using this command:

```
$ conda create --name name-of-your-environment
```

Then, activate it using the following (for all operating systems):

```
$ conda activate name-of-your-environment
```

Installing Taipy

You can then install Taipy from **Python Package Index** (**PyPi**), using `pip` (this is also the way to install Taipy in a Conda environment):

```
$ pip install taipy
```

This will install all the components of Taipy.

When installing, you can specify the version of Taipy. We wrote this book using version 4.1.0. We don't recommend installing an inferior version, since 4.1.0 is a good and stable version of the library.

If you want to contribute to the project or want to install the latest development version, we show how to do it in `/chapter 1` (the README file).

Installing Taipy from a notebook

You can use notebooks to run Taipy applications, both from your local machine and from remote servers, using services such as Kaggle or Colab. We will see an example of this in *Chapter 6*.

You can access the CLI from any notebook by placing an exclamation mark (!) before your command, so you can install Taipy from a notebook running a cell like this:

```
!pip install taipy
```

Formatting and other considerations

We formatted all the code examples of this book with the Black code formatter. You can install it with `pip install black` and use the VS Code extension to do so. It will make your code consistent and clean (it will meet *PEP8* specifications).

We also recommend installing the `isort` library (`pip install isort`) and the extension for VS Code, which automatically sorts your `import` statements. This way, you can focus on what matters: creating great Taipy applications.

Throughout the book, we will use Python libraries and other technologies such as databases or cloud services. All the technologies that we will explore can be part of a data specialist's toolbox. For obvious reasons, it's impossible to replicate everyone's stack; feel free to adapt the examples to your specific tools! The goal is to use diverse technologies so you can adapt them to your use case.

Installing Taipy Studio on VS Code

Taipy Studio is a VS Code extension for visualizing and creating pipelines (Data Nodes, tasks, and scenarios).

Installing Taipy Studio will also provide syntactic help when using the Markdown API (see the next section). In this book, you will mainly discover the Python API.

 To do so, open VS Code, go to **Extensions**, and type `taipy` in the search area. Install **Taipy Studio** (it should come up first, as shown in *Figure 1.2*), and make sure it's created by Taipy:

Figure 1.2 – Installing Taipy Studio, a VS Code extension

In the next section, we'll clarify the structure of Taipy as a project, so you know when to use each one of its components.

Creating your first Taipy application

It's time to create your first, minimal application. This section has two goals:

- Make sure that your setup works fine
- Use the big elements of Taipy in a Hello World! app and see their differences

Creating GUIs with the Python API

To test whether your Taipy installation works well, you can try the following code. Write it in a file called main.py:

```
import taipy.gui.builder as tgb
from taipy.gui import Gui

with tgb.Page() as hello_earth_python:
    tgb.text("# Hello Earth!", mode="md")

page_to_run = Gui(page=hello_earth_python)
if __name__ == "__main__":
    page_to_run.run(use_reloader=True, dark_mode=False)
```

You should see something like this:

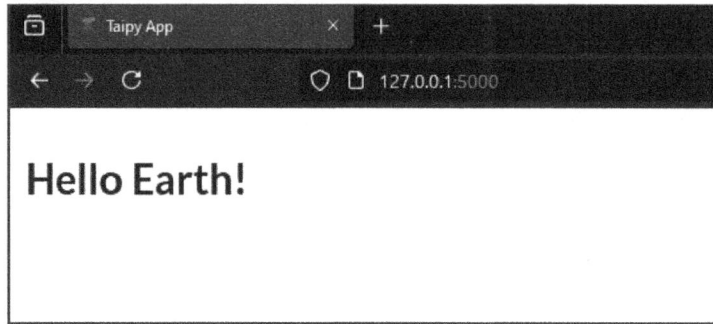

Figure 1.3 – The Taipy application running locally

In this code, we imported the Gui class, which "holds" the Taipy application. It takes a Page element as an argument, which can be of different types, as we saw in the previous section. In this case, we used the Python API by importing the Python application builder (with import taipy.gui.builder as tgb).

We created a variable called hello_earth_python, which is a Page element. Here, you can include lots of visual components. For now, we just added some text (tgb.text).

Then, we created a variable called page_to_run, a Gui element with an assigned Page. To run it, you just need to call the run() method. We will see all this in depth in *Chapter 2*, but notice that, by default, Taipy applications use dark mode (we set dark_mode=False). We also set use_reloader=True, which is for development use. You can edit your code, and the page will reload and show your edits as you code (unless you crash it with an error, of course!).

Also, we placed some of the code under the main guard clause (if _name_ == "main"). It is a good practice; it ensures that the code within the block is executed only once, at launch, which is important as our apps grow so that we don't create new elements constantly.

To run your application, save the file and run it as a usual Python script. If you work with VS Code, open the terminal and go to the directory with your application. You can right-click on the editor and select **Run Python | Run Python file in terminal**.

```
main.py    ×

Getting-Started-with-Taipy > chapter 1 > hello_worlds >  main.py > ...
1    import taipy.gui.builder as tgb
2    from taipy.gui import Gui
3
4    with tgb.Page() as hello_earth_python:
5        tgb.text("# Hello Earth!", mode="md")
6
7    hello_mars_markdown = "# Hello Mars!"
8
9    # Comment or or the other:
10   page_to_run = Gui(page=hello_earth_python)
11   # page_to_run = Gui(page=hello_mars_markdown)
12
13   if __name__ == "__main__":
14
15       page_to_run.run(use_reloader=True, dark_mode=False)
16

PROBLEMS    OUTPUT    TERMINAL    PORTS

∨ TERMINAL
 ○ PS C:\Users\PC\Documents\Local_projects\Getting-Started-with-Taipy\chapter 1\hello_worlds> taipy run main.py
```

Figure 1.4 – Running your Taipy application from the terminal

If this works fine, you're ready to start learning about Taipy! Before that, let's see how the Gui class can take a different type of Page element!

Using the Taipy GUI with the Markdown API

In the previous code, you can replace the element with the following to say "Hello Mars!" instead of "Hello Earth!":

```
hello_mars_markdown = "# Hello Mars!"
page_to_run = Gui(page=hello_mars_markdown)
if __name__ == "__main__":
    page_to_run.run(use_reloader=True, dark_mode=False)
```

If you run this, your application will now say "Hello Mars!". This demonstrates how the same page argument in the Gui class accepts different types of structures (the four types of page builders that you can see in *Figure 1.1*).

You will see different syntaxes for Taipy GUI elements in the documentation and online articles. But they are all analogous

Today, the Python API is gaining traction. It's easier to manipulate it within other Python elements, and it makes your code easier to structure. This is why we'll mainly focus on this syntax in this book.

Hello Planets with Taipy Scenario Management

As we mentioned before, Taipy lets you define pipelines in two main ways: with Python code and with a TOML file (that you can edit from the VS Code extension). We prefer the Python API method, and that's what we will use in this book. We explain Scenario Management in *Chapters 3-5*. The reason we prefer the Python API is that we're used to coding in Python, and it's simple to configure a pipeline with this syntax. Taipy's Config class also has a function to convert your Python code into TOML format, so we can use that in case we want to visualize our pipeline with the VS Code editor.

Scenario Management with the Python API

Here, we will use the "Hello World!" code with the Python API, which you can find in the GitHub repository (main_orchestrator.py). Let's break this code down here (check the file for the complete code):

1. Import the necessary packages. Orchestrator lets you run Scenario Management, and Config lets you define the elements of the scenario pipelines:

   ```
   import taipy as tp
   from taipy import Config, Orchestrator
   ```

2. Define a small Python mock function, say_hello, that adds "Hello" before the input:

   ```
   def say_hello(planet: str):
       return f"Hello {planet}!"
   ```

3. Then, with the Config class, you define two data notes (with Config.configure_data_node()), one for the entry data and the other for the output:

   ```
   planet_data_node_cfg = Config.configure_data_node(
       id="input_planet")
   hello_data_node_cfg = Config.configure_data_node(
       id="hello_from_planet")
   ```

4. You also define a task (with Config.configure_task), which launches a function (in this case, the say_hello function). You also give it the input and the output Data Node that you just defined:

   ```
   say_hello_task_cfg = Config.configure_task(
       "build_msg", say_hello,
   ```

```
            planet_data_node_cfg, hello_data_node_cfg
     )
```

5. Next, you configure a scenario (with `Config.configure_scenario`). You always need at least one scenario:

```
scenario_cfg = Config.configure_scenario(
    "scenario", task_configs=[say_hello_task_cfg])
```

6. Once you set your configurations, you need to run your service with `Orchestrator().run()`.

7. When the service is running, you can use `taipy.create_scenario()` to create a scenario from the scenario configuration file. In the example, the scenario object is in a variable called `planet_scenario`. You can use this scenario more than once; as you can see, it's inside a loop:

```
planet_scenario = tp.create_scenario(scenario_cfg)
```

8. For each planet in the planets list, the input Data Node gets the planet value with the `planet_scenario.input_planet.write(planet)` statement. By default, Data Nodes are pickle files (see more in *Chapter 3*). It's also worth noting that in `planet_scenario.input_planet`, `input_planet` is the `id` value of the Data Node (from the configuration step):

```
for planet in planets:
    planet_scenario.input_planet.write(planet)   # Select by id
```

9. Whenever you want to execute the scenario, you call the `submit()` method:

```
planet_scenario.submit()
```

10. Then, you can access the value of the output Data Node using the `read()` method:

```
print(planet_scenario.hello_from_planet.read())#Select by id
```

11. If you run the preceding code, you will see this output in your terminal:

```
[2024-07-31 20:15:21] [Taipy] [INFO] Development mode: Clean all
entities of version aed1322d-001b-4b23-9b29-72fde4134c4e
[2024-07-31 20:15:21] [Taipy] [INFO] Blocking configuration
update.
[2024-07-31 20:15:22] [Taipy] [INFO] job JOB_build_msg_48fd57e4-
a668-4c17-97a3-96409da4e332 is completed.
Hello Mercury!
...
[2024-07-31 20:15:24] [Taipy] [INFO] job JOB_build_msg_f2ea76e7-
211a-4372-90fe-c22065495389 is completed.
Hello Neptune!
```

We can also replicate the preceding code (*Steps 1-6*) using the Taipy Studio extension.

Scenario Management with Taipy Studio

You can find the code for this example in `main_orchestrator_visual.py`. First, create a Python file called `say_hello.py` with the following function:

```
def say_hello(planet: str):
    return f"Hello {planet}!"
```

Next, you can create your configuration file with Taipy Studio and follow these steps (shown in *Figures 1.5* and *1.6*):

1.   Go to Taipy Studio's extension. To do so, click on Taipy's logo in the side menu (**1** in *Figure 1.5*).

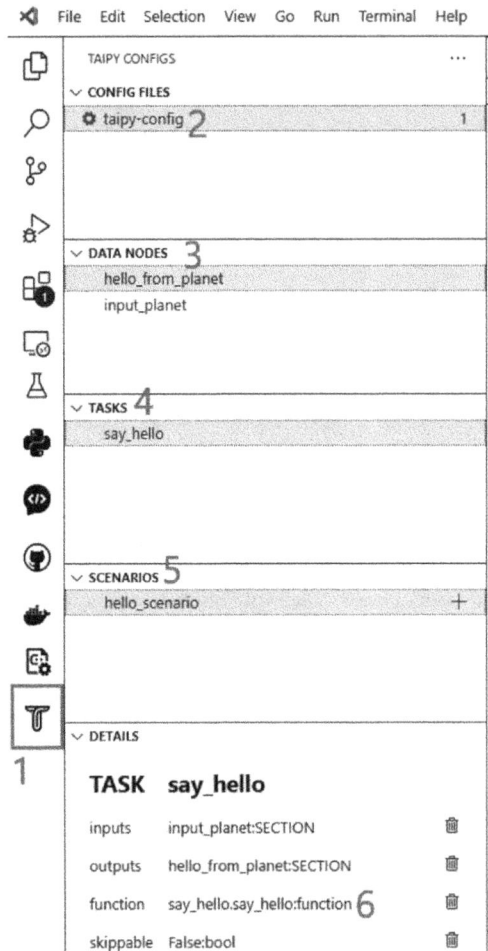

Figure 1.5 – Taipy Studio's main sections

2. In the left pane, next to **CONFIG FILES,** click on the cross: **Create new config file.** Call it `taipy-config` (**2**).

3. Under **DATA NODES**, create two Data Nodes called `hello_from_planet` and `input_planet` (**3**). This will create two blue boxes.

4. Then, go to **TASKS** and create a task. Name it `say_hello` (**4**).

5. Next, go to **SCENARIOS** and create a scenario. Call it `hello_scenario` (**5**).

6. Now that you have all the elements, add a function to your `say_hello` task. Click on `say_hello` in the left pane; this will open a **DETAILS** section. This section lets you edit any element you select (a node, a task, or a scenario). If you click on **function**, it will show you all the files with Python functions within your project (make sure you are in the working directory). Select the right file (`say_hello.py`) and then select the right function (`say_hello`) (**6**).

7. The last step is to link your elements. Each visual element has little boxes in the bottom corner. You can click on them and drag your connections; you will see a dotted arrow come out. Take that arrow toward the desired element. In this case, link `input_planet` with `say_hello`, and then link `say_hello` with `hello_from_planet`. Finally, link `hello_scenario` with the `say_hello` task. You can see the final diagram in *Figure 1.6.*

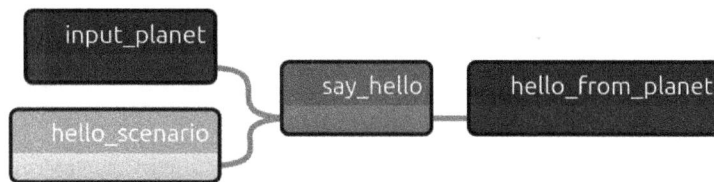

Figure 1.6 – A Taipy Scenario Management basic pipeline

8. Now, come back to your **Files** view on VS Code (exit Taipy Studio). You should see a configuration file called `taipy-config.toml`. You can change the text with your code editor.

9. Now that you have your configuration file, you can use it with `taipy.Congig.load()`, passing the TOML configuration file as an argument. To call the scenario that you defined in the TOML file (`hello_scenario`), you can call it like this: `scenario_cfg = Config.scenarios["hello_scenario"]`.

The rest of the code is the same as the code with the Python API in the previous section.

Using the Taipy CLI

Taipy's documentation of the CLI tool (`https://docs.taipy.io/en/release-4.1/`
`userman/ecosystem/cli/`) is straightforward. You can use the CLI tool from any terminal,
such as the one in VS Code. Let's go over the most important uses of the Taipy CLI.

Starting projects

When you start a project, it can be challenging to be consistent with your file structures, and it
takes some time to create them. The easiest and cleanest way to start a project is using the `taipy`
`create` command.

Starting Taipy applications

Once you run this command, you will have a prompt asking you seven questions. For each question,
you will see a default answer (between parentheses). Just press *Enter* if you like the default, or type
your choice otherwise.

In the following example, you can see that we accepted the default for question 2:

```
$ taipy create
    [1/6] Application root folder name (taipy_application): my_first_
app_from_cli
    [2/6] Application main Python file (main.py):
    [3/6] Application title (Taipy Application): My First Taipy App from
the CLI
    [4/6] Page names in multi-page application? (): Page_1 Page_2
    [5/6] Does the application use scenario management or version
management? (No): Yes
    [6/6] Does the application use Rest API? (No): No
[7/7] Do you want to initialize a new Git repository? (No): Yes
New Taipy application has been created at C:\Users\PC\xxx\my_first_
app_from_cli
```

To start the application, change the directory to the newly created folder:

```
cd C:\Users\PC\xxx\my_first_app_from_cli
```

Then, run the application as follows:

```
taipy run main.py
```

The process is straightforward. One tricky part is [4/6]: when naming pages for a multi-page
application in the command line, use spaces to separate the names (since they are arguments of the
CLI function).

You can name your main files and folders, choose to have a single page or a multi-page application (by naming the pages), and choose whether you want to use Scenario Management or not (that is, to add Taipy Scenario Management to your application).

The file structure that you'll get will be like this:

- `main.py`: Your main application file
- `pages`: Directory for your pages, if you selected a multi-page app
- `configuration`: Directory with a `config.py` file for your configurations, if you selected Taipy Scenario Management
- `algorithms`: Directory with an `algorithms.py` file for your Taipy Tasks, if you selected Taipy Scenario Management
- `requirements.txt`: Add here the libraries that your project uses; you'll need this file to deploy or share your project
- If you select to initialize a Git repo, you'll have a `.gitignore` file

Other Taipy CLI commands

Here are some other important commands that you should be aware of:

- `taipy run`: One way to run your applications from the CLI is to use `taipy run name_of_your_app.py`. Make sure you are in the right directory!
- `taipy help`: Shows information about another Taipy CLI command. You can try to type `taipy help run` or even `taipy help help`.
- `taipy --version`: Shows the version of your Taipy library.

Although you won't be using these two commands, at least for now, we'll introduce them here:

- `taipy migrate` converts older Taipy code (version `3.X`) into Taipy `4.X` applications. As Taipy releases new versions, you may need it in the future!
- `taipy version` helps you manage versions of your Taipy applications. This is an advanced concept, so we won't cover it here.

Why is Taipy different?

Besides Taipy, the Python ecosystem offers solutions to create applications, but none address the issue that Taipy solves: creating production-ready data applications.

For instance, compare the following with Taipy:

- Python has some GUI application frameworks, such as **tkinter**. These are mainly used for simple or experimental GUI apps and are not ideal for production environments, which are typically browser-based. Tkinter also has a difficult syntax.

- You can find web application frameworks for Python users, such as **Django** or **Flask**. While these frameworks are powerful tools for web developers, they may not be the most straightforward option for data scientists looking to quickly build data applications. In fact, Taipy leverages Flask.

- **Plotly Dash** is a great data visualization tool. It allows the creation of complete dashboards for data analysis and can be production-ready. Dash has a harder syntax, and it doesn't offer the same flexibility to compare scenarios.

- **Streamlit** is a popular library for sketch demonstration applications (prototypes) and is easy to learn, with almost no friction. It also supports many Python libraries. Most data professionals can go one step further with Streamlit, but since it's not production-ready, it doesn't fill the entire gap!

- **Gradio** is not suited for production either and focuses on LLMs, such as chatbots and other AI apps. It's also easy to use. With Taipy, you can also create chatbots and use LLMs or other AI technology. And you can take them to production!

This leads us to the next question.

Why is Taipy production-ready?

A production application needs to manage large and complex production data. Analysts and decision-makers need intuitive and responsive tools that load quickly and, more importantly, reload quickly.

Taipy is fast

Taipy uses a cache for the application's graphical components, so you don't need to deal with these complications. This is why Taipy is not (only) a prototyping tool; you can deliver your models to end users in a fully functional manner.

While developing Taipy applications, all you need to understand is how to properly bind elements using **callbacks** (we'll go over this in *Chapter 2*). For resource-intensive applications, you may need to use **Partials** or **asynchronous callbacks** (we'll see this in *Chapter 12*). The complexity is minimal so you can focus on what matters: putting your models and visuals in the hands of end users.

Multiple user applications

When you run Taipy applications in production, each display has a **state** (a `State` object). This "state" is unique for each user and stores the value of the variables in the Taipy application.

We see all this in detail in *Chapter 2*, but what's important here is that multiple users can use the same application at the same time and each user will have their own state. A user may be looking at the data with a certain display, such as sales for a certain store, while another person may be looking at the same chart but with the sales over all the stores of a certain area.

This ensures a personalized experience, which is mandatory in production.

Building pipelines with Taipy

Taipy goes beyond providing GUI components by offering powerful abstractions, such as **Data Nodes**, **Tasks**, and **Scenarios**.

Data Nodes enable interactions with various data sources (CSV and Excel files, Parquet files, databases, etc.), as we'll see in *Chapter 3*.

Tasks hold Python functions and can link to input and output Data Nodes, as described in *Chapter 4*.

Scenarios allow you to create interactive workflows by linking Data Nodes to Python functions. This enables users to test different possibilities and combinations, making it easy to experiment with various scenarios and outcomes, as shown in *Chapter 5*.

Deploying Taipy applications

The last step of a production-ready application is deploying it in a production environment. As we mentioned previously, Taipy is built on top of Flask, which is a well-known Python framework for web development. Taipy takes care of all the complexity within Flask and makes it easy to deploy.

Taipy uses Flask's built-in development server, which is great for testing and local development. However, it's not optimized for production environments, as it can be slow and less secure.

Once the application is ready, you can deploy it in a production server, such as Gunicorn or uWSGI, with minor changes to the code (you can expose your Taipy applications as Flask applications). This ensures better performance, security, and scalability. We'll explore this further in *Chapter 6*.

Summary

In this chapter, you discovered Taipy: an open-source Python library that allows data scientists and data analysts to share their models and visuals in production environments. It also makes it easy to shift between development and production versions of your applications.

After completing this chapter, your setup should be complete. You ran your first applications using different APIs for both Taipy for GUI and Scenario Management, and you used Taipy Studio and the CLI tool.

Now that everything is working and you know the project's structure, you can dive into creating compelling user interfaces with Taipy GUI in the next chapter!

Questions

1. What problems does Taipy solve?

2. What are the main components (or tools) of Taipy? What do you use them for?

3. What is the difference between Taipy GUI and Taipy Scenario Management?

4. How do you create a scenario with Taipy?

5. How do you declare a multi-page application? Tip: create a multi-page GUI application with the Taipy CLI and see how it's coded in the main file.

Answers

1. Taipy turns data models and datasets into fully functional applications that non-technical users can interact with. While many Python tools help data professionals with tasks such as modeling, visualization, and analysis, they cannot often deploy these solutions in production environments for end users.

2. The main components of Taipy are Taipy GUI and Taipy Scenario Management:

   - Taipy Scenario Management is used for managing and automating data workflows. It helps you handle complex data pipelines, schedule tasks, and manage dependencies between different steps in your data processing. It is essential for organizing and running the backend processes of your data applications.

   - Taipy GUI is used for creating the frontend, or user interface, of your data applications. It allows you to build interactive dashboards, forms, and visualizations that users can interact with.

   Next to these two main components, we also have the following:

   - Taipy CLI helps you set up and manage your Taipy projects. It allows you to initialize projects, run applications, and use other Taipy components through simple commands.

   - Taipy Studio is an extension for VS Code that provides a visual way to build and customize workflows.

3. Taipy Scenario Management handles the backend, managing data workflows and automating tasks. Taipy GUI is the frontend, used to build interactive dashboards and visualizations for users. Scenario Management is about processing data, while GUI is about presenting it.

4. You can create a scenario with Taipy in two ways:

   - **Using a configuration file**: Load the configuration from a file, such as `taipy-config.toml`, and then run `Orchestrator`. After that, you can create and manage scenarios based on the configuration.

   - **Using Python code directly**: Define the scenario configuration in your script, create a scenario, and then execute it.

You can access your scenario configuration with `Config.scenarios["name-_of_ scenario"]` and create it with `taipy.create_scenario(scenario_cfg)`.

5. To create a multi-page application, start with defining a dictionary with all the `Page` elements, like this:

```
all_pages = {
    «First_page»: page_1,
    "Second_page": page_2,
}
```

When you create your `Gui` element, you need to use the `pages` parameter instead of `page` (add an extra "s"), something like this:

```
your_gui = Gui(pages=all_pages)
```

Join our community on Discord

Join our community's Discord space for discussions with the authors and other readers:

```
https://packt.link/taipybook
```

2

Creating User Interfaces with Taipy

Taipy for GUI is a complete toolbox for creating web applications. It includes three APIs: Python, Markdown, and HTML syntax; we'll focus on the Python one. **Taipy Designer**, which we'll explore in *Chapter 15*, is also a way to create GUI applications but uses a different approach.

In this chapter, you'll discover how to use all the components of Taipy for GUI. First, you will learn how to structure your page and choose how to display your components. You will also see how to create multiple-page applications and how to personalize the displays (adding favicons or titles to your application). Then, you will see how to add visual elements and **selectors** to your applications, **bind variables** to them, and use **callbacks**. Finally, you will learn how to add style to your applications using the **Stylekit**.

In this chapter, you'll learn about the following topics:

- Creating pages and organizing them with blocks
- Adding visual elements, binding variables, and using callbacks
- Displaying your interactive data visually
- Exploring navigational controls
- Changing your page's styles

Technical requirements

The code in this chapter can be found on the GitHub repository: `https://github.com/PacktPublishing/Getting-Started-with-Taipy/tree/main/chapter_02`

To follow this chapter, it's best to be familiar with Markdown. You can find an excellent tutorial here: `https://www.w3schools.io/file/markdown-introduction/` (in particular, you can focus on the *Heading* section: `https://www.w3schools.io/file/markdown-headings/`).

Creating pages and organizing them with blocks

In this chapter, we'll code a demo app called **Taipy Food**. To start, you'll need two things:

- A `Page` element (one or more). This is where you set up and organize the visual components of your app.

- A `Gui` object with a `run` method and some key settings.

This section shows how to set up your app, and the next section covers visual elements. You can't run a page without visual elements, and you can't add visuals to anything that isn't a page. So, we'll introduce some static visual elements here to give the page some structure. The code for this section is in `/1-organizing-elements/`.

Let's create a basic page:

1. Import `Gui` and the page builder:

    ```
    import taipy.gui.builder as tgb
    from taipy.gui import Gui
    ```

2. Create a `Page` element:

    ```
    with tgb.Page() as welcome_page:
        tgb.text("# Taipy Food 🍜", mode="md")
    ```

3. Create a `Gui` element and call the `run()` method. It's important to use Python's **main guard** before running your Taipy applications (it makes them more efficient and more stable):

    ```
    taipy_food_gui = Gui(page=welcome_page)
    if __name__ == "__main__": # main guard
        taipy_food_gui.run()
    ```

`tgb.text()` is a visual element. The first parameter is the text value; `mode="md"` means that it's Markdown syntax. The string `"# Taipy Food 🍜"` becomes an `<h1>` tag (a title).

To create a `Gui` element from the `Taipy.gui.builder.Page` element (`welcome_page`), use: `Taipy_food_gui = Gui(page=welcome_page)`. Then, use the `run()` method to launch your app. You can now run it from your terminal with `taipy run main.py`.

Discovering Taipy run parameters

The run() method takes several parameters, which are well documented (https://docs.taipy.io/en/release-4.1/userman/advanced_features/configuration/gui-config/#configuring-the-gui-instance).

Some parameters, such as the Stylekit or theme, adjust the app's style (see the *Changing your page's styles* section). Most are for deployment (see *Chapter 6*). For now, let's focus on the ones that affect the app's visual appearance.

Adding cosmetic elements to Taipy applications

You can add the following arguments to your run method:

- use_reloader=True reloads the page when you save changes in code, (used for development, not a cosmetic element).
- dark_mode=False means that we'll use light mode (defaults to True).
- title adds a title to the page metadata and the browser tab, in the <head> of the web page's HTML, inside the <title> tags. (<title>Taipy Food 🍔</title> – *see Figure 2.1*).
- favicon allows us to add a small burger icon we made using a free online service (favicon.io). To add your favicon, place the file in your images directory (see *Figure 2.1*).
- watermark is how Taipy applications add a watermark that states "**taipy**" inside. You can change this watermark to any value, for example, "**Taipy food**" (see *Figure 2.1*).

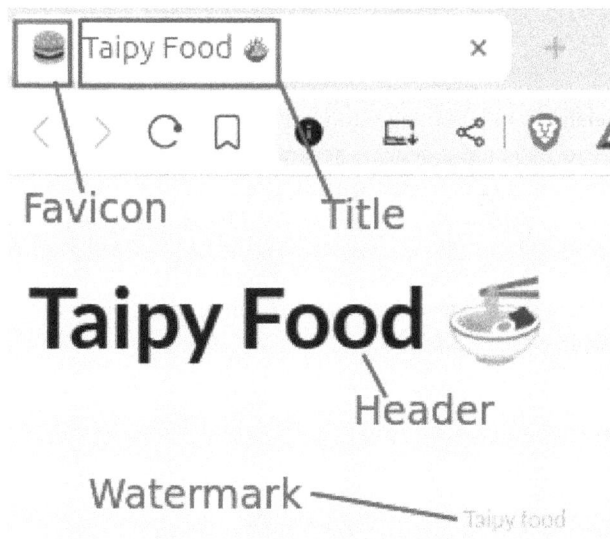

Figure 2.1 – Cosmetic elements in the Taipy Food app

You can see the complete `run` function in `1-organizing_elements/main.py`. Now, let's see how to create pages using the application builder.

Adding static elements

Before we show how to structure an application, let's create a page with text and images.

Adding text

Taipy's `text` element (`https://docs.taipy.io/en/release-4.1/refmans/gui/viselements/generic/text/`) requires a Python string for the `value` parameter. By default, the `mode` parameter is set to `raw`, showing everything as plain text. To use Markdown and make your app look better, set `mode` to `md`. You can add static text in several ways:

- We add more `tgb.text` elements, one with a `<h2>` header and another with plain text.
- We create a file called `description.md` with Markdown-formatted text. We then read this file with Python and assign it to a variable named `description_text`. This approach is handy for long text:

```
with open("description.md", "r") as description:
    description_text = description.read()

with tgb.Page() as welcome_page:
    (...)
    tgb.text(description_text, mode="md")
```

Adding images

You can use an `image` element to add images to your application. Pass either a URL or a file path as a parameter. The `image` object also accepts several optional parameters (`https://docs.taipy.io/en/release-4.1/refmans/gui/viselements/generic/image/`) such as `on_action` (discussed in the *Adding visual elements, binding variables, and using callbacks* section), `id`, and `class_name`.

For now, let's focus on resizing the image with the `width` option. In the following example, we added a photo of food from Unsplash (see *Figure 2.2*):

```
tgb.image(
    url_image,
    width="200px",
)
```

Adding structure with block elements

In this section, you'll learn how to structure content in your Page elements using **blocks**. There are four types: **layout**, **part**, **pane**, and **expandable**.

Block elements group *child* elements (such as charts, buttons, images, and text) together. To create a block with the Python API, use the `with` keyword and indent all child elements under it. You can nest elements (use blocks inside other blocks).

Combining layout and parts

Two block elements are essential to structure your pages:

- `layout` defines a grid structure for all elements within it.

- `part` groups elements together, displaying them with shared properties.

In a grid layout, you set column numbers and sizes with a Python string, using space-separated numbers. Each number represents a column's relative size:

- `layout("1 1 1")` creates 3 columns of equal size.

- `layout("1 2 1 1")` creates 4 columns; the second one is twice as big as the others.

In our app, we want two columns, a small one to the left, and a bigger one (three times bigger) to the right:

```
with tgb.layout("1 3"):
    tgb.text("## Why Choose Taipy Food?", mode="md")
    tgb.text(
        "It's the ultimate tool for making cooking"
        "easier and more fun!",
        mode="md"
    )
    tgb.image(
        url_image,
        width="200px",
    )
    tgb.text(description_text, mode="md")
```

The current code isn't ideal: it displays each element in the grid from left to right and top to bottom, as we can see in *Figure 2.2*.

Taipy Food 🍜

Why Choose Taipy Food?

It's the ultimate tool for making cooking easier and more fun!

Food and data

Taipy Food is your go-to app for all things cooking! Whether you're whipping up a quick meal or experimenting with a new recipe, Taipy Food helps you get it right every time. With our **intuitive unit conversion tool** and a rich database of food facts, you'll have everything you need to cook with confidence.

Key Features:

- Cooking Unit Converter: Easily convert between different units of measurement (cups, grams, ounces, etc.) to ensure your recipes turn out perfectly every time.
- Calorie Calculator: Get quick calorie estimates for different foods to help you make healthier choices.
- Recipes of the world: Visualize food facts so you can learn insights and show your friends how much you know about food.

Taipy Food is designed to make your time in the kitchen more enjoyable and efficient. Whether you're a beginner or a seasoned chef, you'll find valuable tools and insights to enhance your cooking experience.

Figure 2.2 – Static Taipy Food app without the block structure

What we want is to group the first three elements (the `<h2>` header, the plain text, and the image) in the first column and place all the text from the `description_text` variable in the second column. We can achieve this by grouping the first three elements under a `part` statement:

```
with tgb.layout("1 3"):
    with tgb.part():
        tgb.text("## Why Choose Taipy Food?", mode="md")
...
    tgb.text(description_text, mode="md")
```

Our app now displays content in blocks, as you can see in *Figure 2.3*.

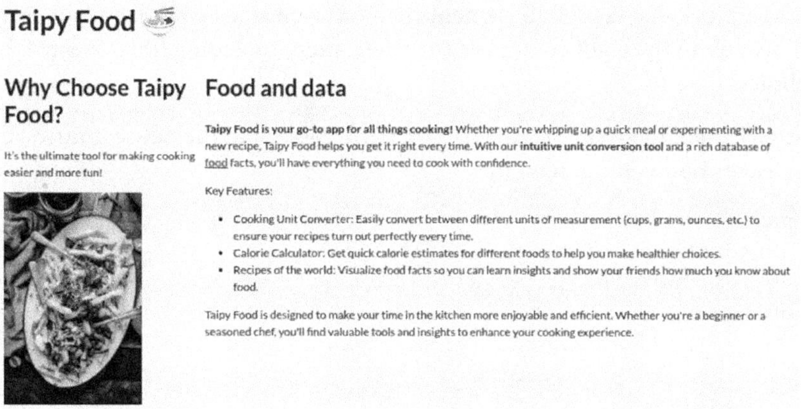

Figure 2.3 – Static Taipy Food app with the block structure

`part` blocks do *much* more than just group elements:

- **Dynamic rendering**: The `render` parameter controls whether the block is displayed. It's optional and `True` by default. If you set `render=False` (e.g., `with tgb.part(render=False):`), the entire block is hidden. You can also use a Boolean variable to show or hide blocks based on conditions.

- **Iframes**: The `page` argument allows you to embed content with iframes (see *Chapter 14*).

- **Partials**: The `partial` argument offers a finer control over your application (see *Chapter 12*).

Next, we'll explore two special types of blocks: panes and expandables. These are essentially `part` blocks with additional features.

Adding panes

A pane appears over your page when the `open` argument is set to `True` (the default is `False`). Users can close the pane by clicking outside of it.

You control the pane's visibility with a button or other trigger. For now, define an open_pane variable set to False, and create a pane with **contact info**. Later, you can set the variable to True to display it (see *Figure 2.4* – we add content to this pane later on, and we add a button to open it in the *Opening a pane with a button* section).

```
open_pane = False  # set to True to see display
with tgb.Page() as welcome_page:
    with tgb.pane(open="{open_pane}"):
        tgb.text("## Contact information", mode="md")
        tgb.text("taipy_food@taipy_food.com")
```

Adding expandables

An expandable block displays child elements in a collapsible area. We'll add an "External Resources" section to the right column of the application, including links to official food and agriculture websites.

We'll use a part element to group the description_text and the new expandable block (see *Figure 2.4*). Here's how you can set it up:

```
with tgb.part():
    tgb.text(description_text, mode="md")
    with tgb.expandable("External Resources", expanded=False):
        tgb.text(
            "* [Food and Agriculture Organization (FAO)]"
            "(https://www.fao. org/)",
            mode="md",
        )
        tgb.text(
            "* [United States Department of Agriculture (USDA)]"
            "(https:// www.usda.gov/)",
            mode="md",
        )
```

Our app now has a side panel with contact information, as well as an expandable section external resources, as you can see in *Figure 2.4*.

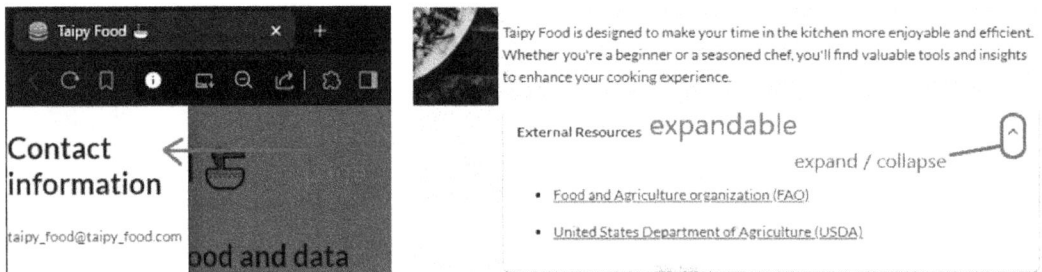

Figure 2.4 – A pane element (left) and an expandable element (right)

Creating multi-page applications

You can create a multi-page application with tabs to switch between pages. You'll find the code in /2-multipage_callbacks:

1. To organize your multi-page app, place each Page element in its own Python file within a pages directory, at the same level as main.py.

2. Create a pages folder with three Python files (we'll add code to them later):

   - welcome.py: contains the content from the previous section

   - unit_converter.py: for a unit converter

   - food_facts.py: for displaying chart

3. In each file, import the application builder (import taipy.gui.builder as tgb) but not the GUI element (which takes the Page elements and which you can run from the main file).

4. Move the variables and the welcome_page creation statement from main.py to welcome.py.

5. In main.py, keep only the import of taipy.gui, the GUI creation (taipy_food_gui = Gui(page=welcome_page)), and taipy_food_gui.run().

6. Import the page element into main.py to make this work:

   ```
   from pages.welcome import welcome_page
   ```

7. For the remaining two Python files, create a minimal Page element with a title and import both page elements to the main.py file, just like with welcome_page:

   ```
   import taipy.gui.builder as tgb
   with tgb.Page() as converter_page:
       tgb.text("# Unit converter 🖩", mode="md")
       # tgb.text("# Food facts 📊", mode="md") #For food_facts.py
   ```

Creating a multi-page element

With your three pages ready, create a Python dictionary with names for each Page element, such as taipy_food_pages. Pass this dictionary to the Gui class, but change the parameter name from page to pages:

```
taipy_food_pages = {
    "welcome": welcome_page,
    "unit_converter": converter_page,
    "food_facts": food_fact_page,
}
taipy_food_gui = Gui(pages=taipy_food_pages)
```

Running this code displays the welcome page, as it's the first page in the dictionary. Switch the order to see other pages or navigate to them directly in your browser (e.g., `http://127.0.0.1:5000/ food_facts`). However, there's a better way to navigate – let's explore that now!

Adding a root page and a navbar to your multi-page application

A **root page** is a `page` element that renders above all other pages in your application. For our app, we moved the `<h1>` header from `welcome.py` to a `root_page` element and added a `tgb.navbar()`. This code is placed in `main.py` since it's minimal and shared by all pages. Here's how it looks:

```
with tgb.Page() as root_page:
    tgb.text("# Taipy Food 🍜", mode="md")
    tgb.navbar()
```

To include the `root_page` in our app, we need to declare it in our dictionary with the following key: `"/"` (just a slash as a Python string, to reference the "root" of your app). Here is how the dictionary looks now (see *Figure 2.5*):

```
taipy_food_pages = {
    "/": root_page,
    "welcome": welcome_page,
    "unit_converter": converter_page,
    "food_facts": food_fact_page,
}
```

As you can see in *Figure 2.5*, our multiple-page app has now a root page with a shared `<h1>` title and a navigation menu.

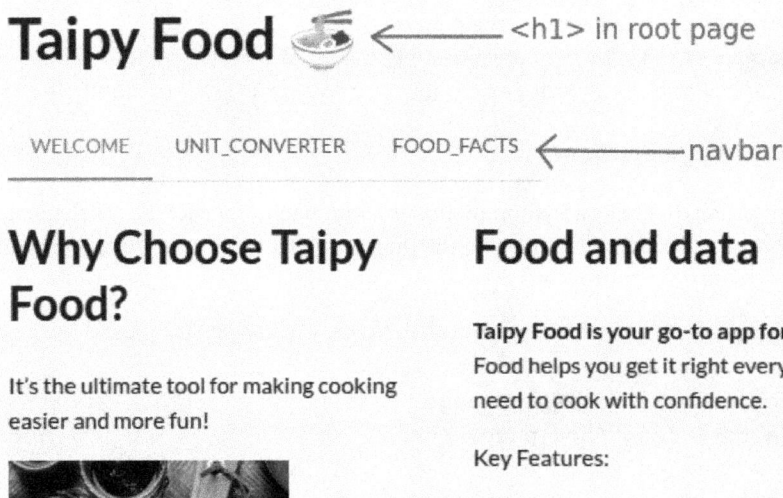

Figure 2.5 – A multi-page app

Page scope

In Taipy, variables are scoped to the page where they're defined. For example, variables in `unit_converter.py` only exist there, and using them on another page causes an error. This is different from **scenario scope** (see *Chapter 4*) and doesn't apply to single-page apps. To share variables across the app, define them in `main.py` for "**global scope**" (different from Python's globals). This way, you can set parameters on one page and use them on another.

Now you know how to create and structure a Taipy application and add static elements such as text and images. While static elements are useful, the main goal of an app is to let users interact with it and visualize data. Let's see how to do that!

Adding visual elements, binding variables, and using callbacks

Taipy applications let users interact with visual elements, such as buttons or charts. You can bind Python variables to some visual elements, and let users change the values of the variables through the application. You can also bind Python functions to the visual elements, with callbacks, and let users trigger the callback functions from the visual elements.

Python's documentation defines a callback as "*a subroutine function that is passed as an argument to be executed at some point in the future*" (`https://docs.python.org/3/glossary.html#term-callback`). In the case of a Taipy application, users interact with the frontend of the application, that is, the buttons, input forms, selectors, and so on that appear in the browser. When users change values from the frontend element, these actions send a message to the backend (the server rendering the app) via sockets (`https://socket.io/docs`), and that's where Python functions are executed (and the result is sent back to the frontend).

Features of visual elements

Taipy's documentation divides visual elements into controls and blocks. Blocks structure content, as we've already discovered; **controls** let users interact with the application. Here's an overview of their notable features:

- **Navigational versus functional**: Navigational controls (such as `navbar` and `menu`) manage the app's layout, while functional controls (such as input fields and buttons) let users interact with data or trigger actions.

- **Variable binding**: Some elements, such as text inputs and charts, bind to variables. Others, such as buttons and file selectors, don't. Controllers can bind to types such as `numbers` for numeric values or `input` for strings.

- **Input/output**: Output elements (such as charts and text) change based on variables but don't interact directly. Input controllers (such as buttons and inputs) handle user input. Some, such as images, can display content and generate actions when clicked.

> **Important note**
>
> Plotly charts allow user interaction, such as zooming, but don't alter the fig object (users interact with the object in the frontend). Taipy charts primarily display data but also support callbacks that trigger functions on the server side (backend interaction).

- **Input scope**: When it comes to the type of data that the users input, we can consider the following:

  - **Binary**: Actions such as clicking a button or image.

  - **Discrete**: Selecting from predefined options.

  - **Free selection**: Entering any value with input or number controllers, with possible restrictions.

- **Actionable or not**: Buttons and some controllers trigger actions (e.g., calling Python functions), while elements such as text don't.

> **Important note**
>
> Taipy's Scenario Management *controllers* interact with Taipy Scenario Management *objects*, covered in *Chapters 3-6*.

Control types and arguments

When you code an application, you add controllers as Python functions. These functions can have four of the following main arguments:

- value: The value they bind to

- lov (**List Of Values**): Used for selectors such as dropdown menus

- on_action: References the function to call when the user presses a button or a key

- on_change: References the function to call when the user changes a value

Controller functions include arguments for styling, labeling, and constraints (e.g., max/min values). We'll focus on key cases in the book, but you can refer to this table for a summary of most of them: https://github.com/PacktPublishing/Getting-Started-with-Taipy/tree/main/chapter_02/taipy_controls.

Binding variables to a controller

Binding variables means linking a Python variable to a controller, allowing updates. Variables can change due to user input or Python functions.

Now, let's add controllers and bind variables! We'll use `number` controllers in `unit_converter.py` for converting units such as teaspoons, tablespoons, milliliters, grams, and ounces. In this example, we'll use *metric and US legal units* with approximations. Feel free to add more units and experiment on your own!

We set variables with initial values (all to `0`) before creating the `Page` element:

```
grams = cups = ounces = tablespoons = teaspoons = milliliters = 0
```

Then we can add the `number` controller and bind the variables. We add the elements with `tgb.number()` function calls. The `value` parameter is the number that the `number` box shows in the UI.

`value` can receive a hard-coded value, as long as it's of the right type. For example, for a `number` controller, you can pass `value=5`. This, however, would not be very useful!

Bind variables by using quotes and curly braces. If you pass the variable name as an argument, the value of the first load will never change! Check *Adding callbacks* to understand this better:

- **Right way**: `value="{cups}"`. It will update as intended.

- **Wrong way**: `value=cups`. Since `cups` equals `0` for its initial value, it will remain set as `0`.

You can also perform operations within the `value` argument. For example, to display kilograms from `grams`, use `{grams/1000}`. Here's how we added `number` elements with layout and text elements for display, including kilograms in a `text` visual element:

```
tgb.text("## Volume units", mode="md")
with tgb.layout("1 1 1 1"):
    tgb.number(value="{cups}", label="Cups")
    tgb.number(value="{tablespoons}", label="Tablespoons")
    tgb.number(value="{teaspoons}", label="Teaspoons")
    tgb.number(value="{milliliters}", label="Milliliters")

tgb.text("## Weight units", mode="md")
with tgb.layout("1 1 1 1"):
    tgb.number(value="{grams}", label="Grams")
    tgb.number(value="{ounces}", label="Ounces")
    tgb.text("") # skip this cell
    tgb.text("") # skip this cell

tgb.text("{grams} grams is {grams/1000} kilograms", mode="md")
```

Now that you know how to bind variables to a visual element, let's see how to bind visual elements to Python functions using callbacks.

Adding callbacks

Taipy uses callbacks to update the app based on user interactions. Callbacks are Python functions (executed in the backend) triggered by events such as clicks or key presses (in the front end). Visual elements often include on_action and on_change parameters to handle these events, updating only the necessary parts of the app for better performance.

Callbacks use **State** (https://docs.taipy.io/en/release-4.1/refmans/reference/pkg_taipy/pkg_gui/State/) which holds the current status of all application variables. State is always the first argument in callback functions, essential for accessing and modifying variable values.

Adding on_change callbacks

Let's add callback functions to our converter app. We've separated volume and weight units, so you can convert between grams and ounces, but not to cups, for example. We'll define a function for each unit type.

The functions called by on_change have two parameters after State, which are var_name, which refers to the variable bound to the element, and value, which is the current value of the variable. You can directly call the variable name and access its value with State, but you can use these optional parameters to use the same function in different elements.

Variables bind to State, so you can use them as children of this element. You can find the change_weight function at /3-final_app/food_converter_functions/change_weight_callback.py.

Notice how we used the round() function so the number elements don't exceed two decimals. You can use *anything Python* in these functions and call any Python library. Also, notice we didn't use a return statement, instead, we used the callback function to reassign values to bounded variables with the State class.

To call callback functions, you need to pass their name (no parameters or parentheses) the callback variables; in this case, we pass it to on_change:

```
tgb.number(label="Grams", value="{grams}", on_change=change_weight)
tgb.number(label="Ounces", value="{ounces}", on_change=change_weight)
```

> **Important note**
> The State lets multiple users interact with the application independently without overwriting each other's variables. Test this by opening your app in two different browsers; they should operate independently.

Now we can add the function for the volume conversions (as well as update the controllers as in the previous example), which is available at /3-final_app/food_converter_functions/ change_volume_callback.py.

If you play with the converter, you'll notice that values update when you change a unit. If you adjust your weight units, the kilogram value will also update.

Adding on_action callbacks

Some elements, such as buttons, use the on_action parameter to trigger a callback on events such as clicks. We'll add three buttons to reset values: one for all variables, and two for resetting weight or volume individually.

The on_action callback function receives an id parameter, which returns the button's unique ID. This allows you to use the same function for different buttons by checking the ID. The payload argument is not needed here. Let's create a reset callback function: see 3-final_app/food_ converter_functions/reset_callback.py.

Create three buttons in the Page element: one to erase all the elements, one to erase weight units, and one to erase volume units, all with their id element:

```
tgb.button(
    label="Reset weight values",
    on_action=reset, id="reset_weight",)
tgb.button(
    label="Reset volume values",
    on_action=reset, id="reset_volume")
tgb.button(
    label="Reset all values",
    on_action=reset, id="reset_all")
```

You can also use **lambda notation** to define your callbacks. The lambda notation takes state as a parameter. To reset the weight values, you could use the following, instead of referencing a function:

```
tgb.button(...
    on_action=lambda state: [setattr(
        state, unit_name, 0) for unit_name in ["grams", "ounces"]]
)
```

If you play with the app, you'll see that when you reset it, all the values turn to 0 (see *Figure 2.6*).

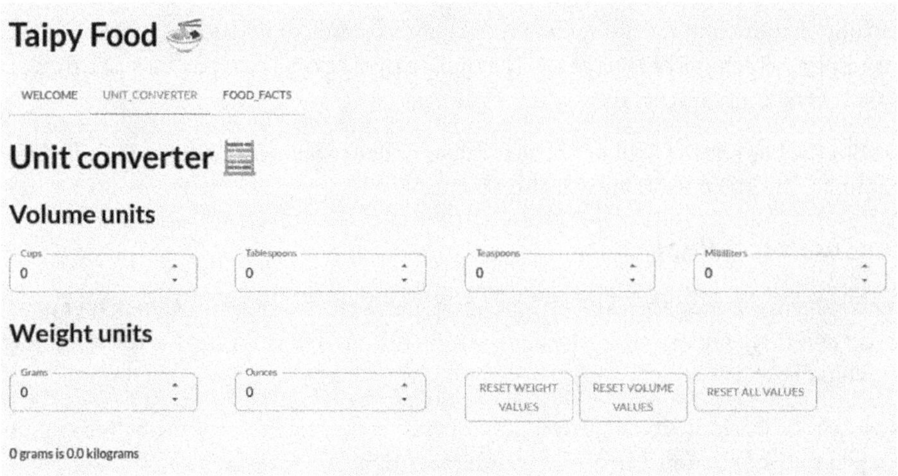

Figure 2.6 – A unit converter

Now, let's dive into handling complex data types such as tables and charts, as well as using selectors and additional features such as side menus and file uploads.

Displaying your interactive data visually

We'll work with a small dataset from the USDA (https://www.ers.usda.gov/data-products/food-expenditure-series/). This dataset tracks US **food spending at home** (**FAH**) and **away from home** (**FAFH**) over time. Nominal sales show the amount spent in current dollars, while constant-dollar sales account for inflation, making prices comparable across different years. We'll use a file named state_sales.csv, we place it in the data directory (/3-final_app/data/state_sales.csv).

First, we need to create a pandas DataFrame to work with tables and Plotly charts. We create two functions in a separate file and import them to food_facts.py:

- clean_sales_data cleans the CSV file and formats an initial DataFrame. It uses the us package (install with pip install us)
- update_df_sales selects a subset of the DataFrame, with a Boolean adjust_inflation parameter; it returns a DataFrame with nominal columns (if True) or with constant sales.

You can find the code for both functions in /3-final_app/food_fact_functions/initiate_sales.py.

In the file food_facts.py, we create the DataFrame like this:

```
df_sales_original = clean_sales_data(sales_csv_file)
df_sales = update_df_sales(df_sales_original)
```

Working with tables

To create a table within your Page element, use tgb.table. You can customize its size with the width and height arguments. For example, to make it smaller, set the height to 60vh. For users to filter the data in your table, add the filter=True parameter. You can add a hover_text to display a small message when the user hovers over a table cell. Use nan_value to replace missing values with a specific value (e.g., 0):

```
tgb. table(
    data="{df_sales}",
    height="60vh",
    filter=True,
    editable=True,
    hover_text="USDA Data ",
    on_edit=edit_note,
    on_add=add_row,
    on_delete=delete_row,
    nan_value = 0,
)
```

The filter button appears in the top left of the table (see *Figure 2.7*); when you click on it, you can choose your column and the conditions to filter. You can let users edit cells, add rows, or remove rows. There are three callback functions for this, but if you choose to use any, you'll need to make your table editable with editable=True. Let's now see the three types of callback functions for tables.

Editing tables

Tables are not just a great way to display data. You can add the options to add or delete rows and to make data editable.

To edit, we use the on_edit callback and create a Python function called edit_note. Keep in mind that when you add on_edit, all columns will show a pencil icon, meaning they're editable. However, without a working function, changes won't be saved.

The on_edit callback has two arguments: var_name, which, in our example, returns the pandas DataFrame df_sales; and payload, which gives details about the column and row where the change occurred. Since we only want users to edit the "Note" column, we need to set up a function to handle this. The function calls another function, add_note(), and it uses it twice, once for each DataFrame (/food_fact_functions/edit_note_callback.py).

The function can use var_name instead of df_sales, but since the function always works with the same DataFrame, it doesn't matter.

> **Important note**
>
> Users can change the DataFrame, and changes persist when reloading the app. You'll lose these changes if the app shuts down and restarts. You could change the function to save data to a file or database.

Adding and removing rows from tables

Tables have two additional callbacks for adding and deleting rows: on_add and on_delete. The on_add callback adds a small plus (+) sign in the top-left corner of the table, while the on_delete callback adds a trash bin icon for each row. Without a valid callback function, you won't be able to add or delete rows. The functions provided add and delete rows in the pandas DataFrame, but you could also change them to update a CSV file or a database.

When adding a row, you can either insert an empty row or one with predefined values. For example, if you want each new row to have "New Index" under the "Note" column, see the add_row_callback.py file (3-final_app/food_fact_functions/add_row_callback.py).

Conversely, the delete_row_callback.py file shows the function to remove the pandas row (3-final_app/food_fact_functions/delete_row_callback.py).

> **Important note**
>
> In our example, when we add a row, it is almost empty, but only the "Note" column is editable (because it's the only column included in the edit_note function). Feel free to adjust the parameters and experiment with the functions!

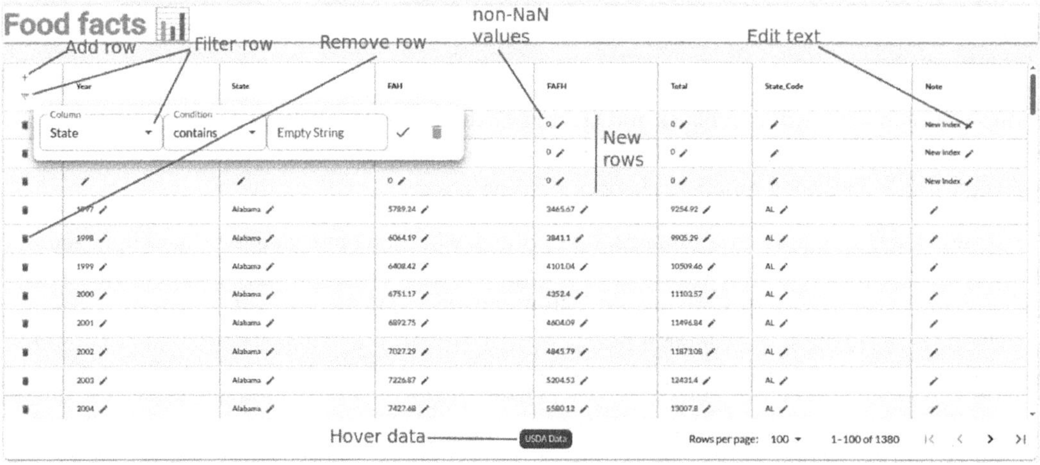

Figure 2.7 – A table and its main components

Adding selection controls to your application

Selection controls let you interact with data. You can select subsets of a DataFrame or single values to narrow your display or to perform operations of those values.

Adding toggle buttons

Let's make a binary toggle button to select whether we want `df_sales` to adjust the data to inflation. Toggle buttons let users pick between options. The `value` parameter binds to a variable that updates when a selection is made. Use the `lov` parameter to create a button for each value in a list. Without a list, the toggle acts as a binary switch, with the `value` variable set to `True` or `False`.

We create an `adjust_inflation = False` variable, and then we create a toggle button inside the `Page`, like this:

```
tgb.toggle(
    value="{adjust_inflation}",
    label="Adjust for inflation",
    on_change=update_sales,
)
```

Next, we code the callback function, `update_sales`, which will call the second function that we defined to initiate the DataFrame, `update_sales`, passing `adjust_inflation` as an argument:

```
def update_sales(state, var_name, payload):
    df_sales_copy = update_df_sales(
        state.df_sales_original, state.adjust_inflation)
```

We can add toggle buttons from a list of elements. Our data has three metrics: FAH, FAFH, and Total spending. Before we add dynamic charts, we want to create a variable that updates the metric to use for display. This won't change the DataFrame. To do so, we initiate a list of values and the `metric` value, like this:

```
lov_metrics = ["FAH", "FAFH", "Total"]
metric = "Total"
```

On the page, we add a toggle button with `metric` as a bound value and the list of possible values assigned to the `lov` parameter. We also add an `on_change` callback, and we leave the `update_charts` function empty (use `pass` or try to print values with `var_name` (refer to the *Adding charts to your applications* section to see how it's coded). Here is the code for the toggle button:

```
tgb.toggle(value="{metric}", lov=lov_metrics, on_change=update_charts)
```

Adding selectors

Taipy has a `selector` element that lets you choose a value from a list. It supports the creation of dropdown and multiple selection lists.

We have two categorical columns in the DataFrame, `Year` and `State` (for US states). We're going to create a list to select values for each category, so users can filter the DataFrame to display specific years or states.

1. First, set up the default initial values and the list of options for the dropdown. For the year list, we also append an "`All`" value, so users can select a specific year, or all years:

```
lov_year = list(df_sales["Year"].astype(str).unique())
lov_year.append("All")
selected_year = "All"
```

2. We also create a list and an initial value for the states:

```
lov_states = list(df_sales["State"].unique())
selected_states = lov_states
```

3. Next, we define our `selector` elements. Both selectors will call the same callback, `update_sales`, the one that we defined in the *Adding toggle buttons* section, and that we're going to extend to filter the DataFrame.

    For the years, we only want users to select one value (one of them is `All`), and we want a dropdown list. We code the selector like this:

```
tgb.selector(
    value="{selected_year}",
    lov="{lov_year}",
    on_change=update_sales,
    label="select year",
    dropdown=True,
)
```

4. For the US states, we want users to have a multiple selection option, with checkboxes. Taipy doesn't (yet) offer a dropdown checkbox list, and we have 50 options, which would take up too much space in our app. To work this around this, we create a variable called `open_states`, with its initial value set to `False`. We then use this value to create a side pane, and we add the list to the pane:

```
with tgb.pane(open="{open_states}"):
    tgb.text("## Select states", mode="md")
    tgb.selector(
        value="{selected_states}",
        lov="{lov_states}",
```

```
        on_change=update_sales,
        label="select states",
        multiple=True,
        mode="checkbox",
    )
```

5. We also add a button, with the other selection elements, so we can open the side pane:

```
tgb.button(label="select states", on_action=open_state_selector)
```

6. Then, we create the `open_state_selector` function:

```
def open_state_selector(state):
    state.open_states = True
```

7. Now, we change the callback function to add the filters. We start by creating a mask as a pandas Series of all `True` values (`pd.Series([True] * len(df_sales))`). Then, we update this mask with each condition in a loop, using the bitwise operator `&=` (`https://docs.python.org/3/reference/expressions.html#binary-bitwise-operations`). You can find the complete function in `3-final_app/food_fact_functions/update_sales_callback.py`.

    You can see all the selectors (except for the checklist in the side pane) in *Figure 2.8*.

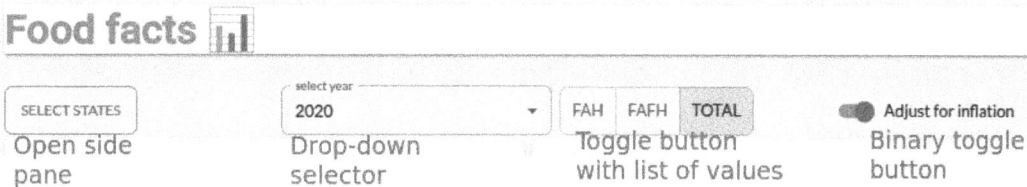

Food facts

SELECT STATES	select year 2020 ▾	FAH FAFH **TOTAL**	⬤ Adjust for inflation
Open side pane	Drop-down selector	Toggle button with list of values	Binary toggle button

Figure 2.8 – Toggles and selectors

Now, let's see how to add some charts to your applications.

Adding charts to your applications

Taipy integrates with Python Plotly, one of the biggest libraries for data visualization and one that has the advantage of making interactive visualizations. Plotly has two main sub-libraries: **Plotly Express** (`https://plotly.com/python/plotly-express/`), for quickly creating common charts, and **Plotly Graph Objects** (`https://plotly.com/python/`) (**Plotly GO**), which is more complex but offers greater customization. You can create a `fig` object with either library.

In Taipy, you have two ways to create your charts, but they both use the `tgb.chart()` control:

- Using a predefined chart from the chart catalog (https://docs.taipy.io/en/release-4.1/refmans/gui/viselements/generic/chart/)
- Using a Plotly `fig` element (Plotly Express or Plotly GO)

Adding charts from the chart catalog

While Taipy's user manuals are useful, they might not list all possible arguments for each chart type. The current documentation (see the bar chart at https://docs.taipy.io/en/release-4.1/refmans/gui/viselements/generic/charts/bar/) shows only the **Key Properties**. To find all arguments, use VS Code and **Ctrl + click** on the function name to see its arguments, as each chart has different options.

Let's create a bar chart and a heatmap. The values will update when you change selections because the DataFrame is bound with `data="{df_sales}"`. Each chart type requires specific arguments: the `chart` uses `x` and `y` for its axes, while `heatmap` also needs a `z` value; we use the `metric` variable to define the values that the chart needs to plot. We bind this variable to `y` or `z` (see the *Adding toggle buttons* section to see how this variable updates). For the charts to update, we need to add the argument `rebuild=True` argument, which is only required when binding variables to parameters that aren't `data` (`x` and `y` in this case):

```
tgb.chart(
    data="{df_sales}",
    type="bar",
    x="State",
    y="{metric}",
    title=f"Value per State",
    rebuild=True,
)
tgb.chart(
    data="{df_sales}",
    type="heatmap",
    x="State",
    y="Year",
    z="{metric}",
    title="Value per year and State",
    rebuild=True,
)
```

Adding custom Plotly charts

To add custom charts, you first need to create a Plotly figure. In this case, we'll create a choropleth map, since it's not (yet) in Taipy's catalog. The function takes a `metric` parameter to know which column to use for the numerical values to display (see the code that creates the function in `charts.py`).

In the `food_facts.py` page, we use this function to initialize a chart object: `fig_states = create_fig_states(df_sales, "Total")`.

Now you can add the chart using the `chart` element and the `figure` parameter; remember to bind your variable:

```
tgb.chart(figure="{fig_states}")
```

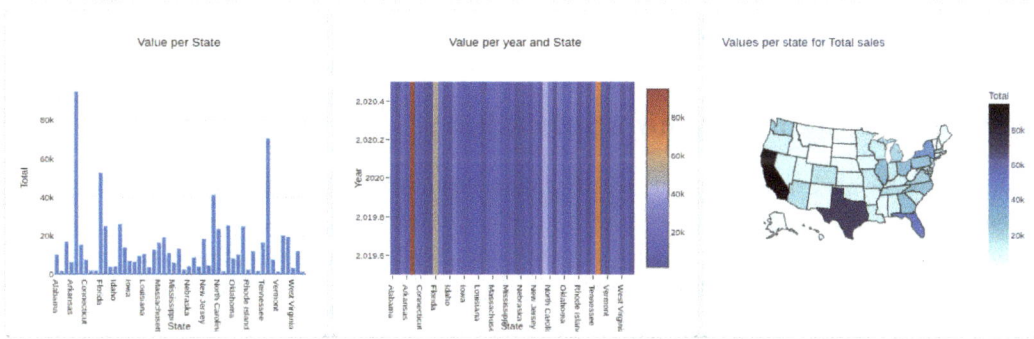

Figure 2.9 – Charts in the application

Updating the charts

We have two callback functions. The first one, `update_sales`, updates `df_sales`. This DataFrame is bound to the bar chart and the heatmap, which update automatically. To also update the maps, add the following line of code at the end of the function:

```
state.fig_states = create_fig_states(state.df_sales, state.metric)
```

The second one, `update_charts`, is triggered when users change the metrics with a toggle button. We add the same line. We could have called the same callback, but it would perform unnecessary steps, so having a lighter function here is more efficient. You can check the code in `/3-final_app/food_fact_functions/update_charts_callback.py`.

Exploring navigational controls

You can use controls to interact with your page layout. We've already used the `navbar` control. We also created a side pane earlier, but it doesn't render yet. We need to add a button so users can open it. Additionally, we'll look at how to add a navigation side menu, which is a cosmetic alternative to the sidebar.

Opening a pane with a button

Once you create a pane, you just need a button that sets the show value to True. Side panes will automatically set this value to False, so you don't need to handle that. The pane is in welcome. py. We created the following callback function:

```
def open_pane_callback(state):
    state.open_pane = True
```

We add the button in the page. When you click on it, it should open your side pane:

```
tgb.button(
    label="Show Contacts",
    on_action=open_pane_callback,
)
```

Adding a side menu to your application

You can replace the navbar with a menu, which is more customizable but also more complex to set up. To add a menu, replace tgb.navbar with tgb.menu in main.py. Unlike navbar, menu takes arguments such as a menu label, a list of values (tuples with the name to display and the page they link to), and the on_menu callback:

```
tgb.menu(
    label="Navigation_menu",
    lov=[
        ("welcome", "welcome_page"),
        ("unit_converter", "converter_page"),
        ("food_facts", "food_fact_page"),
    ],
    on_action=on_menu,
)
```

Now, your menu should show in the left part of your app, with letters for each page. To make it work, you need to import the navigate function (https://docs.taipy.io/en/release-4.1/refmans/reference/pkg_taipy/pkg_gui/navigate/) from taipy.gui, and create this callback:

```
from taipy.gui import navigate

def on_menu(state, var_name, info):
    page = info["args"][0]
    navigate(state, to=page)
```

The `navigate` function is a special callback that takes the `state` parameter and the `to` parameter to change pages. The `info` value is a dictionary, where `"args"` is a list with a single value (the name of the page to navigate to).

Adding icons

Taipy has an `Icon` function that lets you add SVG or PNG icons to your buttons or menu (see *Figure 2.10*). We'll use this to add icons to our navigation menu. We got our icons with iconmonstr (`https://iconmonstr.com/`). We made three icons, one for each page, and saved them in the images folder. First, import the `Icon` class:

```
from taipy.gui.icon import Icon
```

Then, we replace the display name in the `lov` from `tgb.menu()` with an `Icon()` object. `Icon` takes the `path` to the logo and the text to display next to it as parameters:

```
(
    "welcome",
    Icon(
        path="./images/utensils_dark.png",
        text="Welcome!",
    ),
),
```

Figure 2.10 shows the side menu we created for our application.

Figure 2.10 – Side menu in the application

Uploading and downloading files

You can let users upload and download files from the application. Let's see how.

Uploading files

Users may need to upload files for various tasks, such as images for analysis, large PDFs for NLP, or CSV files for tabular data. Let's add a *"favorite restaurants"* section in welcome.py, where users can upload a CSV file with their favorite restaurants. We'll use a sample CSV with imaginary data (yumyum.csv) for this.

We need to use tgb.file_selector, which takes content as its first argument. This is where the file will be uploaded. It also has an on_action callback to specify how to read the file and optionally store it permanently. First, let's define our variables: a file path variable (initially set to None, which the selector will update automatically) and an empty DataFrame:

```
favorite_restaurants_url = None
favorite_restaurants = pd.DataFrame()
```

Here's how the selector is set up. We also added a table to display the DataFrame once it's loaded. We restrict file type to CSV files with extensions=".csv":

```
with tgb.expandable("Favorite Restaurants", expanded=False):
    tgb.file_selector(
        content="{favorite_restaurants_url}",
        label="Upload restaurants",
        on_action=upload_restaurants,
        extensions=".csv",
        drop_message="Yum Yum!",
    )
    tgb.table("{favorite_restaurants}", height="60vh", rebuild=True)
```

Figure 2.11 shows the uploading button, and the table from the uploaded CSV file.

Favorite Restaurants   ⌃

| ⬆ UPLOAD RESTAURANTS |

Restaurant Name	Phone	Email
The Bistro	123-456-7890	info@thebistro.com
Pasta Palace	234-567-8901	contact@pastapalace.com
Burger Haven	345-678-9012	support@burgerhaven.com
Sushi World	456-789-0123	hello@sushiworld.com
Taco Town	567-890-1234	info@tacotown.com

Rows per page: 100 ▾   1-5 of 5 |< < > >|

Figure 2.11 – Upload button and uploaded CSV showing as table

Downloading files

Your applications might generate files or have stored files. You can add a download button to let users retrieve these files. These buttons also have an `on_action` callback, but we won't use it here. Since `food_facts.py` displays data from a CSV file, we can add a button to allow users to download this CSV. We include a `name` parameter to specify the filename; otherwise, the default is an arbitrary set of characters:

```
tgb.file_download(
    content="{fao_csv_file}",
    label="download dataset",
    name="fao_dataset_eu_2019-2024.csv",
)
```

Adding notifications

Notifications are small pop-up messages that alert users about important events, such as a successful operation, an error, or a warning. To add a notification, use the `notify` function and import it like this:

```
from taipy.gui import notify
```

You can call the `notify` function from within any callback function. It takes a `state` parameter (the same as in your callback) and two main arguments:

- `notification_type`: Accepts four values – `information` (default), `warning`, `success`, or `error`
- `message`: The text of the notification

For example, to add a warning notification in `unit_converter.py` when the user sets values to 0, you could include the following code in the `reset` function:

```
notify(state, notification_type="warning", message="Values set to 0")
```

Changing your page's styles

Web applications use CSS to style their elements. With Taipy, you don't need CSS to build your apps. We created a mockup with many components without adding any CSS. Taipy provides a default style that's clean and sufficient for starting your applications. Also, some functions we used, such as `layout()`, create a CSS grid behind the scenes.

Eventually, you might want more customization. We'll cover some parameters and tricks to further customize your app and how to add your own CSS code.

Taipy Stylekit

Taipy includes a predefined set of classes and CSS code called the Stylekit (`https://docs.taipy.io/en/release-4.1/userman/gui/styling/stylekit/`) to style your application. You might have noticed that the buttons are orange and the app's background isn't plain white.

CSS works by linking HTML elements (through classes, IDs, or tags) with style rules (such as color, size, or font) and their values (e.g., hex codes for color, and numbers for size). The Stylekit has documented classes (`https://docs.taipy.io/en/release-4.1/userman/gui/styling/stylekit/#css-classe`) with predefined styles. You can use the Stylekit in two ways:

- Add class names to your application's elements to apply the styles
- Override the default Stylekit parameters

Each class in the Stylekit has one CSS property, but you can apply multiple classes to an element.

Adding Stylekit classes

First, we can add Stylekit classes to `class_name` arguments. For example, we could add `color-primary` to the `text` controller for our `<h1>` header:

```
tgb.text("# Taipy Food 🍜", mode="md", class_name="color-primary")
```

You can add other Stylekit classes similarly, such as `color-secondary` for `<h2>` titles, or adjust margins and padding with classes such as m0 (to remove all margins) and p0 (to remove padding). For example, you can use `class_name = "p0 m0"` for `tgb.table` and `tgb.chart` elements to make them look tighter. You can pass multiple classes to `class_name` by separating them with a space, without any other separator.

The Stylekit also includes four special classes, known as **styles** sections. We added three of these to `welcome.py` (see *Figure 2.12*):

- `container`: Limits the block's width, adjustable via `--container-max-width`. It helps center content or create a focused section on the page.
- `card`: Adds elevation and padding around content, making sections stand out on the page.
- `header`: Creates an elevated bar, commonly used for headers.
- `sidebar`: Creates a full-height, scrollable section that stands out from the background, with spacing and responsiveness managed by `--element-padding` and `--sidebar-min-width`.

Changing the Stylekit

You can also change the Stylekit's properties, but you can't add new classes. For this, you need to create a dictionary in `main.py`, like the following; we just changed two properties, the main colors (see the result in *Figure 2.12*):

```
stylekit = {
    "color_primary": "#E91E63",  # hot pink
    "color_secondary": "#00BCD4",  # aqua blue
}
```

Then, you need to pass the dictionary as an argument to the `stylekit` parameter in the `run()` method:

```
    stylekit=stylekit,
```

Figure 2.12 shows the styles we added to pour application.

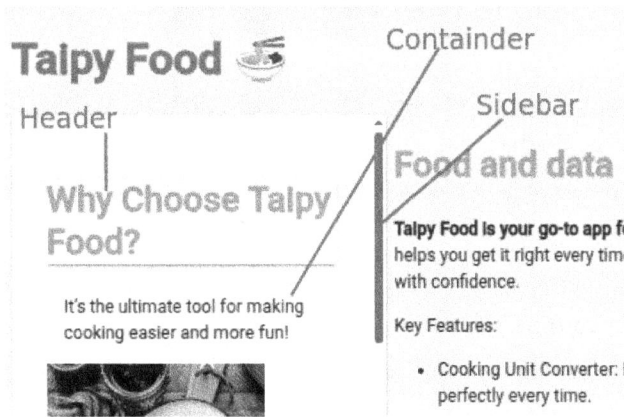

Figure 2.12 – Some added styles in `welcome.py`

In this section, we covered some styling considerations to further personalize your applications. This ends our chapter about creating UIs, and you should now be able to create simple apps using Taipy!

Summary

In this chapter, we covered the essentials of Taipy for GUI. You should now understand the key components needed to build an application: the `Gui` class, the `run()` method, and single-page versus multi-page apps. We also introduced you to important Taipy page concepts, such as the `Page` element, binding visual elements to Python variables, the `State` element, and callbacks.

Moreover, you now know how to structure and arrange elements on a page, add visual components, and focus on the key ones. The documentation on visual elements (`https://docs.taipy.io/en/release-4.1/refmans/gui/viselements/`) is excellent and will continue to expand as Taipy evolves. Finally, you learned how to personalize themes and styles using Taipy's simple commands, the Stylekit, and CSS files. You can find real-life cases (that interact with ML models, enterprise data, LLMs, and so on) in *Chapters 7-11*.

Now that you know how to create UIs with Taipy, let's see how to use Data Nodes and integrate them into Taipy applications!

Questions

1. How do you bind visual elements to variables, and why is this important?

2. Using the documentation (`https://docs.taipy.io/en/release-4.1/refmans/gui/viselements/#generic-controls`), can you change the number selectors from `unit_converter.py` to a `slider` type? Can you increase the maximum value of the slider?

3. Using the documentation (`https://docs.taipy.io/en/release-4.1/refmans/gui/viselements/generic/table/`), how would you hide a column (for example, the column `State_Code` column) in a table? Why is this different than removing it from the DataFrame?

4. How would you add a notification that displays a success message when the user changes a metric to display the charts?

5. How would you style a single element of your Taipy application using its ID?

Answers

1. To bind a variable, you first need to create a Python variable, before the `Page()` element. This variable has an initial value, for example, `my_variable=0`. To bind it to a visual element, you need to use the quotes and curly brackets syntax, for example:

   ```
   tgb.number(value="{my_variable}"
   ```

   This is important because if the variable isn't bound, it won't be part of the `State` object. In that case, the selector will take the initial value (when the server loads), but it will never update.

2. To add a slider, just use `tgb.slider() instead of tgb.number`. It accepts the same `on_change` callback and it works with numerical values, so there won't be problems. There is also a `label` argument, so that will work.

   The problem in this case is that the slider has values between `0` and `100`. This is why this is not an ideal controller here. You can adjust the maximum value with the `max` parameter:

   ```
   tgb.slider(
       label="Grams", value="{grams}",
       max=10000, on_ change=change_weight
   )
   ```

3. To hide a column, you need to use the optional `columns` parameter. The default is showing all, when you use it, you have to specify all the columns that you want to keep. For our example, we want to keep all columns except "`State Code`". We would add this argument to `tgb.table`, keeping all the columns we want:

```
columns=[
    "Year",
    "State",
    "FAH",
    "FAFH",
    "Total",
    "Note",
],
```

When we hide a column, it only affects the display, as opposed to removing the column from the DataFrame. In this case, we use "`State_Code`" to plot the states on a map, so we can't remove it from the DataFrame. If we didn't use the column at all, we could have dropped it from the DataFrame instead.

4. First, import the `notify` function (from `taipy.gui import notify`).

The toggle button that changes the value of the `metric` variable triggers the callback function `update_charts` callback function. You can place the following code at the end of the function:

```
notify(
    state, notification_type="success",
    message=f"Selected metric: {payload}"
)
```

Here, we used the three arguments of the callback:

- `state`: You have to pass this to notify (mandatory)

- `var_name`: This needs to be in the second position, even if we don't use it here

- `payload`: This gives us the value of the bound variable, so we can use it to add a more specific message.

5. In the unit converter, we added IDs to three buttons (we used the `id` variable in the callback function). For example, one button has: `id="reset_all"`. All we have to do now is add some color to this ID in `main.css`:

```
#reset_all {
    color: #0e0e0e;
    background-color: red;
}
```

Unlock this book's exclusive benefits now

Scan this QR code or go to packtpub.com/unlock, then search this book by name.

Note: Keep your purchase invoice ready before you start.

3

Connecting to Data Sources with Data Nodes

As we saw in *Chapter 2*, you can create complete Taipy applications with a UI and use Python data structures or pandas DataFrames to back these applications. However, Taipy offers a different way to access your data: **Data Nodes**. Data Nodes are part of Taipy Scenario Management and let you create pipelines to transform data and run models. You can also use Data Nodes alone, without creating a **scenario**. You can access Data Nodes using Python functions, the **user interface** or **UI** (through a visual element), or within a scenario.

In this chapter, you'll learn what Data Nodes are, why they're important, and what types of data sources they accept. You'll see how to configure and create them. Then, you'll discover how to bring your Data Nodes to your UI and let users interact with them.

We'll cover the following topics:

- Data Nodes and data sources
- Connecting your Data Nodes with your GUI

Technical requirements

The complete code used in this chapter can be found on the GitHub repository: `https://github.com/PacktPublishing/Getting-Started-with-Taipy/tree/main/chapter_03`. Throughout the chapter, we'll mention the names of the GitHub files we're using so that you can pick them up from the repository when needed.

Some examples use the beautifulsoup4 library, which is an HTML parser (`https://pypi.org/project/beautifulsoup4/`). You can install it with `pip install beautifulsoup4`. Knowing about the library will make those examples easier to understand, but it's not required. Since Data Nodes help us connect to data sources, some examples will require basic knowledge and access to the following technologies (you don't have to test every type of connection to understand the overall concept!):

- SQLite databases
- PostgreSQL databases
- AWS S3 storages – you'll need to create an account (`https://aws.amazon.com/s3/`)

Data Nodes and data sources

Data Nodes offer a simple and **clean interface to access data**, but they aren't data: they are an abstraction where we can declare the data source (a file, a database, and so on) and the output (a string, a pandas DataFrame, etc.…), and read and write to them. **Abstraction** means simplifying complex systems by focusing on the essential details while hiding the underlying complexity. In this case, the Data Node hides the interaction steps with the data source, making it easier to work with.

Using Data Nodes simplifies complex data connections, separates data access from your app's logic (such as in hexagonal architecture; see `https://alistair.cockburn.us/hexagonal-architecture/`) and makes code more modular and robust. It also helps with easy migration between data sources and tracks changes in data over time. And of course, Data Nodes are the entry point to Taipy Scenario Management, which we cover in *Chapters 4* and *5*!

Data Nodes support standard file formats (like CSV or JSON), several **Database Management Systems** (**DBMSs**), and Amazon S3 storage. A **generic Data Node** type lets you customize how to access data, using a Python function. Let's now see how we create these Data Nodes!

Working with Data Nodes

Using Data Nodes is a three-step process (see *Figure 3.1*):

1. **Create your configuration objects**: With the Python API, or a TOML file (usually with Taipy Studio). You create a configuration object using a function from the `Config` class.
2. **Create the Data Nodes**: Next, you create the Data Nodes by using a Taipy function such as `taipy.create_global_data_node` or creating your Data Nodes as part of a scenario with `taipy.create_scenario`.
3. **Access Data Node information**: Finally, you can access information about the Data Node using associated methods, such as the `read()` method to retrieve data, or `write()`, to write it.

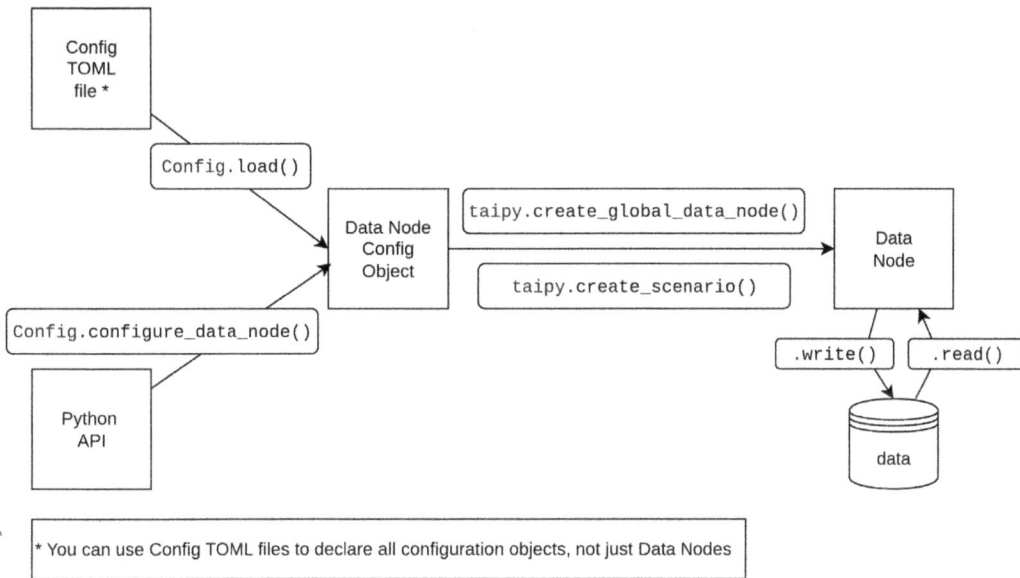

Figure 3.1 – Steps to create a Data Node

As *Figure 3.1* shows, you have two ways to create configuration objects (Python API or via TOML file). You have to choose one or the other, and the objects they create are identical. You also have two functions to create Data Nodes from configuration files, but they create different objects (**Global Data Node** versus **Scenario Data Node**); they're not equal.

In this section, we cover how to create a default `Data Node configuration` object (with the Python API) and then how to create a Data Node from the configuration objects. Afterward, we'll learn how to create specific Data Nodes.

Creating configuration objects

To configure a Data Node, import the `Config` class (`from taipy import Config`). Note that `Config` has a default Data Node configuration function, plus specific ones for different data sources. All Data Node configuration functions share three key attributes:

- `id`: A **unique identifier** for the Data Node; it has to be a string.

- `scope`: The default is `Scope.SCENARIO`. A scenario is a group of Data Nodes and **tasks**; it's useful for **what-if analysis** (see *Chapter 5*). You can choose `Scope.GLOBAL` to make your Data Nodes accessible throughout the application.

- `validity_period`: Sets how long the Data Node stays "fresh" after its last update. It's an orchestration-related concept that we'll cover in *Chapter 5*.

You can add any other custom argument to your Data Nodes, to use it as metadata, or use it as an argument for the functions in the pipelines (refer to *Chapters 4 and 5*).

Let's create a Data Node configuration object (check the file in 1-data_nodes_examples/default_data_nodes.py); we'll store country names in it. Set the scope to "Scope.GLOBAL" (import taipy.Scope):

```
from taipy import Config, Scope
country_node_config = Config.configure_data_node(
    id="input_country", scope=Scope.GLOBAL,
    additional_argument="A cool country!"
)
```

Once you have created your configuration object, you can directly access its properties by using dot notation:

```
print(f"The id of the config object is: {country_node_config.id}")
print(f"We also added a custom argument: {country_node_config.
additional_argument}")
```

The output is as follows:

```
The id of the config object is: input_country
We also added a custom argument: A cool country!
```

Creating Data Nodes

To create a global Data Node from a configuration file, you need to use the taipy.create_global_data_node() function. In this example, we create two Data Nodes from the same country_node_config configuration object. We also import Orchestrator and taipy for Data Nodes:

```
import taipy as tp
from taipy import Config, Orchestrator, Scope

if __name__ == "__main__":
    orchestrator = Orchestrator()
    orchestrator.run()
    country_data_node_1 = tp.create_global_data_node(
        country_node_config)
    country_data_node_2 = tp.create_global_data_node(
        country_node_config)
```

You can write values with the `write()` method, and read them with `read()`. Values can be of any data type, and you can overwrite them, and even change the data type:

```
country_data_node_1.write("Senegal")
senegal = country_data_node_1.read()

country_data_node_2.write("Nigeria")
nigeria = country_data_node_2.read()

print(senegal)
print(nigeria)

country_data_node_1.write(12.6) # different data type
not_senegal = country_data_node_1.read()
print(not_senegal)
```

This should output the following (along with some Taipy configuration messages):

```
Senegal
Nigeria
12.6
```

Let's now take a look at specific Data Nodes, and how to configure and use them. For now, we'll keep `scope=Scope.GLOBAL`. For each Data Node type, you'll find a small piece of code that you can run to see how Data Nodes interface with data. We'll show how to use the default `scope=Scope.SCENARIO` in *Chapter 4*, when we create our pipelines. For our demonstrations, we created small datasets with the 10 biggest cities of the world (`https://github.com/PacktPublishing/Getting-Started-with-Taipy/tree/main/chapter_03/data`) in different formats to connect to them with dedicated Data Nodes.

Working with Pickle

Pickle (`https://docs.python.org/3/library/pickle.html`) is a Python-specific format (serialized Python objects). Pickle files are useful to store data in the intermediate steps of a pipeline (for caching, for example). There are two ways to create configuration files for Pickle Data Nodes: from Pickle files or Python objects. These are the arguments you can use:

- `default_path`: For a Pickle file, add the path to it.

- `default_data`: From a Python object. It can be a variable or hardcoded (it needs to be a JSON serializable).

- If you don't choose any path, Taipy will handle it (it creates arbitrary filenames and stores the files in a `user_data` directory).

In the example file, we will create a Data Node configuration object from a Pickle file called `cities.p` (which holds a pandas DataFrame), and we will also create a Data Node configuration object from a Python string (`1-data_nodes_examples/pickle_data_node.py`).

Working with in-memory Data Nodes

In-memory Data Nodes store data in the computer's memory. It could be a good choice for intermediate steps because it's fast to read and write the data, but the data isn't saved for long-term usage. To create an in-memory Data Node, you need to add a Python serializable object to the `default_data` parameter, like for Pickle files (`1-data_nodes_examples/in_memory_data_node.py`).

Working with tabular data files

Tabular files such as CSV, Excel, and Parquet are common for sharing and analyzing data, with CSV/Excel being suited for smaller datasets and Parquet for large-scale analytics.

Working with CSV files

To configure a **CSV Data Node**, use `Config.configure_csv_data_node()`. These are the extra parameters:

- `default_path`: The default location of the CSV file (optional parameter; Taipy handles it if not provided).

- `encoding`: By default, it uses `utf-8`.

- `has_header`: Tells whether the file has column names – defaults to `True`.

- `exposed_type`: The returned data type: `pandas` (default) `numpy`, or a custom Python class.

The code is in `1-data_nodes_examples/csv_data_node.py`.

Working with Excel files

To configure an **Excel Data Node**, use `Config.configure_excel_data_node()`. Excel files can have several tabs. The `sheet_name` parameter specifies which sheet(s) to read from:

- If not set, it returns all sheets as a dictionary with sheet names as keys

- If given as a string, it returns data from the named sheet

- If given as a list, it returns a dictionary with sheet names as keys

In our example, we created an Excel file with two tabs, one with the table that contains the city information in it (the tab called `cities`), and another one with some metadata (called `description`): `1-data_nodes_examples/excel_data_node.py`.

Working with Parquet files

Taipy doesn't natively support Parquet files but offers dependencies to solve this lack; you can install the needed dependencies with `pip install taipy[parquet]`. To configure a **Parquet Data Node**, use `Config.configure_parquet_data_node()`. Here are the extra parameters:

- `engine`: The Parquet library to use: `fastparquet` or `pyarrow` (default)

- `compression`: The compression type to apply. The options are `snappy` (default), `gzip`, `brotli`, or `None` for no compression.

- `read_kwargs`: A dictionary of extra options for the `pandas.read_parquet` method (`https://pandas.pydata.org/docs/reference/api/pandas.read_parquet.html`). These can override the `engine` and `compression` settings.

- `write_kwargs`: A dictionary of extra options for the `pandas.DataFrame.to_parquet` method (`https://pandas.pydata.org/docs/reference/api/pandas.DataFrame.to_parquet.html`). Like `read_kwargs`, these can also override the `engine` and `compression` settings when writing data.

The code is in `1-data_nodes_examples/parquet_data_node.py`.

Working with databases

Taipy supports the following four DBMSs (details of their requirements are listed here too):

- **SQLite**: No special requirements other than installing it)

- **Microsoft SQL Server**: Use `pip install taipy[mssql]` and install the Microsoft ODBC driver

- **MySQL**: Use `pip install taipy[mysql]` and install the MySQL driver

- **PostgreSQL**: Use `pip install taipy[postgresql]` and install the Postgres driver

Taipy provides two Data Node configuration functions for database connections, with arguments for both the SQLite (database file path) and general database server parameters.

The two Data Node configuration functions are as follows:

- `configure_sql_table_data_node`: To work with single tables, it's easier but less flexible. Use the `table_name` parameter to specify it.

- `configure_sql_data_node`: For more complex queries, such as tables with filters or aggregates, or joined tables, or for specific ways to input data. You need to pass two arguments:

  - `read_query`: A Python string with a SQL query to read the data

- `write_query_builder`: A callable function that returns a Python string with a SQL statement (to write into the database)

The following parameters are shared by both functions:

- db_name: Name of your database.
- db_engine: Database engine: `sqlite`, `mysql`, `mssql`, or `postgresql`.
- table_name: Name of the table you're working with.
- db_username/db_password: Username and password (for server-based).
- db_host/db_port: Host and port to connect to the database. Defaults to `"localhost"` and `1433`.
- sqlite_folder_path/sqlite_file_extension: For SQLite, define the folder and file extension. The default file extension is `.db`.
- exposed_type: The returned data type: `pandas` (default), `numpy`, or a custom Python class.

For our examples, we'll use two database systems: SQLite and PostgreSQL.

Working with SQLite

We created a small database with the most populated countries, with two tables: CITIES and COUNTRIES (the code to create the tables is in `data/cities-sqlite.sql`).

To configure a Data Node for a single table, such as CITIES, we use the `configure_sql_table_data_node()` configuration function.

To use the custom `configure_sql_data_node`, we created a query that joins both tables; this way, we have a more readable format. We keep it as a string (`cities_and_countries_query`). We also add a callable function (`create_cities`) that inserts a pandas DataFrame as the new data in the CITIES table (it deletes all and charges the complete DataFrame).

All of the code, using both configuration options, is in `1-data_nodes_examples/sqlite_data_node.py`.

Working with PostgreSQL

The code to create cities tables with PostgreSQL is in `data/cities-postgresql.sql`.

To configure a Data Node with a server-based DBMS such as PostgreSQL (or for **MySQL** or **Microsoft Server**), you need to pass all the connection parameters to the configuration function (refer to the beginning of this section and the code examples).

To configure a custom **SQL Data Node**, you can use the same connection parameters and use the same functions as the ones in the *Working with SQLite* section (the SQL code works the same). The complete code is in `1-data_nodes_examples/postgresql_data_node.py`.

Working with hierarchical data files (JSON)

JSON files allow to work with hierarchical data (trees). You can configure a **JSON Data Node** using `Config.configure_json_data_node()`. Here are the key parameters:

- `default_path`: File path for reading and writing JSON data.
- `encoding`: Encoding for the JSON file, default is `utf-8`.
- `encoder` and `decoder`: Optional parameters for custom serialization and deserialization of data using `json.JSONEncoder` and `json.JSONDecoder`.

When reading from a JSON Data Node, the returned object is a list of dictionaries. The complete code is in `1-data_nodes_examples/json_data_node.py`.

Working with S3 storage

You can retrieve data from your S3 bucket using a Taipy Data Node. To configure it, use the `configure_s3_object_data_node` function. The key parameters are as follows:

- `aws_access_key`: Your AWS account identity
- `aws_secret_access_key`: Key for authentication
- `aws_region`: Region of your AWS infrastructure
- `aws_s3_bucket_name`: Name of the S3 bucket
- `aws_s3_object_key`: Name of the object (file) in the S3 bucket
- `aws_s3_object_parameters`: Extra parameters for AWS interactions

In our example, we uploaded the `cities.csv` file to the S3 bucket. *Using the* `read()` *method returns a string, but you can convert the string to a DataFrame using* `io.StringIO`*!* Check the code in `/1-data_nodes_examples/s3_data_node.py`.

Working with custom data connections

While Taipy offers dedicated configuration files for most common data sources (and more data sources will come over time), you sometimes will need custom Data Nodes. In this case, you need to create a function that reads your data and a function that writes it, and then use the `configure_generic_data_node()` configuration function. Here are the main arguments:

- `read_fct`: A Python function to read data from a source
- `write_fct`: A Python function to write data to a destination
- `read_fct_args`: A list of extra arguments for `read_fct`
- `write_fct_args`: A list of extra arguments for `write_fct`

All these arguments are optional, meaning you can create a Data Node that reads data without writing it. We can imagine three cases where you would use the generic Data Node:

- Your data source does not have a dedicated Data Node, as with an API call or data from a URL – for example, retrieving data from a Wikipedia table (see the code in `1-data_nodes_examples/wikipedia_data_node.py`).

- Your data type, such as image or sound data, is not covered. For example, you can read satellite images with **rasterio** (`https://rasterio.readthedocs.io/en/stable/`) and return a NumPy array (see the code in `1-data_nodes_examples/image_data_node.py`).

- You need to transform your data with a function. For example, filtering your pandas DataFrame from a CSV file.

Overriding and reusing Data Node configuration

By default, Taipy uses Pickle Data Nodes and a scope set to `SCENARIO`. You can override this with `Config.set_default_data_node_configuration()` for specific types, such as SQL tables or CSV files. New Data Nodes inherit the default configuration unless the storage type differs. For example, you can override the default to read CSV files with a header and a `GLOBAL` scope (look at `1-data_nodes_examples/change_config.py`).

Taipy also lets you create Data Nodes from an existing configuration using `Config.configure_data_node_from()`, making it easy to duplicate setups while adjusting properties such as table names or scope. This is useful for handling multiple similar Data Nodes. In this example, we reuse a CSV Data Node, and we expose the data in two different types (pandas DataFrame and NumPy). You can check it in `1-data_nodes_examples/reuse_config.py`.

Now that you know how to create Data Nodes, let's see how to use them in the GUI!

Connecting Data Nodes with a GUI

In the preceding examples, we saw how to configure and create (global) Data Nodes. We're going to see three examples of how to use Data Nodes in a Taipy graphical application. We're going to create an app with three pages, one for each case.

The structure of the application includes a `configuration` directory with a `config_data_nodes.py` file, which holds the configuration files for three different Data Nodes, and a `main.py` file, which imports three `Page` objects from a `pages` directory and the configuration object. The `main.py` file runs both the `Gui` and the `Orchestrator` under the main guard. This is also where we create all our initial scenario objects (in this case, our global Data Nodes, which leads to faster and more stable applications. The application code is in the `2-data_node_visual_elements` directory.

Using Data Nodes to create data objects

As we saw in *Chapter 2*, you can create complete applications starting from a pandas DataFrame, so the first way to use Data Nodes in your graphical applications is by creating your DataFrames from global Data Nodes. This allows to read and write data to the data source, such as a CSV file. You can see a minimalist example in the following code: it creates a `table` from `df_cities`, a DataFrame that we create from a `biggest_cities` Data Node in the `main.py` file. The `on_edit` callback modifies the DataFrame but also calls `biggest_cities.write(state.df_cities)` to change the values in the CSV file. The code is in `data_node_visual_elements/pages/simple_data_node.py`.

Using the Data Node selector element

Taipy applications offer a visual element, `data_node_selector`, that allows users to select specific Data Nodes. Creating the `data_node_selector()` element, with no extra arguments, will show all the Data Nodes.

The **Data Node selector** has several parameters to organize the display. Some only make sense in an orchestrated pipeline. Here are some of them:

- `show_pins`: Defaults to `True`; we keep it as is. It allows users to pin several scenarios and then restrict the display to pinned scenarios (you can think about it as *Favorites*).
- `multiple`: Allows you to select more than one Data Node.
- `filter`: Allows you to search for Data Nodes based on a filter.
- `datanodes`: By default, the selector displays all the Data Nodes, but you can create a list of Data Nodes to display, or restrict Data Nodes to a scenario (we'll see all this in *Chapter 4*).

Data Node selectors also have an on_change callback: this way, users can perform actions using the Data Nodes. See how we define the bound variable (selected_data_node) within the Page element, and the on_change callback uses a lambda state to update the variable.

In our demonstration example, we create a pandas DataFrame within the table element (with table.read()), so users can change the table by selecting a Data Node. The code is in data_node_visual_elements/pages/data_node_selector.py.

Figure 3.2 shows a Data Node selector and a table, which changes depending on the selected Data Node.

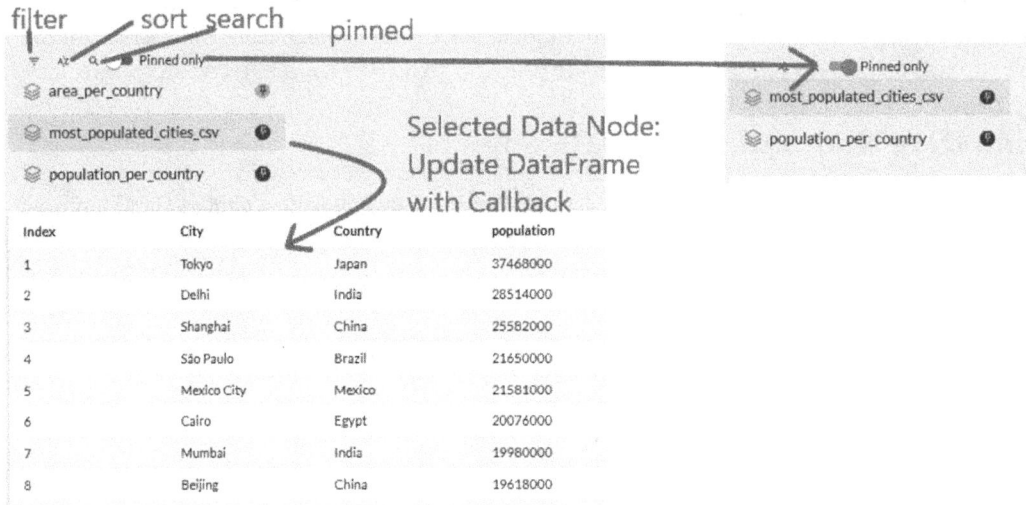

Figure 3.2 – A Data Node selector

The Data Node selector lets us filter, sort and search for Scenarios, as well as pin them, to work with them. Now, let's see the last visual element for Data Nodes: the Data Node viewer.

Using the Data Node viewer element

The **Data Node viewer** element is a complete widget that allows users to interact with the Data Node and with the data itself (using the visual interface). For our example, we create a data_node element using the CSV data about the 10 biggest cities in the world. We just need to pass the following parameter: data_node="{biggest_cities}". It's important to bind the variable; otherwise, you'll see an empty expandable object.

The data_node visual element creates a block with tabs within it. The function has several optional parameters that add tabs with options. Here are some of them; we'll set them all to True so we can play around and discover them, but keep in mind that displaying more elements impacts performance:

- show_data (defaults to True): This shows the data in a suitable format (e.g., a table for tabular data), and it has options to show data as a chart.

- `show_properties` (defaults to `True`): Displays the custom properties of the Data Node. Allows users to add, edit, or delete properties.
- `show_history` (defaults to `True`): Shows a chronological list of changes made to the Data Node, in a dedicated tab.
- `show_owner` (defaults to `True`): Displays the owner (scenario or cycle) of the Data Node, with options to change the selected owner.
- `show_config`: Shows the configuration properties of the Data Node, in a dedicated tab.
- `show_edit_date`: When the Data Node has edits, Taipy keeps track of the dates. You can choose to display that information.
- `show_expiration_date`: If your Data Nodes have a `validity_period` value, then you can render it (defaults to the edit date).

Figure 3.3 shows a Data Node viewer. The code is in `data_node_visual_elements/pages/data_node_viewer.py`.

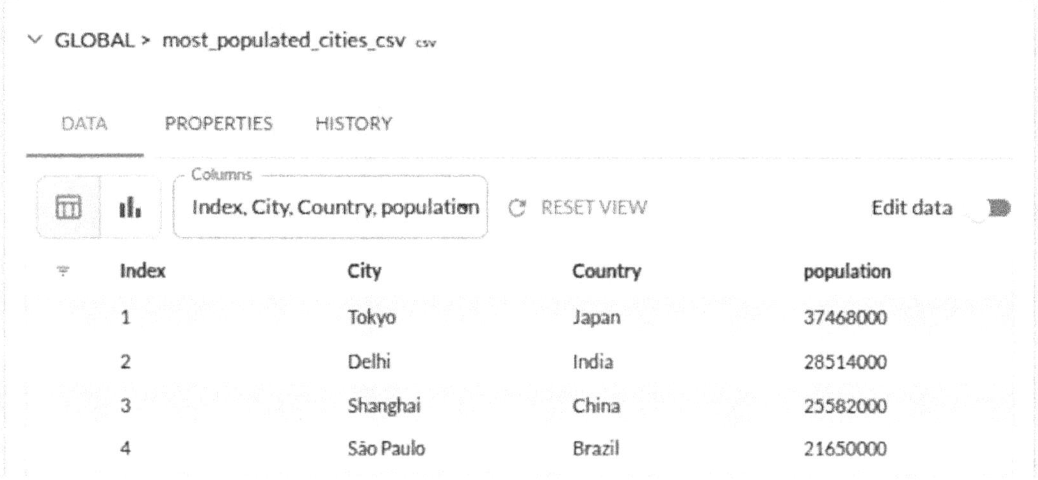
GLOBAL > most_populated_cities_csv csv
DATA
PROPERTIES
HISTORY
Columns
Index, City, Country, population
RESET VIEW
Edit data
Index
City
Country
population
1
Tokyo
Japan
37468000
2
Delhi
India
28514000
3
Shanghai
China
25582000
4
São Paulo
Brazil
21650000

Figure 3.3 – A Data Node viewer

Data Node viewers allow users to explore the data, and even edit it. Data Node selectors and Data Node viewers, can be combined to explore the data inputs and outputs of our data applications.

Summary

In this chapter, we explained what Data Nodes are and how to create and configure them. You should be able to interact with (read and write) all types of data sources using Data Nodes, as well as being able to use dedicated graphical components to visualize their data (and metadata).

We chose to create all Data Nodes with Scope.GLOBAL for two reasons: first, for pedagogical purposes, as Data Nodes are an important concept to focus on and creating them with GLOBAL scope allows us to avoid discussing other concepts. Second, not all Taipy applications require Scenario Management capabilities, but even so, you can leverage Data Nodes as a data interface for your applications.

In the next chapter, we'll cover orchestration with Taipy. Unlike GUI applications, where you may or may not use Data Nodes, orchestrated pipelines always need them to interact with tasks. The content covered here should greatly help you in *Chapter 4*.

Questions

1. In the *Working with Excel files* section, we read the tabular data from a specific tab in the Excel sheet and displayed it as a pandas DataFrame. Can you access the table without specifying the tab name and display it as a NumPy array?

2. Using the example with the 10 biggest cities, how would you select, from the Parquet Data Node configuration, the cities with a population greater than 20,000,000 people?

3. You work on a project that requires creating lots of Data Nodes, in an enterprise environment (with enterprise DBMS). How would you make your life easier (and your code lighter)?

4. Can you change the Taipy Foods application from *Chapter 2* to create its DataFrames from Data Nodes?

5. Following on from the previous question, can you replace the table from *Chapter 2* with a Data Node viewer? Create a minimalistic display, focusing on displaying the data in a table.

Answers

1. To display your data as a NumPy array, you need to change the exposed_type parameter, like this: exposed_type="numpy".

    If you remove the sheet_name="cities" parameter, the Data Node's read() method will return a dictionary, with a data structure for each sheet (in this case, a NumPy array). The keys of the dictionary will match the sheet name. You can access it like this:

    ```
    dict_cities = cities_excel_data_node.read()
    np_cities = dict_cities["cities"]
    ```

2. The `configure_parquet_data_node` function allows the addition of a `read_kwargs` argument. Add the following line:

```
read_kwargs={"filters": [("population", ">", 20000000)]},
```

3. Connecting to enterprise databases requires the `Config.configure_sql_table_data_node()` or `Config.configure_sql_data_node()` function. Most likely, all your configuration objects will have the same `db_username`, `db_password`, `db_engine`, and even `db_name`. To reduce the code, you can create a first Data Node, and then reuse it using `Config.configure_data_node_from()`.

4. For simplicity, we'll add all the code to the same page, but if you decide to work with Data Nodes, you should put all your configuration functions in a dedicated directory.

    First, we need to import the configuration and orchestration libraries:

```
from taipy import Config
import taipy as tp
from taipy import Config, Orchestrator, Scope
```

    Then, create the configuration and the Data Node:

```
sales_csv_file = "./data/state_sales.csv"
sales_configuration_file = Config.configure_generic_data_node(
    id="cities_from_wikipedia",
    read_fct=clean_sales_data,
    read_fct_args=[sales_csv_file],
    write_fct_args=None,
    scope=Scope.GLOBAL,
)
orchestrator = Orchestrator()
orchestrator.run()
sales_data_node = tp.create_global_data_node(
    sales_configuration_file)
df_sales_original = sales_data_node.read()
```

5. You need to replace the `table` visual element with a `data_node` instance. The `value` argument is no longer a bounded pandas DataFrame but a bounded Data Node. To keep it minimal, you can set to `False` all the parameters that default to `True` (except for `show_data`). Here is how the element looks:

```
tgb.data_node(
    "{sales_data_node}",
    show_properties=False,
    show_history=False,
    show_owner=False,
    show_config=False,
)
```

Join our community on Discord

Join our community's Discord space for discussions with the authors and other readers:

`https://packt.link/taipybook`

4

Orchestrating Taipy Applications

Data orchestration is the management and automation of different data transformation steps. Taipy's orchestration process has three main components: **Data Nodes**, which connect to data (as we saw in *Chapter 3*), **Tasks**, which connect to Python functions, and **Scenarios**, which group Tasks and Data Nodes. Scenarios allow you to structure your algorithms and create data pipelines (a succession of Tasks using Data Nodes).

As opposed to the usual "data pipelines" that data engineers create with **Extract Transform Load** (ETL) tools and that are backend-only, users can access Taipy pipeline components from the UI, with dedicated visual components (we already covered some in *Chapter 3*). Taipy orchestration pipelines abstract complex setups, such as parallel processing or scaling, so you can focus on your app and algorithms.

In this chapter, you'll learn about the main components and steps of orchestration in Taipy. We'll create pipelines, starting with simple ones, and make them more complex over time. We'll also see how to bring Scenarios to your UI.

In this chapter, we cover the following:

- Fundamentals of Taipy orchestration
- Creating your first Scenario
- Bringing Scenarios to your graphical interface
- Creating complex Scenarios

Technical requirements

You can find the complete code used in this chapter can on the GitHub repository: `https://github.com/PacktPublishing/Getting-Started-with-Taipy/tree/main/chapter_04`. Throughout the chapter, we'll mention the names of the GitHub files we're using so that you can pick them up from the repository when needed.

The example we use in this chapter uses the scikit-learn Python library (`https://scikit-learn.org/`). It's best if you're familiar with it and with machine learning, but it isn't required to understand how Scenarios work.

Fundamentals of Taipy orchestration

Let's start with an overview and key concepts of Data Nodes, Tasks, and Scenarios. We'll first see how to configure them, and then we'll cover how to run a Scenario.

Configuring Scenarios

We covered Data Nodes in *Chapter 3*: they provide an interface to access data. We configured them with `scope = Scope.GLOBAL`, and we accessed the Data Nodes directly from any part of the application (either the UI or from Python functions). In this chapter, we'll be using the default `scope=Scope.SCENARIO`.

Within a Scenario, Data Nodes are the input and/or the output of Tasks.

Just as Data Nodes are an interface to data, but they're not data, *Tasks are an interface to Python functions*, but they're not functions. Tasks have a dedicated configuration object, `Config.configure_task`. The arguments are as follows:

- `id`: A unique identifier, so we can assign it to a Scenario
- `function`: The Python function bound to the Task
- `input` (optional): It can be empty if the function takes no argument, otherwise, it references the ID of Data Nodes, or a list of IDs if there is more than one input
- `output` (optional): Also references one or more Data Nodes:

    - `skippable`: If `True`, the function isn't run if the inputs haven't changed (the default is `False`).

Scenarios reference an ordered group of Tasks (which are also linked to Data Nodes): they are an interface to data pipelines. Taipy's orchestration happens within Scenarios: they create a succession of inputs, functions, and outputs (which can be inputs of the next function). Scenarios also have a dedicated configuration object: `Config.configure_scenario`, as well as dedicated visual elements (refer to the *Linking Scenarios to your graphical interface* section). The arguments of the Scenario configuration function are as follows:

- `id`: A unique identifier, as a Python string
- `task_configs`: A list of Task configuration IDs, *in execution order.*
- `additional_data_node_configs`: Some Scenarios may have Data Nodes that aren't used by any Task, but that aren't global Data Nodes either. You can add them here.
- `frequency`: This is to attach a Scenario to a Cycle (refer to *Chapter 5*).
- `comparators`: A list of functions used to compare Scenarios (refer to *Chapter 5*).
- `sequences`: A dictionary of Scenario subsets (refer to the *Using sequences* section).

As a rule of thumb, do the following to create your Scenario configurations:

1. Start defining your Python functions (in a dedicated `.py` file).
2. Then, create your Data Node `config` objects. Each function argument should have a Data Node (except for maybe some optional parameters), as well as each returned statement.
3. Next, create your `Tasks`, which use Data Nodes and reference the Python functions.
4. Finally, create your `Scenarios`, which use `Tasks`.

> **Important note**
>
> Two (or more) different `Tasks` can access the same Data Node. Two (or more) `Scenarios` can use the same `Task`. But the same Data Node can't belong to more than one `Scenario` (if it has a `SCENARIO` scope).

Submitting Scenarios

Creating a Scenario is like creating a global Data Node: you create a configuration object (with `Config.configure_scenario`) and you use it to create the Scenario with `taipy.create(scenario)`. `Scenario configuration` objects use `Task configuration` objects and `Data Node configuration` objects (with `Scope=SCENARIO`).

Once you create a `Scenario` object, you can trigger it using the `.submit()` method. This will run the pipeline, using the Data Nodes (with the current state of data) and running the Tasks one after the other. *Each submission returns a job object for each Task.*

Figure 4.1 shows all the processes, from configuration to creation and then submission.

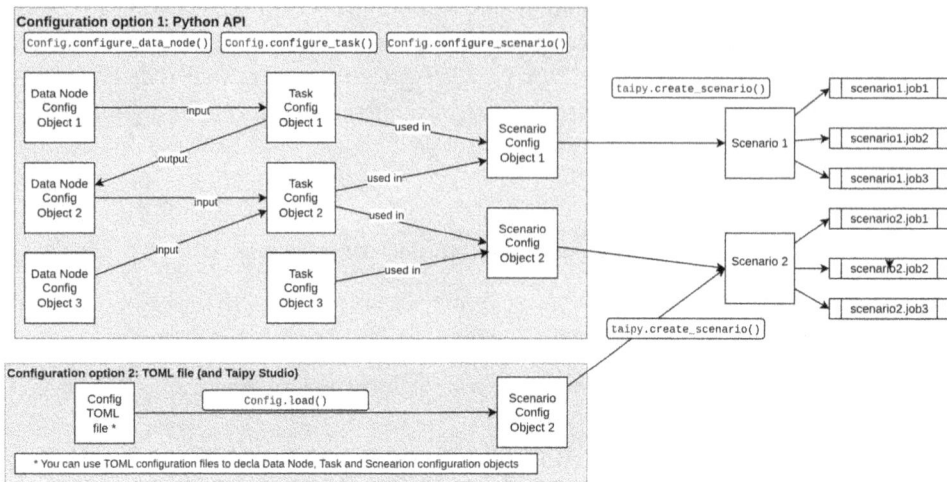

Figure 4.1 – Taipy orchestration process

Now that you see the big picture, let's create our first Scenario!

Creating your first Scenario

We'll construct two pipelines. The first will be a minimal example, while the second will show a functional approach. For the second example and the rest of the chapter, we'll be using the auto-mpg dataset (`https://www.kaggle.com/datasets/uciml/autompg-dataset`), which tracks various features of cars and their corresponding **miles per gallon** (**mpg**). This classic dataset allows us to explore how different car characteristics influence fuel efficiency using linear regression, a **machine learning** (**ML**) technique.

> **Important note**
>
> The dataset on Kaggle contains the CSV file that we need. The original source of this dataset is as follows: *Quinlan, R. 1993*. Auto MPG. UCI Machine Learning Repository. `https://doi.org/10.24432/C5859H`.

Creating the smallest pipeline

In this section, we'll introduce the fundamental components of a pipeline by creating the simplest possible Scenario (see the code in `/minimal_pipeline`). We're creating it without any Data Nodes. These are the steps:

1.   We create a `minimal_function` function that prints a statement.

2. We create a `Task configuration` object, with `Config.configure_task()`, we introduce a (mandatory) `id` and we reference `minimal_function`, without any Data Nodes (since the function has no inputs, and doesn't return anything).

3. We create a `Scenario configuration` object with `Config.configure_scenario()`, we add an `id`, and we reference the `Task configuration` object.

4. We run the `Orchestrator()` inside the main guard.

5. We create the Scenario with `taipy.create_scenario()`.

6. We submit the Scenario using `.submit`. You can find the code in the `minimal_pipeline.py` file in our GitHub repository. When you run it, you should see it print "`I'm super minimal!`"

Creating a simple pipeline

Let's now consider a more realistic example. We have the auto-mpg dataset in the `data` directory. We create a pipeline that reads the CSV file as a pandas DataFrame and returns a subset of the DataFrame with at least two columns, where one of the columns is always mpg and the others come from a list.

To create this, we need two input Data Nodes, one that references the DataFrame created from the CSV file (we configure it with `Config.configure_csv_data_node()` and we name it `auto_data`) and a default Data Node (we use `Config.configure_data_node()`, naming it `column_subset`), and we give it a default value with `default_data`, which is all the columns of the dataset. During the orchestration process, we can write the Data Node with a newer list of column names.

The pipeline also needs an output Data Node, which will store the output of the function that the Task triggers. This output will be a DataFrame with two or more columns (mpg and the ones defined in the `column_subset` Data Node). We name this Data Node `filtered_auto_df`.

The pipeline has a single Task, that references the two input Data Nodes, stores the result in the output, and calls a function called `select_subset`. We place this pipeline in a Scenario called `auto_scenario` (we name the configuration object `auto_scenario_config`).

Once the configuration is over, we do the following:

1. We run the `Orchestrator`.

2. We create the Scenario with `tp.create_scenario(auto_scenario_config)`.

3. We can write the `column_subset` Data Node with a list of column names (in the example, we commented on this step – feel free to experiment with it!). This is optional because the Data Node has a default value!

4. We submit the `Scenario`.

5. We read the value from the `filtered_auto_df` Data Node: we have a subset of the original DataFrame, with two columns.

You can find the code to run the Scenario in `select_subset_pipeline.py`. Let's now see how to interact with Scenarios from a UI.

Bringing Scenarios to your graphical interface

While you can use Taipy orchestration as a backend-only process (and that may make sense in some cases), you can put the Scenario Management components in the hands of end users through an application's UI, using visual elements.

One way to bring Scenario Management to your UI is by accessing Scenario components with various methods, such as Data Nodes' `read()` or `write()`, or Scenarios' `submit()`, and using them inside callback functions, or using the resulting data to create tables or charts. You can combine your Scenario Management with almost all "regular" visual elements (the ones we covered in *Chapter 2*).

Another way to bring Scenario components to your UI is by using dedicated Scenario visual elements.

In this section, we'll see how to use Scenarios from "regular" visual elements, and we'll introduce Scenario-specific visual elements. We covered Data Node visual elements in *Chapter 3*. We'll present the `scenario_selector` and the `scenario` elements that let you select a Scenario from a list and interact with a Scenario respectively (similar to the `data_node_selector` and `data_node` elements), as well as the `scenario_dag` and `job_selector`.

Visual element	Binds to	Main usage
`scenario_selector`	Scenario and list of Scenarios	Select one Scenario from a list of Scenarios
`scenario`	Scenario	Interact with a selected Scenario (submit, edit…)
`scenario_dag`	Scenario	Show the Scenario's DAG representation
`data_node_selector`	Data Node and list of Data Nodes	Select a Data Node from a list of Data Nodes
`data_node`	Data Node	Interact with a selected Data Node (see the data it connects to)
`job_selector`	Job or list of jobs	A job is the execution of a Task

Table 4.1 – List of Scenario visual elements

Let's create a UI application, using the simple pipeline from the previous section. The structure will have the following:

- A `data` directory, with the `auto_mpg` CSV file.
- A `configuration` directory with a `config.py` directory. This file has all the configuration objects, but we don't run them here.
- An `algorithms` directory. The Tasks that we create have all their functions here (we don't add all the callback and page-specific functions, just the orchestration ones).

- A pages directory, with five pages, that will have our visual elements: regular_ui.py, dag.py, scenario_element.py, scenario_selector.py, and job_selector.py.

- A main.py file with a root page, where we run the Gui and the Orchestrator objects.

  The complete app is in /visual_elements.

Let's now see how to interact with scenarios through a GUI.

Using regular visual elements

You can imagine many ways to interact with Scenarios and their components (Tasks, Data Nodes) from the various visual elements. For example, you can use the read() method from a Data Node, create a Pandas DataFrame, and then create a table visual element (we saw this in *Chapter 3*).

Our Scenario has a Task that takes a list of column names. We can create a selector element that allows multiple value selections and write the column_subset Data Node each time the user changes the values of the list. The selector element uses the on_change parameter to call a change_column function, like this:

```
On_change = lambda state: state.auto_scenario.column_subset.write(
    State.selected_column
)
```

💡 **Quick tip**: Enhance your coding experience with the **AI Code Explainer** and **Quick Copy** features. Open this book in the next-gen Packt Reader. Click the **Copy** button (**1**) to quickly copy code into your coding environment, or click the **Explain** button (**2**) to get the AI assistant to explain a block of code to you.

```
function calculate(a, b) {
   return {sum: a + b};
};
```

Copy   Explain
 ①   ②

🔒 **The next-gen Packt Reader** is included for free with the purchase of this book. Scan the QR code OR go to packtpub.com/unlock, then use the search bar to find this book by name. Double-check the edition shown to make sure you get the right one.

When the user triggers the function, it updates the Data Node. To write the Data Node, it uses a list of values from the `selector` visual element (at its current `state`) to update the Data Node.

We also create a button that calls a `submit_scenario` function, which triggers the Scenario submission, and looks like this:

```
on_action=lambda state: state.auto_scenario.submit(),
```

We also add a `table` with the original data, and a Data Node viewer to show the data after the transformation. (See `visual_elements/pages/regular_ui.py` for the code.)

Adding a Scenario DAG

The `scenario_dag` visual element creates a representation of the Scenario. It shows the links between Data Nodes and Tasks. This is a great way to generate documentation about your pipeline (technical or project documentation). You can also include it in your apps if you want end users to know the process. *Figure 4.2* shows how this renders in the application (see `visual_elements/pages/dag.py`).

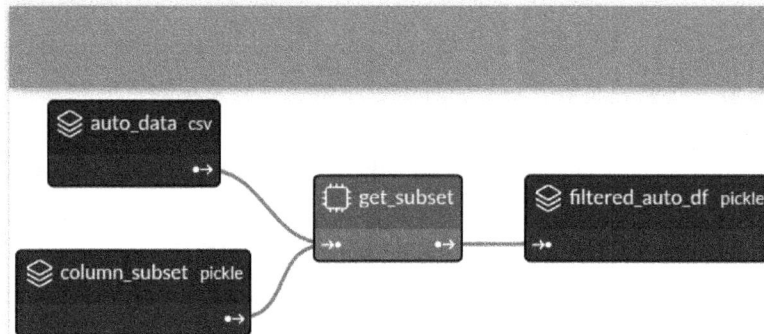

Figure 4.2 – A DAG from the scenario_dag element

The `scenario_dag` element shows the pipeline's DAG and allows users to visualize how tasks and Data Nodes are connected. Let's now take a look at the Scenario element!

Adding a scenario element

The `scenario` visual element helps users interact with Scenarios: they can change Scenario parameters, such as its label, add tags, or add new sequences. *This element allows users to submit scenarios from the UI. Figure 4.3* shows the `scenario` element (with the complete code in `scenario_element.py`). You can use it to submit the same Scenario as the one from the *Using regular visual elements* section. You just have to bind the Scenario as a variable and don't need to code the Scenario submission. We use the `scenario` visual element in a more comprehensive example in the *Creating complex Scenarios* section.

You can customize the `scenario` element by adding or removing components (such as to show the creation date, show cycles, or hide the submission button; *Figure 4.9* shows a richer `scenario` element) using boolean parameters (you can see them all in the documentation: `https://docs.taipy.io/en/release-4.1/refmans/gui/viselements/corelements/scenario/`).

You also have an `on_submission_change` callback argument. For our example, we create a `change_scenario` function, which displays a notification. We also create a smaller than default `scenario` element, since our current Scenario is simple.

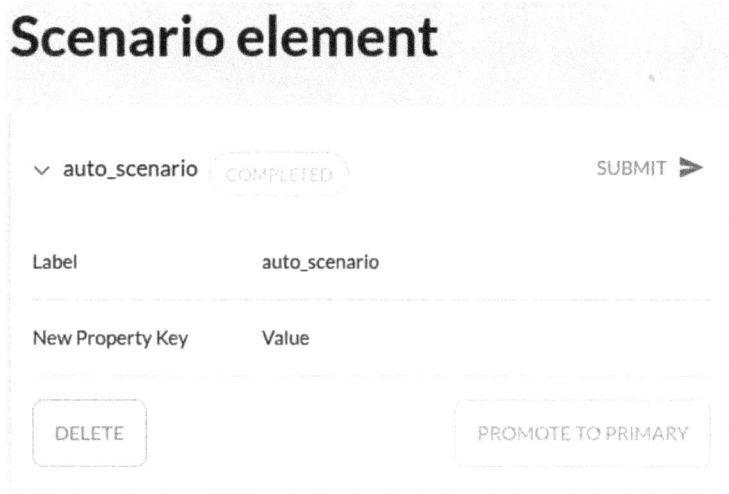

Figure 4.3 – The Scenario visual element

The Scenario element lets us submit the Scenario, and see some associated metadata, such as labels. Let's now take a look at the Scenario selector!

Adding a Scenario selector

Taipy offers a `scenario_selector` visual element that lets users select Scenarios from a list of Scenarios. In our current example, we're only using one Scenario, but we'll use this element in *Chapter 5*, where we'll be able to select different Scenarios to compare them to each other. You can check the documentation to see all the options (`https://docs.taipy.io/en/release-4.1/refmans/gui/viselements/corelements/data_node_selector/`). Here are the function's parameters:

- `scenarios`: The default is to show all the Scenarios, but you choose a restricted list of values
- `show_pins`: This adds a way for users to restrict the Scenarios the selector shows (just like `data_node_selector`)

This selector has two callbacks:

- `on_change`: This triggers a function when the selected Scenario changes
- `on_creation`: This triggers a function when you create a new Scenario

In the following example, we add a `scenario_selector` with pins, and two callback functions that trigger notification message functions. *When you change the selected Scenario from the* `scenario_selector`, *it changes in the Scenario selector as well* (if they are bound to the same Scenario). You can see the result in *Figure 4.4* (and the corresponding code in `scenario_selector.py`):

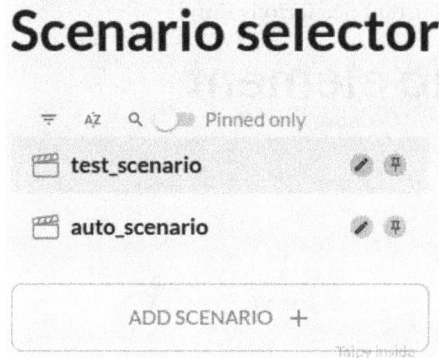

Scenario selector

≡   A̅Z̲   Q   ⬤ Pinned only

🎬 **test_scenario**   ✏ 📌

🎬 **auto_scenario**   ✏ 📌

ADD SCENARIO +

Figure 4.4 – A Scenario selector (a user created a test_scenario with the ADD SCENARIO + button)

Next, we'll take a look at the job selector.

Adding a job selector

The last visual element for Scenario Management is the `job_selector` (see the doc here: `https://docs.taipy.io/en/release-4.1/refmans/gui/viselements/corelements/job_selector/`). A **job** is a Scenario's execution. Users can run a Scenario several times, and Taipy records each job. The `job_selector` element lets you visualize all the app's jobs.

Like other Scenario selectors, `job_selector` lets you customize the information that it displays (ID for the job, ID of the Scenario, job label...). It also comes with two callback arguments:

- `on_change`: You can select jobs using the checkboxes. Each time you select a job, it will trigger the `on_change` callback.
- `on_details`: By default, when you click on the Details button (the little "document" symbol – there is one per line), the selector displays detailed information about the job. You can override it using this callback.

Figure 4.5 shows a `job_selector` with four jobs. You can check the code to create a `job_selector` in `job_selector.py`.

Job selector

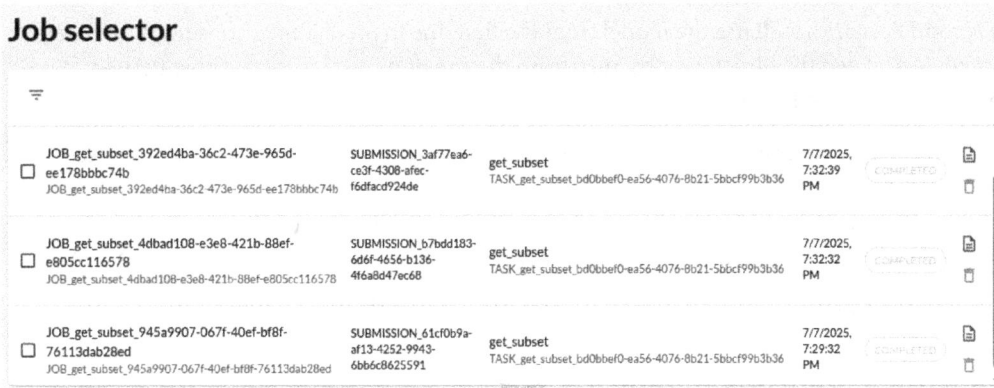

Figure 4.5 – A job selector, showing four jobs

Now, let's create a more complex Scenario!

Creating complex Scenarios

We're going to create a simple ML Taipy application using the auto-mpg dataset. We'll create two Scenarios and each one will be a separate pipeline. We'll be using the scikit-learn library. The application will have a UI for users to select car characteristics (such as the number of cylinders, production year...) and will use a regression model to predict the mpg consumption. You can see the UI in *Figure 4.6*.

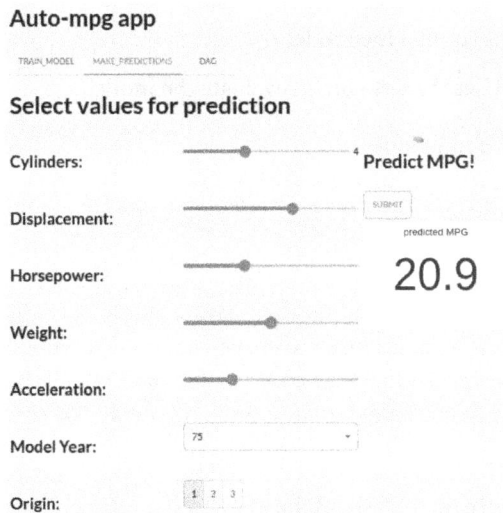

Figure 4.6 – Auto-mpg prediction application

In the first Scenario, users will be able to select the columns they want to include as predictors for the car's mpg consumption as we did earlier in this chapter, but the process will then continue with training a simple linear regression model.

In the second Scenario, we'll use the model from the first one to predict mpg consumption based on user input. We'll keep the directory structure from the previous section, with three Python files on pages: `train_model.py`, `make_predictions.py`, and `dag.py`.

The application uses boolean variables to "remember" whether a model used a column for testing in the `make_predictions.py` (for example, the `show_cylinders` variable is `True` if the user selected the `Cylinders` column when they trained the model – this boolean variable is then the argument of the `active` parameter in the selectors from the `make_predictions.py` page).

You can find the complete application in. Let's now see some of the key elements.

Configuring complex Scenarios

To configure a complex Scenario, you can start creating your Python functions (in the `algorithms` directory). Ideally, your functions should do single Tasks. In our case, we reuse the `select_subset.py` file from the previous section, and we add two files – one to fit (or train) the model, and one to predict outcomes using the model.

The `fit_pipeline.py` file has these functions:

- `preprocess_data`: Uses a scaler to transform the data and it removes missing values. It returns the scaled values and the scaler, which we'll use in the prediction pipeline as well.

- `split_data`: Splits the data into train and test subsets.

- `train_model`: Trains (or fits) the model.

- `evaluate_model`: Uses the test data to evaluate the model.

The `predict.py` file has two functions:

- `create_prediction_dataframe`: Creates a pandas DataFrame with a single column, so it can be input for the model.

- `make_predictions`: Uses the input DataFrame, the model, and the scaler to make a prediction.

Once you have your functions, it becomes easier to create your configuration files. In this example, we created two Scenarios, for a better demonstration. We could have put all the Tasks in the same one. All the Data Nodes, Tasks, and Scenarios are in the `config.py` file. Take the time to look at the file.

1. You can create a Data Node for each input and output of your functions. A Data Node can be the output of one or more functions and the input of other functions as well. The Data Nodes represent most intermediate steps of the ML pipeline, such as the dataset splits for training and testing; notice how the `regression_model_node_config` Data Node stores a scikit-learn model! You can create a Task for each Python function, referencing all the input and output Data Nodes.

2. Then, you create a Scenario, grouping all the Tasks.

Voilà! You're *almost* set. For most intermediate and final steps, you can use the `Config.configure_data_node()` configuration function. This creates pickle files in a directory called `user_data`, but you can customize them further – for example, you may want to store data from the final or intermediate steps as files or in a database. In our file, we used some `Config.configure_pickle_data_node()` functions. We'll discuss the reason in the next section (*Using files in different scenarios*).

In the UI application, we left a `dag` page to show both scenarios. It's a great way to visualize and document them. *Figure 4.7* shows the pipeline to train the model. You can see how any serializable Python object can end up as a Pickle file and be used in a Data Node, including objects such as models or scalers. This graph also documents pretty well the splitting of the test and train data.

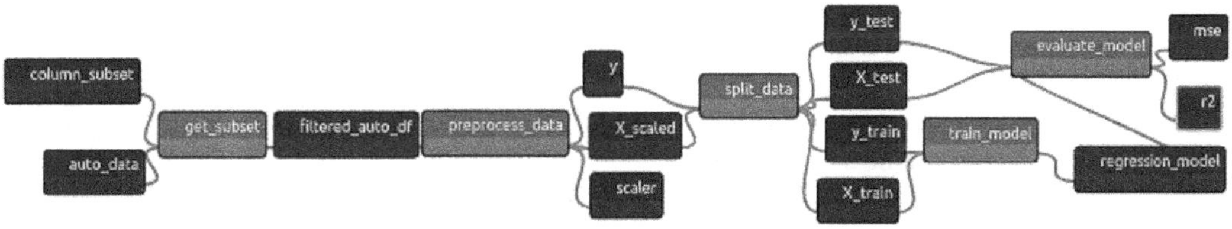

Figure 4.7 – Training DAG

Figure 4.8 documents the prediction pipeline. You can see how single inputs (number of cylinders, acceleration, model year...) go into a pandas DataFrame, which is used, along with the model and the scaler, to predict the car's mpg consumption.

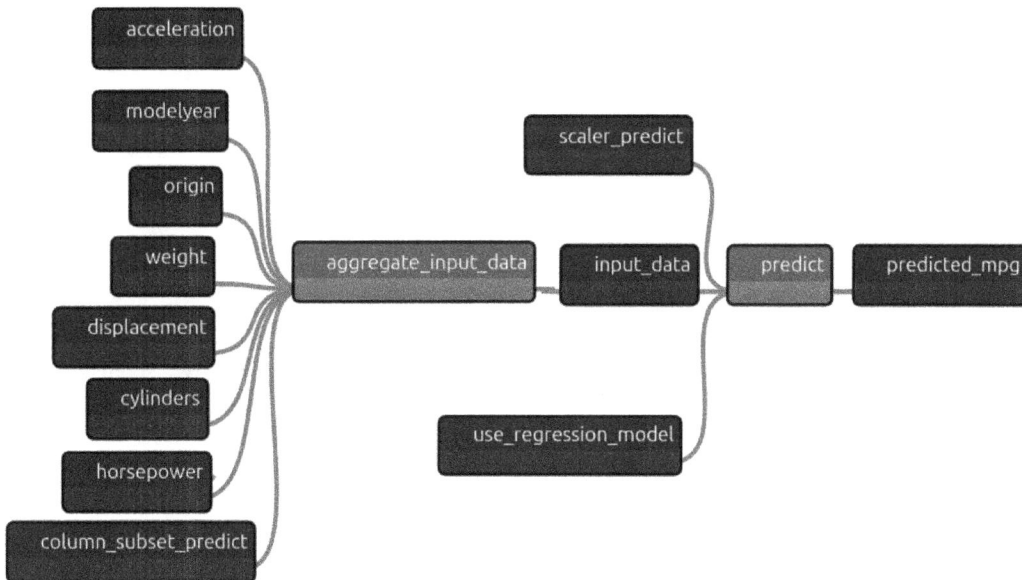

Figure 4.8 – Prediction pipeline

In the next section, we'll discuss how to specifically link Data Nodes to certain files, and how to use them across Data Nodes.

Using files in different scenarios

The default `Scope` for Data Nodes is `Scope.Scenario`. This means that if you have two different scenarios, you can't use the same Data Node in them. In our example, the first scenario uses a list to create a subset of the DataFrame, and it generates a model and a scaler. In our prediction pipeline, we need to reuse the list, so we can also have the same subset for our input data (if we didn't train based on a certain column – for example, the number of cylinders, then we shouldn't allow the input of the number of cylinders either). We also need to reuse the model and the scaler!

Since we can't reuse the Data Nodes, what we can do is provide a specific type and a path. Remember that *Data Nodes are* **interfaces***, so two Data Nodes can interact with the same file!* In our file, we used pickle Data Nodes. For example, this is how we defined the Data Nodes for the model in the training scenario and in the prediction scenario (two Data Nodes with the same `default_path`):

```
regression_model_node_config = Config.\
    configure_pickle_data_node(
        id="regression_model",
        default_path="./user_data/model.p"
    )
...
use_regression_model_node_config = Config.\
    configure_pickle_data_node(
        id="use_regression_model",
        default_path="./user_data/model.p"
    )
```

Using sequences

Taipy scenarios allow you to create Task sequences. To do so, you should use the `sequences` parameter in the `Config.configure_scenario()` configuration function. The argument is a dictionary, each key is the name of a sequence, and the values are a list of Tasks. *All the Tasks of a sequence need to be in the* `task_configs` *argument!* In our example, we created two sequences in the training Scenario: one that generates the DataFrame subset, and one that trains the model based on an input DataFrame.

Here is how the function looks:

```
train_auto_pipeline_config = Config.configure_scenario(
    "train_pipeline",
    task_configs=[
        filter_df_task_config,
```

```
        preprocess_data_task_config,
        split_data_task_config,
        train_model_task_config,
        evaluate_model_task_config,
    ],
    sequences={
        "filter_sequence": [filter_df_task_config],
        "train_sequence": [
            preprocess_data_task_config,
            split_data_task_config,
            train_model_task_config,
            evaluate_model_task_config,
        ],
    },
)
```

Once you have a sequence, and after you create your scenario (with `taipy.create_scenario`), you can either submit the complete scenario (for example, `train_pipeline.submit`) or submit a single sequence (for example, with `train_pipeline.train_sequence.submit()`).

You can also use the `scenario` visual element to either submit the complete Scenario or a sequence. You can even create new sequences using the visual element, as you can see in *Figure 4.9*.

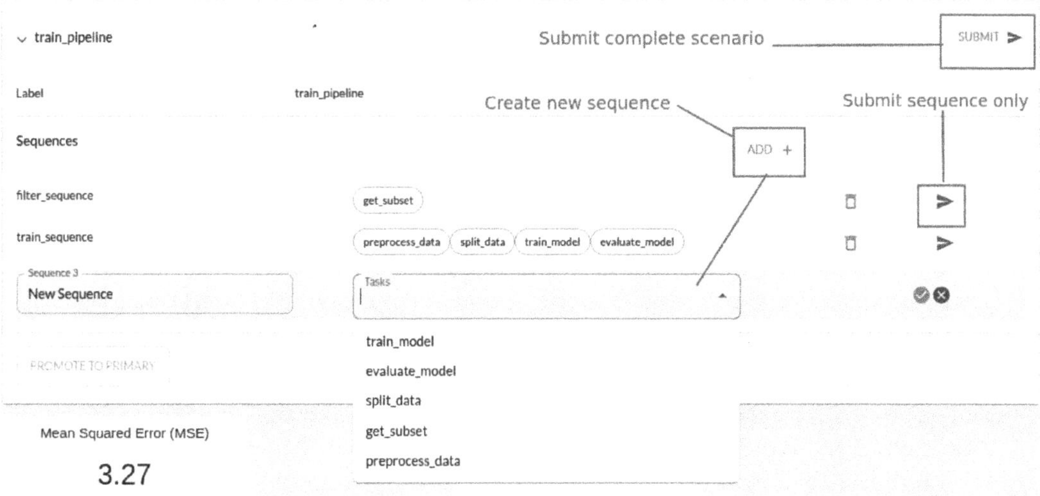

Figure 4.9 – Scenario selector with sequence management options

Scenario subscription

Taipy offers a special function to track the execution of each Task of a Scenario. This function is `taipy.subscribe_scenario`. It's used when the `Orchestrator()` is running, before the `taipy.create_scenario` statement. The function takes three arguments:

- `callback`: A function that's executed after Task execution.

- `scenario` (optional): If it's not defined, it will apply to all Scenarios. If you define it, it will apply to the specified Scenario.

- `params` (optional): Extra parameters that you can use in the function (pass them as a dictionary).

The `callback` function has two arguments, `scenario` and `job`. You can use them for monitoring or debugging. You can check the `main.py` file to see how we used the Scenario subscription.

Summary

In this chapter, you learned how to orchestrate processes with Taipy's Scenario Management tools. You learned how to configure pipelines, create them from the configuration objects, and bring them to a UI. We also created some complex Scenarios, with several Data Nodes and Tasks, and we covered some important concepts such as Scenario sequences. We also demonstrated how to bring ML algorithms to a UI for end users!

We have now covered all the distinct elements of Taipy Scenario Management, and all the visual elements to interact with them. But we still haven't covered them all in depth! Taipy Scenario Management brings lots of opportunities to compare scenarios and improve decision-making. We'll see all that in *Chapter 5*!

Questions

1. In the *Create your first pipelines* section, we started with a minimal pipeline that didn't reference any Data Nodes. Can you create a minimal pipeline without any Tasks (don't create a global Data Node)?

2. Looking at the Task configuration documentation (`https://docs.taipy.io/en/release-4.1/refmans/reference/pkg_taipy/pkg_core/pkg_config/TaskConfig/`), is there a way to make your Tasks run faster when you run your scenario several times? How could you apply it to the auto-mpg example? Could there be any limitations? (`https://docs.taipy.io/en/release-4.1/tutorials/articles/skippable_tasks/`)

3. Can you create a pipeline (without a UI) that reads the auto-mpg dataset, calculates the average for each column, and stores it in a plain `.txt` file?

4. Taipy orchestration lets you submit scenarios, but also Tasks! How would you create a `button` that submits the `filter_df_task_config` Task (this would be like submitting the `train_pipeline.filter_sequence` sequence, which has a single Task)?

5. Sometimes, less is more: could you make a single-page application where users can train the model and run it from the UI? Use scenario visual elements to interact with scenarios (use regular visual elements to select values for prediction). Don't include Data Node viewers or display training results.

Answers

1. You can create a scenario configuration object that doesn't reference any Task configuration objects but references a single Data Node using the `additional_data_node_configs()` argument. This is probably not useful, but it's certainly possible. Here is an example: `/exercises/answer_1.py`.

2. You can use the optional `skippable` parameter and set it to `True`. This way, if your Tasks receive the same input from the Data Nodes as the previous execution, it's skipped, and the Scenario execution continues, using the output Data Nodes from the previous execution. *It's a fantastic way to make your apps more efficient.* If your function is not deterministic (it uses the `random()` function or an LLM), you may not want to ever skip the Task. In auto-mpg, we could have created all our Tasks, setting `skippable = True`, but there is one Task where we could have thought differently. If you look at the `split_data()` function from the `fit_pipeline.py` file, you can see that we used `random_state=42`. This makes the dataset split in a deterministic manner. The Task that references this function (in `config.py`) is `split_data_task_config`. If we want our split to happen randomly, by removing the `random_state` value, then we should avoid setting `skippable` to `True` in the Task configuration.

3. You can do this in several ways. We chose to create a function and a Task to return the averages as a Python dictionary, and to use a generic Data Node with a custom-writing function to store the results in a file. You can check the code in: `/exercises/answer_3.py`.

4. To submit a Task using a button, create a `button` element, and define a callback function that accesses the Task from the Scenario object, like this:

```
# Inside the Page() element:
tgb.button(
    label="Submit Task",
    on_action= lambda state: state.training_scenario.\
        get_subset.submit()
)
```

5. You can do this in several ways! One example can be found here: `/exercises/answer_5.py`

Unlock this book's exclusive benefits now

Scan this QR code or go to packtpub.com/unlock, then search this book by name.

Note: Keep your purchase invoice ready before you start.

5

Managing Scenarios with Taipy

Here, we'll dive into Scenario Management. In *Chapter 4*, we discovered the orchestration process, and how the `Scenario` element plays a central role. Task orchestration is a technical concept that involves data transformation. Scenario Management leverages task orchestration, but it goes beyond that by adding functionalities that allow users to compare estimates or predictions, run data science or optimization algorithms, and compare outcomes at different periods in time, or with other hypotheses (such as comparing optimistic versus pessimistic predictions).

This chapter covers transforming your orchestration pipelines into Scenario Management tools. We'll introduce important concepts such as cycles and Scenario comparison.

Taipy is all about bringing your algorithms to end users. This chapter is a fantastic opportunity to think about the business side (or the functional side) of your Taipy applications. You can imagine Data Nodes as abstractions that represent KPIs or business metrics. You can conceive Scenarios as business problems. Business analysts and other users may rely on analyzing data that evolves to make informed decisions. We'll see the tools that we can use to empower users with recurrent data.

Scenario Management and comparison allow users to perform **what-if analysis**, which involves changing input variables and observing how the output changes. What-if analysis is often used for scenario planning and risk assessment, or to predict future outcomes based on different assumptions or hypotheses.

In this chapter, we'll cover what-if analysis with Taipy and, more precisely, the following:

- Working with recurrent Scenarios
- Comparing Scenarios

Technical requirements

You can find the complete code used in this chapter in the GitHub repository: https://github.
com/PacktPublishing/Getting-Started-with-Taipy/tree/main/chapter_05.
Throughout the chapter, we'll mention the names of the GitHub files we're using so you can pick them
up from the repository when needed.

Working with recurrent Scenarios – scope, cycle, and frequency

Recurrent scenarios are business cases where at least some of the data evolves at a set pace. Examples
of recurrent business data include daily past sales, quarterly financial results, monthly website traffic,
weekly customer support tickets, or yearly carbon emissions. A business scenario can mix recurrent
and non-recurrent data. For instance, if you're predicting your team's optimal schedule, the team
members might stay the same over long periods, while your workload predictions may vary each week.

To create recurrent Scenarios with Taipy, you can set the Data Node's scope to Scope.CYCLE.
Cycles are a set of Scenario properties that group Scenarios under a certain time frame. You can
think of cycles as a "*time box*" that groups all the Scenarios that come from the same configuration
object and were defined within the same time window. When you work with cycles, your Scenario
configuration object should also have a frequency, which is an optional parameter with a None
default value (which we'll explain in the next section).

You can create Scenarios from the same Scenario configuration several times (this will create a new
Scenario object and other Scenario Management objects such as Tasks and Data Nodes). For recurrent
Scenarios, the creation date will determine the Scenario cycle (along with the frequency).

Let's now see the configuration options, and how to run multiple Scenarios, and then we'll create a
small application that demonstrates these concepts.

> **Important note**
>
> The library may sometimes seem unstable during development. If you get a warning to reload
> your page, deleting the .taipy folder and changing use_reloader=False to True will help.

Setting the scope for Data Node configuration

As we saw in *Chapters 3* and *4*, Scenarios use Data Nodes as interfaces to data. We've seen how to
create global Data Nodes and Scenario Data Nodes with the scope argument on the configuration
side. Let's take a look at the third option (Scope.CYCLE), and how they compare to each other.

The `scope` argument can take three values:

- **Scope.GLOBAL**: This will create a single Data Node for all the Scenarios (from the same Scenario configuration)
- **Scope.CYCLE**: This will create a single Data Node for all the Scenarios within the same cycle
- **Scope.Scenario**: This will create one distinct Data Node for each Scenario

Setting the Scenario configuration frequency

If your Scenario configuration uses Data Node configuration objects with `scope` set to `Scope.CYCLE`, you need to assign a value to `frequency`. The default value for `frequency` is None. This means that even if you assigned a `Scope.CYCLE` to your Data Nodes, if their Scenario configuration object has no `frequency`, they will behave like Data Nodes with `Scope.SCENARIO`!

The `frequency` determines the time frame for a cycle. To assign values to this parameter, you need to import the Frequency class (`from taipy import Frequency`).

The values are self-explanatory; you can choose between the following:

- `Frequency.DAILY`
- `Frequency.WEEKLY`
- `Frequency.MONTHLY`
- `Frequency.QUARTERLY`
- `Frequency.YEARLY`

Submitting Scenarios from the same configuration object

You can create a Scenario with the Scenario configuration object and its `taipy.create_scenario()`. This creates all the Data Node and Task objects. When you create a second Scenario from the same configuration object, it may or may not create new Data Nodes, depending on their `Scope` and the Scenario's cycle.

The `taipy.create_scenario()` function has a `creation_date` parameter. It takes a `date.datetime` value type. The default value for this parameter is the current timestamp. If your Scenario has Data Nodes with the `scope` configuration set to `Scope.CYCLE`, Taipy will assign your Scenario to the cycle that matches the `creation_date` and `frequency`.

For example, let's say you create two Scenarios from a single Scenario configuration file and that Scenario configuration has one single Data Node configuration:

- If the Data Node has a `Scope.GLOBAL`, you will get one Data Node, no matter what
- If the Data Node has a `Scope.SCENARIO`, you will get two Data Nodes, no matter what

- If the Data Node `scope` is `Scope.CYCLE`, the Scenario has a `Frequency.MONTHLY`, and both Scenarios are created in the same month (of the same year!), then they belong to the same Scenario cycle, and this will create a single Data Node

- If the Data Node `scope` is `Scope.CYCLE`, the Scenario has a `Frequency.MONTHLY`, and the Scenarios are created in different months, then they belong to different Scenario cycles, and this will create two Data Nodes, one for each month, as you'll see in the following example

Once you have a Scenario, you can submit it with the `.submit()` method.

You can also access information about the Scenario's cycle using the `.cycle` attribute (to read or to write), which has the following attributes as well:

- `scenario.cycle.creation_date`: The cycle's creation date and time
- `scenario.cycle.end_date`: The date and time marking the end of the cycle
- `scenario.cycle.frequency`: The frequency at which this cycle repeats
- `scenario.cycle.id`: A unique identifier for the cycle
- `scenario.cycle.name`: The name given to the cycle
- `scenario.cycle.properties`: A dictionary for any extra cycle properties
- `scenario.cycle.start_date`: The start date and time of the cycle

The `taipy` library also offers two methods to retrieve information about the application's cycles:

- `taipy.get_cycles()` returns a list with all the cycle objects
- `taipy.get_scenarios(cycle_object)` takes a cycle object as a parameter and returns all the Scenarios within it

    All elements in Scenario Management (such as Data Nodes, Scenarios, sequences, jobs, and cycles) have two methods to retrieve their labels:

- `get_label()` – Returns the full label of the entity as a unique, human-readable string. The full label is created by combining the simple labels of its parent elements. This ensures that each entity has a distinct name across the system.

    - Example: A Data Node for a `forecast` in Scenario A of the January cycle might have the label `January > A > forecast`.

- `get_simple_label()` – Returns a simplified version of the entity's label. This label is not necessarily unique across the system, but it can still differentiate elements within the same scenario.

    - Example: The same `forecast` Data Node mentioned above would have a simple label of just `forecast`. If another `forecast` Data Node exists in Scenario B of the February cycle, it would also have the simple label `forecast`, making it ambiguous outside its scenario.

Figure 5.1 summarizes all the key steps for cycle management, from configuration to orchestration.

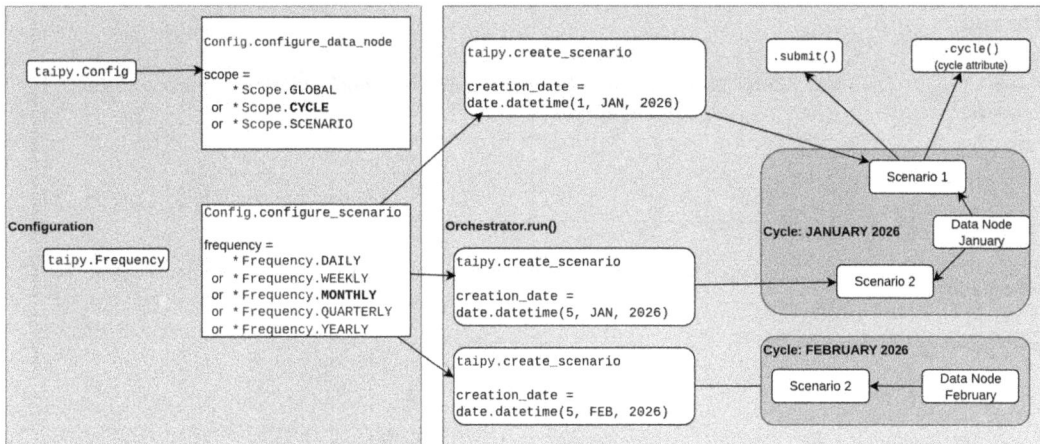

Figure 5.1 – Recurrent Scenario Management

Let's now see a practical example.

Creating a recurrent Scenario

We'll create a simple Scenario that uses three Data Nodes, one with a GLOBAL scope, one with a CYCLE scope, and one with a SCENARIO scope.

Suppose we want to compare the final price of a product (say, a small cup of coffee), and we want to compare different Scenarios depending on how much profit our company makes on the product. In our simple Scenario, we calculate our final price with these three factors:

- **Buying price**: We buy our products monthly, and the price of those products can change monthly. We'll use a Data Node with Scope.CYCLE to represent this.

- **Markup**: This is a multiplying factor, where the minimum value is 1. If the markup is set to 1.5, this means we make a 33% margin on our product. To calculate the final price, we multiply the final price by the markup value. We'll use a Data Node with Scope.SCENARIO to represent this, because we want each Scenario to have a different markup value (we ultimately want to test different markup values at different moments to see what the final price would be).

- **VAT**: Let's say that VAT (value-added or consumption tax) is at 20%, as it is in France. This means that we multiply the buying price by the markup and by 1.2. This tax stays constant for all Scenarios and all cycles (we can't change the taxation level). We set a Data Node with its scope set to Scope.GLOBAL.

We're going to create a small GUI (see *Figure 5.2*) to run different Scenarios.

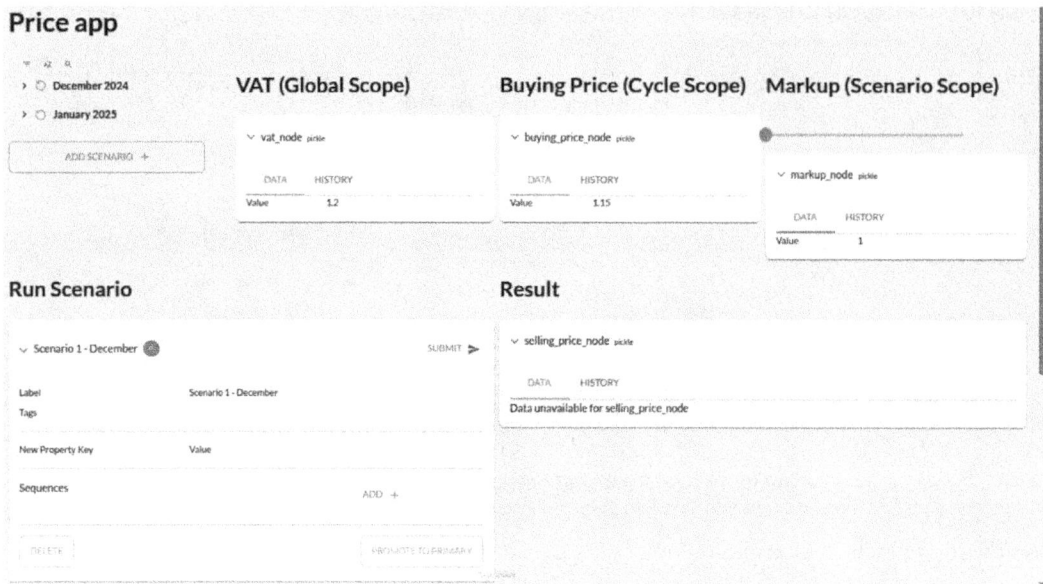

Figure 5.2 – A price calculation app

This mock-up app will allow users to answer what-if questions – for example, "*WHAT happens to the final price IF I increase my markup by 50% or 20%?*"

Let's first see how we could configure this Scenario using Taipy configuration objects.

Scenario configuration

The code for this section is in `price_app/`. To configure this business case, we need to configure four Data Nodes: one for each of the three factors we mentioned (the GLOBAL VAT tax Data Node, the CYCLE buying price Data Node, and the SCENARIO markup Data Node), and a fourth Data Node to store the output (with `scope` set to `Scope.SCENARIO`). This is how the Data Node configuration looks (pay attention to the `scope` parameter):

```
vat_data_node_config = Config.configure_data_node(
    id="vat_node", scope=Scope.GLOBAL, default_data=1.2
)
buying_price_node_config = Config.configure_data_node(
    id="buying_price_node",
    scope=Scope.CYCLE,
)
```

```
markup_node_config = Config.configure_data_node(
    id="markup_node",
    scope=Scope.SCENARIO,
)
selling_price_node_config = Config.configure_data_node(
    id="selling_price_node",
    scope=Scope.SCENARIO,
)
```

Our Scenario configuration also needs a Task and function to calculate the price from the three input variables. The function takes three input parameters and returns their product, like this:

```
def calculate_price(buying_price, markup, vat_tax):
    final_price = buying_price * markup* vat_tax
    return final_price
```

The Task configuration object looks like this:

```
calculate_price_task_config = Config.configure_task(
    id="calculate_price_task",
    function=calculate_price,
    input=[
        buying_price_node_config,
        markup_node_config,
        vat_data_node_config
    ],
    output=selling_price_node_config,
)
```

Once we have our Data Node and Task configuration objects, we can create the Scenario configuration object. When we defined our use case, we stated that our buying price could change monthly. This is why we set frequency to Frequency.MONTHLY, like this:

```
scenario_config = Config.configure_scenario(
    id="pricing_scenario",
    task_configs=[calculate_price_task_config],
    frequency=Frequency.MONTHLY,
)
```

Figure 5.3 shows a representation of the pipeline we configured.

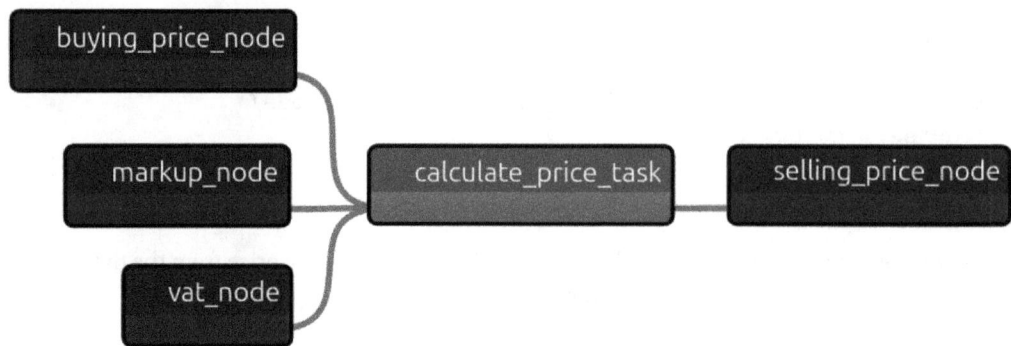

Figure 5.3 – Price application pipeline

Let's now create and run some Scenarios to better understand cycles.

Running multiple Scenarios

Now that we have our configuration files, and before we create a GUI, let's run the Orchestrator and figure out some key concepts of Taipy Scenario Management. You can see all the code in / prices_app/pipeline.py (remember to run the code from within the directory).

In our example, we'll create four Scenario objects from the same scenario_config object. Two Scenarios will have a creation_date in December of 2025, and two of them will have a creation_date in January of 2026. For example, this is how we created the first Scenario (pay attention to the creation_date parameter):

```
scenario_december_1 = tp.create_scenario(
    scenario_config,
    creation_date=dt.datetime(2025, 12, 22),
    name="Scenario 1 - December",
)
```

Now that we have our first Scenario, we can write the data to the input Data Nodes, like this (you can experiment and change the values!):

```
scenario_december_1.vat_node.write(1.2)   # Not necessary because
                                          # has default data
scenario_december_1.markup_node.write(1.5)
scenario_december_1.buying_price_node.write(2)
```

We can then submit the Scenario and read from the output Data Node:

```
scenario_december_1.submit()
price_december = scenario_december_1.selling_price_node.read()
print(
    f"The price for December with is {round(price_december, 2)}")
```

We strongly suggest playing around with different Scenarios and trying to access different values.

In our example, we can access the value of `scenario_december_2.buying_price_node` because it's the same Data Node as `scenario_december_1.buying_price_node`. It's the same Data Node because both scenarios are in the same month cycle, and the Data Node has `scope` set to `Scope.Cycle`.

You can also access all the attributes from the Scenario's `cycle`, as in this example:

```
december_1_cycle = scenario_december_1.cycle
print(december_1_cycle.creation_date)
# Output: 2024-12-22 00:00:00
```

Now that we've covered the essential elements of recurring Scenario Management, let's bring these concepts to a UI.

Creating a GUI with recurring Scenarios

We're going to create a small application that allows users to test different Scenarios, selecting the markup to compare different final price outcomes. The app will also show the GLOBAL VAT Data Node (with a visual element) as well as the buying price Data Node. Users will be able to create and select new Scenarios, with different dates and, therefore, different cycles.

The configuration files are the same as in the previous section. We also create a mock-up dataset; it's a CSV file that we place in a `data` directory. This file contains monthly buying prices from 2024 and 2025. You can see it in `/prices_app/data`.

We create a single-page app. The complete code for the main application is in `/prices_app/main.py`. Let's see the main components of the app.

Adding a Scenario selector and a Scenario element with cycles

After the `Orchestrator()` runs, we create four Scenarios, two in December of 2024, and two in January of 2025. We also create a `selected_scenario` object, like this (line 112 in `main.py`):

```
Orchestrator().run()
scenario_december_1 = tp.create_scenario(
    scenario_config,
    creation_date=dt.datetime(2024, 12, 1),
    name="Scenario 1 - December",
```

```
    )
    (...)
selected_scenario = scenario_december_1
```

In the `Page` element, we add a `scenario_selector` and a `scenario` element, like this:

```
tgb.scenario_selector(
    "{selected_scenario}",
    on_change=update_scenario
)
(...)
tgb.scenario("{selected_scenario}")
```

The callback function for the `scenario_selector` looks like this:

```
def update_scenario(state, var_name, value):
    state.selected_scenario = value
```

Figure 5.4 shows how a Scenario selector with cycles looks. When users change the Scenario in the selector, it changes it in the `scenario` element as well.

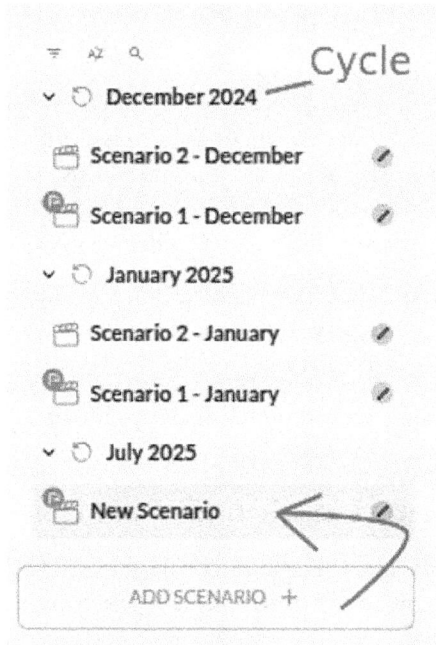

Figure 5.4 – A `scenario_selector` with cycles

We created four Scenarios in `main.py`, as you can see, but users can create new Scenarios with the Scenario selector.

Next, we can create four `data_node` elements. Since we have several Scenarios (and users can create new ones), we can assign the values of the `data_node` parameters using the `selected_scenario` variable, so the Data Nodes will change when we change the Scenario.

We define all Data Nodes in the same way – here's an example:

```
tgb.data_node(
    data_node="{selected_scenario.vat_node}",
    show_properties=False,
)
```

Our markup Data Node has to be easy for users to interact with. We want users to `write()` into the Data Node so they can compare different final prices based on different markup levels. For this, we create a `markup` variable and bind it to a `slider` element. The callback to this function writes the value into the markup Data Node. We also add a statement to the `update_scenario` callback, to change the value of the `markup` variable when we change the scenario (otherwise, changing Scenarios would overwrite the markup). Here are the relevant code snippets from `main.py`:

```
markup= 1.0 #Initial value
def change_markup(state):
    state.selected_scenario.markup_node.write(state.markup)
def update_scenario(state, var_name, value):
    (...)
    state.markup = state.selected_scenario.markup_node.read()
# Inside Page():
    tgb.slider(
        "{markup}", step=0.01, min=1, max=2,
        on_change=change_markup
    )
```

The last important element of the application is how it updates the monthly values for the Data Nodes with a cycle scope. The buying price is in a CSV file. We can read it with a function that creates a pandas DataFrame and returns the right value:

```
def get_monthly_price(
    scenario_ym, price_file="./data/buying_prices.csv"
):
    df_prices = pd.read_csv(price_file)
    try:
        price = df_prices.loc[
            df_prices["month"] == scenario_ym, "price"
        ].iloc[0]
```

```
        return price
except:
    print("no data for this period")
    return 0
```

If you look at the CSV file, you'll notice that the `scenario_ym` variable has to be a string in the `mm-yyyy` format. Lucky for us, *we can access the value of the scenario's cycle creation date* to determine the right value!

Here is how we start the value. We also add a similar statement to the `update_scenario` function, so we also update the `buying_price` variable for the Data Node:

```
scenario_date = selected_scenario.cycle.creation_date
scenario_cycle_ym = f"{scenario_date.month}-{scenario_date.year}"
buying_price = get_monthly_price(scenario_cycle_ym)
selected_scenario.buying_price_node.write(buying_price)
```

You can run the application, *change the values of the markup Data Node with the slider first*, and submit your Scenarios. You can also create new Scenarios. As you create and submit more Scenarios, you'll be able to compare the final prices from different `markup` levels. You can also use the `data_node` visual elements to change the values of the Data Nodes directly. Feel free to experiment with the application!

Primary Scenarios

When users compare multiple Scenarios, they can choose one **primary Scenario** (typically their best case) per cycle. Primary Scenarios will show a **P** symbol next to them in the `scenario_selector` element (refer to *Figure 5.4*). *The primary Scenario is just a tag; it has no other functionality, but it's useful to flag the Scenario to use in production*. Taipy also offers ways to retrieve primary Scenarios, which is something your applications can leverage.

You can make a Scenario primary in two ways (by default, it will be the first Scenario):

- The first one is to use the `taipy.set_primary()` function and pass a Scenario name to it.
- The second way is to use the `scenario` visual element. When you select a non-primary Scenario, it will show a **PROMOTE TO PRIMARY** button at the bottom right.

You have two ways to access primary cycle information:

- `taipy.get_primary_scenarios()` returns a list of all primary Scenarios (doesn't take arguments)
- `tp.get_primary(cycle_name)` takes a cycle object as an argument and returns the primary Scenario for that cycle.

Let's now see how to compare Scenarios with Taipy!

Comparing Scenarios

In the previous section, we created a small application that lets users submit several Scenarios with different inputs, compare the results using visual elements, and switch between Scenarios. This could be a way to compare Scenarios quickly and perform some superficial Scenario comparisons. This could also be fine with a few Scenarios.

In this section, we'll explore Taipy's Scenario comparison capabilities to take our users one step further. We'll continue using our price comparison example.

Configuring Scenario comparison

You can see the code for this part in the `comparison_app/` directory.

Taipy's **scenario configuration function** (`Config.configure_scenario()`) takes an optional `comparators` argument. This argument takes a dictionary as a value. The dictionary takes Data Node configuration IDs as keys and a comparison function as a value.

For example, we created a variant configuration file (`config_comparison.py`), and this is how the Scenario configuration looks:

```
scenario_config = Config.configure_scenario(
    (...)
    comparators={selling_price_node_config.id: compare_price},
)
```

Now, we need to code a `compare_price` function. A Scenario comparison function has a single argument that uses the `*args` syntax. Using the `*args` syntax means that the function takes any number of parameters. The values of those parameters are the Scenario's Data Nodes we're comparing.

You can create complex and elaborate functions, but this would be a minimal comparison function that returns a list with all the Data Node values:

```
def compare_price(*prices):
    return list(prices)  # prices is a set
```

You can use the preceding function to display the comparison result in a table. We could also return a comparison value as a ratio or a difference between two items in the list.

The `comparators` argument can take as many dictionary keys as the Data Nodes the Scenario has. Also, the same Data Node can take more than one comparison function; in this case, all the functions are in a list.

Running Scenario comparison

Once your Scenarios have one or more comparison functions, you can use the `taipy.compare_scenarios()` function to run the Scenario comparison. This function takes any number of Scenarios (from the same configuration!), and returns a dictionary object with the results for each comparison function.

It's important to keep in mind that the `taipy.compare_scenarios()` function doesn't submit the Scenarios! In our example, we configured the function to compare the results of the output Data Nodes, but if the Scenario was never submitted, the output would be None.

The function returns a dictionary of dictionaries. The keys of the first dictionary are the Data Node IDs (the Data Nodes we're comparing), and the keys of the nested dictionary are the name of the Scenario comparison function.

This is how to execute the function (when the `Orchestrator()` is running) and how to access the results:

```
comparison = tp.compare_scenarios(
    scenario_december_1, scenario_december_2)
selling_prices = comparison[
    "selling_price_node"]["compare_price"]
```

Scenario comparison in a UI

With all the concepts we have covered so far in this book, you should be able to bring Scenario comparison to a UI. You can find one example in `/comparison_app/main.py`. This app uses the configuration file we saw in the *Configuring Scenario comparison* section, and it's a variant of the price comparison application we created in the first section of this chapter.

Figure 5.5 shows how the application looks.

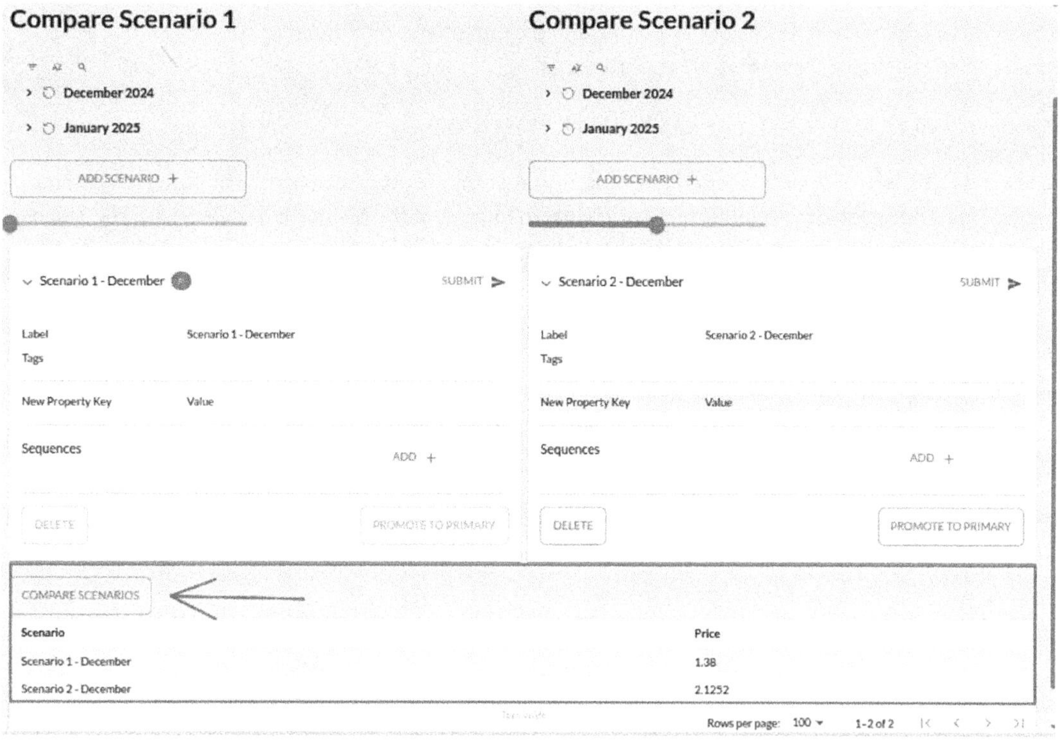

Figure 5.5 – Price comparison app

To create this application, we used two Scenario objects (we created them with `tp.create_scenario` from configuration objects). Then, we manage each Scenario with the following controls (as you can see in *Figure 5.5*, one Scenario is managed in the left part of the app, the other in the right one):

- Two `scenario_selectors` to choose the Scenarios to compare
- Two sliders to assign the values of the `markup` Data Nodes for each Scenario
- Two `scenario` selectors to submit each Scenario

To display the comparison results, we create a `table` element and bind it to a `comparison_table` variable, with the initial value set to None, like this:

```
tgb.table("{comparison_table}", rebuild=True)
```

We also added a button that triggers the function that compares the Scenarios. The function creates a pandas DataFrame with two columns – one with the name of the Scenario and one with the Price value for that Scenario – and then assigns the DataFrame as a value for the `comparison_table` variable, to display the results.

Here's how the function looks (in `main.py`):

```python
def compare_scenarios(state):
    comparison = tp.compare_scenarios(
        state.selected_scenario_1,
        state.selected_scenario_2
    )
    selling_prices = comparison[
        "selling_price_node"]["compare_price"]
    df_compared_prices = pd.DataFrame({
        "Scenario": [
            state.selected_scenario_1.name,
            state.selected_scenario_2.name,
        ],
        "Price": selling_prices,
    })
    state.comparison_table = df_compared_prices
```

Summary

In this chapter, you learned how to perform a what-if analysis with Taipy. You discovered the main components to configure your Data Nodes and Scenarios and how to orchestrate them to achieve comparisons. You saw how to bring these comparisons to the UI, and how to set up applications where users create, submit, and compare Scenarios. You also learned about cycles, scopes, and frequency, and how to combine these concepts to compare Scenarios over time.

With this chapter, we've introduced all the main Taipy concepts. You should now be able to create complete applications! In *Chapters 7-11*, we'll create realistic applications, where we'll combine all the knowledge from *Chapters 2-5*, and in *Chapters 12-15*, we'll discover advanced functionalities to take your apps to the next level. But before that, in the next chapter, we'll explore the last part of a production-ready project: deploying your Taipy apps.

Questions

1. In our multiple-Scenario example (`pipeline.py`), we submitted `scenario_december_1`. We could also submit `scenario_december_2` to generate a value for the `scenario_december_2.selling_price_node` Data Node. Is there a way to write into `scenario_december_2.selling_price_nodeScenario's Data Node` without interacting with `scenario_december_2`?

2. Can you create, and use, a function that prints the minimal value for the final price *within the cycle* that's selected in the `price_app`? This function is triggered when the user changes Scenarios.

3. In our Scenario comparison UI example, we created a table, from a pandas DataFrame, that displayed the Scenario name and the final price. Let's imagine that your results are in a magical currency, where 1 unit = 1.2 US dollars. Can you change the configuration file and the functions in `main.py` to add a column with the price in USD, next to the local price, as well as the `markup` levels, to allow for better comparison?

4. Can you add a button to the comparison UI app that creates a table with three columns: one for each cycle, one that lists the Scenario with the lowest final price for that cycle, and one with that Scenario's price? Also, this function promotes each lowest price Scenario to primary.

5. Can you create a chart that compares all the Scenarios that users submit in the comparison app?

Answers

1. A way to do this could be to assign a `scope=Scope.CYCLE` (or `scope=Scope.GLOBAL`) to the `selling_price_node_config`. This way, the output Data Node would be shared and written after submitting the `scenario_december_1` scenario.

    But this wouldn't be a good idea! We want to compare the outcomes of each Scenario, so if Scenarios share the output Data Node with other Scenarios (globally or at a cycle level), the results will override each other.

2. You can code a `calculate_minimum` callback function, and call it from the `update_scenario` callback. You can leverage the `selected_scenario` cycle and the `taipy.get_scenarios` function. Once you have all the Scenarios for the cycle, you can read the values of the output Data Nodes and select the minimal value. The code is in `answer_2.py`.

3. You can see the code in the `answer_3.py` file. In the configuration file, you can create a specific function to return the price values multiplied by 1.2 and then use 2 functions for the price Data Node and one function for the `markup` Data Node in the `comparators` argument, like this:

```
comparators={
    selling_price_node_config.id: [
        compare_values, compare_price_usd],
    markup_node_config.id: compare_values,
```

Then the callback can retrieve the data from all the comparison results and append it to a DataFrame like this:

```
markup_values = comparison[
    "markup_node"]["compare_values"]
selling_prices = comparison[
    "selling_price_node"]["compare_values"]
selling_prices_usd = comparison[
    "selling_price_node"]["compare_price_usd"]
df_compared_prices = pd.DataFrame({
    "Scenario": [
        state.selected_scenario_1.name,
        state.selected_scenario_2.name,
    ],
    "Markup": markup_values,
    "Price": selling_prices,
    "Price (USD)": selling_prices_usd,
})
```

4. You can see the code in `answer_4.py`. The goal here is to leverage several functions to select all cycles (`taipy.get_cycles()`) and get the Scenarios for each cycle (with `get_scenarios(cycle)`).

5. You can use charts or other visual elements to display your Scenario comparisons! For example, you could add this bar chart to your application:

```
tgb.chart(
    "{comparison_table}", type="bar",
    x="Scenario", y="Price"
)
```

Join our community on Discord

Join our community's Discord space for discussions with the authors and other readers:

`https://packt.link/taipybook`

6

Deploying Your
Taipy Applications

Taipy builds production-ready web applications. This means you should be able to deploy your applications in production environments that end users can access from their web browsers.

In this book, we mainly work with Taipy's default server, which is ideal for local testing and fast iteration. In this chapter, you'll learn how to package and deploy your Taipy application as a standard Flask app, leveraging the breadth of the Flask ecosystem to run in any production environment. We'll walk through converting your Taipy project into a WSGI-compatible Flask application and discuss best practices for hosting it on real servers. Finally, we'll explore alternative workflows, such as running Taipy inside Jupyter notebooks for quick demos and exploratory development, so you can choose the right approach for every stage of your project.

When we talk about production environments, each organization has its standards and rules, so we will just cover the generic and common aspects of deployment. We'll see some specific examples of deployment on **Linux servers** and in **Docker containers**. At the end of the chapter, we'll briefly discuss how to deploy some popular online services, which can be a good way to share prototypes, proof-of-concept apps, personal projects, or public applications.

In this chapter, we'll cover the following topics:

- Running Taipy applications
- Deploying Taipy applications
- Deploying Taipy applications in popular services

Technical requirements

The complete code used in this chapter can be found in the GitHub repository: `https://github.com/PacktPublishing/Getting-Started-with-Taipy/tree/main/chapter_06`. Throughout the chapter, we'll mention the names of the GitHub files we're using so you can pick them up from the repository when needed.

The deployment part assumes some knowledge of Linux commands. Knowing about cloud services (we'll use Google Cloud as an example) and Docker is also recommended.

Running Taipy applications

Throughout the book, we use two `run()` methods to activate our Taipy services: one for `Gui()` objects and another one for `Orchestrator()` objects. You can run both objects in the same application. We also saw in *Chapter 1* that it's recommended to use these `run()` methods under the main guard (`if __name__ == "__main__":`), along with other instantiations, such as creating scenarios or defining variables (when you work with Taipy's default server).

For all our examples in this chapter, we'll use a minimal application that runs both a `Gui()` and `Orchestrator()` object. The app displays some text; you should be able to run any Taipy application in the same way.

We're now going to focus on the Gui class's `run()` method. We already saw some cosmetic parameters in *Chapter 2*. The Orchestrator class's `run()` method doesn't take any extra parameters; we'll be running it, but that's it. Let's now look inside Gui's `run()` method.

The run() method

The `Gui` class is Taipy's `run()` method has optional parameters that let us configure how the app runs. In this section, we'll cover the most important parameters to run our applications (we'll discuss some extra parameters in the deployment sections of this chapter).

Development, production, and observability

For **development**, we've been using `use_reloader` set to `True` (the default is `False`). When we do this, the server reloads any time we make a change in our code files and save them. When running in production, you should set this parameter to `False`.

If you don't want the reloader to work, but you still want to test your application, you can set the debug parameter to `True`. This will print some useful error messages in the terminal. If `use_reloader` is `True`, it activates the debugger, so you don't need to activate it twice. Both options will set the `async_mode` parameter to `"threading"` (see the *Async mode* section).

There is also a `flask_log` parameter, which defaults to `False` and creates a complete real-time log from the Flask server if you set it to `True`. *Figure 6.1* shows real-time logs from Taipy's debugger and from the Flask server.

```
[2024-11-03 09:32:03.801][Taipy][INFO] Updating configuration with command-line arguments...
[2024-11-03 09:32:03.802][Taipy][INFO] Managing application's version...
[2024-11-03 09:32:03.803][Taipy][INFO] Development mode: Clean all entities of version 9ca88349-c670-41bb-9988-a08049e87b9a
[2024-11-03 09:32:03.846][Taipy][INFO] Checking application's version...
[2024-11-03 09:32:03.847][Taipy][INFO] Blocking configuration update...
[2024-11-03 09:32:03.847][Taipy][INFO] Starting job dispatcher...
[2024-11-03 09:32:03.848][Taipy][INFO] Orchestrator service has been started.
[2024-11-03 09:32:04.049][Taipy][INFO] job JOB_task_35405fd3-a801-44b9-928b-b518a88980e0 is completed.
```
Taipy log

```
hi Flask!
 * Debugger is active!
 * Debugger PIN: 891-479-856
127.0.0.1 - - [03/Nov/2024 09:32:04] "GET /socket.io/?EIO=4&transport=polling&t=c31bh6fa HTTP/1.1" 200 -
127.0.0.1 - - [03/Nov/2024 09:32:04] "POST /socket.io/?EIO=4&transport=polling&t=c34pw5ub&sid=yE-vB0wDswj8q7PEAAAA HTTP/1.1" 200 -
127.0.0.1 - - [03/Nov/2024 09:32:04] "GET /socket.io/?EIO=4&transport=polling&t=c34pxynr&sid=yE-vB0wDswj8q7PEAAAA HTTP/1.1" 200 -
∏
```
Flask log

Figure 6.1: Logs from Taipy's debugger and the Flask server

Async mode

`async_mode` determines which asynchronous backend Flask-SocketIO will use to handle WebSocket and long-polling connections in the WSGI server (a synchronous web server interface standard used by frameworks such as Flask). The default value is `"gevent"`, which enables asynchronous handling of WebSocket connections for better performance. You can also set it to `"threading"` or `"eventlet"`, depending on the needs of your application.

The `"threading"` mode creates a new thread for each connection, making it simple to use but less efficient for handling high numbers of users due to increased memory usage.

The `"eventlet"` and `"gevent"` modes both use cooperative multitasking (via monkey-patching; see `https://www.gevent.org/intro.html#monkey-patching`) to handle many simultaneous connections efficiently. `gevent` is generally faster and more optimized for production use (`https://python-socketio.readthedocs.io/en/latest/server.html#id8` and `https://eng.lyft.com/gevent-part-3-performance-e64303fa102b`), while eventlet is easier to use but is no longer actively maintained. We do not recommend using eventlet unless you have a specific reason (`https://eventlet.readthedocs.io/en/latest/`).

Setting host and ports

Web applications run on a server, and users can access them with a combination of a hostname and port number.

The `host` parameter defaults to `"localhost"` (`127.0.0.1`) for development, but you can add any IP address you want, as long as it's opened in your network. For local development, all addresses in the range `127.0.0.1` to `127.0.0.8` should work (in case you want to test or have a good reason to change this; otherwise, we recommend sticking to the default `localhost`).

You can change the `port` parameter, which defaults to `5000`. There's a second parameter, called `port_auto_ranges`, that you can use if you set `port` to `"auto"`, and you can pass a value as a list of tuples. For example, to automatically connect to any port between `50000` and `55000`, you would write `port_auto_ranges = [(50000, 55000)]`.

Setting time zones

Time zones are a sensitive problem in data analysis and data engineering. Understanding how your application displays and collects data is important to prevent problems (you don't want to display different date and time values in your charts depending on user location, and you need a standardized way to store your date and time data).

The `run` method has a `timezone` parameter. The default value is `client` (the user's computer determines the time zone). It also accepts `server` (the app uses the server's time zone for all users), or a custom parameter as a TZ identifier (Taipy's doc links to Wikipedia to know the right identifier: `https://en.wikipedia.org/wiki/List_of_tz_database_time_zones`).

> **Note**
> Taipy applications store all the dates in UTC, but the date selectors display them in the selected format.

Advanced configuration

The `server_config` dictionary supports configuring Flask, Flask-CORS, and Flask-SocketIO. Each configuration object is itself a dictionary. You can reference the respective documentation for detailed configuration options. For SSL support, you can provide a simple string or tuple for the `ssl_context` key, but this might not work with async modes such as `eventlet` or `gevent`.

Here is an example of how your `server_config` could look:

```
server_config={
    "flask": {"root_path": "/home"},
    "socketio": {"manage_session": False},
},
```

Running your applications on a Flask web page

You can add your Taipy application to a Flask-based website. To do so, you need to add the name of your Flask app to the `flask` parameter in the `Gui()` object:

```
flask_app = Flask(__name__)


@flask_app.route("/home")
```

```
def home_page():
    return "<h1>The home page.</h1>"
(...)
gui = Gui(page=page, flask=flask_app)
```

You can look at `/run_with_flask` for a complete example. When the application runs, you can go to `/localhost:5000/home`, and you'll see the content of Flask's website (it shows the `<h1>` tag with the text **The home page**).

Running your applications in a notebook

While notebooks are not the ideal environment to develop complete applications, they're a familiar tool for data scientists and data analysts. It's possible to run a Taipy application from a notebook, and you can use Taipy's GUI to change values and then use them from the notebook.

If you run a Taipy app from a notebook, don't use the main guard (`if __name__ == "__main__":`). Using a notebook, you won't be able to create multiple-user UIs, and `async_mode` will always be `"threading"`.

A cool thing you can do with notebooks is to access the values of a bound variable from notebook cells with `Gui().state.variable_name`. You can see an example in `/run_in_notebook`.

Let's now see how to deploy your applications in external servers.

Deploying Taipy applications

There are endless deployment possibilities and company standards that affect how you'll effectively share your application with others for demonstration, or even bring it to a production stage. In this section, we cover the deployment on a Google Cloud Linux server, but the process should be similar with other cloud providers. We also cover deployment in Docker containers, which are a popular way to deploy applications in enterprise environments, as well as some popular hosting services.

Deploying on Linux servers

To demonstrate deployment on a Linux server, we'll use a Google Cloud **Virtual Machine** (**VM**). We selected a Debian-based distribution (**Ubuntu 24**). You can create one for free to test your applications (but be careful not to exceed the usage limits if you don't want to be charged).

You can find a tutorial to set up a machine in Google Cloud's documentation (`https://cloud.google.com/compute/docs/create-linux-vm-instance`). *Figure 6.2* shows some key configuration elements of our VM. You can access the VM's terminal with the SSH button. Once we deploy our app, we'll access it from the external IP address.

Other popular VM services include Microsoft Azure VMs and AWS EC2 instances. Make sure you open port 80 (allow HTTP access).

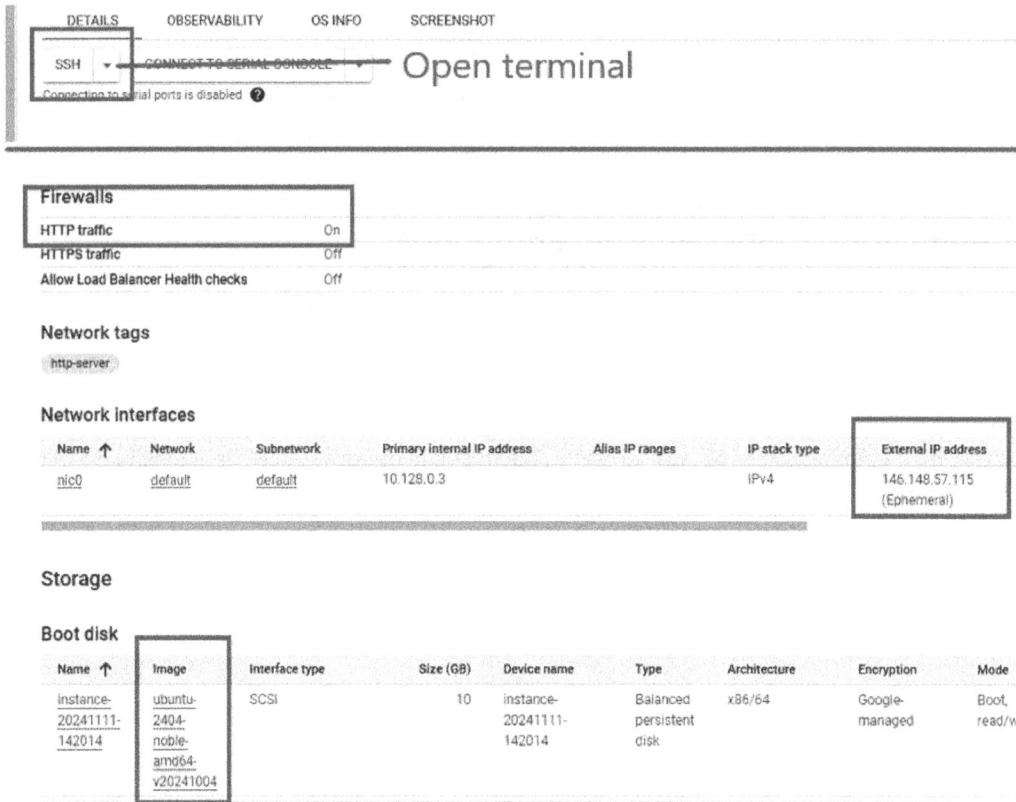

Figure 6.2: Example of Google Cloud's VM panel

This screenshot shows the SSH button to open the terminal, that HTTP traffic is available, the external IP address, and the selected image (Ubuntu 24).

Taipy applications run in a **uWSGI** server that runs WSGI-compatible apps by acting as a bridge between the web server (nginx) and the Python app. **WSGI** stands for **Web Server Gateway Interface** and is a standard that defines how web servers communicate with Python web applications, allowing for scalable, production-ready deployments.

Preparing your main.py file

The code for this section is in the /deploy_linux directory. To run your application in an nginx server, you need to run your app with the run-server parameter set to False, and you need to create a Flask app object using the get_flask_app() method (from the Gui object). Here is how it looks:

```
gui = Gui(page=page)
gui.run(debug=False, run_server=False)
app_to_deploy = gui.get_flask_app()
```

> **Note**
>
> To deploy your application in a server, you need to skip the main guard (if __name__ == "__main__") because uWSGI imports the app directly, so the code under the main guard doesn't execute.

Setting an nginx server

To set up an nginx server, connect to your VM using SSH and update it. You need to install the nginx server, as well as pip for the next steps:

```
sudo apt update
sudo apt install -y python3-pip nginx
```

Next, you can start and enable the nginx server:

```
sudo systemctl start nginx
sudo systemctl enable nginx
```

On your Google Cloud instance page, under **Network interfaces**, you should see an external IP address. Browse to that address. You should see the nginx welcome page (*Figure 6.3*).

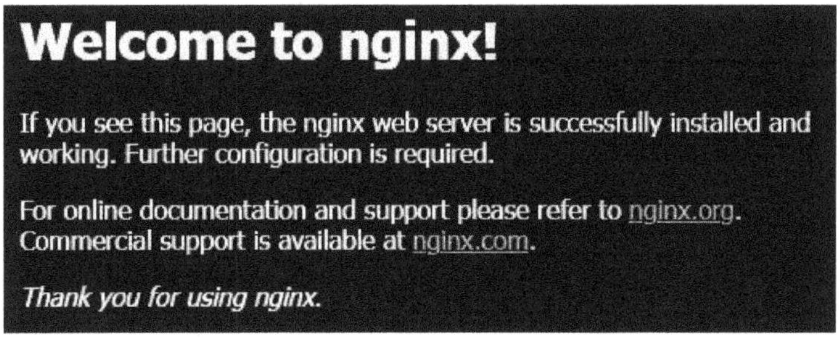

Figure 6.3: nginx welcome page

Setting your Taipy app on the server

Once your `nginx` server runs, go to your Taipy project's directory (you can `git clone` the book's Git repository or any other app you have to try this out). You need permission to read and execute the files (you can use the `chmod` command for this). Create a new environment and enter it. For example, we have created a `taipy` environment (you need to install `venv`; in the following example, we're using `Python 3.12`. Adapt this to your case):

```
sudo chmod -R 755 /path/to/your/directory
sudo apt install python3.12-venv
python3 -m venv taipy
source taipy/bin/activate
```

Next, you need to use `pip install` to install your app's packages, that is, `taipy`, `uwsgi`, and `gevent`:

```
pip install uwsgi gevent taipy
```

Next, you need to create an `app.uwsgi.service` file. You can use the following command to generate the file from the CLI. *You need to execute it from the application's directory* (it uses the pwd variable).

It's important to change the `ExecStart` line. You should add the path to the `uwsgi` directory. This directory is inside your virtual environment's directory (`taipy` in our example). It was created with `pip install uwsgi`.

The last part of the `ExecStart` line shows `main:app_to_deploy`. This references the file (`main.py` and the name of the Flask object, `app_to_deploy`):

```
echo """
[Unit]
Description=App
After=syslog.target

[Service]
ExecStart=/path/to/uwsgi --http 127.0.0.1:5000 --gevent 1000 --http-
websockets --module main:app_to_deploy
WorkingDirectory=`pwd`
Restart=always
KillSignal=SIGQUIT
Type=notify
StandardError=syslog
NotifyAccess=all
User=`whoami`

[Install]
WantedBy=multi-user.target
""" > app.uwsgi.service
```

Then, you can move the file to its directory, and start your application with the following:

```
sudo mv app.uwsgi.service /etc/systemd/system/app.uwsgi.service
sudo systemctl start app.uwsgi.service
sudo systemctl enable app.uwsgi.service
```

To connect `nginx` to your app, you need to change the content of `/etc/nginx/sites-enabled/default` with the following. You have to replace `server_name`'s IP address with your Google Cloud external IP address:

```
server {
    listen 80;
    server_name 123.456.78.910;

    location / {
        proxy_pass http://127.0.0.1:5000;

        # Preserve the client's original host and IP information
        proxy_set_header Host $host;
        proxy_set_header X-Real-IP $remote_addr;
        proxy_set_header X-Forwarded-For $proxy_add_x_forwarded_for;
        proxy_set_header X-Forwarded-Proto $scheme;

        # Support for WebSocket connections(if needed by your app)
        proxy_set_header Upgrade $http_upgrade;
        proxy_set_header Connection "upgrade";
    }
}
```

Next, restart `nginx` and your application should run:

```
/etc/nginx/sites-enabled/default.
```

We just saw how to deploy our directly in a remote Linux server. Next, we'll see how to run our app using Docker containers.

Deploying Taipy using Docker containers

Taipy's documentation describes how to create a Docker image from your Taipy project (`https://docs.taipy.io/en/latest/userman/run-deploy/deploy/docker/`). We'll discuss how to deploy a development app in a Docker container. Docker containers *package applications with all their dependencies* into a lightweight, portable, and isolated environment for *consistent execution* across any machine with Docker installed. The code is in the `/deploy_docker` directory.

In our case, we're using Docker Desktop with Windows and **Windows Subsystem for Linux (WSL2)** (check Docker's documentation to install this setup: `https://docs.docker.com/desktop/features/wsl/`).

Since we are running a development app, we can run it with Taipy's default server and keep the main guard. To build a Docker image for your app, you need to organize your files in a single directory. This directory will serve as the **Docker build context**. It should include:

- Your Taipy app, with `main.py` at the directory's root, and all other directories it may have.

- Your `requirements.txt` (in our minimal app, we just wrote `taipy==4.1.0`).

- Your Dockerfile (see its content in the repo). Our Dockerfile sets up a `Python 3.11` environment, exposes port `5000`, copies the app files, installs dependencies, and runs `main.py` in debug mode on host `0.0.0.0`.

Once you have all your elements, access your directory from your terminal and build your image with `docker build -t name-of-your-app` (in our case, we named it `taipy-app`). When you have your image, you can run it with `docker run -p 5000:5000 taipy-app`. It's important to specify your port with the `-p` flag.

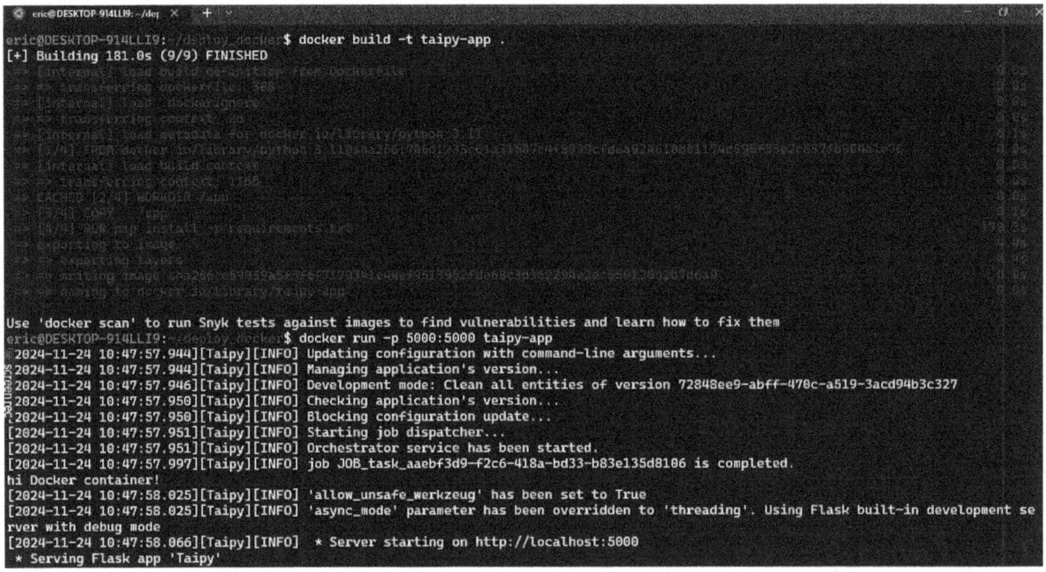

Figure 6.4: Linux terminal showing how to create and run a Taipy image

If you browse to `localhost:5000`, you should see your app running! Let's now look at some popular ways to deploy Python applications to share your Taipy apps.

Deploying Taipy applications in popular services

Since Taipy applications are Flask-based, you can choose to deploy yours using hosting services that support (or even specialize in) Python frameworks. Most have a free tier if you're just getting started, or just want to share a quick proof of concept.

We can't cover each platform, but here is a small list of services to look into:

- **Heroku** (`https://www.heroku.com/`): A platform-as-a-service offering that allows deploying using Git.

- **PythonAnywhere** (`https://www.pythonanywhere.com/`): Lets you upload your Flask app and set it using a WSGI configuration file.

- **Koyeb** (`https://www.koyeb.com/`): A serverless platform that lets you deploy web apps from a Git repository and use a Gunicorn WSGI server.

- **DigitalOcean** (`https://www.digitalocean.com/`): Offers virtual private servers (Droplets) and an app platform for easier deployments. There is plenty of documentation about this service.

- **Ngrok** (`https://ngrok.com/`): Offers a way to run your applications locally. External users can access it from their browser (Ngrok uses a secure tunnel between your local machine and their servers).

Deploying with Ngrok

You can deploy a Taipy application on your local machine and share it with others using Ngrok; this is useful for testing and presenting your proof-of-concept/prototype apps. You can see the code to deploy on Ngrok in `/run_ngrok`.

The first step is to install `pyngrok`:

```
pip install pyngrok
```

To deploy your app on Ngrok, create an account there. Ngrok will offer you the executable file to install when your account is set. You will then have a token (you can find it in the **Your Authtoken** section).

> Important
>
> We recommend you create an environment variable for your token. In Windows, open your CLI and type `setx NGROK_AUTHTOKEN "your_ngrok_authtoken"`. In Linux or Mac, type `export NGROK_AUTHTOKEN="your_ngrok_authtoken"`. Restart your computer, and then you can use the environment variable using this Python line: `NGROK_AUTHTOKEN = os.getenv("NGROK_AUTHTOKEN")`.

To deploy your app on Ngrok, Taipy's `run` method comes with a special argument to add your Ngrok token. You need to add it like this:

```
gui.run(
    ngrok_token=NGROK_AUTHTOKEN,
)
```

Now, you can run your app locally. Once it's running, you can access it from Ngrok's URL. To find your URL, go to **Endpoints**. Your URL should look like this: `https://00ff-00ff-00f-00ff-00ff-00ff-00ff-00ff-00ff.ngrok-free.app/`. You can share this link to make demonstrations and show your application. If you stop your application locally, you will also stop it for your remote users.

Summary

In this chapter, you discovered how to interact with the `run()` method to select the appropriate ways to run your Taipy application efficiently and switch between development and production states. You also discovered how to deploy your application on a Linux server in a cloud provider's VM: we used Google Cloud, but the process would be similar in any other service. You saw how to run your Taipy application in a Docker container and how to share your locally running app with Ngrok.

With this chapter, you've finished the first part of this book: you are now able to create complete projects using Taipy, from developing your UI and Scenario Management applications to sharing them as prototypes or proof of concept and even deploying them in production environments. In the next section, we'll create applications that leverage different Taipy components to solve real enterprise problems.

Questions

1. Can you run your application in an eventlet server, letting the app choose its port in a range of `1000-2000`, using the Maldives time zone?

2. Looking at Taipy's documentation, how would you set up a Docker server to deploy production applications?

3. Could you create a small chart animation using a Taipy app and a notebook? For example, plot $y = x^i$ where `i` changes from 0 to 4.

Answers

1. Taipy's documentation links to eventlet's documentation (`https://flask.palletsprojects.com/en/stable/deploying/eventlet/`) for this task.

    As you see there, the first step is to install the eventlet with the following:

    ```
    pip install eventlet
    ```

    You can find the requested `run` function in `/answers/answer_1/answer_1.py`.

2. You can find the app in `/answers/answer_2`. Here are the main changes compared to the development deployment:

    - The Dockerfile creates a non-root Taipy user for security, configures a secure working directory and path, updates `pip`, installs dependencies, copies application files, and runs `main.py` with an `ENTRYPOINT` command without a reloader.

    - Using Docker Compose with `nginx` makes your setup more modular, secure, and production-ready!

3. You can find a possible answer in `/answers/answer_3.iynb`.

    The key here is in the last cell, where we use `gui.state` to assign values in a loop. We also use `time.sleep(1)` to allow the callbacks to update the chart and make an animation.

Part 2:
Building Real-World
Applications with Taipy

In this part, you'll walk through four practical examples that demonstrate how to build complete data applications with Taipy. These tutorials will help you under-stand how to integrate various types of algorithms into your applications, including time series analysis, optimization algorithms, and geospatial processing. You'll also build a chatbot and discover how to interact with large language models (LLMs) from a Taipy interface. This part will introduce some advanced concepts that are dis-cussed in more detail in Part 3, such as partials and long-running callbacks.

This part of the book includes the following chapters:

- *Chapter 7, Taipy for Finance: Sales Forecasting and BI Reports*
- *Chapter 8, Taipy for Logistics: Creating Supply Chain Management Apps*
- *Chapter 9, Taipy for Urban Planning: Creating a Satellite Image App*
- *Chapter 10, Building an LLM Chatbot with Taipy*

7
Taipy for Finance: Sales Forecasting and BI Reports

In this chapter, we put on our business analyst suit and focus on a case study. We'll build an app to track sales and predict future transactions for our sales department. We'll consider all the process steps, including the interactions with our clients, and see how to narrow our scope and understand our data, as well as how to prepare our data.

We'll then start building the backend. We'll perform time-series predictions, using the **sktime library**, so our final users can forecast sales based on different scopes (by client or product type) and with various assumptions. We'll build the GUI with two main parts (a sales dashboard and forecasting app). We'll try to make an app that's intuitive and comfortable to use by our end users. We'll also cover some deployment and documentation considerations.

In this chapter, we'll cover the following:

- Understanding business needs
- Preparing data for our app
- Building the app
- Bringing the app to production

Technical requirements

You can find the complete code used in this chapter in the GitHub repository: `https://github.com/PacktPublishing/Getting-Started-with-Taipy/tree/main/chapter_07`.

Being familiar with time series and the sktime (`https://www.sktime.net/`) and statsmodels (`https://www.statsmodels.org/stable/index.html`) libraries, as well as knowing some data modeling concepts, will help you understand the chapter, but it's not mandatory. To reproduce the preprocessing steps (optional), you need to create a small PostgreSQL database and query it using SQL and SQLAlchemy (all of the code is provided).

Understanding business needs

We work for a company that sells different types of bikes and related accessories. The sales department needs a dashboard to analyze past sales and forecast future trends. Before we meet with our clients, we will have a quick look at the data from our data warehouse.

Discovering our data

We'll work with a simplified version of AdventureWorksDW's database by Microsoft. The code to create the tables and fill them with data can be found here: `https://github.com/enarroied/AdventureWorksSimplified`.

> **Important**
>
> If you can't create a PostgreSQL database—or don't want to—we still recommend following the first section of this chapter, since the considerations apply to most projects. The app uses Parquet files (after extracting data from the database). We have provided those files in the main repo, so you'll be set for further steps.

We have a **star-schema database**, with one fact table (`factinternetsales`) and three dimension tables (`dimproduct`, `dimdate`, and `dimcustomer`) that store categorical information about our products, dates, and customers. Dimension tables have a primary key that we can link to the fact table (one-to-many relationship). The data in dimension tables has historical information, with `startdate` and `enddate` columns, which show the time frame in which information is valid. For example, the unit price of a bike model can change over time, which leads to two (or more) lines in the `dimproduct` table, for the same product (with different price information). The fact table always references the dimension at the time of the sale. *Figure 7.1* shows the relational model for our app.

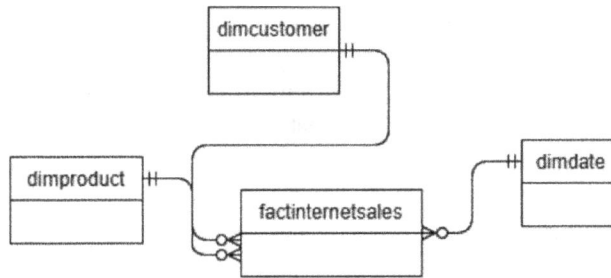

Figure 7.1: Sales database schema

Meeting with our clients

Meeting with our clients is an essential step in building our app. Here are some important issues that impact how we'll code our app or process our data:

- Understand the needs: Customers need to predict sales (money and items), segment product and customer data, access historical sales, and use predictions for inventory and resource planning.

- Focus on the essential: Avoid adding unnecessary elements—they waste time, clutter the app, and limit performance. Clarify unneeded data to filter it out. In this case, we just want data about bike sales, so we can exclude all the other items.

- Ask about data quality or concerns: Analysts can detect some issues, but operational anomalies may need clarification. For example, were there periods without records due to server issues? Are sales from missing days recorded elsewhere? Have any exceptional events (such as strikes or supplier issues) affected operations and should we consider them in our forecasts? In this case, everything seems fine and up to date!

- Share our concerns with the clients: It's appropriate to communicate limitations, such as insufficient data. For example, predicting sales by year of birth or for specific bike models could be challenging. Could we group by generation (e.g., "Gen X") or bike type, color, or style? The quantity column currently only shows 1; should we remove it? (In this case, the client prefers to keep it as is, as sales with more than one bike are possible.)

Ask clients what they want the app to feel like and what questions it should answer—for example, "How much cash will come from mountain bike sales in the next 30 days?" Clients want conservative and optimistic predictions, detailed tables, and charts showing trends over time and by weekday.

Now that we know our customers' needs, let's build a pipeline to retrieve our data for the app!

Preparing data for our app

The app uses Data Nodes to interface with Parquet files, which we retrieve from the database (our data warehouse) using a SQL query and a data pipeline—which we simulate with the notebook in `pre_process/select_data.ipynb`.

Selecting the right data

In this example, we don't have data quality issues that could lead to inaccurate forecasting. We also don't have empty (NaN) values, which can be problematic when creating visuals or when running forecast algorithms. This is always the first thing to address. The SQL query that retrieves the data is in `pre_process/bike_sales_subset.sql` (it's also in the notebook that simulates the pipeline). Here are some considerations about this query that directly impact our final app:

- We use `JOIN` on the fact table (`factinternetsales`) and the three dimension tables.

- We filter the data to keep bikes only, using `WHERE productsubcategorykey IN (1, 2, 3)` (mountain, road, and touring bikes, respectively). Removing unnecessary data increases the app's performance.

- We limit the number of columns with the `SELECT` clause. This increases performance in the database engine (when retrieving the data), and makes smaller files and smaller DataFrames (which is also better for performance!).

- We use `CASE WHEN...` statements to add a column for customer generation or product type. We calculate the sales price `with unitprice * orderquantity AS sales` (even if—for now at least—`orderquantity` is always 1). We create a `day` column with a `CASE WHEN` transformation, to retrieve days as two-letter codes.

- We use `TRIM` on the data that comes from `CHAR` columns, getting rid of extra spaces.

- We rename columns to make them meet our `snake_case` naming standards.

The goal is to not have any transformations of our DataFrames (except for maybe some data type changes) in our Taipy apps before any user interaction. Carrying out these transformations at the database level is also better for maintainability: ANSI SQL (a feature of SQL that's shared by all dialects) is stable (in general, what changes is each dialect's specific terms). Taipy and all the Python libraries your app will use evolve way faster. The more transformations you can do with SQL, the better (and faster).

When you select your data for your app, always think about the following:

- Data quality: Fix duplicates, missing values, outliers, and inconsistencies. Standardize categories. Clean and organize data early to save time later.

- App performance: Fetch just the needed rows and columns. Use `WHERE` clauses and calculate/aggregate data at the database level when possible.

- Visualization impact: Simplify data for better display (e.g., shorter labels and organized tables). Ensure visuals are clear and optimized for the app's layout. In our example, we have created two-letter codes for days, which is easy to understand if we place them in the right order in a bar chart with a proper title.

Data pipeline

The pipeline creates a DataFrame, df_sales, from the SQL query (see the previous section, Selecting the right data). Non-numerical data appears as object, which is hard to work with. Integers such as birth come out as floats, causing issues such as unnecessary decimal points (e.g., 1987.0). The next step is to give appropriate data types to our DataFrame, using the .astype() method:

- We set the date column as datetime64[ns]. We'll use this column for forecasting and to plot data over time!

- We set all categorical data as category.

- We keep name as str.

- We set the birth column as int.

The Sales Forecast app will use the df_sales DataFrame to display raw data in a table. We'll create three more DataFrames from this original one:

- df_sales_simplified: Groups sales by a large subset of columns. It creates a slightly smaller DataFrame compared to df_sales (14,242 versus 15,205 lines). Pre-aggregating the DataFrame reduces the app's workload for data aggregation. The size reduction is probably insufficient and wouldn't justify using a partially aggregated DataFrame like we're doing, but we kept it as an element for thought.

- df_sales_by_customer: This is an aggregated DataFrame with customer data for the app. We'll just use it for display (as a table). It won't be re-aggregated.

- df_sales_by_product: Same as for customers, but for products.

We created all these DataFrames using the group_by_dimensions_and_facts function. Here is the function:

```
def group_by_dimensions_and_facts(
    df, dimension_columns, orderby="sales"
):
    df_copy = df.copy()
    df_grouped = df_copy.groupby(
        dimension_columns, observed=True
    ).agg(
        sales=("sales", "sum"), items=("items", "count")
    )
```

```
df_grouped = df_grouped.sort_values(
    by=orderby, ascending=False)
df_grouped = df_grouped.round(2)
df_grouped = df_grouped.reset_index()
return df_grouped
```

The pipeline saves the DataFrames as Parquet files. Let's now discuss this file format!

💡 **Quick tip**: Enhance your coding experience with the **AI Code Explainer** and **Quick Copy** features. Open this book in the next-gen Packt Reader. Click the **Copy** button

(**1**) to quickly copy code into your coding environment, or click the **Explain** button

(**2**) to get the AI assistant to explain a block of code to you.

```
                                              Copy    Explain
function calculate(a, b) {                      1        2
    return {sum: a + b};
};
```

The next-gen Packt Reader is included for free with the purchase of this book. Scan the QR code OR go to `packtpub.com/unlock`, then use the search bar to find this book by name. Double-check the edition shown to make sure you get the right one.

File format choice

One important reason for choosing Parquet files over a straight database connection (with a SQL Data Node) is that it could be challenging for some readers of this book to reproduce the database, but in an enterprise environment, a direct database connection could be a great option.

IMPORTANT:
We added an alternative configuration file that creates SQL Data Nodes from the database directly. You can find it in the /sql_data_nodes directory.

We cover the generic aspects of file format selection in *Chapter 13*. For our specific case, Parquet works well because it offers a compact storage size (10x smaller than CSV), saving space. In addition, it's especially useful for periodic (daily) updates, which suit our app's needs. Parquet's faster read/write speeds improve efficiency and reduce reliance on external database servers. It retains data types directly from pandas DataFrames, optimizing memory use and avoiding extra in-app transformations. Pre-setting data types (e.g., category) reduces memory use and improves performance. Our example reduced memory from 8.32 MB to 3.27 MB, but if we don't store data as Parquet files, we'll need to load the bigger DataFrame first, and then reduce its size (from the Taipy app).

Now that we have our data, let's build our Taipy app!

Building the Sales Forecast app

Our app has two parts (you can see how the app looks in an animated GIF in the app's README file):

- A small sales dashboard, with charts, tables, and some big numbers (see *Figure 7.2*)

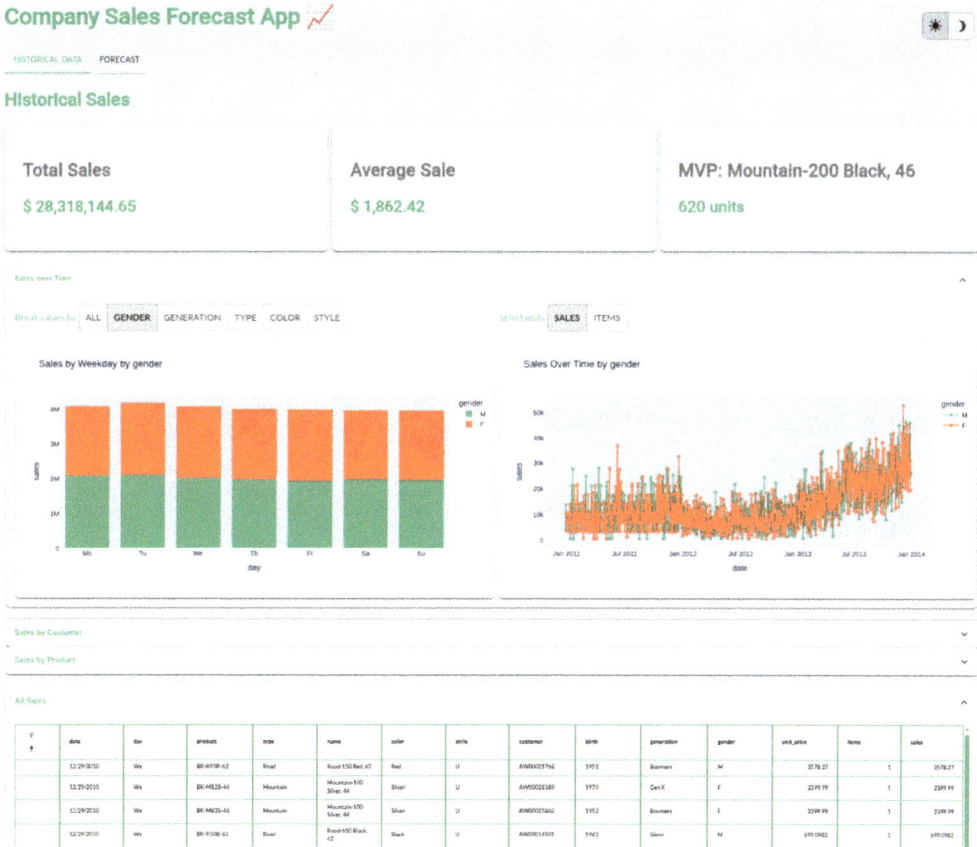

Figure 7.2: The sales dashboard we're going to build

🔍 **Quick tip:** Need to see a high-resolution version of this image? Open this book in the next-gen Packt Reader or view it in the PDF/ePub copy.

🔒 **The next-gen Packt Reader** and a **free PDF/ePub copy** of this book are included with your purchase. Scan the QR code OR go to `packtpub.com/unlock`, then use the search bar to find this book by name. Double-check the edition shown to make sure you get the right one.

- A forecasting pipeline that users can launch from the GUI that shows the forecasting results (see *Figure 7.3*)

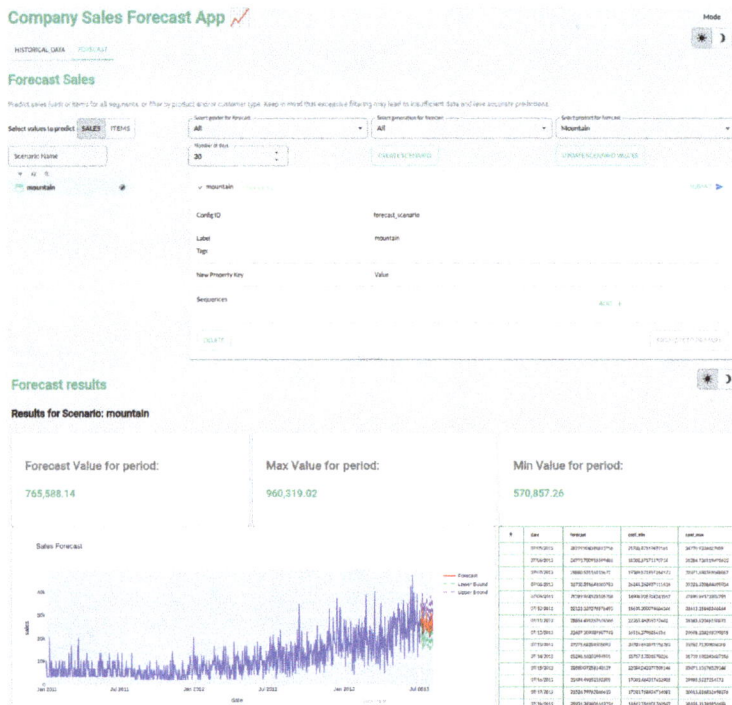

Figure 7.3: The forecast app we're going to build

We'll first see how to build the app's scaffold. We'll then cover the construction of the sales dashboard, and we'll finish with the forecast app. The complete app can be found in the `src` directory.

Building the app's scaffold

The first step is to create our folders and the basic files. Here is the app's directory structure (the root is the `src` directory):

- `algorithms`: The directory with the Python files with functions
- `configuration`:
  - `config.py`: The configuration for `Orchestrator`
- `css`: A directory with a main.css file
- `data`: We put our Parquet files here
- `images`: Our app doesn't show images, but we put our favicon in here
- `pages`: The directory with our app's pages, since it's a multiple-page app
  - `sales`: A directory with the information for the sales dashboard:
    - `sales.py`: The main sales page
  - `forecast`:
    - `forecast.py`: The forecast page
- `main.py`: The main page!

Now that we have our filesystem, let's add the scaffold code!

Initiating the main page

Before dealing with the main page, you can add a minimal `Page` element to both the `sales.py` and `forecast.py` pages. This allows us to import the pages in `main.py` and build our scaffold. We'll add the content to these pages later. This is how `forecast.py` looks now (do the same with `sales.py`):

```
import taipy.gui.builder as tgb
with tgb.Page() as forecast_page:
    tgb.text(
        "## Forecast Sales", mode="md",
        class_name="color-primary"
    )
```

In an enterprise environment, it could be a good idea to have some style templates, with a dedicated font, colors that match your corporate identity, company logos, and so on. In our case, we added a simple favicon to the images directory, and we added fonts to the `main.css` file (lines 1-6).

In the `main.py` file, we need to do the following:

1. Import the necessary libraries as well as the app's pages (`sales.py` and `forecast.py`). We can add imports as we build and need them, but we know that we need most `taipy` imports and pandas, as well as the app's pages (`sales.py` and `forecast.py`).

2. Create the `root` page. We will add a theme toggle button for users to switch between light and dark mode:

```
with tgb.Page() as root_page:
    tgb.toggle(theme=True)
    tgb.text(
        "# Company Sales Forecast App ",
        mode="md", class_name="color-primary"
    )
    tgb.navbar()
```

3. Create a dictionary with all the app's pages:

```
sales_forecast_pages = {
    "/": root_page,
    "historical_data": sales_page,
    "forecast": forecast_page,
}
```

4. Add a Stylekit dictionary (we recommend doing this now so you can add all the class names to your code; you can always change the colors and other parameters later):

```
stylekit = {
    "color_primary": "#66C2A5",
    "color_secondary": "#A9A9A9", # metallic dark grey
                                  # (dark gray)
}
```

5. Under the main guard, add the `gui` element, giving the `pages` dictionary to the `pages` argument (add the CSS file name to the `css_file` argument). We also run the page, setting the title and referencing the favicon file and the Stylekit, as well as using the reloader for development.

```
if __name__ == "__main__":
    sales_forecast_gui = Gui(
        pages=sales_forecast_pages,
        css_file="./css/main.css")
    ...
    sales_forecast_gui.run(
        use_reloader=True, # For development
        title="Sales Forecast",
```

```
                    favicon="./images/favicon.ico",
                    stylekit=stylekit,
        )
```

You should now have a running app. Let's build the dashboard!

Building the dashboard app

The first step is to add our data.

Adding global Data Nodes

Our dashboard doesn't need Scenario Management, but we can use global Data Nodes as a data interface. We can use the `Config.configure_parquet_data_node()` function to access the parquet file and configure the Data Nodes, for example:

```
from Taipy import Config, Scope

sales_node_config = Config.configure_parquet_data_node(
    id="sales",
    default_path="data/sales.parquet",
    exposed_type="pandas",
    scope=Scope.GLOBAL,
)
```

Once we create our four Data Node configuration objects, we create the DataFrames in the `main.py` file. We import the configuration objects, and we read the Data Nodes, as follows:

```
sales_node = tp.create_global_data_node(sales_node_config)
df_sales = sales_node.read()
```

Aggregating data

We won't be detailing the functions that aggregate the data; you can find them in `algorithms/preprocess.py`. They are as follows:

- `calculate_big_numbers`: Returns a dictionary with the total historical sales, the average sale cost, and the most sold product

- `group_by_dimensions_and_facts`: We explained this function in the Data pipeline section

- `group_by_weekday`: A special function to group by weekday, with custom sorting in weekday order (starting Monday)

We create the DataFrames for the app in the `main.py` file. For example, this is how we create the DataFrame that will generate the product stats chart:

```
product_stats = group_by_dimensions_and_facts(
    df_sales_simplified, ["type", "color"]
)
```

Dashboard layout

We use block elements in the `sales_page` page object, in the `sales.py` file. We place the three big cards together, using text elements inside a card, which is a `part()` element with `"card"` passed as a parameter, like this:

```
with tgb.layout("1 1 1"):
    with tgb.part("card"):
        tgb.text(
            "## Total Sales ", mode="md",
            class_name="color-secondary"
        )
        tgb.text(
            "### $ {total_sales}",
            mode="md",
            class_name="color-primary",
        )
    ...
```

You can see this three-card section in *Figure 7.4*, it lets users grasp the big numbers of their sales.

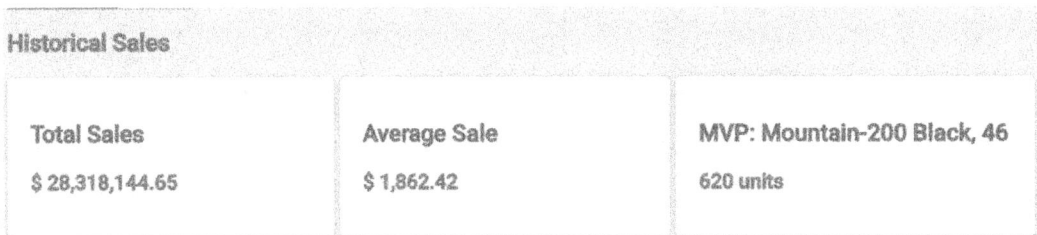

Historical Sales

Total Sales	Average Sale	MVP: Mountain-200 Black, 46
$ 28,318,144.65	$ 1,862.42	620 units

Figure 7.4: The app's big number section

We include all four major parts of our app (sales over time, sales by customer, sales by product, and the "**All Sales**" table) inside `expandable` block elements, so users focus on the analytical axis they prefer. For example, for the sales by customer section, we have the following:

```
with tgb.expandable(
    "Sales by Customer",
    class_name="color-primary",
```

```
        expanded=False,
    ):
```

Creating charts and tables

To create charts, we use the functions in `algorithms/create_charts.py`. These functions create Plotly `fig` objects, and they need variables to update the charts. The time-based charts also need to be created ahead of time, in `main.py`:

```
time_break_by = "All"
z_axis_customer = "sales"
...
date_fig = create_time_scatter(date_stats, y_axis_time)

# in sales.py
tgb.chart(figure="{date_fig}")
```

In the case of `date_fig` and `weekday_fig`, we need to update them from a callback function, `change_time_charts`. This callback updates a set of elements using the `with` syntax for better performance (refer to *Chapter 12* to understand why). It starts re-creating the DataFrames, reading from the Data Node, and using the functions to group the elements by dimensions. It also updates the chart elements. Here is the function (we omit one chart update):

```
def change_time_charts(state):
    with state as s:
        df_time = s.sales_simplified_node.read()
        is_all = s.time_break_by == "All"

        # Grouping and visualization parameter:
        break_by = None if is_all else s.time_break_by

        # Group and visualize weekday stats
        s.weekday_stats = group_by_weekday(
            df_time, extra_col=break_by)
        s.weekday_fig = create_weekday_chart(
            s.weekday_stats,
            y_axis=s.y_axis_time,
            break_by=break_by
        )
        ...
```

The other two charts don't need an external callback, since we don't need to filter the DataFrame. We just update the chart's axis using a toggle button. In this case, we can directly use the bound variable and the chart creation function in a lambda expression, like this:

```
tgb.toggle(
    value="{z_axis_customer}",
    lov=["sales", "items"],
    label="Select units",
)
tgb.chart(
    figure=lambda customer_stats, z_axis_customer:
        create_customer_heatmap(
            customer_stats, z_axis_customer
        )
)
```

Let's now see how we chose the visual representations for our app!

Visual presentation

Here is how we chose our visuals:

- For the sales by weekday, we're showing numerical values for one or two categories. Sales by product shows the numerical values for two distinct categories. A bar chart with the eventual color for the sub-category is ideal for this kind of data.

- The sales-by-date representation shows numerical values against a continuous scale. A scatter plot with distinct colors for different categories is a good choice.

- Sales by customer also shows two distinct categories against a numerical value. We chose to represent this data as a heatmap, with a color scale for the continuous numerical values.

An important aspect when creating charts is to select a good color scale for your plots. You'll find plenty of built-in color scales, but it is important to choose the right type. Ask yourself: "*What am I using colors for?*" In our example, we have the following reasoning:

- The bar charts plot categorical data and the scatter chart plots continuous data—but they both use colors to represent discrete categories, so we need a *categorical scale*. We chose the Set2 scale, and we pass it to the `color_discrete_sequence` parameter, like this:

- `color_discrete_sequence=px.colors.qualitative.Set2.`

- The heatmap uses color to represent continuous data (the value of sales or a count of items). We need a *continuous scale*, so we chose `algae`. We define it like this:

- `color_continuous_scale="algae"`

For our table elements, we add some styling in the `main.css` file, to make the data smaller, and color the lines with the same color as our Stylekit's `color-primary`. We also create a special styling for a `col-number` class, like this:

```
.col-number {text-align: right !important;}
```

Aligning numbers to the right can be a good idea (or a straight request!). It's a common practice in accounting. To add this styling to some columns only, we can use the `cell_class_name_COLUMNNAME` argument. For example, in the All Sales expandable in `sales.py`, we added the following:

```
cell_class_name__sales=lambda _: "col-number",
```

In this section, we covered the most important parts of creating our sales dashboard. Let's build the forecast app!

Designing the forecast app

The forecast app uses the sktime library. This Python library uses the sklearn standard processes (select a model, train—or fit—it, eventually validate it, and then use it with production data) and offers an interface to plenty of time-series models For our demo, we'll use the exponential smoothing algorithm from Statsmodels.

> **IMPORTANT**
> We created a notebook that explains all the algorithms and functions we use in the chapter. You can find it in `/how_to_help/time_series.ipynb`.

Creating the forecast pipeline

We build a pipeline using a Taipy Scenario, which we define in `configuration/config.py`. All the functions that the tasks use are in `algorithms/forecast_tasks.py`. *Figure 7.5* shows a representation of the pipeline.

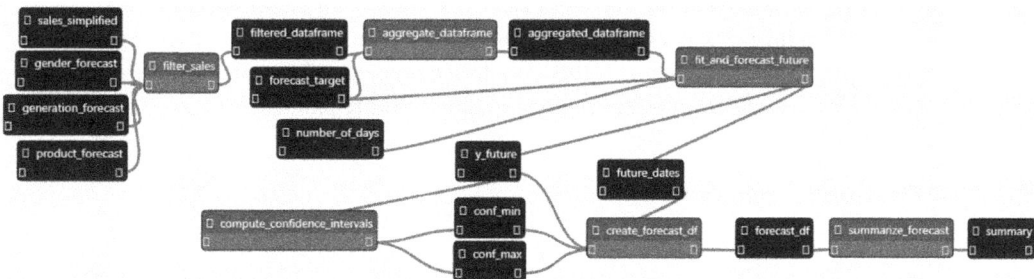

Figure 7.5: Forecasting scenario pipeline

Here are some comments about the pipeline:

- `filter_sales` task:

  - Takes in data from the `sales_simplified` GLOBAL Data Node. This is the only Data Node of this scenario that has a global scope, and we defined it earlier, for the sales dashboard.

  - Users will write the other three Data Nodes from the GUI.

  - This task selects a subset of the data before running the forecast on it.

- `aggregate_dataframe`: This takes in the subset DataFrame from the previous step, as well as `forecast_target`, which refers to the column that we'll use as the target for our prediction. It can be either **"sales"** or **"items,"** depending on what we want to forecast. This Data Node will also be defined by the user from the GUI. This returns a DataFrame aggregated by dates with the selected target column. In other words, it creates a DataFrame with a format that we can feed to our forecast model.

- `fit_and_forecast_future`: This takes the aggregated DataFrame and `number_of_days`, an integer between 1 and 365. It returns the predictions for the next `number_of_days` (`y_future`), as well as the corresponding dates, as a pandas Series.

- `compute_confidence_intervals`: This creates upper and lower confidence intervals for each forecasting value.

- `create_forecast_df`: This returns a DataFrame with the future dates, the values for the forecast, and the maximum and minimum intervals.

- `summarize_forecast`: This returns the sum of the forecast and the maximum and minimum intervals. This is the total forecast value for the next `number_of_days`.

If we look into the Python functions (`algorithms/forecast_tasks.py`), here are some choices worth explaining:

- The forecasting pipeline (the `create_pipeline` function) defines the forecasting process using `ForecastingPipeline` from `sktime.forecasting.compose`. It allows us to combine preprocessing steps and forecasting models in one reusable object. It uses **exponential smoothing**, a method for predicting future data based on patterns such as **trends** (long-term growth or decline) and **seasonality** (regular patterns that repeat, such as sales increasing every December).

  This is the relevant line of code:

```
ExponentialSmoothing(
    trend="add",
    seasonal="mul",
    sp=91,
    initialization_method="estimated",
```

```
            use_boxcox=True,
            optimized=True,
            method="L-BFGS-B",
    ),
```

Here, we've set the trend to `add` or additive (steady increases or decreases over time) and seasonality to `mul` or multiplicative (seasonal changes that get bigger or smaller based on the overall level) (check the `thetime_series.ipynb` notebook for more information about it!).

For more on exponential smoothing, see the *Further reading* section.

> **Important**
>
> We hardcoded these values. We could have chosen to let users experiment with different values (or even select different models to put in the pipeline!). In this case, we can consider that the data science department validated the right type of model and the optimal parameters, and that's what we give to the final users (both approaches can make sense; it all depends on the app you need!).

- **Fitting and forecasting** (the `fit_and_forecast_future` function) fits the pipeline to historical data and predicts future values. Here are the main steps:

    I.   Extract the target series (`y`) from the prepared DataFrame.

    II. Fit the pipeline on the entire historical data.

    III. Define `ForecastingHorizon` with future dates to specify the prediction timeline. `ForecastingHorizon` represents the time points to forecast.

    IV. Predict values for `ForecastingHorizon`.

Once we define our scenario configuration, we import it to `forecast.py`. We aren't creating a scenario in the `main.py` file, but we create an initial binding scenario variable with a `None` value in the main file, `selected_scenario = None`.

Let's now create our visual app!

Creating the forecast app's GUI

We build the forecast app's GUI in two parts (in `pages/forecast.py`): a part to select parameters and create and run scenarios, and a second part to visualize the scenario results.

Creating scenarios and callbacks

First, the users can select the data subset to forecast, the unit target (sales or items), and the days to forecast. *Figure 7.6* shows this component.

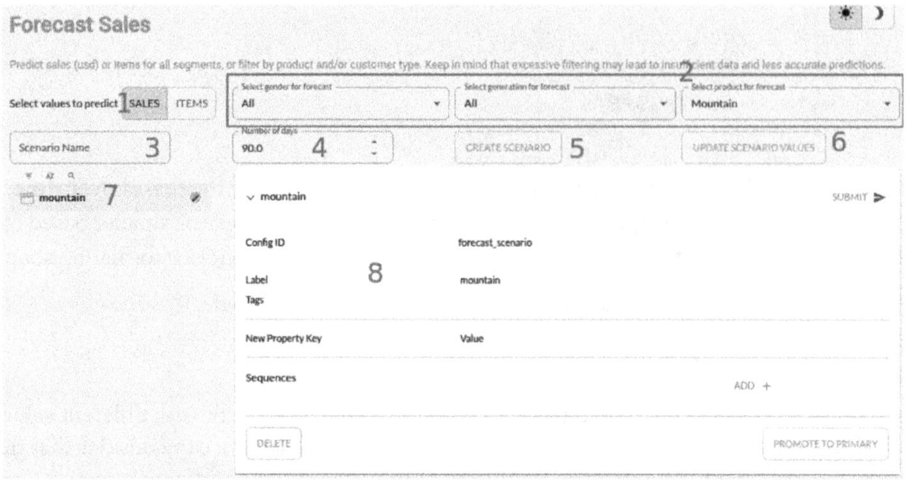

Figure 7.6: Scenario creation from the forecasting app

Here are the important parts of the figure, which have been labeled:

- **1:** The app uses this toggle selector to write the `forecast_target` Data Node.
- **2:** These selectors are bound to the variables that callback functions use to write the Data Nodes used to filter the data.
- **3:** We need to give a name to the scenario; otherwise, the `create_scenario` callback returns a warning. It's defined like this:

```
if state.scenario_name == "":
    notify(state, "w", "The Scenario needs to have a name")
```

- **4:** This is a `number` selector with `min=1` and `max=365`. It is used to add a value to the `prediction_number_days` Data Node we can predict values for up to one year).
- **5:** Create scenario `button`. This triggers the `create_scenario` callback, which creates a scenario with the provided name and selected forecast parameters, sets the new scenario as the selected one, writes the input Data Nodes, clears the scenario name input, and displays a success message with `notify`.

> **Important**
> We create the scenarios this way because the scenario selector callbacks don't allow us to interact with the scenario they create (because the function returns it). We want to create a scenario and write the Data Nodes in the same step.

- **6:** This button updates the selected scenario's input Data Nodes' values with `update_scenario`. It displays a warning message if there's no selected scenario.

- **7**: Scenario selector: we create it with `show_add_button=False` because we use the button in *step 5*. This triggers the `change_scenario` callback, which updates the selected scenario, but also reads the input Data Nodes for the scenario and updates the selectors.

  Technically, this is what `change_scenario` does: when a scenario is selected, it retrieves its forecast parameters and populates the corresponding state variables (target, gender, etc.). It checks whether the scenario has run a forecast before (has forecast data available). If yes, it retrieves the forecast results, updates the chart and summary, and calls `update_chart` and `update_summary`. If no, it initializes the forecast results with an empty DataFrame, clears the chart and summary, and sets their values to 0.

- **8**: This is a `scenario` visual element to run the selected scenario. It triggers the `update_results` callback. When the submission ends (COMPLETED), it reads the forecast results from the selected scenario and updates the state variables with the scenario name and forecast results. It calls `update_summary` and `update_chart` to update the summary and chart based on the new results.

Visualizing the scenario results

The results visualization has three parts. You can see them in *Figure 7.7*:

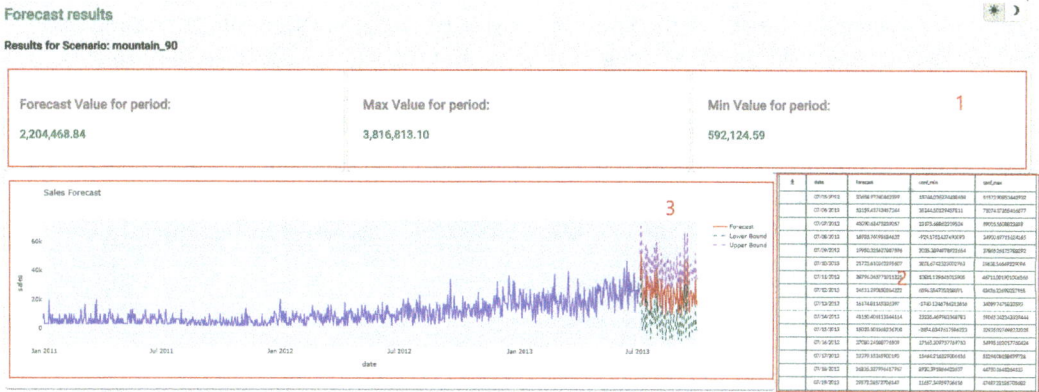

Figure 7.7: Visualizing the scenario results

Here is an explanation of the labeled areas:

- **1**: Three cards with the totals for the forecast and the maximum and minimum confidence predictions.
- **2**: A table that shows the DataFrame from the forecast pipeline
- **3**: A chart that shows historical data for the selected subset (solid blue line) and the forecast (solid red lines), the minimum confidence interval (green dotted line), and the maximum value (purple dotted line). The function that creates this chart is `plot_forecast`. You can find it in `algorithms/create_charts.py`.

Bringing the app to production

Deploying your app to production is a process that depends heavily on your organization's standards and the technologies that you use. However, taking your app to production involves more than *just* deploying your app, such as documenting it properly. Let's discuss this briefly!

Deploying your app

To deploy your app, it's important to remove—or comment—`use_reloader=True`. Since we're using Parquet files, we also set `use_arrow=True` for better performance.

We added a `requirements.txt` file, which you'll likely need in most deployment cases (we included the libraries you'll need in the notebooks but not in the app).

Documenting your app

We used the README file to document some aspects of our app. Adding references to the data sources is a good idea. In an enterprise environment, you could add information about your department and your customers and some context about why they requested this app.

You can document the `Orchestrator` pipelines using Taipy's representation with the `scenario_dag` visual element, but if the pipeline is long, you may want to change or re-arrange the elements (as we did for *Figure 7.5*). If you configure your pipelines with **Taipy Studio**, you can do it directly (you can also duplicate the TOML configuration file and use one to create an image and leave the other one as your app's config file). You can also create a TOML file from your Python config, and then use Taipy Studio to document your pipeline. For this, just use

```
Config.export():
Config.export("./configuration/config.toml")
```

Summary

In this chapter, we created a small BI sales dashboard and forecast app. The app's data influences the results' quality (garbage in, garbage out), the performance, and the visualization; it may even have legal and policy-related implications. In this chapter, we chose to give considerable weight to preprocessing techniques because they are the foundation of our Taipy apps and because they're common considerations in enterprise environments. We also covered the main steps to create a complete application that displays historical data and runs time-series algorithms, focusing on aspects such as data visualization, documentation, and trying to polish the user experience, which is important if we want to bring our apps to a production stage.

In the next chapter, we'll see how to create a location intelligence application to help users choose the optimal location for their store!

Further reading

- Kimball, R., & Ross, M. (2013). The Data Warehouse Toolkit: The complete guide to dimensional modeling (3rd ed.). John Wiley & Sons, Inc.

- NIST/SEMATECH e-Handbook of Statistical Methods, `https://doi.org/10.18434/M32189`, What Is Exponential Smoothing?. `https://www.itl.nist.gov/div898/handbook/pmc/section4/pmc43.htm`

Questions

1. Using the Sales Forecast app, how many red bikes (of all types) did we sell?

2. Using the Sales Forecast app, what is a conservative (minimal) estimate for the sales of the next 90 days for road bikes?

3. How can the data be preprocessed even more for a more efficient app?

4. How would you add a different forecasting model to the pipeline (look at the sktime documentation, `https://www.sktime.net/en/latest/api_reference/forecasting.html`. There are plenty. Try ThetaForecaster)? How would you let users decide which model to use?

5. Could you add a `data_node` element instead of a `table` element to display the forecast results?

Answers

1. To see this information, we can go to Sales by Product in the Historical Data menu, select Items, and look for the red bikes. We can hover over the chart to see the results. First, we see that there have only been red road bikes, so we can just see how many red road bikes we've sold: 2,542.

2. If we go to the forecasting part of the app, we can select "Road" type bikes as a "product to forecast" and 90 days. We run the scenario, and the "Min Value for period" value is 1,259,653.48.

3. One thing we could have done is to move the `calculate_big_numbers` preprocessing function to the data pipeline since these big numbers are not being re-calculated. The dictionary could be stored as a Pickle file, or we could save the results as a CSV or Parquet file, and we could then interface it with a Data Node. A reason to keep them this way would be if we plan to add a dynamic component to this element in the future.

4. Another improvement we could test is to add fact columns to a DataFrame for the "Sales over Time" dashboard. This dashboard organizes the data by All, Gender, Generation, Type, Color, and Style. We could add 10 columns to the DataFrame to add the sales and items sold for each dimension (the All columns exist already, so we have five dimensions x two facts). We could also create an additional DataFrame that follows the same strategy to break the data by day of the week. The compromise here is to load more data in memory (more and bigger DataFrames), but it requires less computing since the data is previously aggregated.

You can see the code in `answers/answer_4/answer_4.txt`. Here are the main steps:

1. Import the new algorithms and change the functions to use the correct algorithm depending on a parameter (such as `theta_forecaster` or `exponential_smoothing`).

2. Change the configuration file to add a Data Node to take the new parameter for the function to select the proper algorithm. Change the task also.

3. Add a button to select the correct algorithm from the UI.

4. Change the callbacks to update the Data Node depending on the selected algorithm.

5. You can see the code in `answers/answer_5/answer_5.txt`.

Join our community on Discord

Join our community's Discord space for discussions with the authors and other readers:

`https://packt.link/taipybook`

8

Taipy for Logistics: Creating Supply Chain Management Apps

In this chapter, we assume the role of logistics analysts for *EuroDuctPipe*, a fictitious European pipe manufacturer. We'll develop an app to help strategic departments find optimal warehouse locations based on cost and carbon emissions. Optimization is widely used in industries such as finance (tax-efficient investments), energy (grid balancing), and agriculture (crop yield maximization). It also includes subcategories such as route optimization and scheduling problems.

We use linear programming techniques and specialized software known as solvers to solve optimization problems. Understanding the algorithms isn't essential; what matters is correctly formulating the problem. PuLP, a Python library, works for small to medium problems, while larger ones require commercial solvers such as CPLEX or Gurobi. PuLP uses declarative syntax to define and solve problems.

The Taipy app can use any solver, whether it's within the app (like in this chapter's example) or on a distant server. Taipy can help us create a UI where users can define the problem using selectors (introduce the variables, values, and constraints for the problem). Optimization problems strongly benefit from Scenario Management and comparison: while a problem may have an optimal solution, it's often useful to test different assumptions by exploring multiple versions of it.

We'll go through a full case study, starting with business needs and developing the algorithms for the business logic. Then, we'll cover the Scenario Management pipeline before moving on to building the UI.

This app is inspired by Taipy's supply management demo app (`https://docs.taipy.io/en/latest/gallery/articles/supply_chain/`). They gave us access to the code, and we created our simplified version. We thank them greatly for that!

In this chapter, we'll cover the following topics:

- Understanding and implementing business logic
- Creating the Scenario Management pipeline
- Creating the UI

Technical requirements

The complete code used in this chapter can be found in the GitHub repository: `https://github.com/PacktPublishing/Getting-Started-with-Taipy/tree/main/chapter_08`. This chapter solves linear programming and optimization problems using PuLP (`https://pypi.org/project/PuLP/`). Being familiar with these concepts and the library will help, but we'll explain every step; we won't be diving deep into the topic, so don't worry about not being able to follow along!

Understanding and implementing business logic

In this section, we'll cover the steps that come before creating the app. Our clients want an app to help them decide the best location for their warehouses. *EuroDuctPipe* is a fictitious Western European company; the company sells to retailers. The company wants to change their warehouses, and they need an app to make informed decisions.

To help you understand the functions, we created a notebook with more detailed explanations and with all the functions so you can run (and play with) them. You can find it in `/how_to_help/how_to_help.ipynb`.

Let's see what the customer needs are!

Meeting our customers

Our clients need an app that shows potential warehouse locations and customer distribution on a map to help determine the optimal facility locations. Customer data, including yearly orders, comes from the company database. The warehouses under consideration are for-rent facilities, and our client provides a list of potential locations, along with relevant information such as annual operating costs and **CO_2e emissions** (meaning **carbon dioxide equivalent emissions**, which account for several greenhouse gases using standardized conversion factors). Note that in the code and throughout the chapter, we may refer to them simply as CO_2 emissions for simplification.

You can find the notebook to create the data in `/create_data.ipynb` and the datasets in `/src/data`. You can see the description of the dataset in the README file (at the end, under the Data header).

The goal is to minimize costs—both warehouse operating costs and transportation costs from warehouses to retailers—while also reducing CO_2 emissions. This problem is a classic case of optimization, where we look for the best combination of warehouse locations that achieves the lowest cost and environmental impact, subject to constraints such as available facilities and demand fulfillment.

We tell our clients that we can create an app that solves the optimization problem, as long as we can calculate the routes and distances between the warehouses and customers. Given the cost and CO_2 emission estimates per kilometer, we can determine the total impact for each route. Users can select these values in the app's UI, with default rates set at €4/km (including fuel, wages, maintenance, and tolls) and 2 kg CO_2/km. In our example, one client is always connected to the same warehouse. The total yearly cost for a warehouse comes from this calculation:

```
total_cost_of_warehouse = warehouse_operation_cost + Sum(
    distance_to_customer x price_per_km x orders_per_year_by_customer)
```

Our clients want to explore different scenarios when planning warehouse locations. One common request is to make sure that certain countries always have at least one warehouse. This might be because some customers prefer local suppliers, or because certain countries offer business advantages that go beyond what this app handles (such as tax incentives, government contracts, or subventions). In optimization, we call this kind of requirement a **constraint**—a rule that the solution must follow. In this case, the constraint is that there must be at least one warehouse in the selected countries, and we can build that directly into the optimization model.

Our clients want the app to display the price and CO_2 emissions of each scenario as big numbers since they are the main **key performance indicators** (**KPIs**) to compare scenarios. They also want to know the cost and emissions per shipping, and they want to keep each shipment under €2,000 and 1 ton of CO_2 emissions.

> **Note**
>
> This scenario is simple. A realistic case would involve calculating real distances by road, adapting consumption and cost by road type (also adding tolls), considering employee time and extra cost for long trips (overnight compensation), considering country-based differences (gas, wages, and so on), or by having trucks that supply more than one customer in one trip, just to name a few!

We know the kind of app we need to code, but before we code it, let's develop the functions that will hold the app's logic!

Calculating routes

Our app uses a **vectorized implementation** of the **Haversine formula** to efficiently compute the great-circle distance between two sets of geographic coordinates. This implementation uses NumPy's broadcasting to avoid explicit Python loops. Here is the `haversine_vectorized` function (in `/algorithms/distances.py`):

```python
def haversine_vectorized(lat1, lon1, lat2, lon2):
    lat1 = np.radians(lat1[:, np.newaxis])
    lon1 = np.radians(lon1[:, np.newaxis])
    lat2 = np.radians(lat2[np.newaxis, :])
    lon2 = np.radians(lon2[np.newaxis, :])
    dlat = lat2 - lat1
    dlon = lon2 - lon1
    a = (
        np.sin(dlat / 2) ** 2
        + np.cos(lat1) * np.cos(lat2) * np.sin(dlon / 2) ** 2
    )
    c = 2 * np.arcsin(np.sqrt(a))

    R = 6371.0  # Radius of Earth in km
    return R * c
```

The function takes two arrays of latitude and longitude: one for the first set of points and one for the second. It reshapes the inputs to compute all pairwise distances using broadcasting and applies the Haversine formula with vectorized NumPy operations. The output is a 2D array of distances in kilometers: each row corresponds to a point in the first set, and each column to a point in the second.

> **Note**
> Calculating straight distances is not the best approach in real scenarios. To calculate real routes, you could use services such as `https://openrouteservice.org/`.

Next, we can create a matrix (as a pandas DataFrame) with all the distances for our warehouses (20) and customers (94), so we can calculate the costs. To do so, we create a `calculate_distance_matrix` function in `algorithms/distances.py`:

```python
def calculate_distance_matrix(df_warehouses, df_customers):
    lat_wh = df_warehouses["latitude"].to_numpy()
    lon_wh = df_warehouses["longitude"].to_numpy()
    lat_cu = df_customers["latitude"].to_numpy()
    lon_cu = df_customers["longitude"].to_numpy()
    distance_matrix = haversine_vectorized(
        lat_wh, lon_wh, lat_cu, lon_cu)
```

```
return pd.DataFrame(
    distance_matrix,
    index=df_warehouses.index,
    columns=df_customers.index
)
```

Now that we can calculate our distances, let's take a look at our app's actual "brain": the `optimization` function!

Optimization problem and solver

Optimization finds the best solution, such as minimizing costs or emissions, while satisfying a set of constraints. Linear programming solves optimization problems by representing both the goal (objective function) and the required conditions (constraints) as linear equations. **PuLP** is a Python library that simplifies the creation of these optimization models by allowing us to define decision variables, objectives, and constraints in a declarative way and then solve them using external solvers. In our app, we use these concepts to select warehouse locations based on various criteria, such as rental costs, transportation expenses, and CO_2 emissions. This is done with the `create_pulp_model` function (in `/algorithms/optimization.py`). Let's break it down step by step. To make the function easier to test and read, we create a dataclass (`ProblemData`, in `/algorithms/problem_data.py`). This makes the function interfaces cleaner and ensures consistent use of input data throughout the model. We also create several helper functions. Let's take a look at them.

The `create_pulp_model` function delegates work to these helpers:

- `_initialize_problem()`: Initializes a new PuLP minimization problem

- `_define_variables(data)`: Defines the binary decision variables:

  - `warehouse_var[w]`: 1 if warehouse, w, is selected

  - `assignment_var[(w, c)]`: 1 if a customer, c, is assigned to a warehouse, w

- `_compute_transport_cost_term()`: Calculates total transportation cost based on distance, orders, and price per km

- `_compute_transport_co2_term()`: Calculates total transportation CO_2 emissions based on distance, orders, and price per km

- `_compute_warehouse_cost_term()`: Adds fixed costs or emissions for running each warehouse

- `_set_objective_function()`: Combines all cost or CO_2 terms into a single objective for the solver to minimize

- `_add_customer_assignment_constraints()`: Ensures every customer is assigned to exactly one warehouse

- `_add_warehouse_selection_constraints()`: Ensures customers can only be assigned to open warehouses

- `_add_number_of_warehouses_constraints()`: Limits how many warehouses can be selected, for example, exactly 3, or any

- `_add_country_constraints()`: Forces the model to select at least one warehouse from each country in a list

- `_interpret_solution()`: Reads back which warehouses were selected and which customers were assigned where

- `_format_results()`: Creates two final DataFrames with warehouse summaries and customer assignments

At the core of our optimization logic is a **minimization objective**: we want to find the lowest possible total cost or CO_2 emissions while still fulfilling all the requirements of the scenario. To do this, we define the problem using **binary decision variables**, which are simple yes-or-no choices: whether to select a warehouse (1 or 0) and whether to assign a customer to a specific warehouse (1 or 0). These binary variables allow the solver to explore all valid combinations of warehouse selections and customer assignments to find the most efficient setup.

Once we define the objective and decision variables, we add a series of constraints to ensure the solution makes sense. For example, each customer must be assigned to exactly one warehouse, and only to those that are open. The optimization model, built using the PuLP library, uses this setup to evaluate all possible configurations and selects the one that best meets the objective. This approach ensures we always generate scenarios that are both optimal and satisfy the constraints.

The `/algorithms/calculate_total_numbers.py` files have a `calculate_total_numbers` function that takes the resulting DataFrame from the `create_pulp_model` function and calculates aggregated results (total cost and total CO_2 emissions per scenario and per truck trip).

Now, we're going to create a Scenario Management pipeline to create different scenarios with different constraints and assumptions.

Creating the Scenario Management pipeline

Our app uses Scenario Management to execute the optimization pipeline. The pipeline is a three-step process (refer to *Figure 8.1*); you can see the code in `/src/configuration/config.py`. Here are the main tasks:

- It calculates the distances between customers and warehouses and generates a distance matrix

- It runs the optimization algorithms and generates the two DataFrames with the optimal solutions

- It runs a task to create the scenario's big results (total cost and total CO_2 emissions)

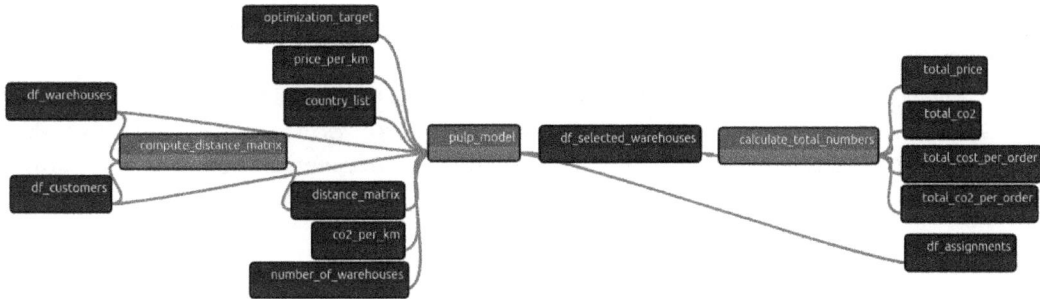

Figure 8.1: App's scenario pipeline

Let's now see how we can configure the pipeline.

Pipeline configuration

To configure the pipeline, we add three global Data Nodes to the model. We create two CSV Data Nodes to read the input files (`warehouses_data_node_config` and `customers_data_node_config`). The `distance_matrix_data_node_config` configuration holds the output of the `calculate_distance_matrix` function. These Data Nodes won't allow user interaction, and all scenarios will share them. By providing a default path and a GLOBAL scope to both input Data Nodes, we ensure that our app can display the data (using Taipy's visual elements such as `table`, `chart`, or with a `data_node` visual element) at any time. Here are two global Data Nodes:

```
customers_data_node_config = Config.configure_csv_data_node(
    id="df_customers",
    default_path="./data/customers.csv",
    scope=Scope.GLOBAL
)
distance_matrix_data_node_config = Config.configure_data_node(
    id="distance_matrix",
    scope=Scope.GLOBAL,
    validity_period=dt.timedelta(days=1)
)
```

We can see in the preceding code that `distance_matrix_data_node_config` has a one-day validity period (`validity_period=dt.timedelta(days=1)`). This allows for caching, as long as this node is in the output of a skippable task (refer to *Chapter 12*). The Data Node configuration object is the output of `compute_distance_matrix_task_config`. **We make this task skippable because all the scenarios will share the same distance matrix**. Here is how the task configuration looks:

```
compute_distance_matrix_task_config = Config.configure_task(
    id="compute_distance_matrix",
    function=calculate_distance_matrix,
    input=[warehouses_data_node_config,
           customers_data_node_config],
    output=distance_matrix_data_node_config,
    skippable=True,
)
```

In this case, we could have pre-computed the distance matrix to avoid handling the computation at the app's level; however, we can imagine a use case where our customers will add new warehouses over time, and the file with those warehouses could be provided daily from a batch process. In this case, having a daily cache and re-computing the matrix once a day seems like a good compromise.

The rest of the scenario pipeline is straightforward; take a look at it! Here are some things worth commenting on:

- Outside of the two input Data Nodes, we create most configurations with `Config.configure_data_node`, which generates intermediate Pickle files. We use CSV Data Nodes for the two main output Data Nodes (`df_selected_warehouses_node_config` and `df_assignments_node_config`). This allows easier file inspection.

- We provide `default_data` values to all Data Nodes that are an input to the model. This allows us to read them without errors in the app.

- We export the configuration as a `.toml` file with `Config.export("config.toml")`; this allows us to document the pipeline (we used this to create the pipeline in *Figure 8.1*).

Adding scenarios to the app

In `main.py`, we import our `Scenario` configuration, and we start `Orchestrator` under the main guard. We create a first scenario, called `selected_scenario`, and submit it (since all input Data Nodes have default values, we don't need to write any of them).

By having a default scenario, we avoid having missing elements in the app when it starts, which can be somewhat unappealing. It can also be interesting to start scenarios with code, instead of from the UI, like we did with the `create_test_scenarios` function (in `/src/create_test_scenarios`):

- Having several scenarios from the start can be useful for development. Every time the app reloads, we lose all the scenarios, so creating them when the app starts avoids creating them from the UI over and over again. We can remove this function when we launch to production.

- We may need some scenarios no matter what, such as default or baseline scenarios, so creating them beforehand can be useful.

Here is how we start our scenarios:

```python
if __name__ == "__main__":
    tp.Orchestrator().run()
    create_test_scenarios(warehouse_scenario_config)
    selected_scenario = tp.create_scenario(warehouse_scenario_config)
    selected_scenario.name = "Default Scenario"
    selected_scenario.submit()
```

We now have our scenario configuration and all the functions that hold the business value. Let's create the UI for our users so they can select the variables and constraints to run the optimization model and then compare the results of different models!

Creating the UI

We have our clients' needs, the main algorithms, and the Scenario Management pipeline. Let's create the UI! Our multiple-page app will have four tabs:

- **Analysis**: This tab will show the raw data so users can get an intuition of our customers' and warehouses' geographic distributions and some basic stats.

- **Scenario**: This is the tab where users will select the main parameters and run their scenarios. They'll also see the scenario's outputs.

- **Comparison**: Here, users will be able to select two scenarios, side by side, and compare them.

- **Admin**: This tab will allow you to check all the `Scenario` objects and monitor the scenario and its submissions.

Let's code our app!

Creating the app's layout and style

The app's layout is a classic multiple-page app, with four pages held in the /src/pages directory. We created a logo for our fictitious company, *EuroDuctPipe*, and we placed it in the app's header, inside the root_page element (in main.py). To reduce the header size, we placed all the elements in the same line, placing the navigation bar in the top left and the company name and logo in the top right. We use a 12-column grid layout to define the root page, like this:

```
with tgb.Page() as root_page:
    with tgb.layout("10 1 1"):
        tgb.navbar()
        tgb.text("# **EuroDuctPipe**", mode="md")
        tgb.image("./img/logo_nbg.png", width="100px")
```

Our company's color is a sort of *European blue*; the hex code is #003399. We'll use this color in the charts (unless we need to add specific color maps) and also add it as the app's primary color in the stylekit, like this:

```
stylekit = {"color_primary": "#003399"}
```

We customize /src/main.css by adding company colors to <b> tags and table borders, reducing the table font size, and creating a .col-number class to right-align numbers. Using color on <b> tags lets us style titles (e.g., Available Warehouses) with Markdown. Also, Taipy's html component allows HTML tags such as horizontal lines: tgb.html("hr"). We also create dedicated classes (such as content-block or side-bar) to give a specific style to specific blocks (we use part blocks and the class_name argument to group the styled content).

Now that we have our main style that fits our corporate identity, let's build the actual app!

Showing the raw data

The code for the app's first page is in /src/pages/analysis/analysis.py. You can see the page in *Figure 8.2*. This page shows the two input DataFrames, df_warehouses and df_customers, as tables, side by side (using layout("1 1")), in an expandable block element.

ANALYSIS   SCENARIO   COMPARISON   ADMIN

EuroDuctPipe

Available Warehouses

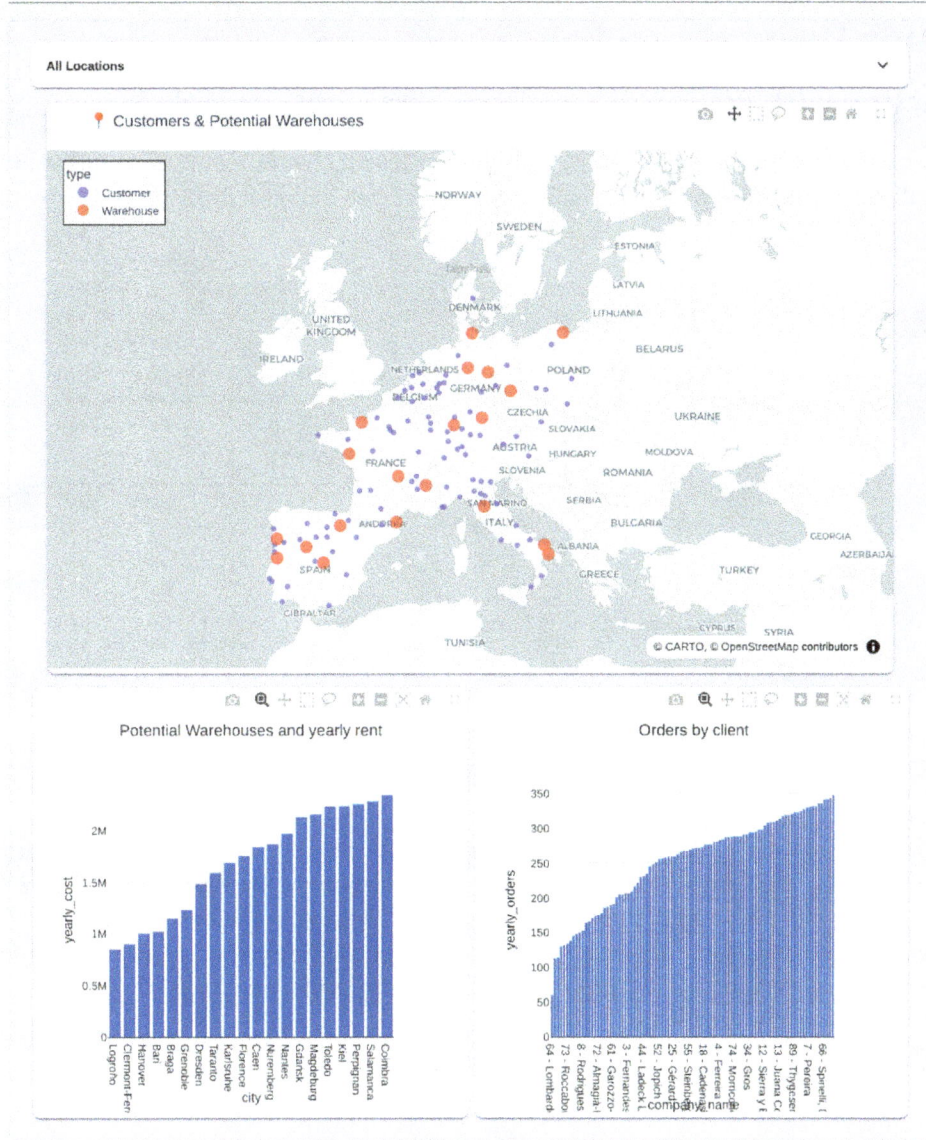

Figure 8.2: Analysis page

The page displays a map with all the warehouses and customers. The code to create the map is in `/src/analysis/create_charts.py`. This function takes the two DataFrames (with customers and warehouses), adds a column type to both, and concatenates them; this way, we can plot both of them as a single DataFrame and use the type distinction to make markers have different sizes and colors. We use a plain background for the map (`mapbox_style="carto-positron"`), and we add a margin at the top to isolate the title and a legend to the top left of the map, where there is no actual data.

Interacting with scenarios

The code for the scenario page is in `/src/pages/scenario/scenario.py`. The top of the page has all the scenario selection and submission elements; you can see it in *Figure 8.3*.

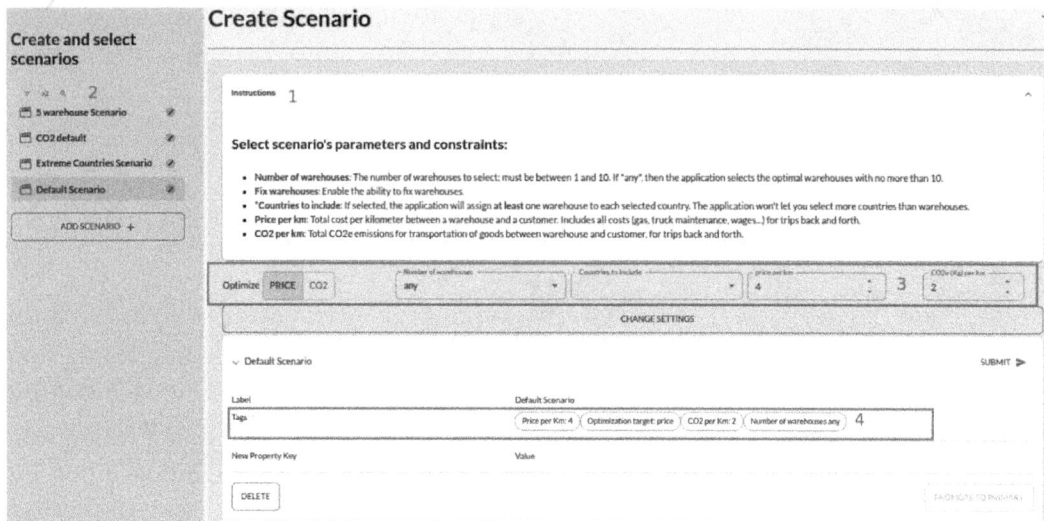

Figure 8.3: The app's scenario selectors

The app has a `"1 4"` (or 20-80) layout, with a `scenario_selector` visual element in the left part (*Figure 8.3*; see label *2*), and the selectors that let users change the scenario's values (*Figure 8.3*; see label *3*), along with the `scenario` element on the right. The page has an `expandable` element with instructions so users know how to operate the app (*Figure 8.3*; see label *1*). The `scenario_selector` visual element has two callback functions, `on_change=change_scenario` and `on_creation=deactivate_scenario`:

```
with tgb.layout("1 4", columns__mobile="1"):
    with tgb.part("sidebar"):
        tgb.text(
            "**Create** and select scenarios", mode="md")
        tgb.scenario_selector(
```

```
            "{selected_scenario}",
            on_change=change_scenario,
            on_creation=deactivate_scenario)
```

deactivate_scenario is a function that sets the active_scenario variable (defined in main.py) to False, and this variable is passed as a value to the scenario's active argument. This trick makes the scenario not submittable until the active_scenario variables become True again, which happens when users validate the new settings for the Scenario. It's a way to force users to validate their settings, even if the Scenario has default values.

The selectors to assign values to the model are the usual ones; we can apply values to all the input Data Nodes for the model:

```
with tgb.layout("1 1 1 1 1"):
    tgb.toggle(
        "{optimize}",
        label="Optimize",
        lov=["price", "co2"])
    tgb.selector(
        "{number_of_warehouses}",
        lov=["any", 1, 2, 3, 4, 5, 6, 7, 8, 9, 10],
        dropdown=True, label="Number of warehouses")
    tgb.selector(
        "{country_list}", lov="{all_countries}",
        label="Countries to Include", multiple=True,
        dropdown=True)
    tgb.number(
        "{price_per_km}", label="price per Km",
        min=1, max=10, step=0.1)
    tgb.number(
        "{co2_per_km}",
        label="CO2e (Kg) per km", min=1, max=10, step=0.1)
```

To change the settings, users need to click on the button (notice class_name="fullwidth", which creates an element with 100% width), and it triggers the change_settings callback. This callback has a first part that ensures that users don't select more countries than warehouses, which leads to an impossible problem (for example, we can't select two warehouses in three different countries). If the function doesn't return, it assigns the values from the selectors to all Data Nodes using the .write() method. Then, it adds tags to the Scenarios using add_tags_to_scenario (this is discussed in more detail in the following paragraph), and it notifies us of success at the end:

```
def change_settings(state):
    if state.number_of_warehouses != "any":
        if len(state.country_list) > int(
```

```
                state.number_of_warehouses
        ):
            with state as s:
                s.active_scenario = False
                notify(
                    s, "e",
                    "Don't select more countries than warehouses!"
                )
                return
    with state as s:
        s.selected_scenario.optimization_target.write(
            s.optimize
        )
        ...
        s.selected_scenario = add_tags_to_scenario(
            s.selected_scenario,
            ...
        )
        s.active_scenario = True
        notify(s, "s", "Changed Scenario settings")
```

The `add_tags_to_scenario` function adds tags to the Scenario, which help users understand its characteristics (the variables and constraints) since the `scenario` element displays them (*Figure 8.3*; see label *4*). Here's the function:

```
def add_tags_to_scenario(
    scenario, optimize, number_of_warehouses,
    country_list, price_per_km, co2_per_km):
    tags = [
        f"Optimization target: {optimize}",
        f"Number of warehouses {number_of_warehouses}",
        f"Price per Km: {price_per_km}",
        f"CO2 per Km: {co2_per_km}",
    ]
    if len(country_list) > 0:
        tags += (f"Fixed countries {country_list}",)
    scenario.tags = tags
    return scenario
```

The `change_scenario` function, from the `scenario_selector` element (the first one we covered in this section, in *Figure 8.3*; see label *2*), assigns the values of the selected Scenario to the visual elements, using the `read()` method. This way, when users change Scenarios, they can easily see the values (they also have the tags), and they can change Scenario values from the correct starting point:

```
def change_scenario(state):
    with state as s:
        s.optimize = s.selected_scenario.optimization_target.read()
        ...
        refresh_results_of_scenario(s)
```

The preceding function calls itself `refresh_results_of_scenario`, which updates all the output Data Nodes in a similar manner; the `refresh_results_of_scenario` function is shared with the `submission_changed` callback, and it has an `if/else` condition to prevent reading Data Nodes that haven't been written before (in that case, it assigns a None value to the bound variables).

The `submission_changed` function is the scenario's element callback. It updates all the output Data Nodes if the Scenario runs successfully. When it's done running, it also notifies users:

```
def submission_changed(state, submittable, details):
    if details["submission_status"] == "COMPLETED":
        print("Submission completed")
        refresh_results_of_scenario(state)
        notify(state, "s", "Submission completed")
    elif details["submission_status"] == "FAILED":
        notify(state, "error", "Submission failed")
```

We just covered all the callbacks and all the elements that allow users to run their models. *Figure 8.4* shows a summary of all the selectors and the associated callbacks.

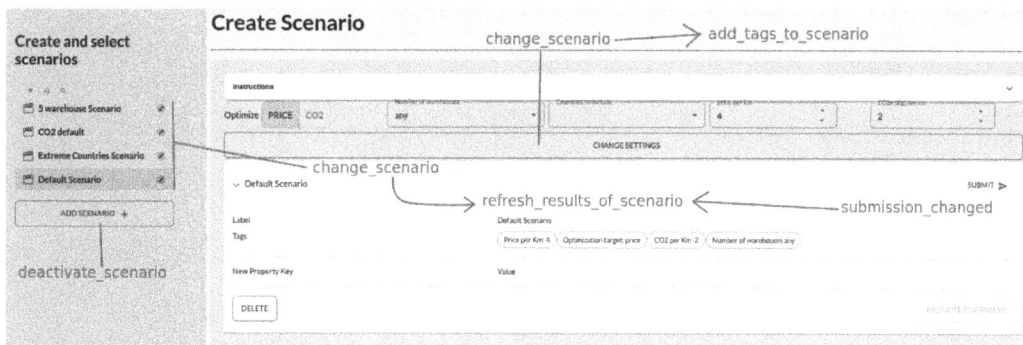

Figure 8.4: Scenario Management from the UI and associated callbacks

We see that our UI has four elements that trigger callbacks: the **Add Scenario** button, the scenario selectors in the `scenario_selector` element, the **Submit** button in the `scenario` element, and the **Change Setting** button element. We also see that the `refresh_results_of_scenario` function is shared by two callbacks, `change_scenario` and `submission_changed`. Let's see how the app renders the Scenario results!

Showing Scenario results

Once a Scenario is submitted, users can visualize the results in two places: the **Scenario** tab, where they'll see the result right after it's completed (they can also change the scenario with the selector), and in the **Scenario comparison** tab (the code is in `/src/comparison/comparison.py`). Let's take a look at some of these visualizations!

Adding maps and charts

The **Scenario** tab creates visualizations from the output Data Nodes. *Figure 8.5* shows a map and three bar charts.

To create the map, we use `plot_assignments`, in `/src/pages/scenario/scenario_charts.py`. This function is like the one from the **Analysis** page, except for the lines that connect each warehouse to a customer. We do it with these lines:

```
lons = []
lats = []
for _, row in df_assignments.iterrows():
    lons.extend([row["warehouse_lon"],
                 row["customer_lon"], None])
    lats.extend([row["warehouse_lat"],
                 row["customer_lat"], None])

fig.add_trace(
    go.Scattermapbox(
        lon=lons,
        lat=lats,
        mode="lines",
        line=dict(width=1, color="#003399"),
        showlegend=False))
```

The plot_customer_by_warehouse function (in /src/pages/scenario/scenario_ charts.py) generates a bar chart showing customer orders for each selected warehouse. It uses a Set3 qualitative color map to differentiate customers. We also add two Taipy bar charts to display the cost and the CO_2 emissions for each Scenario.

We have a general vision of the Scenario, but we can add some specific indicators to track our KPIs. Let's see that.

Adding metrics and KPIs

The metric visual element is perfect for displaying big numbers and KPIs, which are essential for BI analysis. You can see some examples in *Figures 8.5* and *8.6*. To create a simple card like the ones on the left side of *Figure 8.5*, we just need to add the value, a title, the format parameter, which will display the units, and, eventually, hover_text:

```
tgb.metric(
    value="{total_price}",
    title="Scenario's Total Price",
    format=" €",
    type="none",
    hover_text="Estimated total price.",
    class_name="mb2 mt2")
```

The type parameter lets us create semi-circular visuals with a gauge (default), like the ones on the right side of *Figure 8.5*. To create an indicator with a gauge, add a max value as well; for example, to display the cost per order, use the following:

```
tgb.metric(
    value="{total_cost_per_order}",
    max=6_000,
    threshold=2_000,
    format=" €",
    title="Avg cost/order",
    type="circular",   # default
    hover_text="Estimated average transportation cost per truck
                shipping.",
    class_name="mb2 mt2 pb1")
```

Figure 8.5 shows the metrics we follow for this Scenario: The grand total for our two main variables, total price and total CO_2 emissions, and the average values per order.

Figure 8.5: Scenario tab metrics: Big numbers and KPIs

We now have an app that creates Scenarios and displays their main results. However, users would like to compare Scenarios with one another. We'll look at that next!

Comparing Scenarios side by side

The Scenario comparison tab shows a `scenario_selector` visual element, along with cards, charts, and KPIs; you can see the display in *Figure 8.6*. This tab shows a different approach to show Scenarios side by side for better comparison. The idea here is to create two Scenario elements and split the app into two halves (`with tgb.layout("1 1")`), creating the same visual elements bound to each Scenario.

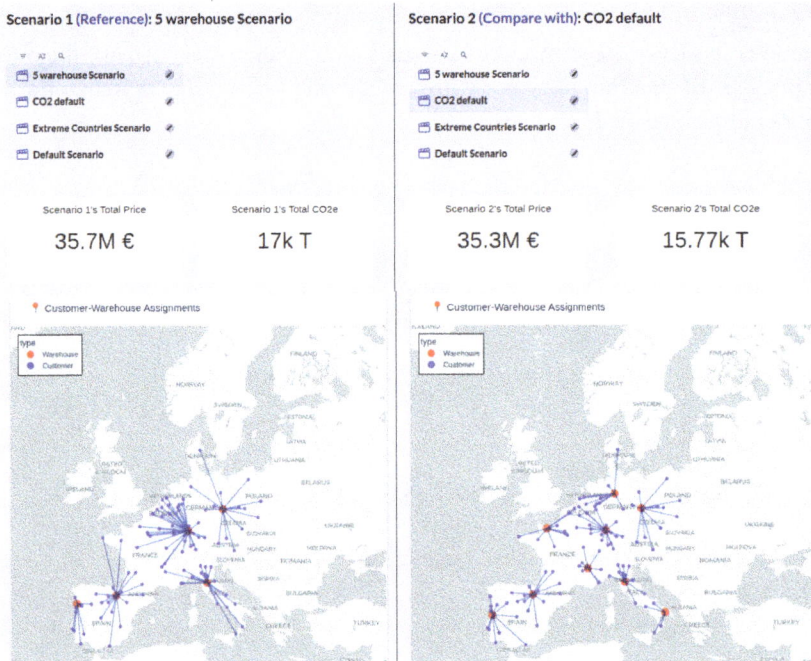

Figure 8.6: Scenario comparison tab: Side-by-side visuals

To compare KPIs, we can use the `delta` parameter in the metric visual element. We can also add custom colors to our KPI metric elements using the `color_map` parameter. Here is how we can reproduce the indicators in the bottom right of *Figure 8.7*:

```
tgb.metric(
    lambda scenario_1, scenario_2: (
        scenario_1.total_cost_per_order.read()
        if scenario_1 and scenario_2
        else None
    ),
    delta=lambda scenario_1, scenario_2: (
        scenario_1.total_cost_per_order.read()
        - scenario_2.total_cost_per_order.read()
        if scenario_1 and scenario_2
        else None
    ),
    delta_color="invert",
    type="linear",
    max=6_000,
    threshold=lambda scenario_1, scenario_2: (
        scenario_2.total_cost_per_order.read()
        if scenario_1 and scenario_2
        else 1
    ),
    format=" €",
    title="Avg cost/order",
    hover_text="Estimated average transportation cost per truck
                shipping.",
    class_name="mb2 mt2 pb1",
    color_map={
        0: "#90EE90",
        2_000: "#FF6347",
    },
    bar_color="#003399")
```

We saw how to add a comparison page. Now, we can add an admin page with some extra information about the scenario and the job runs.

Adding an admin page

We create an **Admin** tab to centralize all the scenario-related information. The code is in `/src/pages/admin/admin.py`. This tab has all the Scenario Management visual elements, including `scenario_dag`, which lets users see the scenario pipeline, and the `job_selector` element, which gives information about each job, such as the time it was run or the submission status. This tab is valuable to monitor how users use the app and how it behaves.

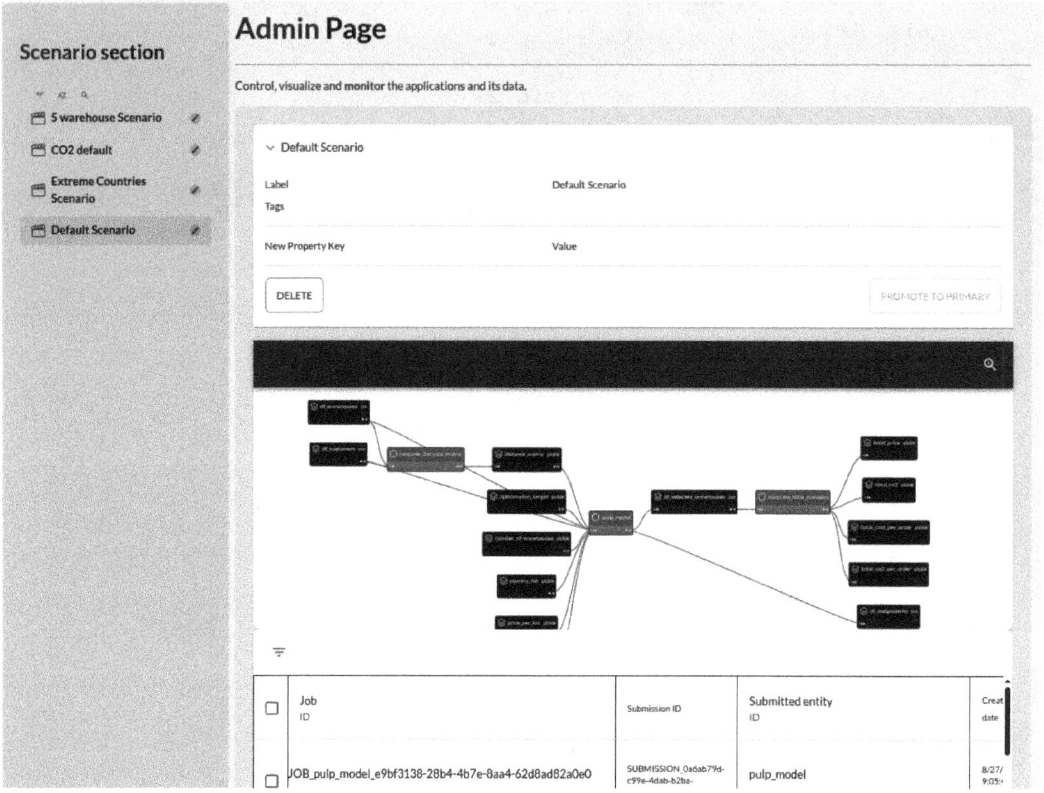

Figure 8.7: Admin page

With this last step, our app is complete. It provides users with an overview of all warehouse options and customers, an interface to create scenarios based on a few assumptions, a comparison page, and a page to monitor the scenarios and how users interact with the app.

Summary

In this chapter, we saw how to create an optimization app using a logistics company as an example. While the problem was simple, this project showcases how Taipy can help us create a production app for analytic, operational, or strategic departments, in almost any economic sector. Taipy's UIs let users define and run their optimization problems using selectors such as drop-down menus or toggle buttons. Taipy Scenario Management allows us to keep track of different scenarios for comparison or analysis. Users can visualize scenario results with charts and maps and compare essential KPIs in no time.

From the perspective of the analytics department, the biggest challenge was defining the optimization problem. Using Taipy, we were able to create an app rather quickly, for a proof of concept first, but to deploy in production later. In the next chapter, we'll see how Taipy can help us create satellite image processing applications.

Further readings

- Article about the Haversine formula: `https://community.esri.com/t5/coordinate-reference-systems-blog/distance-on-a-sphere-the-haversine-formula/ba-p/902128`

- PuLP documentation: `https://coin-or.github.io/pulp/index.html`.

- standards for CO_2 emissions trucks and buses in the European Union: `https://theicct.org/publication/eu-co2-emissions-trucks-manufacturers-2021-reporting-dec24/`

Questions

1. Use the data we provided in the repo and create two scenarios. In both scenarios, we have three warehouses, with at least one in France. One Scenario is optimized for cost reduction, while the other one optimizes CO_2 emissions. What is the difference between them?

2. Our clients want to have a set of default scenarios that use a fixed number of warehouses, from 1 to 10, with all default values. Can you do that for them?

3. Can you change the optimization function and the `scenario.py` page to add an exclusive constraint, like countries not to be included in the Scenario?

4. Can you add cycles to the Scenario and make the Scenario's price per km a monthly based variable?

5. Can you add a page to the app called `total_comparison.py` that compares all the submitted Scenarios? Add charts and a table that ranks Scenarios.

Answers

1. You need to create two scenarios in the **Scenario** tab (for example, 3_france_price and 3_france_co2), and set the number of warehouses to 3 and the countries to include to **France** (leave the default €4 per km and 2 kg of CO2e per km). For the first scenario, select the **PRICE** option using the **Optimize** toggle button, and select **CO2** for the second scenario. In the **Comparison** tab, select both scenarios. The scenario that optimizes price costs €42.6 million per year, versus €43.1 million for the scenario that optimizes CO2e reductions. On the other hand, the scenario that optimizes CO2 emissions saves 60 T in global emissions a year.

2. The answer is in /src/answer_2. Just add the scenario creation in a loop, like this:

```
def create_test_scenarios(scenario):
    for fixed_warehouse in range(1, 11):
        default_scenario = tp.create_scenario(
            scenario
        )
        default_scenario.number_of_warehouses.write(
            fixed_warehouse
        )
        default_scenario.name = (
            f"Default Scenario - {fixed_warehouse}"
        )
        default_scenario.submit()
```

You can add this function to main.py (or better, import it like we did with create_test_ scenarios.py) and execute it inside if __name__=="__main__".

3. The answer files are in /src/answer_3. We need to change the _add_constraints function, adding a no_country_list argument and the following constraint to ensure that warehouse_var is closed for the warehouses located in the restricted countries:

```
if no_country_list:
    for country in no_country_list:
        wh_in_country = df_warehouses[
            df_warehouses["country"] == country
        ]["id"].tolist()
        prob += pulp.lpSum(
            warehouse_var[w]
            for w in wh_in_country
        ) == 0
```

It's also important to ensure that there are enough warehouses to assign. For example, if a user excludes all countries except for Poland, where there is only one warehouse, and requests a solution with more than one warehouse, the solution is impossible. To prevent this, we add the following to the change_settings function (in scenario.py):

```
if len(s.no_country_list) > 0:
    df_warehouses = s.df_warehouses.copy()
    count_warehouses = df_warehouses[
        ~df_warehouses["country"].isin(
            s.no_country_list
        )
    ].shape[0]
    if count_warehouses < number_of_warehouses:
        s.active_scenario = False
        notify(s,"e","There are not enough warehouses...")
        return
```

We add a condition to ensure that a country can't be selected in both the include and exclude scenarios. We also add the selector and the Data Node to the Scenario.

4. The /src/answer_4 directory has the modified files to answer this question. Let's discuss the key elements. First of all, we need to add Scope.CYCLE to our price_per_km_data_node_config, and we add a Frequency.MONTHLY to our Scenario configuration frequency argument:

```
price_per_km_data_node_config = Config.configure_data_node(
    id="price_per_km", default_data=4, scope=Scope.CYCLE
)
...
warehouse_scenario_config = Config.configure_scenario(
    ...
    frequency=Frequency.MONTHLY
)
```

For this small task, we create a km_prices dictionary with distinct prices for each month. On the scenario.py page, we remove all the selectors to change the price per km since it's now a fixed monthly value. Each time we submit a new Scenario, we retrieve the month and year, and we use the dictionary to write the price_per_km Data Node, like this:

```
scenario_date = f"{state.selected_scenario.creation_date.month}-
{state.selected_scenario.creation_date.year}"
    if scenario_date in state.km_prices.keys():
        km_cost = state.km_prices.get(scenario_date)
        state.selected_scenario.price_per_km.write(km_cost)
    else:
```

```
                        notify(state,"w", "No Data for km price...",
                        )
```

5. The answer is in /src/answer_5. This exercise requires two main parts: first, retrieve all the Scenarios using taipy.get_scenarios(). We place this command inside the refresh_all_scenarios() callback, which users can trigger from the UI. Once we have our Scenarios, we need to create a pandas DataFrame with all the summary information for each. This is what the create_comparison_df() does: it passes all the Data Nodes' information to lists using list comprehension to create the DataFrame. You could imagine further data transformations. Once you have your DataFrame, you can display it as a table, and you can also create any chart you wish (in our example, we add two bar charts for total cost and total CO_2e, and a total cost versus total CO_2e scatter plot). Don't forget to add the new page to your pages dictionary in main.py:

```
    "total_comparison": total_comparison_page,
```

Add the import to __init__.py:

```
    from .total_comparison.total_comparison import *
```

9

Taipy for Urban Planning: Creating a Satellite Image App

In this chapter, you'll step into the role of a land use analyst working for a public agency in Paris, France. Your mission: to build an application that allows users to select specific parks and gardens across the city and analyze their vegetation health using the **Normalized Difference Vegetation Index (NDVI)** over a growing season. Users will be able to compare NDVI data across multiple seasons to monitor how urban green spaces change over time.

This project showcases how Taipy can go beyond standard tabular data workflows. You'll learn how to work with geographic data and satellite imagery, which is relevant in fields ranging from agriculture and forestry to climate research, urban planning, and environmental monitoring. The app will use the compute infrastructure of the **European Space Agency (ESA)**, which will show how to connect Taipy to external APIs and manage long-running background processes. This application will use data from **Sentinel 2**, a constellation of satellites that retrieves the type of information we need to calculate the NDVI.

While the app we'll build is simplified and not a fully realistic NDVI analysis tool (since small urban parks often don't provide strong NDVI signals, and real-world use would incorporate additional data such as weather patterns or growth cycles), it introduces powerful image-processing techniques and architectural patterns you can apply to more advanced scenarios.

In this chapter, we'll cover the following:

- Implementing geographical problems
- Creating the scenario's pipeline
- Creating the UI

Technical requirements

You can find the complete code used in this chapter in the GitHub repository: `https://github.com/PacktPublishing/Getting-Started-with-Taipy/tree/main/chapter_09`.

This chapter talks about geographical data, so being familiar with the basics will help, but we'll explain the concepts, and, as usual, all the code is provided. Specifically, we'll use the following tools:

- GeoPandas (`https://geopandas.org/`)
- `rasterio` (`https://rasterio.readthedocs.io/en/stable/`) to handle geographical information
- openEO (`https://openeo.org/`) to connect to the ESA's Copernicus service (satellite images)
- We'll also use SciPy (`https://scipy.org/`) to render some time-series data (but there will be minimal use of this library)

Implementing geographical algorithms

Our application brings together two types of geographical data: vector-based representations of Parisian parks (essentially groups of coordinates defining shapes) and raster-based satellite imagery (images where each pixel holds a data value—often continuous, such as reflectance, but sometimes discrete, such as land cover classifications). In this section, we'll walk through how we source, process, and integrate these distinct formats within our app. The end goal is to build a tool that monitors urban parks and calculates their NDVI values for a given year. Let's explore how we put all the pieces together!

Getting Paris' parks as polygons

Our data comes from the City of Paris' open data portal, available at `https://opendata.paris.fr/explore/dataset/espaces_verts`. To retrieve and prepare this data, we've created a notebook located in `/data_preparation` in the GitHub repository. This notebook fetches the full dataset of parks from the city's public API, filters out the fields relevant to our app, translates field names from French to English, and saves the cleaned data in two formats:

- A CSV file with tabular information (e.g., park names, surface areas)
- A GeoPackage (`.gpkg`) file that contains the spatial data

We use GeoPandas, a library that lets us manipulate geographical datasets, to work with the `.gpkg` file. It includes two layers of geographical data:

- Polygons, representing the boundaries of the parks
- Points, representing the centroids (central points) of each park

Both resulting files are stored in /src/data and will be used throughout the app to link geographic shapes with satellite-derived vegetation data.

We have our data; let's see how we can manipulate it to extract some insights!

Manipulating vector data

In this section, we're going to discuss the functions that allow us to manipulate vectorized geographical information. With vectorized information, the basic unit is a point that is defined by coordinates (latitude and longitude, and sometimes also altitude—although we won't use altitude in this app). Other types of vector data are lines and polygons, which are defined by groups of points. In our example, Paris parks are represented as polygons and stored in GeoPackage files (.gpkg). In this section, we discuss how to access this type of data.

> We created a notebook (in /how_to_help) so you can test the functions that we'll use in the application.

The first part of the demonstration notebook shows how to access the layers in the .gpkg file with GeoPandas:

```
geopackage_path = "../src/data/paris_parks.gpkg"
layer_names = gpd.list_layers(geopackage_path)
gdf_paris_parks = gpd.read_file(
    geopackage_path, layer="parks_polygons")
gdf_park_centroid = gpd.read_file(
    geopackage_path, layer="parks_centroids")
```

In the .gpkg file, we included both park polygons and their centroids to make plotting easier and more flexible. This allows us to visualize a selected park while using its centroids to automatically center the map view. Since both the polygon and centroid layers share a common id, we can reliably match each polygon with its corresponding centroid. Plotly supports GeoDataFrames as input, so we can build a function that takes care of the filtering and plotting in one go:

```
def plot_park_with_centroid(
    gdf_parks, gdf_park_centroid,
    id_name, map_style="open-street-map"
):
    park_polygon = gdf_parks[
        gdf_parks["id_name"] == id_name
    ].copy()
    id = int(id_name.split("-", 1)[0])
    park_centroid = gdf_park_centroid[
```

```
        gdf_park_centroid["id"] == id
].copy()
if park_polygon.empty or park_centroid.empty:
    return None
centroid_point = park_centroid["geometry"].iloc[0]
center = {
    "lat": centroid_point.y,
    "lon": centroid_point.x
}
fig = px.choropleth_map(
    park_polygon,
    geojson=park_polygon.geometry.__geo_interface__,
    locations=park_polygon.index,
    center=center,
    map_style=map_style,
    zoom=15,
    opacity=0.5,
    hover_name="name",
    hover_data={
        "name": True, "type": True,
        "category": True, "area_sqm": True,
    },
)
fig.update_layout(
    margin={"r": 0, "t": 0, "l": 0, "b": 0}
)
return fig
```

This code creates a map like the one labeled as *2* in *Figure 9.1*, which shows the `general_info` page for our app.

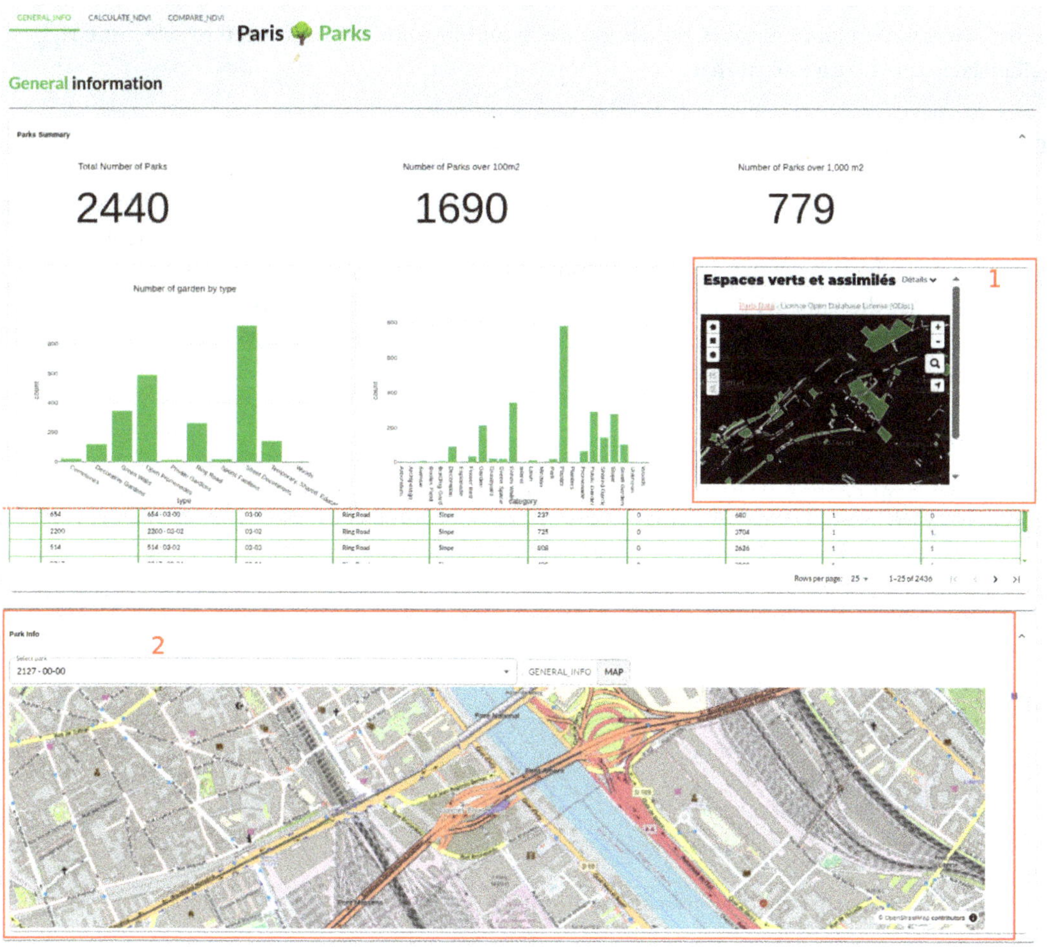

Figure 9.1: General information page. Notice the embedded map (1) and
the Plotly map, with a dedicated selector for each park (2)

We just saw a way to plot polygons, which we use in our app, but we'll also need to select the right satellite data. Let's take a look at that!

Retrieving satellite data with openEO

openEO is a Python client that offers a unified interface for several Earth observation services. This means that we can use it to connect to a specific service; in our case, it's the Sentinel-2 satellites from the ESA, and to interact with that service (we could connect to other services, from the ESA or other agencies, and use the same API). In this section, we'll see how to connect to our service and how to manipulate the satellite data. Note that we're still explaining the code in /how_to_help, and all these functions will then be used in our Taipy app!

Selecting polygons

Before we dive into **openEO**, we need to code a function to retrieve specific polygons from our GeoDataFrame, using a unique identifier (we'll need this in the spatial_extent argument in the connection.load_collection() function in the *Creating NDVI data cubes* section). Here's the function:

```
def get_polygon(gdf_paris_parks, id_name):
    polygon = gdf_paris_parks[
        gdf_paris_parks["id_name"] == id_name
    ].geometry.__geo_interface__
    return polygon
```

Let's now explore openEO's capabilities!

Creating an account and testing the service

To retrieve data from ESA's Copernicus Data Space Ecosystem, you'll first need to create a free account at https://dataspace.copernicus.eu/. The sign-up process is straightforward, and both account creation and API access are completely free.

Once your account is set up, you'll need to create an OAuth credential (under your user settings; you can see a screenshot in the repo's README). This will give you the necessary client ID and secret to authenticate your API requests. You can create an openEO connection object (openeo.rest.connection.Connection) using openeo.connect. The following function returns a connection object:

```
def connect_to_copernicus(
    client_id, client_secret,
    url="https://openeo.dataspace.copernicus.eu"
):
    connection = openeo.connect(url)
    connection.authenticate_oidc_client_credentials(
```

```
            client_id=client_id, client_secret=client_secret)
    return connection
```

We highly recommend storing your ID and secret using a secure system, such as environment variables. Now, let's take a look at openEO's data cubes!

Creating NDVI data cubes

A data cube is a multi-dimensional structure used to represent satellite data. One of its dimensions is time, which refers to the specific moments when satellite images were captured (Sentinel-2 satellites, for example, take images approximately every three days). In addition to time, two spatial dimensions define the geographic extent of each image. Each spectral band captured by the satellite adds another dimension to the cube. Sentinel-2 includes 12 spectral bands (see `https://custom-scripts.sentinel-hub.com/custom-scripts/sentinel-2/bands/`), which means the data cube used in our app has 15 dimensions in total: 12 bands, 2 spatial dimensions, and 1 time dimension. A spectral band is a specific range of light wavelengths that a satellite sensor, such as Sentinel-2, can detect to help observe things such as vegetation, water, and land features.

The number of dimensions can vary depending on the satellite or data provider, and openEO supports connecting to different sources, including satellites from ESA and other agencies. For a deeper understanding, we recommend checking the demonstration notebook and reading openEO's documentation on data cubes.

In the demonstration notebook (and in the app), we create a `get_ndvi` function that takes in a polygon object and a year (an integer). The key aspect here is that we can use a specific park's polygon to retrieve the satellite image. We do that in the `create_datacube` function, which uses `connection.load_collection()` to retrieve the data cube.

Note how we pass the satellite name (`"SENTINEL2_L2A"`) as an argument to the `connection.load_collection()` function and the dimensions for the cube:

```
datacube = connection.load_collection(
    "SENTINEL2_L2A",
    temporal_extent=[start, end],
    spatial_extent=polygon,
    bands=["B04", "B08", "SCL"],)  # Red and NIR for
                                   # NDVI and SCL for clouds
```

In this case, the `start` and `end` parameters represent the first and last days of the year passed as input parameters in `get_ndvi`. We select three spectral bands (the ones we need to calculate the NDVI and process our data):

- Band 04 is for a red wavelength (sometimes referred to as R).

- Band 08 is for an infrared wavelength (sometimes referred to as N).

- The SCL band is a special band that we can use for masking (look at the `mask_clouds` function). Cloud masking is the process of identifying and removing cloudy or cloud-shadowed areas from satellite images to ensure only clear, usable data is analyzed.

The reason we have red and infrared is that the NDVI's formula is calculated as follows:

$(N - R) / (N + R)$

We can create a data cube from another data cube, by calculating the index from the previous data cube's bands. See how we use `datacube.band` in the `create_ndvi` function:

```
ndvi = (datacube.band("B08") - datacube.band("B04")) / (
datacube.band("B08") + datacube.band("B04"))
```

We have created our NDVI object, which is a data cube with four dimensions: two spatial dimensions (a grid representing the terrain surface), time, and one synthetic band—the NDVI index we calculated from the original bands. This means that each pixel in space, at each point in time, has a single NDVI value between -1 and 1. There are ways to simplify and aggregate this data to extract meaningful insights. Let's look at them here:

- Time reduction, where we summarize the NDVI values for each pixel across the entire observation period. In our case, we use the median. The result is a 2D array where each pixel holds the median NDVI value over time, effectively collapsing the time dimension (the `reduce_by_time` function). Here's the main statement:

```
ndvi_time_reduced = ndvi.reduce_dimension(
    dimension="t", reducer="median")
```

- Spatial aggregation works in the opposite direction, and instead of reducing across time, we reduce across space. For each observation date, we calculate the median NDVI value across all pixels in the image. This gives us a time series—a single NDVI value per date—that reflects the overall vegetation condition of the entire area across time (the `get_time_series` function). Here's the main statement:

```
timeseries = ndvi.aggregate_spatial(
    geometries=polygon, reducer="median")
```

Data cubes are objects that hold the instructions to process the data, but the data isn't processed (always processed on the server side) until we retrieve the results. Let's take a look at that!

Executing functions on the server

When applying the reduction and aggregation functions, we get 2D objects that we can plot. The `reduce_by_time` function creates an object we can download as a TIFF image using `ndvi.download()`. We can calculate the time series using the `execute_batch` function, and download them as CSV files with `get_results().download_file()`:

```
def download_ndvi(ndvi, park_id_name, year):
    ndvi.download(f"{park_id_name} - {year}.tiff")
    return 0


def download_time_series(ndvi_timeseries, park_id_name, year):
    title = f"{park_id_name} - {year}"
    job = ndvi_timeseries.execute_batch(
        out_format="CSV", title=title)
    job.get_results().download_file(f"{title}.csv")
```

These two functions are the ones that do the actual work, and they take quite some time (about five minutes for both)! Once we have the data on our own server, we can manipulate it outside the openEO API. Let's see how to plot our TIFF and CSV files!

These are the steps we need to follow to plot the NDVI data:

1. We can open the TIFF file using `rasterio` (and return a NumPy array) with the `read_tiff` function:

    ```
    def read_tiff(id_name, year):
        tiff_image = f"{id_name} - {year}.tiff"
        with rasterio.open(tiff_image) as src:
            ndvi_image = src.read(1) # NDVI is one band
        return ndvi_image
    ```

2. We then use `plotly.express.imshow()` to create an NDVI image, which is what we do with the `plot_ndvi` function, which we use in the app. We set the range color between -1 and 1, which are the limits for NDVI (this way, we ensure all images have the same scale and comparable colors). We also choose the RdYlGn (red, yellow, green) color scale, which is appropriate for this index (refer to *Figure 9.2*, label *4*, to see how this looks in the app):

    ```
    def plot_ndvi(np_image):
        fig = px.imshow(
            np_image,
            color_continuous_scale="RdYlGn",
            range_color=(-1, 1),
            labels={"color": "NDVI"}
        )
    ```

```
fig.update_traces(
    hovertemplate="NDVI: %{z}<extra></extra>")
fig.update_layout(
    title="NDVI Map",
    coloraxis_colorbar=dict(title="NDVI")
)

return fig
```

3. We can also visualize the distribution of pixel values in the NDVI image by creating a box plot or a violin plot. The following function accomplishes this by flattening the NDVI array and generating a violin plot that highlights the spread and density of NDVI values for a given park and year, with helpful visual references at key threshold levels (refer to label 5 in *Figure 9.2*):

```
def plot_box(ndvi_array, id_name, year):
    flattened_data = ndvi_array.flatten()
    fig = px.violin(
        y=flattened_data,
        title=f"NDVI distribution for {id_name}, {year}",
        labels={"y": "NDVI"},
        color_discrete_sequence=["#12b049"],
    )
    fig.update_layout(
        showlegend=False,
        yaxis_title="NDVI Value",
        xaxis_title="",
        plot_bgcolor="rgba(240,240,240,0.8)",
        paper_bgcolor="rgba(240,240,240,0.5)",
        font=dict(family="Arial", size=12),
        margin=dict(l=20, r=20, t=40, b=20),
    )
    # NDVI range for scale: (-1 to 1)
    fig.update_yaxes(range=[-1, 1])
    # Add horizontal lines at important NDVI thresholds
    fig.add_hline(
        y=0, line_dash="dot", line_color="gray")
    fig.add_hline(
        y=0.5, line_dash="dot", line_color="gray")
    fig.add_hline(
        y=-0.5, line_dash="dot", line_color="gray")
    return fig
```

Figure 9.2 shows the `calculate_ndvi` page, which holds representations of the TIFF image with the median yearly values and median yearly NDVI distributions:

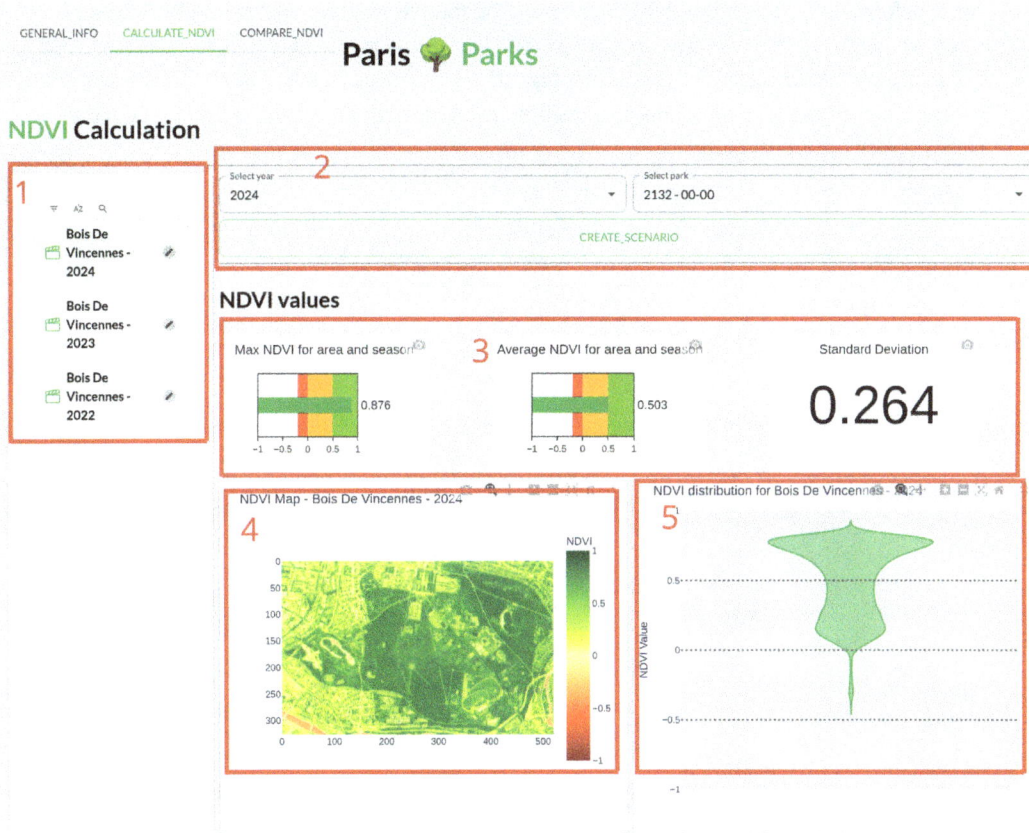

Figure 9.2: calculate_NDVI page (doesn't show the time-series chart). Notice the scenario selector (1), the selectors to create a scenario for a given park and season (2), the cards (3), the NDVI map (4), and the NDVI violin plot (5)

4. To create the time series, we create a pandas DataFrame from the CSV file (see the `read_time_series` function). We use **Savitzky-Golay's function** (`from scipy.signal import savgol_filter`, `https://docs.scipy.org/doc/scipy/reference/generated/scipy.signal.savgol_filter.html`), which smooths the NDVI signal by reducing noise while preserving important features such as peaks and trends. This is useful for ecological or vegetation analysis, where raw NDVI values can be noisy due to cloud cover or sensor variation.

We also interpolate missing values (`df_time_series.interpolate(method="time")`) to ensure the time series is continuous. Interpolation estimates missing data points based on the values before and after a gap, which is important for analysis and smoothing functions that expect evenly spaced data. We also use the date as the DataFrame index (`pd.to_datetime(df_time_series.index)`) to take advantage of pandas' time-based indexing and resampling features. This allows for operations such as time-aware interpolation and sorting, and simplifies working with temporal patterns:

```python
def read_time_series(id_name, year):
    time_series_name = f"{id_name} - {year}.csv"
    df_time_series = pd.read_csv(
        time_series_name, index_col=0)

    df_time_series.index = pd.to_datetime(
        df_time_series.index)
    df_time_series = df_time_series.rename(
        columns={"band_unnamed": "ndvi"})
    df_time_series = df_time_series.drop(
        columns="feature_index")
    df_time_series.sort_index(inplace=True)
    df_time_series = df_time_series.interpolate(
        method="time")
    df_time_series["date"] = df_time_series.index
    # Apply Savitzky-Golay Smoothing
    window_length = 5
    polyorder = 2
    df_time_series["ndvi"] = savgol_filter(
        df_time_series["ndvi"],
        window_length, polyorder
    )
    df_time_series["date"] = df_time_series.index

    return df_time_series
```

5. Once we have our time-series DataFrame, we plot it with the following function. Note how we add three horizontal lines using `fig.add_traces`, to indicate reference NDVI thresholds (*Figure 9.4* shows a similar chart with several traces):

```python
def plot_ndvi_timeseries(df, title):
    df = df.copy()
    df["date"] = pd.to_datetime(
        df["date"]).dt.date
    title = f"NDVI Trend: {title}"
    fig = px.line(
```

```
        df,
        x="date",
        y="ndvi",
        title=title,
        labels={"ndvi": "NDVI Value", "date": "Date"},
        color_discrete_sequence=["#12b049"],
        template="plotly_white")

    fig.update_traces(
        line_width=2.5,
        hovertemplate=(
            "<b>Date</b>: %{x|%b %d}<br>"
            "<b>NDVI</b>: %{y:.2f}",
        )
        mode="lines")

    fig.update_layout(
        yaxis_title="NDVI Value",
        xaxis_title="",
        yaxis_range=[-1, 1.05],
        hovermode="x unified",
        plot_bgcolor="white",
        font=dict(family="Arial"),
        margin=dict(l=50, r=50, t=60, b=30) )
    # NDVI reference lines
    for y, color, name in [
        (0.5, "#8BC34A", "Healthy"),
        (0, "#FFC107", "Neutral"),
        (-0.2, "#F44336", "Barren"),
    ]:
        fig.add_hline(
            y=y,
            line_dash="dot",
            line_color=color,
            opacity=0.5,
            annotation_text=name,
            annotation_position="right",
            annotation_font_size=10,
        )
    return fig
```

We saw the main functions to create our algorithms and our main charts. Let's now see how we can orchestrate all the main tasks together using Taipy's Scenario Management!

Creating the scenario's pipeline

In this section, we'll see how we adapt all the processing to a scenario pipeline. This way, we'll benefit from the scenario capabilities, which allow us to orchestrate the tasks and compare the output Data Nodes in our app. Let's take a look at it!

Adapting functions for orchestration

To create the pipeline, we place the processing functions in `/src/algorithms/algorithms.py` (we'll see how we handle the visualization functions in the next section). We make some changes to our functions to better orchestrate them.

We can improve pipeline orchestration in two ways. The first one is to adapt our functions so they can return objects that we can persist as Data Nodes. The second one is to think about performance issues in our pipeline.

If you look at the `download_time_series` function, you'll notice that we merged the function that downloads the time series as a CSV file and the one that reads it as a pandas DataFrame into a single one. This function acts as a *bridge* between the remote ESA server, which does all the heavy processing, and our app, which saves the original CSV in a dedicated directory (it's a good practice to save the original documents) and generates a DataFrame with the extra features (extrapolation and smoothing) and the proper indexing for the plots.

In terms of performance, we saw in the previous section that downloading images from ESA's server takes a long time (minutes). The `download_time_series` function gets results from historical data, which means it should never yield different results for the same combination of park and year. To make our app more efficient, we can add a condition to not download the file if it already exists, but keep the reading process, to return the DataFrame:

```
def download_time_series(ndvi_timeseries, park_id_name, year):
    filename = f"./data/time_series/{park_id_name} - {year}.csv"
    if not os.path.exists(filename):
        ...
    # outside of the if statement:
    df = pd.read_csv(filename, index_col=0)
    ...
```

We use the same technique in the `download_ndvi` function, for the same reasons, but this function reads the TIFF image using `rasterio` and returns a NumPy array. Let's now take a look at our configuration file!

Creating the pipeline

The configuration file is in `/src/configuration/config.py`. You can see the pipeline in *Figure 9.3* (we can use `Config.export("config.toml")` to generate the configuration TOML file and edit it with Taipy Studio).

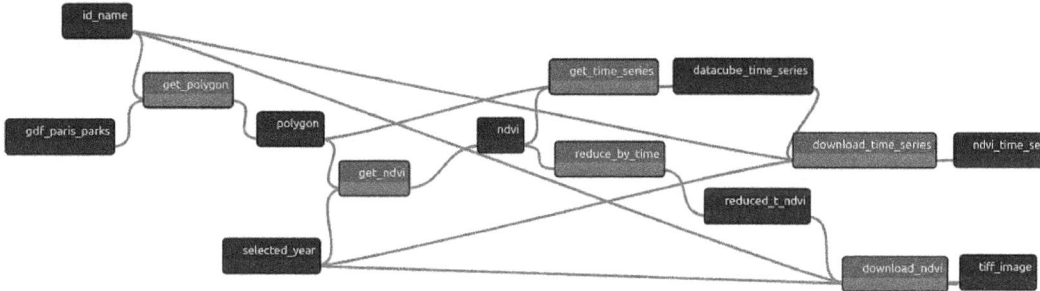

Figure 9.3: Scenario's pipeline

🔍 **Quick tip**: Need to see a high-resolution version of this image? Open this book in the next-gen Packt Reader or view it in the PDF/ePub copy.

📖 **The next-gen Packt Reader** and a **free PDF/ePub copy** of this book are included with your purchase. Scan the QR code OR go to `packtpub.com/unlock`, then use the search bar to find this book by name. Double-check the edition shown to make sure you get the right one.

The pipeline has three Data Node configuration objects with global scope. `df_paris_parks_node_config` reads the CSV file with Paris parks, and we just use it to later display some summary stats and a table with all parks; we don't use it in the scenario.

gdf_paris_parks_centroids_node_config and gdf_paris_parks_node_config are generic Data Nodes; that is, they use a dedicated function to read specific files, in this case, a GeoPackage file, and they return a GeoPandas GeoDataFrame. We use both GeoDataFrames to visualize the park location on the **General information** page (refer to *Figure 9.1*, label *2*):

```
def read_gpkg(file, layer):
    gdf = gpd.read_file(filename=file, layer=layer)
    return gdf

gdf_paris_parks_node_config = Config.configure_generic_data_node(
    id="gdf_paris_parks",
    read_fct=read_gpkg,
    read_fct_args=["./data/paris_parks.gpkg", "parks_polygons"],
    scope=Scope.GLOBAL)
```

The scenario pipeline we create reproduces the flow to create the two objects to analyze NDVI data (the NDVI time series and the average NDVI for the area). The get_polygon task takes in the park's id_name, which will be user-selected, and the park's GeoDataFrame to retrieve a polygon object. Note how we can create a polygon Data Nodes by storing a geometry.__geo_interface__ object in Pickle format!

We use the resulting polygon object and a user-selected year to create an ndvi object, which has an openeo.datacube data type!

The ndvi object is then used by two tasks to create two objects with the reduction commands (reduction by time and spatial aggregation). Each resulting object is then processed by its corresponding task, by executing the downloading tasks (they also take in the park's id_name for file naming), and they return our final Data Node objects, which reference a NumPy array (for the TIFF image) and a pandas DataFrame (for the time series).

When we look at the pipeline, we could imagine that running the get_time_series and reduce_by_time tasks in parallel would make sense, especially since they're the two functions that take time to run. However, this would cause errors since the ESA's servers don't allow running parallel tasks, at least with our free accounts.

Our pipeline is in place; let's see how we create an app to run and compare results.

Creating the UI

The application has three tabs (you can see them in *Figures 9.1, 9.2,* and *9.4*, respectively). The main. py page initializes all the bound variables under if __name__ == "__main__". We create a classic *root page* with a simple *navbar* and a simple stylekit dictionary to define a primary color (#12b049). The CSS file, in /src/css, is similar to other files we have created throughout the book, so we won't discuss it further (but notice how we pass it to the Gui object in main.py: gui = Gui(pages=pages, css_file="./css/main.css")).

In this section, we'll discuss the main elements we used to create the three pages, focusing on the most relevant aspects.

Submitting initial scenarios

Our application uses Scenario Management to launch our data generation functions. When we launch the application, we can create some initial scenarios (we also did this in *Chapter 8*. The code for this section is in /src/create_test_scenarios.py). Generating initial scenarios has at least two potential uses: it makes development easier, and we can use this approach to generate scenarios that we're sure our users will need, which can be reference scenarios or standard scenarios. It's especially useful if scenarios take a long time to run and we want to cache some.

To launch scenarios, we can create a create_and_submit_scenario function that takes in the park identifier, the season's year, and the scenario configuration, and then creates a new scenario, writes its input Data Nodes, and submits it:

```
def create_and_submit_scenario(id_name, year, scenario_config):
    scenario_name = f"{id_name} - {year}"
    scenario = tp.create_scenario(
        config=scenario_config, name=scenario_name)
    scenario.selected_year.write(year)
    scenario.id_name.write(id_name)
    scenario.tags = [f"year: {year}", f"park: {id_name}"]
    scenario.submit()
    return scenario
```

We can then call this function from another function to initialize as many scenarios as we want. In our case, we start the scenarios for the *1679 - Bois de Vincennes* park, for the years 2020 to 2024. Note how we return one specific scenario, so we can have an initial selected scenario in our app (look at the selected_scenario = create_test_scenarios(ndvi_scenario_config) statement in main.py):

```
def create_test_scenarios(
    scenario_config, parks_file="./data/paris_ parks.csv"
):
    vincennes = "1679 - Bois De Vincennes"
    for year in range(2020, 2024):
        create_and_submit_scenario(
            vincennes, year, scenario_config)
    # return a specific Scenario for selection
    return create_and_submit_scenario(
        vincennes, 2024, scenario_config)
```

Notice how we assign tag names with `scenario.tags`. This is useful to group scenarios by different analytical axes. In our example, we add a year tag (which we could use to compare all scenarios of the same year, without using cycles), and then we add `f"park: {id_name}"`, so all the scenarios for the same park share this tag, which is a crucial component of our comparison step (refer to the *Selecting scenarios for comparison* section).

Creating the General information page

The code for the **General information** page is in `/src/pages/general_page`. The top part of the page has an `expandable` element that groups basic metrics and charts with information about Paris' parks. The values for the charts, the table, and the metrics come from `main.py`, as usual:

```
df_paris_parks_node = tp.create_global_data_node(
    df_paris_parks_node_config)
df_paris_parks = df_paris_parks_node.read()
number_parks = len(df_paris_parks)
number_parks_over_100 = df_paris_parks[
    "is_over_100_sqm"
].sum()
number_parks_over_1_000 = df_paris_parks[
    "is_over_1_000_sqm"
].sum()
```

The charts and metric elements are straightforward. Notice how we used the same green color to be consistent across the app (`color="#12b049",`). The expandable element also shows a small map of Paris' parks, which comes from a widget (refer to *Chapter 14* for more information). The code for the widget (an iframe) is in `/src/widgets`, and we place it in the app using a `part` element:

```
tgb.part(page="./widgets/paris_parks_widget.html", height="420px")
```

The bottom part of the page has another expandable element, and displays either some general information about parks or a map of the park, using a partial block (refer to *Chapter 11*). A selector allows selecting a specific park, and a toggle button allows selecting the display; both elements call the same callback, `change_selection`. We insert the partial element with the following:

```
tgb.part(partial="{park_partial}")
```

The `change_selection` callback uses the `with` statement, which is more efficient than using individual state statements (refer to *Chapter 11*). Notice how we also used an `if` statement to test whether we have a selected park. This is because the selector element has a `filter=True` argument, which allows users to search for information by typing in the box, but can also generate empty strings, which could lead to errors. The callback calls `create_park_info_partial`, which we can find in `/src/pages/general_page/park_partial.py`:

```
def change_selection(state):
    with state as s:
        if s.selected_park: # Avoid doing anything if empty string
            park = s.selected_park
            df_parks_cp = s.df_paris_parks.copy()
            s.selected_park_row = df_parks_cp[
                df_parks_cp["id_name"] == park]
            s.selected_park_dict = s.selected_park_row.to_dict(
                orient="records")[0]
            create_park_info_partial(s)
```

The `create_park_info_partial` function creates a different page element, depending on the value of the toggle button. This is a neat way to use the same dedicated space to show different elements, in this case either a text-based general information statement (which uses `selected_park_dict` with distinct values of the selected DataFrame's row) or a map (which uses the `plot_park_with_centroid` function, which we explained in the first section, *Implementing geographical problems*):

```
def create_park_info_partial(state):
    if state.info_display == "general_info":
        with state as s:
            park_type = state.selected_park_dict.get("type")
            category = state.selected_park_dict.get("category")
            area = state.selected_park_dict.get("area_sqm")
            perimeter = state.selected_park_dict.get("perimeter")
        with tgb.Page() as park_info:
            tgb.text(
                f"""## General Information: {state.selected_park}
- **Park Type:** {park_type}
- **Park Category:** {category}
- **Area:** {area} sqm.
- **Perimeter:** {perimeter} m.
""",
                mode="md",)

    elif state.info_display == "map":
```

```
        with tgb.Page() as park_info:
            tgb.chart(
            figure=lambda gdf_paris_parks,
            gdf_paris_parks_centroids,
            selected_park: plot_park_with_centroid(
                gdf_paris_parks,
                gdf_paris_parks_centroids,
                selected_park if selected_park else None,))
    else:

        ...

    state.park_partial.update_content(state, park_info)
```

An important step to add the partial to our app is to add it to our `gui` element in `main.py` (all of this is explained in *Chapter 11*):

```
park_partial = gui.add_partial(page="")
```

The **General information** page lets users see basic information about the city parks. Now, we'll code the page that will let them calculate the NDVI values for the parks they monitor.

Creating the NDVI calculation page

The code for this section is in `/src/pages/calculate_ndvi`. The `Page()` element shows a `scenario_selector` visual element in the left part, which allows changing scenarios but not submitting them (we add `show_add_button=False`). On the right part of the page, we add two selectors, one to select the year and one to select the park name; we add a big button (with `class_name="fullwidth"`) to create and submit the scenarios (`on_action=create_scenario`).

We chose this setup because the NDVI scenarios we create are simple (they take in a park and a year, nothing else), and they don't ever need to be recalculated: once we get the NDVI values for a park and a year, that's it; it will never change. It's historical data, not predictive data based on assumptions.

It's important to note that the two selectors and the submission button have the same bound variable for the active parameter, `show_scenario_selectors` (defined at the beginning of the file):

```
active="{show_scenario_selectors}",
```

The reason for this is that our tasks take a long time to run, and we don't want users to trigger new callbacks when one is running (nor change the park variables).

Creating a long-running callback

The `create_scenario` function is the main element of the `calculate_ndvi` page.

It retrieves the `id_name` value to use as a parameter for our scenario pipeline. It also gives a name to the scenario based on the park name and the year. The reason why automatic naming is important is that we don't want to create more than one scenario with the same assumptions (we disabled the scenario creation option from the `scenario_selector` for the same reason).

Once we get our scenario name, we check whether it exists using `taipy.get_scenarios()`. If it does exist, we notify the user, and we're out of the callback.

If the scenario doesn't exist, then we're ready to launch our long-running scenario! The first step is to make the selectors and the submit button inaccessible (with `s.show_scenario_selectors = False`), and then we create a new scenario, write the input Data Nodes with the values from the bound variables, and launch the scenario submission with an `invoke_long_callback` function (refer to *Chapter 11* to understand how long-running callbacks work):

```python
def create_scenario(state):
    with state as s:
        id_name = s.selected_park_ndvi
        scenario_name = f"{id_name} - {s.selected_year}"
        existing_scenarios = [
            scenario.name for scenario in tp.get_scenarios()]
        if scenario_name in existing_scenarios:
            print("Scenario already exists!")
            notify(
                s, "w",
                f"Scenario {scenario_name} already exists"
            )
        else:
            s.show_scenario_selectors = False
            new_scenario = tp.create_scenario(
                config=ndvi_scenario_config)
            new_scenario.selected_year.write(s.selected_year)
            new_scenario.id_name.write(id_name)
            new_scenario.name = scenario_name
            new_scenario.tags = [
                f"year: {s.selected_year}",
                f"park: {id_name}"
            ]
            invoke_long_callback(
                s, submit_scenario,
                [new_scenario], update_status, [], 2000
            )
```

The `invoke_long_callback` function is adapted to our current use case because it launches the long-running callback in a separate thread. Our callback takes a long time to run, but it runs on a different server (for the most part). If the task had been running on our server, we may have thought about running it asynchronously, but in this case, launching it in a separate thread allows users to continue using the app while the task runs.

`invoke_long_callback` triggers the `submit_scenario` function, which submits the scenario (this is all it does, and the reason we have a dedicated function is so it can be running in a separate thread!).

The `update_status` function is a special callback, with a special status parameter (refer to *Chapter 11*) that returns an integer while the long callback runs, and equals `True` when it's done. This way, we can notify the users that the long-running callback is still running; we choose to do it every minute. When the long callback is done, we can update the selected scenario with the new, fresh result, change all the other values with the `change_scenario` function (we will explain it right after this one), make the selectors available again (`s.show_scenario_selectors = True`), and notify users of completion:

```
def update_status(state, status, scenario):
    if isinstance(status, bool):
        if status:
            with state as s:
                s.selected_scenario = scenario
                change_scenario(s)
                s.show_scenario_selectors = True
                update_compare_selector(s)
                notify(
                    s, "s",
                    f"New Scenario created - {scenario.name}!"
                )
        else:
            notify(state, "e", "Scenario Generation Failed")
    else:
        if is_multiple_of_60(status):
            notify(
                state, "i",
                f"{status/60} min... Calculations running"
            )
```

The `update_status` function also calls the `update_compare_selector` function, which we import from the `/src/update_callback.py` file; this step updates the `scenarios_to_compare` list, which we use in the `compare_ndvi` page (refer to the *Selecting scenarios for comparison* section). Let's now take a look at the scenario update process.

Updating the scenarios

`scenario_selector` allows us to change the scenario and update the charts and the selector values (as we saw earlier, we added `show_add_button=False` to remove scenario creation capabilities). The function to change the values relies on reading the newly selected scenario's Data Nodes and is a "classic" process:

```
def update_selectors(state):
    with state as s:
        s.selected_year = s.selected_scenario.selected_year.read()
        s.selected_park_ndvi = s.selected_scenario.id_name.read()


def change_scenario(state):
    with state as s:
        if (s.selected_scenario.tiff_image.is_valid
            and s.selected_scenario.ndvi_time_series.is_valid
        ):
            print(
                f"changing Scenario: "
                f"{s.selected_scenario.name}")
            s.selected_np_tiff = (
                s.selected_scenario.tiff_image.read())
            s.selected_df_time_series = (
                s.selected_scenario.ndvi_time_series.read())
            s.selected_scenario_name = (
                s.selected_scenario.name)
            update_selectors(state)
            notify(
                s, "i",
                f"Changed Scenario - {s.selected_scenario.name}")
        else:
            notify(s, "w", "Scenario is incomplete")
```

The relevant part of this function is in the validity checking (`if s.selected_scenario.tiff_image.is_valid`). We add this statement because when we create a new scenario, it takes a long time to run, but the selector shows the new scenario immediately, so if we let users select it, the output Data Nodes aren't written (this is what `is_valid` checks). If the Data Nodes aren't written, then we notify users that their selection is impossible.

We've now covered the logic in our callbacks. Let's discuss how we created the metrics page in our app!

Adding charts and metrics to the page

The page shows the NDVI values as charts and metrics. The charts are the ones we described in the first part of the chapter (you can see the code to create them in `/src/pages/calculate_ndvi/charts.py`). We then create the chart elements using the functions and lambda expression. We've done this in previous chapters. Here's an example to create the violin plot with NDVI distribution for the selected scenario:

```
tgb.chart(
    figure=lambda selected_np_tiff,
    selected_scenario_name: plot_box(
        selected_np_tiff, selected_scenario_name) )
```

The application also shows two metrics (look at *Figure 9.2, label 3*). To create these metrics, we use the `tgb.metric` element, with a linear type, to put the metric in a certain context. The value is either the maximum NDVI or the average NDVI (based on the median values). To add context to the metric, we define min and max values (between -1 and 1, which is the NDVI range) and we pass a dictionary to the `color_map` argument with a "traffic light" scale indicating thresholds for the NDVI values (red for -0.2 to 0, yellow for 0 to 0.5, and green for above 0.5):

```
tgb.metric(
    value="{float(selected_np_tiff.max())}",
    type="linear",
    min=-1,
    max=1,
    title="Max NDVI for area and season",
    hover_text="Maximum NDVI value for selected area and given year.",
    color_map={
        -0.2: "#F44336",
        0: "#FFC107",
        0.5: "#8BC34A",
    },
    bar_color="#12b049",)
```

We've covered the most important aspects of the `create_ndvi` page, let's now create a page to compare results.

Creating the NDVI comparison page

The code for the `compare_NDVI` page is in `/src/pages/compare_ndvi`. You can see how it looks in *Figure 9.4*.

Figure 9.4: compare_NDVI page lets users compare different scenarios

This page is simple: it has a drop-down selector that shows park names (`id_name`) and overlays the time-series charts for all the scenarios for that park. This page has two important elements to it: it plots all time series together (for a given park) and it allows selecting parks that have at least one valid scenario. Let's take a look at them!

Plotting multiple years together

The first important element for this page is in the `charts.py` file, which has the `plot_ndvi_multi_timeseries` function. To plot and compare all our time series, we need to get all the resulting DataFrames and all the associated scenario names as inputs, in the form of lists.

Notice how the function checks whether the two input lists (one with all the scenario DataFrames and one with the scenario names) are equal. This matters because if one scenario exists but has no valid Data Node, we could have errors (this should be taken care of on the callback side, but we add an error check in case).

The main trick to compare different years in one single chart is to combine all DataFrames into a single one, adding a `trace_name` column to distinguish them and plot them in separate lines, as well as changing the dates to make them share the same year. We chose 2020 as an arbitrary year; however, we made sure to choose a leap year to avoid problems. It's also important to change the chart's x-value display to not show the year! This is what we do with `xaxis_tickformat="%b %d"` (where `%b` stands for an abbreviated month notation, such as `Jan` or `Feb`, and `%d` stands for the day of the week):

```
def plot_ndvi_multi_timeseries(df_list, trace_names, title):
    if len(df_list) != len(trace_names):
        raise ValueError(
            "df_list and trace_names must have the same length"
        )
    combined_dfs = []
```

```
for df, name in zip(df_list, trace_names):
    df = df.copy()
    df["date"] = pd.to_datetime(df["date"])
    # We use 2020 as an arbitrary year for comparison -
    # chart won't show year
    # 2020 is leap year, which could prevent Feb-29 errors
    df["date_std"] = df["date"].apply(
        lambda x: x.replace(year=2020)
    )

    # Add trace name for identification
    df["trace_name"] = name
    combined_dfs.append(df)
combined_df = pd.concat(combined_dfs)
fig = px.line(
    combined_df,  x="date_std",  y="ndvi",
    ...
)
# Update layout to ensure the x-axis is correctly formatted
fig.update_layout(
    yaxis_title="NDVI Value",
    xaxis_title="Date (Month-Day)",
    yaxis_range=[-1, 1.05],
    hovermode="x unified",
    xaxis_tickformat="%b %d", # Display only month and day
    xaxis_range=[
        "2020-01-01",
        "2020-12-31",
    ], # We use arbitrary 2020 )
    ...
    return fig
```

We can plot several years together for the same park. Let's see how we select all the scenarios for comparison!

Selecting scenarios for comparison

The compare_ndvi.py file has a simple compare_page Page element, with a drop-down selector showing the parks that have a scenario (the scenarios_to_compare list) and a chart with the time series. Most of the intelligence in this page is in its callback function (select_scenarios), which we call from the selector and in the /src/update_callbacks.py file. Let's take a look at it!

The first important element of this page is that the drop-down selector shows the parks with at least one completed scenario. This is possible because `scenarios_to_compare` gets updated by the `update_compare_selector` function, and this function gets called every time a new scenario is submitted and completed (we also call it from the `on_init` special callback, in `main.py`). Since all scenarios have a tag that starts with `park:`, followed by the park name, we can get the distinct park names:

```
def update_compare_selector(state):
    all_tags = [
        scenario.tags for scenario in tp.get_scenarios()]
    all_tag_set = set()
    for tag in all_tags:
        all_tag_set.update(tag)
    all_park_scenario = [
        tag.replace("park: ", "")
        for tag in all_tag_set if "park: " in tag
    ]
    state.scenarios_to_compare = all_park_scenario
```

If we go back to our `compare_ndvi.py` page, in the callback, we see how we use the same approach to retrieve all the scenarios that have the selected park name in the tag (`tp.get_scenarios(tag=tag_name)`):

```
def select_scenarios(state):
 if state.select_park_name_comp:
    with state as s:
        tag_name = f"park: {s.select_park_name_comp}"
        scenarios_to_compare = tp.get_scenarios(tag=tag_name)
```

After this, we create the inputs for the `plot_ndvi_multi_timeseries` function. We get the scenario names with `scenario.name` and the time-series DataFrames by reading the dedicated Data Node. Note how both lists include the `if scenario.ndvi_time_series.is_valid` statement, which prevents errors in case we select a park whose values are being calculated (the scenario may exist, but the output Data Node isn't yet written):

```
s.scenario_comp_names = [
    scenario.name
    for scenario in scenarios_to_compare
    if scenario.ndvi_time_series.is_valid
]
s.selected_time_series_list = [
    scenario.ndvi_time_series.read()
    for scenario in scenarios_to_compare
    if scenario.ndvi_time_series.is_valid
]
```

Finally, note that we update the `figure_ndvi` object directly within the callback instead of using a `lambda` expression. This is because the callback changes several variables that are required by the `plot_ndvi_multi_timeseries` function. Using a lambda in this context could lead to inconsistencies—some variables might be updated while others are still in their previous state, potentially resulting in value errors when generating the figure.

Summary

In this chapter, we explored how to integrate third-party services into our applications, using long-running callbacks to create smoother, more responsive user experiences. We also showed how to work with geographic data and images in Taipy, going beyond traditional tabular data. The example app showcased advanced concepts such as partials for cleaner navigation and HTML iframe embedding to incorporate external data sources.

We also used lambda expressions to generate customized charts, highlighting Taipy's powerful integration with Plotly. This example illustrates Taipy's flexibility, enabling you to tap into nearly any Python library. Whether you're working with image classification, video or audio processing, or unstructured text, the possibilities for building rich, interactive apps are virtually unlimited. In the next chapter, we'll develop a different type of application: an AI chatbot!

Questions

1. Using the app, select the park named *239 - Jardinieres De La Rue Paul Bourget*, and calculate the NDVI for the years 2020 to 2024 (you can use the `create_test_scenarios` function). What do you observe?

   NDVI is one out of many spectral indices you can calculate from a satellite image! Using the following information, calculate a different index for Paris parks, for example, Bare Soil Index:

   `https://awesome-ee-spectral-indices.readthedocs.io/en/latest/list.html#vegetation`. You can find Sentinel-2 band numbers in the following document: `https://custom-scripts.sentinel-hub.com/custom-scripts/sentinel-2/bands/`. (Note: The "S" band in the SWIR-2 band, is band number 11.)

   Create a page that shows a summary of all scenarios.

2. Add a selector that adds a tag to the scenario (maybe something such as "organic growth" versus "non-organic growth"), and have a page that compares all scenarios with one tag versus all scenarios with a different tag.

3. Add a partial (refer to *Chapter 11*) to the `compare_ndvi` page that compares all scenarios for a certain park.

Answers

1. This park was created in 2020. You can select the years one after the other (using the selectors from the Plotly chart). You'll notice that the NDVI tends to increase, especially during the growing season (spring and summer), which makes sense if the park is so recent (it gets greener over time)!

    To add the data from this park for all years, from the beginning, we can add this code to the `create_test_scenarios` function:

    ```
    answer_1 = "239 - Jardinieres De La Rue Paul Bourget"
    for year in range(2020, 2025):
        create_and_submit_scenario(answer_1, year, scenario_config)
    ```

    The formula to calculate Bare Soil Index, as we see in the documents, is as follows:

    $((S1+R)-(N+B))/((S1+R)+(N+B))$

    In the Sentinel Hub documentation, we can find the right bands (see the commented code):

    ```
    def create_datacube(polygon, start, end, connection):
        datacube = connection.load_collection(
            "SENTINEL2_L2A",
            temporal_extent=[start, end],
            spatial_extent=polygon,
            bands=["B02", "B04", "B08", "B11", "SCL"]
        ) # B02: Blue , B04: Red, B08: NIR, B11 SWIR 1
        return datacube
    ```

    Note that we also get the SCL band for cloud masking.

    Then, we can replace `crerate_ndvi` with the `create_bsi` function, which uses the BSI formula instead of the NDVI one:

    ```
    def create_bsi(datacube):
        numerator = (
            datacube.band("B11") + datacube.band("B04")
        ) - (
            datacube.band("B08") + datacube.band("B02")
        )
        denominator = (
            datacube.band("B11") + datacube.band("B04")
        ) + (
            datacube.band("B08") + datacube.band("B02")
        )
        bsi = numerator / denominator
        return bsi
    ```

To bring this index to the app, you should also change the chart names. You could also change the color scale for the map image, something such as `color_continuous_scale="YlOrBr"`.

The answer is in `/answers/answer_3`. Don't forget to import it (`from answers.answer_3.answer_3 import answer_3_page`) and add it to the pages dictionary in `main.py`! The `rank_scenarios` function creates a DataFrame by creating lists with scenario properties (scenario names and calculated values).

2.   The main answer is in `/answers/answer_4`. You need to import this page into your pages dictionary.

3.   On the `ndvi.py` page, we add a selector with `"organic"` and `"non-organic"` values. To add the label, you can just add it to the tag list in the `create_scenario` function (add `f"type: {organic_tag}"`). We should also add the tags to the `create_and_submit_scenario` function. Here is an example:

```
if year in [2020, 2021]:
    scenario.tags = [
        f"year: {year}",
        f"park: {id_name}", "non-organic"]
else:
    scenario.tags = [
        f"year: {year}",
        f"park: {id_name}", "organic"]
```

On the answer page, we add a button to create the scenario comparison. The callback creates two lists, with the distinct scenarios (`organic_scenarios = tp.get_scenarios(tag="organic")`), and then we access each scenario's properties, such as the name or the Data Node values (using the `.read()` method) with list comprehension. We append it all to a DataFrame. The visual in this case is a violin plot, but you can imagine any chart or table that makes sense.

4.   The answer files are in `/answers/answer_5`. To add images to our partial, we'll need to bring the arrays from the selected scenarios. For this, we add the following to the `select_scenarios` function in `compare_ndvi.py`:

```
s.selected_arrays = [scenario.tiff_image.read()
    for scenario in scenarios_to_compare
    if scenario.tiff_image.is_valid]
```

The partial is in the `answer_5.py` file. The trick is to calculate how many submitted scenarios we have for the selected park, to show the charts next to each other. We create a `variable_layout` object to add as many columns as needed, and then we add the charts in a loop using `range`:

```
number_of_scenaios = len(state.selected_arrays)
variable_layout = "1 " * number_of_scenaios
variable_layout = variable_layout[:-1]

with tgb.layout(variable_layout):
    for index in range(number_of_scenaios):
        tgb.chart(figure=lambda state: plot_ndvi(
            state.selected_arrays[index],
            state.scenario_comp_names[index], )
```

Note that this approach is reasonable because, for a given park, we have a maximum of five distinct values. Finally, to add the partial to our page, we need to add the partial object in `main.py`, with `answer_5_partial = gui.add_partial(page="")` (also initialize the object to hold the selected arrays, like this: `selected_arrays = []`).

We import and add `create_comp_partial(state)` to `main.py` (to add it to `on_init`) and to `compare_ndvi.py` (to add it to `select_scenarios`).

Add the partial to Page (`tgb.part(partial="{answer_5_partial}")`).

Join our community on Discord

Join our community's Discord space for discussions with the authors and other readers:

`https://packt.link/taipybook`

10

Building an LLM Chatbot with Taipy

Generative AI and **Large Language Models** (**LLMs**) have been all over the place ever since the release of ChatGPT in 2022. A handful of big companies, such as OpenAI, Google, Mistral AI, xAI, and Anthropic, provide models and infrastructure through APIs, while others, such as Meta, push open-weight models (think LLaMA) that anyone can run in-house or via third-party infrastructure.

In this new ecosystem, new AI applications pop up every day. Using an application builder such as Taipy will let us build anything from a simple API wrapper (a chat interface that uses an API to let users chat with a specific model) to more advanced interfaces, such as adding buttons with predefined prompts or selectors to change models, and even selecting documents to send to our chat model. Our UI can also help us observe chat usage and history or record user satisfaction. The app's complexity can also happen behind the UI, by constructing **Retrieval-Augmented Generation** (**RAG**) pipelines that use embedding models and vector databases to "assist" our AI models with a specific knowledge base (such as private company documentation), or complete agentic workflows.

In this chapter, we'll build a chatbot incrementally: we'll start by explaining the chat visual element and how to style it, and then we'll connect it to our first AI model. Then, we'll add visual elements and components to create a better user experience.

In this chapter, we'll cover the following topics:

- Creating our first bot
- Creating a chat UI

Technical requirements

You can find the complete code used in this chapter in the GitHub repository: `https://github.com/PacktPublishing/Getting-Started-with-Taipy/tree/main/chapter_10`.

Having some knowledge of the LLM landscape is enough to understand this chapter; we won't dive deep into AI stuff! We'll use LangChain (`https://python.langchain.com/`), a framework to interact with AI models and other tools to build AI applications that can use external data or even to create agents. You'll also need to install the `langchain-mistralai` integration package (`https://pypi.org/project/langchain-mistralai/`).

Creating our first bot

In this section, we'll create our first chatbot using Taipy, which is the entry point to building more complex applications. The code for this application is in `/ai_wrapper`. We'll discover the chat visual element, and we'll see how it builds and displays a list of messages. Once we are familiar with our visual element, we'll connect to Mistral AI's API, to create our first chatbot. We'll also cover some styling considerations for this particular element. Let's go!

Discovering the chat visual element

The chat visual element is a Taipy component to build GUIs, just like most of the components we covered in *Chapter 2*. To get familiar with the component, we'll code an app that takes in a user message from a chat interface and detects whether there is any **Personally Identifiable Information** (**PII**), such as names, phone numbers, or emails, in the text. It also removes the PII data from the text and replaces it with asterisks (`****`) to avoid confidentiality issues. The application is in `/chat_element/main.py`; you can see it in *Figure 10.1*.

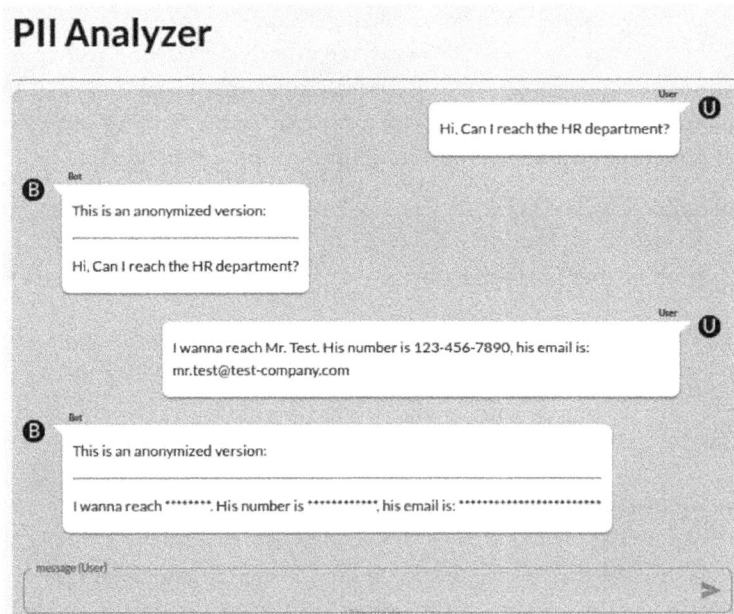

Figure 10.1: A simple chat interface

Our single-page application has a simple `Page` element, with a title, a horizontal line, and a chat element, defined like this:

```
tgb.chat(
    messages="{messages}",
    users="{users}",
    show_sender=True,
    sender_id="{users[0]}",
    with_input=True, #defaults to True
    on_action=chat,
    mode="markdown"
)
```

💡 **Quick tip**: Enhance your coding experience with the **AI Code Explainer** and **Quick Copy** features. Open this book in the next-gen Packt Reader. Click the **Copy** button

(**1**) to quickly copy code into your coding environment, or click the **Explain** button

(**2**) to get the AI assistant to explain a block of code to you.

```
                                              Copy    Explain
function calculate(a, b) {                     1        2
  return {sum: a + b};
};
```

The next-gen Packt Reader is included for free with the purchase of this book. Scan the QR code OR go to `packtpub.com/unlock`, then use the search bar to find this book by name. Double-check the edition shown to make sure you get the right one.

Let's break the arguments down:

- messages: The mandatory bound variable is a list we initialize under if __name__ == "__main__" (messages = []). Each message is a tuple with three values, each one a string: a message identifier, the message, and the message sender's name.

- users: A list with all the usernames. It accepts more than two values, since the chat visual element supports interactions with several users (such as a team multi-chat or a forum app). It also accepts Icon objects (refer to *Chapter 2*), but we'll focus on string names for this chapter.

- sender_id: The name of the user sending from the chat interface, for a specific client. This value can change for each user's account.

- with_input: Defaults to True; if you set it to False, the element becomes a display-only element, without a sending element.

- on_action: Triggers the chat callback function when a user clicks on send; we describe the callback in the next paragraph. This visual element doesn't have other callback arguments.

- mode: Defaults to Markdown, which means the chat display will render Markdown syntax (most LLMs return Markdown text). We can also choose "raw", which displays the text as a chunk with no processing and no paragraphs, and "pre", which keeps extra spaces and newlines and returns the displayed text between HTML <pre> tags. The tgb.chat visual element has other "classic" arguments, such as active, properties (to add custom properties in a dictionary), class_name and id (to add the HTML identifiers), or hover_text.

In our chatbot, to trigger a chat callback, users can write a message and press *Enter* or click the send button. The chat callback has the following arguments:

- state: Like all other GUI callbacks, it's the state of the client's variables

- var_name: The name of the variable bound to messages

- payload: A dictionary with predefined arguments

Each message is stored as a tuple within a list called messages. The first element of each tuple is a string that represents the message's sequence number. This number can be generated by converting the current length of the messages list to a string, using f"{len(messages)}", ensuring it increments with each new message. The next two items in the tuple are user_message and user_id, which are in the payload argument, so we retrieve them and add them to the messages list:

```
chat_arguments = payload.get("args", [])
(_, _, user_message, sender_id) = chat_arguments[:4]
messages.append((f"{len(messages)}", user_message, sender_id))
```

Next, we can process the message using the respond function:

```
result_message = respond(state, user_message)
```

The `respond` function calls a `detect_and_redact_pii` function, which does simple text processing using a regex (for example, `"email": r"\b[\w.-]+@[\w.-]+\.\w+\b",`). Its goal is to identify PII data, and it returns a tuple with the following:

- A string with replaced data

- A Boolean that's true if it finds any PII in the string

- A dictionary with each PII type (email, phone, address, and name) count

After retrieving the data, the chatbot notifies (using the notify function) whether there is any PII in the user's message, and it returns a response:

```
def respond(state, message):
    pii_answer = detect_and_redact_pii(message)
    if pii_answer[1]:
        notify(state, "w", "Your message contains PIIs")
    response = f"""... {pii_answer[0]}""" # The answer message
    return response
```

If we go back to the chat function, we can update the `messages` function with the answer:

```
messages.append((f"{len(messages)}", result_message, users[1]))
```

> **Note**
>
> This example uses a simple function and isn't connected to an AI chatbot. You can already see how to use this element in less complex apps that don't require an LLM!

In this section, we used a simple function to explain the behavior of the chat visual element. While adding LLM APIs and chains of actions would increase the app's value, the way we interact with the visual element is the same; what will change is the function that returns the answer. Let's take a look at that!

Adding an LLM to our chat

We know how to add a chat element to our app and how to add messages and responses. Now we need to add an LLM to it. For this, we'll use Mistral AI's API and LangChain to orchestrate the LLM pipeline. The first step is to create an account and get an API key, and then create a Python function that's able to interact with Mistral AI.

To help with this process, we created a notebook, which can be accessed here: `/how_to_help/mistral_ai_langchain.ipynb`. The code for this application is in `/ai_wrapper`, and you can see how the app looks in *Figure 10.2*.

LangChain has several Python libraries, including `langchain_core` (LangChain's base abstractions) and dedicated model-specific APIs, such as `langchain_mistralai`.

The `ChatMistralAI` class serves as a connector to Mistral AI's APIs. It accepts several parameters, the most important being the model, which specifies which Mistral AI model to use (in our case, the free `mistral-small`), and the `mistral_api_key` value, which we need for authentication. In our example, we omit the API key argument because we've set `MISTRAL_API_KEY` as an environment variable. The chapter's `README` file describes how to set the environment variable to run the chatbot smoothly.

Under the main guard, we can create a `ChatMistralAI` object, called `chat_bot`, and we also initialize a `message_history` list. :

```
from langchain_core.messages import HumanMessage
from langchain_mistralai.chat_models import ChatMistralAI
...
if __name__ == "__main__":
    ...
    chat_name = "mistral-small"
    chat_bot = ChatMistralAI(model=chat_name)
    message_history = [] # Different from "messages"
```

To chat with the model, we create a function that updates the chat message history (on the LangChain side) and creates the response from the model. LangChain provides two abstractions, `HumanMessage` and `AIMessage`, that hold the message content, along with metadata about the conversation. To send the message to the model, we just need to use `chat.invoke(history)`, where the history has the `user` message last:

```
def talk_to_bot(input_message, history, chat):
    history.append(HumanMessage(content=input_message))
    response = chat.invoke(history)
    history.append(response)
    return response, history
```

The reason for this system is that each time we interact with an LLM, the LLM processes the whole conversation to provide an answer to the last question (they don't have "memory"; we force that by sending the entire conversation, each time). We now have a personal AI wrapper; this is great! Let's see how we can style the component before upgrading our app!

Styling the chat component

To style our chat element, we use CSS code. We added our code to /ai_wrapper/css/main.
css. We won't discuss all the styling choices (we advise looking at the CSS file, making some changes, trying your own styling, etc.), but we'd like to mention that the chat element has three classes you can use to style it:

- .taipy-chat: This is for the whole chat box. You can use it to add margins, padding, color, and so on to the whole element.
- .taipy-chat-sent: This styles the sender's (that is, the user's) box.
- .taipy-chat-received: This styles the answer box (the LLM bot in this case).

We can also style HTML tags that will render from the chat's Markdown outputs. For example, we may ask our LLM to produce some Python code; in that case, the LLM will probably surround that code around triple backticks (```), and Taipy's chat element will render it surrounded by HTML <pre> tags, so we can add specific styling to them.

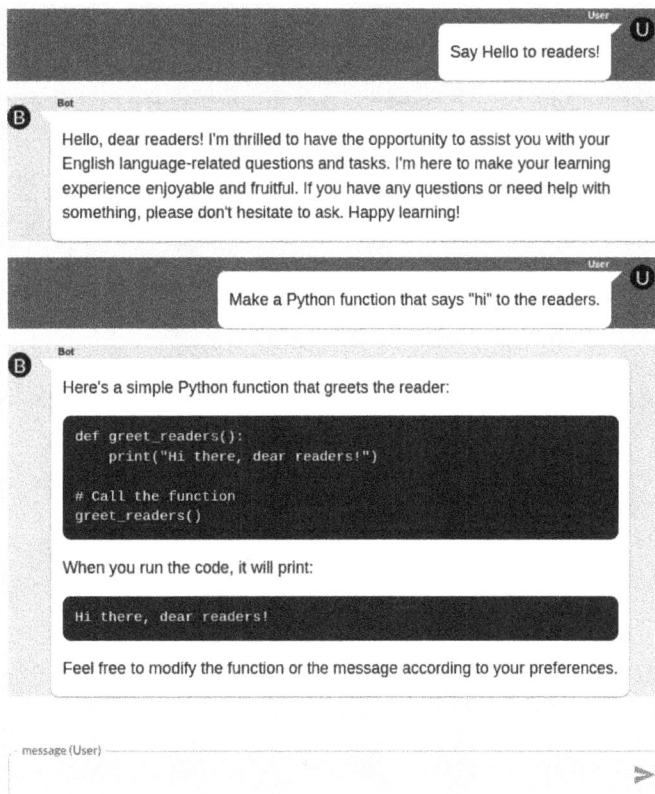

Figure 10.2: An LLM app with Taipy and some CSS styling

As you can see in *Figure 10.2*, we limited the chat's width, added margins to add some spacing to the element, and added distinct background colors for the sender and the bot. We also added some styling to the `<pre>` tag to showcase code outputs. Let's now add more elements to our chatbot!

Creating a chat UI

In this section, we'll cover ways to make a better UI for our chatbot, to enhance user experience, and to better interact with our LLMs. In this section, we'll incrementally build a small **TransiBot** app, an AI chatbot that will answer questions about transit data for New York City.

We created several folders named `/transibot_n` (replace n with 1, 2, 3, etc.), built step by step. Our app is still a single-page application, but the code is more abundant, so we split it into different files. The `/algorithms` directory holds the logic. To make a better-looking app, we enrich the CSS file, add a `stylekit` dictionary, and add a favicon. Now, let's make a better UI for our users!

Managing conversation flow

A limitation of our earlier app was that conversations couldn't restart without reloading the server. To fix this, we'll move the chat into a `Partial` element (see *Chapter 11*), which includes two switchable `Page` elements. We'll also ensure the bot receives a new question after answering the previous one. You can find the code in `/transibot_1`.

To create a `chat_partial` element, we need to declare it under the main guard as an empty page. We create an `update_chat_partial` callback to update it (we explain this in more detail after the code, but we essentially move the chat element there), and we add the partial block to a part element in our `chat_page` element. We also create a `chat_is_active` variable that defaults to `False` and will help us select the right `Page` element in our partial:

```
def update_chat_partial(state):
    ... # We explain this later

def on_init(state):
    update_chat_partial(state)

with tgb.Page() as chat_page:
    tgb.text("# **AI Transit Assistant**", mode="md")
    tgb.html("hr")
    tgb.part(partial="{chat_partial}",
             class_name="color-primary")

if __name__ == "__main__":
    ...
    chat_is_active = False
    chat_partial = gui.add_partial(page="")
```

`update_chat_partial` has two parts, with a conditional `if` statement:

- `if state.chat_is_active`: When the `chat_is_active` variable is `True`, the `Page` block has the chat visual element and calls the chat callback function, as it did in previous examples. We added two buttons, one that calls `change_chat_status` (makes the partial go to the other `Page`, described as follows) and a `clear_current_chat` button that erases the conversation.

- `else`: When the `on_init` function executes the callback, `chat_is_active` is `False`. This is a welcome page with a button that calls `change_chat_status` to go to the other partial's `Page`, the one with the chatbot.

Both conditions end with the partial update statement (`state.chat_partial.update_content()`) and create a different `Page` element. You can see them in *Figure 10.3*:

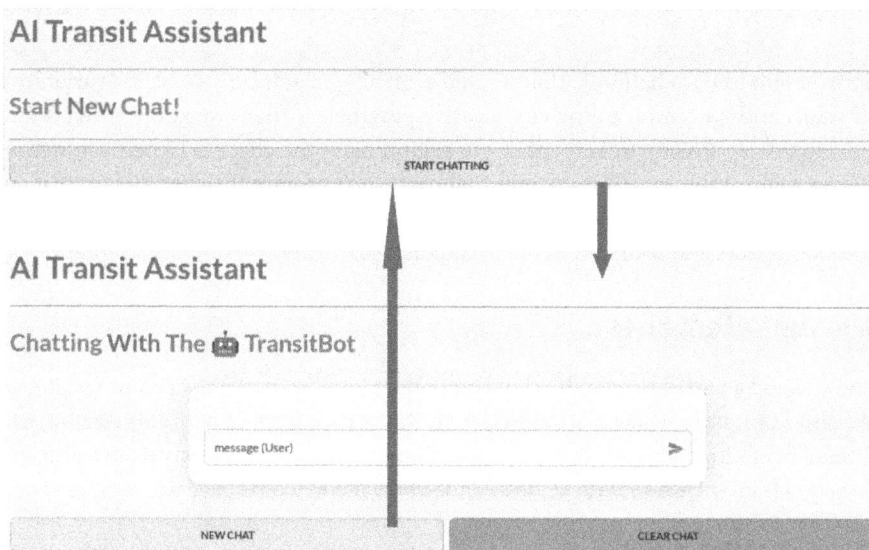

Figure 10.3: Chat's partial with buttons that change the Page element

You can see the two partial `Page` elements in *Figure 10.3*, with the buttons that allow navigation from one to another, and even delete the conversation. The `clear_current_chat` function reassigns the messages and the `message_history` list to an empty string (that is, the list for the visual element's conversation and the list for the LLM's conversation), and it also reloads the GUI (we can use `gui.reload()`, and we can get the GUI element with `state.get_gui()`):

```
def clear_current_chat(state):
    with state as s:
        s.messages = []
```

```
s.message_history = []
gui_to_reload = s.get_gui()
gui_to_reload.reload()
```

change_chat_status calls the clear_current_chat function if chat_is_active is True, then it reverses its value using not and calls the update_chat_partial function. This way, the conversation is "emptied" before going back to the welcome page, and changing the chat_is_active value before updating the partial changes the Page that will render:

```
def change_chat_status(state):
    with state as s:
        current_status = s.chat_is_active
        if current_status:
            clear_current_chat(s)
        s.chat_is_active = not current_status
```

Another improvement to our chatbot is that we add a chat_element_active variable, with a True initial value, and we bind it to the chat's active parameter. Then, we add a state.chat_element_active = False statement at the beginning of the chat callback function, and we make it True again at the end. This ensures that users can't prompt the chatbot before it answers the previous question (the API call can take a bit of time), so it prevents input mistakes. Now that our flow is a bit smoother, let's add some elements to interact and customize our chat element.

Chatbot visual elements

We just saw how to add a partial to split the chat component into two parts: a welcome section and the chat itself. We also saw how to delete a conversation to start a new, fresh one. In this section, we'll add some visual elements to interact with our chat model object and with our conversation history. The code for this section is in /transibot_2. You can see how the welcome page will look in *Figure 10.4*.

Changing the chatbot object

To create our chatbot object, we use LangChain's ChatMistralAI because we're using a model from Mistral AI, and we passed "mistral-small" for the model argument. If we check Mistral AI's API documentation, we see that there are other models (https://docs.mistral.ai/getting-started/models/models_overview/#premier-models), which come with different capabilities and different pricing (at the time of writing this book, they're all accessible from the free tier, with restrictive call limits). ChatMistralAI also has an optional temperature parameter that takes a value between 0 and 1, where 1 makes the model more "creative" and 0 makes it more "predictable" (it defaults to 0.7).

We could choose a different model and set a different temperature, or even better: let users choose it from a drop-down menu and a slider! The first step is to create the variables under the main guard. We'll use two models: the current `mistral-small` and `mistral-large`. We want to abstract this to end users, so we'll call our assistants "The TransitBot" and "The TransitBot PLUS." Here's how we start our values:

```
chat_name = "mistral-small"
temperature = 0.7
bot_name = "The 🚌 TransitBot"
users = ["User", bot_name]
messages = []
models = {
    "The 🚌 TransitBot": "mistral-small",
    "The 🚌 TransitBot 🐝 PLUS": "mistral-large-latest",
}
chat_bots = list(models.keys())
```

Once we have our values, we can add our visual elements to `inactive_chat_page`, since users will select these before starting the chat. For temperature, we can use a slider with values between 0 and 1 that increments by steps of 0.1 (refer to *Figure 10.4, label 2*). In the following code, note how we use `hover_text` and a `labels` dictionary with emojis to make this notion accessible to end users (who may not be familiar with the concept of the "temperature" of LLMs):

```
tgb.slider(
    value="{temperature}",
    min=0,
    max=1,
    step=0.1,
    on_change=change_model,
    labels={
        0.0: "🤓 ",
        1.0: "🤪",
    },
    hover_text="Higher Values make the assistant more creative",
)
```

To select the chat model, we can create a drop-down selector that shows users the name we gave to the bot, not the underlying chat model (refer to *Figure 10.4, label 3*):

```
tgb.selector(
    value="{bot_name}",
    lov="{chat_bots}",
    dropdown=True,
    on_change=change_model,
```

```
    label="Select your Assistant",
)
```

> **Note**
>
> This approach can be interesting if you have various fine-tuned models (https://www.
> packtpub.com/en-us/learning/how-to-tutorials/principles-for-
> fine-tuning-llms) customized for your specific tasks or with specific company knowledge.

Both visual elements call the same `change_model` callback, which interacts with the `ChatMistralAI` object:

```
def change_model(state):
    with state as s:
    model_name = models.get(s.bot_name)
    s.users = ["User", s.bot_name]
    new_bot = ChatMistralAI(
        model=model_name, temperature=s.temperature)
    s.chat_bot = new_bot
```

Now that users can customize the model a bit further, let's see how to customize prompts on our page!

Adding predefined prompts

The emergence of LLMs has created a discipline known as prompt engineering (https://www.
packtpub.com/en-us/learning/how-to-tutorials/prompt-engineering-for-
beginners), which refers to the set of techniques to create prompts that generate the best possible output from LLMs for a given task.

To make a better chatbot, we can add a system prompt, which is a special prompt we place before the chat history and specifies what the model does, what it doesn't, or what its general tone is. This technique is well known and easy to set, but it is also easy for users to bypass (although it's a good practice to set it). Another improvement we could make to our app is to add preset prompts to the welcome page, as well as an input prompt so users can start the conversation right away, instead of clicking a button to go to the chat.

The first step in this implementation is to create the prompts. In our current app, we store them as text files in the `transibot_2/prompts` directory, though a database table could also work. Prompts can rotate over time—either randomly from a pool or based on admin decisions. Predefined prompts offer several advantages:

- They improve the user experience by making it easier to ask common questions
- They can reduce costs if preset questions have preset answers, avoiding LLM queries

- They can promote products or services (e.g., "Tell me about your new product XYZ") or share general information, such as "How will NYC's marathon affect transportation tomorrow?"

Once we create our prompts, we make a function to read them. Notice how LangChain has a SystemMessage class, on top of HumanMessage and AIMessage:

```python
def read_prompt(file_name, type):
    with open(file_name, "r") as prompt:
        prompt_text = prompt.read()
    if type == "system":
        message = SystemMessage(prompt_text)
    elif type == "human":
        message = HumanMessage(prompt_text)
    return message
```

We can then use this function to initialize the bound variables and the messages list (with the system prompt), under the main guard:

```python
system_prompt = read_prompt(
    "./prompts/system_prompt.txt", type="system")
message_history = [system_prompt]
user_prompt_1 = read_prompt(
    "./prompts/user_prompt_1.txt", type="human")
...
user_prompt_first_input = ""
```

Once we have our bound variables, we add our preset questions to the UI. Since there isn't a visual element that's fit for this, we can combine a text element with the prompt and a button that triggers the change_status callback (we're making it evolve too). Here's the code (refer to *Figure 10.4, label 1*):

```python
with tgb.part() as questions_part:
    with tgb.layout("1 1 1"):
        with tgb.part(class_name="card-bg outer"):
            tgb.text(f"{user_prompt_1.content}", mode="md")
            tgb.button(
                label="Ask",
                on_action=change_chat_status,
                id="prompt_1",
                class_name=(
                    "fullwidth plain color-start stick-bottom"
                )
            )
    ...
```

Notice how each button has a distinct id for the callback, and how we added classes for special styling (check the CSS file!). We also add an input element, along with a button to trigger the same change_chat_status callback. Note that they both have the same ID as well (refer to *Figure 10.4, label 4*):

```
tgb.input(
    value="{user_prompt_first_input}",
    label="Ask your Question!",
    multiline=True,
    class_name="fullwidth",
    id="user_custom_message",
    on_action=change_chat_status
)
tgb.button(
    label="Ask",
    class_name="fullwidth plain color-start",
    id="user_custom_message",
    on_action=change_chat_status
)
```

The change_chat_status callback does the following:

- It checks the id value of the element that triggered it. If there's no id, then the callback comes from the chat interface to trigger a comeback to the welcome page.

- It creates a selected_prompt object to get the right prompt to pass to the ask_first_question callback (see the following code block). It calls a select_prompt function for this task.

- Notice how it returns if selected_prompt is an empty string and id isn't an empty string; this avoids the user sending empty prompts to the chatbot.

- Also, notice how it changes current_status before calling the ask_first_question function (it calls it only if there's an ID). This way, if the call is latent, we are at least in the chat interface.

Here's how the functions look:

```
def select_prompt(state, id):
    if id == "prompt_1":
        selected_prompt = state.user_prompt_1.content
    ...
    else: selected_prompt = None
    return selected_prompt

def change_chat_status(state, id, payload):
    selected_prompt = select_prompt(state, id)
```

```
if id != "" and selected_prompt == "":
    return

with state as s:
    current_status = s.chat_is_active
    if current_status:
        clear_current_chat(s)

    s.chat_is_active = not current_status
    update_chat_partial(s)
    if id != "":
        ask_first_question(s, selected_prompt)
    s.user_prompt_first_input = ("")
```

The `ask_first_question` function is a call to the chat function that simulates the `payload` dictionary that would come from the chat visual element:

```
def ask_first_question(state, selected_prompt):
    payload = {"args": ["", "", selected_prompt, state.users[0]]}
    chat(state, "", payload)
```

Figure 10.4 shows the welcome page, with suggested first questions, but also the option to start the conversation right away, as well as options to interact with the chat element!

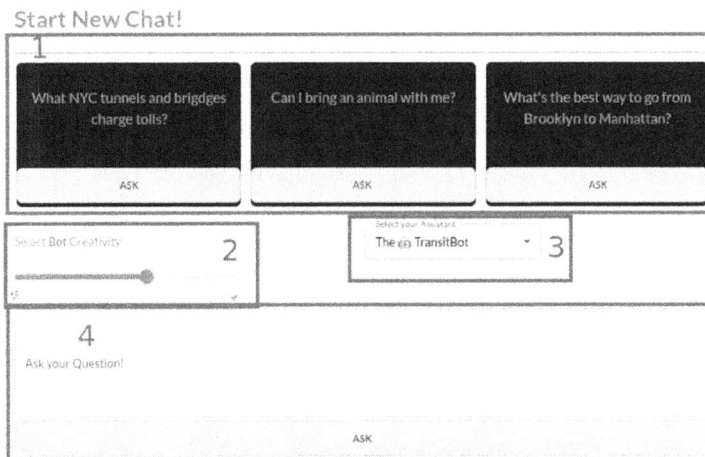

Figure 10.4: A welcome page with preset prompts (1), a slide element to select the model's temperature (2), a drop-down selector to choose the model (3), and a box to send a message (4)

Our current application offers improved usability, making it easier for users to interact with the chatbot, but all conversations disappear once the session ends, which isn't ideal. In the next section, we'll add long-term memory and conversation history to address this.

Adding memory to our chatbot

Our bot now has a flow that allows us to customize it with visual elements, start a conversation, end it, and start a new conversation again. In this section, we'll take our app further by making it record conversation history. The code for this part is in `./transibot_3`. Recording history has at least the following advantages:

- It allows you to restart a conversation after some time.

- You can use historical content for analytics (app analytics and conversation analytics; see *questions 3 and 4 of this chapter*!). You can use this to know what users ask frequently, monitor whether the chatbot is giving wrong or inappropriate answers, and also for legal compliance.

- You can store this history in vector databases to create a caching system (that's an advanced use we won't be covering here).

We will create a custom system that records all the conversations in an NDJSON file. This is how we create the file, and how the app uses it to keep the record and update the conversation:

- **Creating and saving conversation history**: When users start a new conversation, we create a `.ndjson` file. Note the following about this file:

  - It has a unique `name` that uses a unique identifier (with `uuid.uuid4().int`).

  - It uses the `sanitize_filename` function to create a proper filename from the first chat input.

  We chose the NDJSON format so we can build the file row by row, as the conversation increments.

  The first line in the NDJSON history file is metadata, with the `id` value, creation date, bot name, and temperature. To create this metadata, we use the `generate_history_metadata` function and the `HistoryMetadata` dataclass to store the metadata (you'll find both in `chat_algos.py`). We call the `generate_history_metadata` function from the `ask_first_question` callback.

- **Recording messages during conversation**: As more conversations take place, each message from the user (stored as the `HumanMessage` LangChain object) and each message from the LLM (stored as the `AiMessage` object) gets appended to the history file. We use the `save_history` function in `chat_algos.py`; we call this function once from the `ask_first_question` callback to store the system prompt (`SystemMessage`). Then, we call this function twice from `talk_to_bot`: once for the user message and once for the LLM answer.

- **Loading past conversations from a file**: We make a system to load the conversation from memory, with three functions that regenerate the history in the chat display but also load the history in the list for the LLM and select the users involved:

  - `load_history`: Reads an NDJSON file and re-creates the message history with LangChain objects.

  - `create_display_list`: This function generates the conversation list for the chat visual element. This gets the message contents from the `message_history` list, and it also needs the identifiers of the user and the bot, which it gets with the next function.

  - `get_users`: This gets the names of the user and the bot from the conversation metadata, as well as the temperature.

  We call the preceding three functions from the `change_history` callback; the `change_history` callback also calls the following:

  - `change_model` to ensure users chat with the same model and temperature as in previous chats

  - `update_chat_partial` if the user selects a new history from the welcome page (if they're already in the chat area, they don't need to change it!)

  - `Initializing history`: We load the history at application launch. We code an `init_history` function that returns all the `.ndjson` filenames in the history directory as a list. We append all the filenames to the `list_history` list, from `on_init`, like this:

    ```
    state.list_history = init_history("./history")
    ```

  The app creates the conversation at once and extends it progressively; if the user comes back to a previous conversation later on, they can continue chatting and extend the conversation.

- **Selecting previous conversation**: To select previous conversations, we create a selector with `list_history` inside a pane object:

  ```
  with tgb.pane(
      open="{open_pane}",
      on_close=lambda s: s.assign("open_pane", False)
  ):
      tgb.selector(
      value="{selected_history}",
      lov="{list_history}",
      mode="radio",
      on_change=change_history)
  ```

We also create an `open_pane boolean` variable to open the pane from a button:

```
tgb.button(
    "Show History",
    on_action=lambda s: s.assign("open_pane", True)
)
```

Figure 10.5 shows how the chat looks when we open the side pane, which users can open from the welcome page or from the current chat, to change the conversation. The pane displays a selector with radio buttons for single selection.

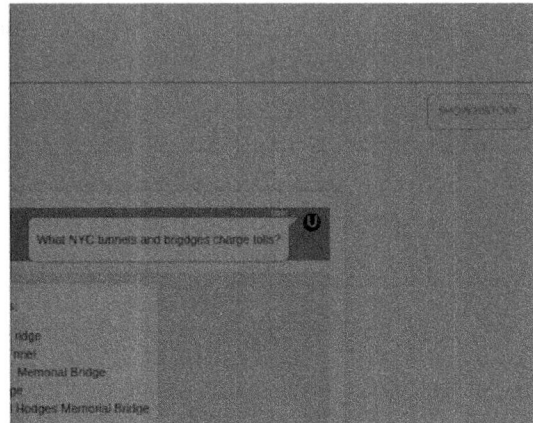

Figure 10.5: A side panel with the chat's history

> **Note**
>
> This technique could give some problems in a multi-user app, since all users would see each other's conversations. Adding the user's ID to the conversation metadata, or creating different user directories, and displaying the right user conversation accordingly could help with this situation!

This ends our chapter about creating chatbots with Taipy. Don't forget to check out the chapter's question, where you can see other ways to build your chatbot!

Summary

In this chapter, we explored how to build a chatbot using Taipy. We introduced the chat visual element, which stands out from other components in the library due to its unique structure and behavior. We connected it to an LLM, learned how to interact with the model, and learned about key parameters such as temperature that shape the responses. We also looked into how to maintain chat history and trigger prompts from other UI elements.

Rather than exploring advanced setups, such as using embeddings for RAG or fine-tuning models, we focused on showcasing how Taipy makes it easy to work with LLMs out of the box. Our goal was to show how to manage user input, handle model responses, and integrate these interactions within your app.

You can, of course, create more complex workflows involving chains, agents, and external tools, using the same Taipy UI components we covered in this chapter. It's also worth noting that you can use LLMs in Taipy even without a chat component, but that wouldn't technically be a chatbot!

This chapter ends our section on simple app tutorials. In the next chapter, we'll look at ways to build efficient Taipy applications.

Questions

1. Add a different model to the list of models—maybe a model from Google AI (give it whatever name you like, but keep the two bots from Mistral AI on the same page).

2. Add predefined answers to the prompts to save chat tokens. Add a toggle button to the welcome page that makes the bot talk like "a real New Yorker from Brooklyn" (by modifying the system prompt).

3. Using chat history, create a second page in your app that monitors the app's usage from the NDJSON files, such as counting input versus output tokens.

4. Create a pipeline with Taipy Scenario Management that reads an NDJSON file from the conversation, creates Data Nodes from the metadata, and summarizes the conversation using an LLM.

5. Create a small app that uses a model that can describe image content, such as Pixtral (look at the notebook in `answer_5/example_pixtral.ipynb` to see how to use it). The app lets users upload a picture from their computer or add an image URL.

Answers

1. You can find the answers to this question in `/answers/answer_1`. You'll find two notebooks:

   - `google_ai.ipynb`: A notebook with instructions on how to set up a Google AI account and get the API keys, which, at the time of writing this book, gives you a free tier.

   `ollama.ipynb`: A notebook to test local models with Ollama (`https://ollama.com/`).

   You can (should!) test other APIs (OpenAI, Anthropic, DeepSeek, etc.) and other ways to run local models (take a look at the Hugging Face community and libraries such as Transformers or llama.cpp).

Whatever option you choose, you can create a dedicated object with LangChain and assign it to the bound `model_name` variable (we also need to add a model alias name for the drop-down selector, then check and run the file!):

```python
def change_model(state):
    with state as s:
        model_name = models.get(s.bot_name)
        s.users = ["User", s.bot_name]

        #### ANSWER 1: Add this conditional statement
        if model_name in (
            "mistral-small", "mistral-large-latest"
        ):
            new_bot = ChatMistralAI(
                model=model_name,
                temperature=s.temperature
            )
        elif model_name in (
            "gemini-1.5-flash", "gemini-1.5-pro"
        ):
            new_bot = ChatGoogleGenerativeAI(
                model=model_name,
                temperature=s.temperature)
        elif model_name in ("smollm2:135m"):
            new_bot = ChatOllama(
            model=model_name,
            temperature=s.temperature)
```

2. The answer to this question is in /answers/answer_2. To add answers to the questions, we transform the text files into JSON files; this way, we can have the question and the answer in the same place. Then, we create a Python function to read the files and return both the question and the answer:

```python
def read_question_from_json(file_path):
    with open(file_path, "r", encoding="utf-8") as file:
        data = json.load(file)
        question = data.get("question")
        answer = data.get("answer")
        return {question: answer}
```

We start the variables like this:

```python
all_qa = {}
all_qa.update(read_question_from_json(
    "./prompts/user_prompt_1.json"))...
user_prompt_1, user_prompt_2, user_prompt_3 = all_qa.keys()
```

A key aspect of this method is to assign these questions to a special function that appends the predefined question and its answer to both the list of the chat element and the one of the chat memory:

```
def ask_and_answer_first_question(state,selected_prompt,):
    answer = all_qa.get(selected_prompt)
    with state as s:
        messages = s.messages
        message_history = s.message_history
        users = s.users
        sender_id = s.users[0]
    messages.append((
        f"{len(messages)}",
        selected_prompt, sender_id
    ))
    messages.append((
        f"{len(messages)}", answer, users[1]
    ))
    message_history.append(HumanMessage(selected_prompt))
    message_history.append(AIMessage(answer))
```

To change the system prompt to make the bot have a Brooklyn "accent," we create a separate file (`answers/answer_2/src/prompts/system_prompt_brooklyn.txt`). We also add a selector in the `Page` block to change the prompt with the following callback:

```
def change_system_prompt(state):
    with state as s:
        prompt_address = transibot_style_prompts.get(
            s.transibot_style)
        s.system_prompt = read_system_prompt(
            prompt_address)
        s.message_history = [s.system_prompt]
```

3. The proposed answer is in `/answers/answer_3`. We turned the page into a multi-page app. The proposed solution is in `src/pages/analytics.py`. We placed all the functions and the page in the same file to separate the answer from other elements of the app, but we could have separated the functional code from the Taipy page and callbacks. `parse_file_summary` reads an NDJSON file (from our conversation history, as created in the *Adding memory to our chatbot* section) and builds a dictionary with information from the first line that has conversation metadata (such as the bot's name, the set temperature, and the date the conversation started) and the last line, which has LangChain-style metadata from the last output of our chatbot, which gives us the total conversation tokens. We can then call this function from `load_history_to_dataframe`, a function that parses all the files in the history directory and returns a pandas DataFrame with the chat's information. Once you have the DataFrame,

you can make tables and charts as usual! You could also add more metadata to your file (to the first line, or using LangChain), which gives you options to handle your chatbot's observability!

4. The proposed answer is in `answers/answer_4`. You'll notice that the algorithms directory now has several files; we split them to avoid circular imports. We also created a two-page app, one page with the chat and one page with the Scenario Management app.

   The pipeline is in the configuration directory, and it's pretty standard; it's worth noticing that `summarize_task_config` has a `skippable=True` argument, which allows it to cache this task, which calls the (not free-to-use) LLM.

   The `scenario_functions.py` file handles functions that load NDJSON conversations, extract token usage and model metadata, build a summarization prompt, and invoke the LLM to generate a summary. These are the functions we use in the configuration pipeline.

   The `ask_for_summary` function uses a system prompt to tell the LLM to summarize the conversation; you can see it in `prompts/system_prompt_summary.txt`. It also appends the conversation as a LangChain `HumanMessage` and returns the model's response.

   It's also interesting to notice the `create_history_scenario.py` file, which creates a scenario and writes the input Data Node with the corresponding filename. This is later called from `init_history` (which creates all the scenarios when the application first loads—once!), and from the `ask_first_question` functions.

5. The proposed answer is in `answers/answer_5/src`. We use the functions from the example notebook, and we create two distinct callback functions, `submit_file` and `submit_url`, which both update a bound variable, `image_description`. The `Page` block uses an input and a button to trigger the callback for the URL, and a `file_selector` element to upload the image file. Notice how we set the `extensions` argument to `".png, .jpeg, .jpg"` to allow certain file formats. The answer is text-based, so we can display it with a text visual element.

Part 3:
Advanced Taipy: Building Efficient and Complex Apps

In this third and final part of the book, you'll explore advanced concepts that will help you build efficient, scalable, and production-ready applications with Taipy. You'll learn how to handle edge cases, optimize performance, and architect robust solutions for real-world scenarios. Topics include managing large datasets, inte-grating data on a scheduled basis or via real-time streams for IoT use cases, and extending your applications with extra Python libraries.

This part also introduces Taipy Enterprise and Taipy Designer—a no-code, drag-and-drop UI builder. To inspire your future projects, you'll find three interviews with real-world Taipy users sharing their experiences and use cases.

By the end of this part, you'll be equipped to build any kind of data application with Taipy, designed not only to function effectively but also to deliver real value to end users.

This part of the book includes the following chapters:

- *Chapter 11, Improving the Performance of Taipy Applications*
- *Chapter 12, Handling Large Data in Taipy Applications*
- *Chapter 13, Creating Real-Time Apps with Taipy*
- *Chapter 14, Embedding Iframes in Taipy Applications*
- *Chapter 15, Exploring Taipy Designer (Enterprise Version)*
- *Chapter 16, Who Uses Taipy?*

11

Improving the Performance of Taipy Applications

In the book's first part, we covered the basics of creating a Taipy application. Some apps may be slow and show non-reproducible errors on the run. In this chapter, we'll cover methods to improve your app's performance.

Your app's performance depends on several external factors. Slowdowns can occur when interacting with databases, APIs, or handling file operations due to network delays, processing time, or large data (see *Chapter 13*). Complex Python functions also affect speed, so optimizing algorithms can help. Hardware limitations are another factor; you may need more resources to increase your app's performance, or you may want to increase your app's performance by other means so you can reduce hardware costs (or you may not have access to more hardware resources).

You can improve your app's performance using some Taipy functions and parameters, and we'll go through the most important ones in this chapter. Performance is inherently challenging to measure with precision. The same process running several times in the same computer may take more or less time, depending on other processes running in that computer, and different computers (different hardware) handle applications differently.

In this chapter, we'll cover the following:

- Improving callback performance
- Using partials
- Improving the performance of Scenario Management

Technical requirements

You can find the complete code used in this chapter in the GitHub repository: `https://github.com/PacktPublishing/Getting-Started-with-Taipy/tree/main/chapter_11`.

This chapter uses mid/advanced Python concepts, such as threads and asynchronous programming, but it's not required to master these concepts to follow the chapter.

Improving callback performance

When users trigger callbacks, these callback functions take in a `state` parameter to access the bound variables. Each user connection generates a `State` instance that's unique, which enables support for multiple-user apps. Each time a user triggers a callback from a visual element, that is, from the browser (the frontend), it sends a message to the server where the Python functions will run (the backend), and the server sends the result back to the frontend. When a callback runs, the client waits for the server's response. Our goal is to reduce this time to make faster apps. A bigger issue arises if the response takes too long, as the communication between the client and server might time out.

Let's first take a closer look at the `State` class to see how we can use it more efficiently, and then we'll look at two ways to deal with functions (or tasks) that take too long to run.

Improving State usage

Taipy's `State` object is a Python context manager, which makes it accessible from a `with` block (`https://realpython.com/python-with-statement/`). A Python context manager typically defines two key methods:

- `__enter__`: Code to run when entering the `with` block
- `__exit__`: Code to run when exiting the `with` block, such as cleanup, batching, or committing updates

If you have a callback function that updates two or more bound variables at the same time, you can increase efficiency by using a `with` statement. The reason for this is that behind the scenes, Taipy performs some operations once for all elements inside the block, in bulk. If you don't use the `with` statement, those operations will happen once per assignment. Here is the basic syntax:

```
def callback_fuction(state):
    with state as s:
        s.var1 = value1
        s.var2 = value2
```

If you're skeptical and want to verify for yourself (as you always should!), check out the code in state/state.py. The application has two buttons that trigger two similar functions. They both calculate and assign random values to four bound variables 1,000 times and display the running time. The difference is that one function, callback_without_with, doesn't use the with block, and the other one, callback_with_with, does. Here is how the function looks:

```
def callback_with_with(state):
    time_test = datetime.datetime.now()
    for _ in range(1_000):
        with state as s:
            s.var1 = random.random()
            s.var2 = random.random()
            s.var3 = random.random()
            s.var4 = random.random()
    state.run_time_with_with = datetime.datetime.now() - time_test
```

If you run the app, you should see the two buttons; you can run one function and then the other, and verify these results (see *Figure 11.1*):

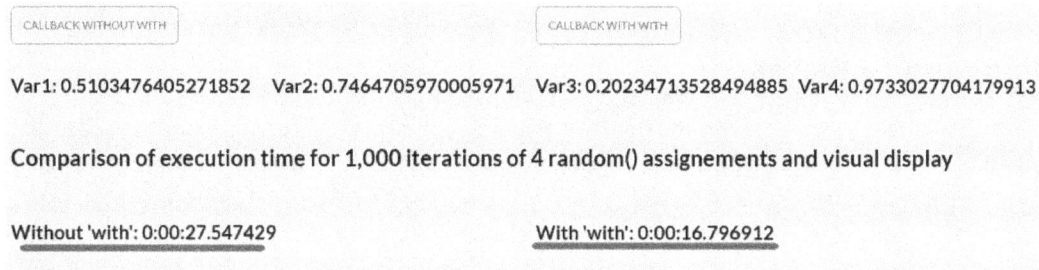

CALLBACK WITHOUT WITH   CALLBACK WITH WITH

Var1: 0.5103476405271852   Var2: 0.7464705970005971   Var3: 0.20234713528494885 Var4: 0.9733027704179913

Comparison of execution time for 1,000 iterations of 4 random() assignements and visual display

Without 'with': 0:00:27.547429   With 'with': 0:00:16.796912

Figure 11.1: Performance comparison, using the with statement to interact with State vs. not using it

Most applications will not have thousands of variable assignments in a callback; thus, the app just helps realize the difference between using versus not using the with block, intuitively. To explore this further, we coded an app that measures the average time of assigning 1 to 10 variables with or without the with block, in milliseconds. You can see the results in *Figure 11.2* and try to code it yourself in *Question 1* of this chapter!

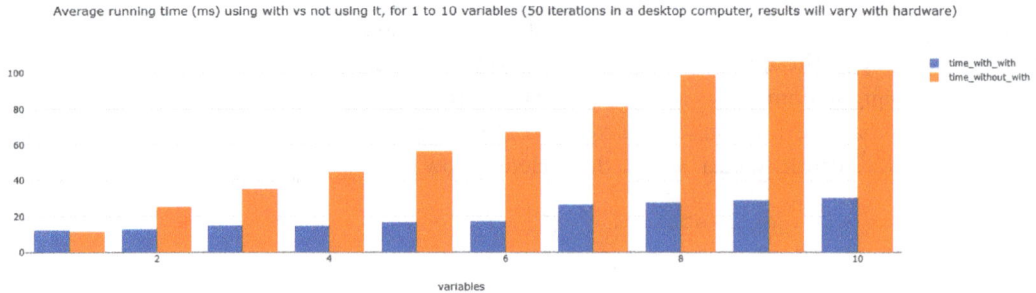

Figure 11.2: Average running time for assigning 1 to 10 bound variables using with vs. not using it

What you can see in *Figure 11.2* is that there is almost no difference between running the state in a with block when we have a single call (it even seems to underperform in that case). As the number of calls increases, the time spent seems to increase proportionally (we get a function that resembles $y = a.x$) without context management (this seems intuitive; each step needs to happen completely, each time). Without the with block, we also get a linear function, but in this case, we have a slope (something that looks like $y = a.x + b$), where the slope is the time spent on all the shared operations.

Using long callbacks

When callbacks take a long time and you don't know how to optimize them further, Taipy has a special function, invoke_long_callback(), that allows you to run these functions in a separate thread and let the application run without breaking.

> **Note**
>
> Taipy will introduce **async callbacks** (using asyncio), though this functionality is not yet officially documented. The method we explain here should, however, remain valid in future versions.

Some callbacks may take a long time to execute, either because they spend a long time waiting for an external response or because they do a complex task. Threads are program units that can run concurrently with other parts of your program (https://realpython.com/intro-to-python-threading/). This is a complex subject, but threads are usually best suited for I/O-bound tasks, where programs spend more time waiting for answers than CPU-intensive work.

The invoke_long_callback() function abstracts the complexity of setting threads manually (which we do in the next section, *Using threads*). It calls two callback functions: one that carries the long-running algorithms, and another that updates the status. Updating the status is optional but allows your app to return a value (or values) to the UI; updating the status also allows you to notify users of how the long task is running.

Here are the arguments for the function. The first three arguments involve the main callback action (the one we are creating a separate thread for), and the remaining three arguments update the status:

- `State`: The `State` argument is the same as other callback functions.

- `user_function`: The function we want to run. It's a callback function (we call it from another function), but it doesn't use a `State` object.

- `user_function_args` (optional): If `user_function` takes arguments, we pass them here as a list.

- `user_status_function` (optional): The function that keeps track of the long-running callback. We will see it in detail later in this section.

- `user_status_function_args` (optional): The arguments for `user_status_function`.

- `period` (optional; the default is 0): The number of milliseconds at which we call `user_status_function`.

Coding your first long callback

You can see a minimal long callback example in `long_callbacks/long_callback.py`. Of course, this minimal example wouldn't require a long-running callback, but it's useful to understand how to set the function's parameters.

The app has a bound variable, `initial_value`, which is 1 at first, and a button that triggers the `multiply_by_2` callback. The goal is to multiply `initial_value` by 2 incrementally, that is, each time the user clicks on the button, it doubles the value. Let's code the `multiply_by_2` callback using the `invoke_long_callback` function, which calls one function, `multiply`, which multiplies and returns the input value by 2. We also print the result, so you can see what happens when you run it. It would look like this:

```
def multiply(initial_value):
    time.sleep(10)  # this will force notification updates
    initial_value = initial_value * 2
    print(initial_value)
    return initial_value

def multiply_by_2(state):
    invoke_long_callback(state, multiply, [state.initial_value])
```

When you run the app with the preceding callback and you click on the button, you should see that the initial 1 value doubles and prints in the terminal, but the status isn't updated. The terminal prints the number 2 all the time, and the value in the UI remains the same. In the next section, we'll explain how to use the `status` function, so the long-running callback can interact with the GUI's state.

The long callback's status function

To update bound variables and interact with the `State` element, you need to define a `status` function, which takes these parameters:

- `State`: Unlike the main algorithm function, this function runs along the GUI (in the same thread) and can update the state.

- `status` (defaults to a Boolean): A special parameter that can be a Boolean value or an integer, but this is automatically set by Taipy. If it's a Boolean, then it indicates that the function ended in success (`True`) or failed (`False`); if it's an integer, it returns the number of elapsed periods since the application started to run. You can define the number of periods in the `invoke_long_callback` function.

- `Other arguments`: This function takes the returned variables from the first `callback` function as arguments.

Let's go back to our demo app and update it. We can check whether `status` is a Boolean, and then whether it's `True` before we update the bound variable:

```
def update_status(state, status, initial_value):
    if isinstance(status, bool):
        if status:
            state.initial_value = initial_value
... # and update the long callback function:
invoke_long_callback(
    state, multiply,
    [state.initial_value],
    update_status
)
```

We can use this Boolean value to display success or failure messages in the UI with `notify()`. We can also display periodic notifications if we set a period value in `invoke_long_callback` and treat the condition as an integer value for `status`. This is how we can change the `update_status` function; to test the following code, we also add `time.sleep(10)` to the `multiply` function, so we force some notification display. Notice how we can display the `status` value in the notification, and it increments at each notification:

```
def update_status(state, status, initial_value):
    if isinstance(status, bool):
        if status:
            # We learned this in the previous section,
            # let's use it!
            with state as s:
                s.initial_value = initial_value
```

```
                notify(s, "s", "the value has been updated!")
        else:
            notify(state, "e", "Oh no! the callback failed!!")
    else:  # if not bool then it's int
        notify(
            state, "i",
            f"The Long callback is still running... {status}"
        )
        ...
invoke_long_callback(
    state, multiply,
    [state.initial_value],
    update_status, [], 2000
)
```

Long-running callbacks may not always improve performance by themselves, but they help avoid communication timeouts. Also, they provide a tool to keep users updated when algorithms take a long time, which can help with how users perceive your app's performance. Let's now see how we can manually set threads in our apps!

Using threads

We can "manually" use Python threading (https://docs.python.org/3/library/threading.html), which can be useful for **input/output (I/O)** operations and for real-time data connections (see *Chapter 13* for more details). This approach gives you more flexibility, for example, if you want to run several threads from a single callback (look at *Question 3!*). Let's see how to use threading in our apps. You can see the code for this section in threads/thread.py.

We can rewrite our previous app to manually set threading. We also need to use the invoke_callback function, which is a special function and not intuitive to use. Here are its arguments:

- gui: The current GUI instance
- state_id: The state's identifier, returned by the get_state_id() function
- callback: The function it calls, which has to have State as the first parameter
- args (optional): Extra arguments for the callback
- module_context (optional): The name of the module where the page that holds the control that triggered the callback was declared

We'll code a similar application to the one from the previous section that multiplies a number by 2 but uses a thread instead of a long-running callback. We first need to import the necessary libraries, and the `multiply` function remains the same. The next step is to code a `multiply_thread()` function, which calls `multiply` and then uses `invoke_callback()` to update the value using `state` (and notify success):

```
def notify_thread_success(state, new_value):
    notify(state, "s", f"The Long Task is over")
    state.initial_value = new_value

def multiply_thread(state_id, initial_value):
    new_value = multiply(initial_value)
    invoke_callback(
        gui, state_id, notify_thread_success, [new_value])
```

Now, we can call the main `multiply_by_2` callback, which is triggered from the UI and runs `multiply_thread` in a thread:

```
def multiply_by_2(state):
    notify(state, "i", "You just triggered the callback")
    thread = Thread(
        target=multiply_thread,
        args=[get_state_id(state), state.initial_value]
    )
    thread.start()
```

Now, let's explore a technique to restrict user interaction, which is useful for long-running tasks.

Hold and resume control

Taipy's `gui` class has two functions that restrict the UI from user interaction: `hold_control()` (blocks user interaction and shows a pop-up window) and `resume_control()` (to restore UI interaction). You can use these functions strategically inside callbacks that take a long time, or even not-so-long ones, to prevent any user interaction before the call of `resume_control()`.

Note that `invoke_long_callback` allows you to deal with this kind of situation too, without blocking the app, so you can use the approach that makes more sense for your use case.

This pair of functions doesn't directly impact performance, but it helps deal with performance-related issues in at least two ways:

- By preventing users from executing more than one action at a (certain) time, we can save resources for heavy processes and avoid conflicts due to simultaneous callbacks running (by preventing double-clicking)

- It acts as a clear notification of "work in progress," which can help improve users' perception of your app's performance

The `hold_control()` function takes the following arguments, while `resume_control()` takes `state` as its only argument:

- `State`: A `state` object that's used by the callback calling `hold_control()`.

- `callback` (optional): A `callback` function. When it's defined, the information panel displayed during the app's holding displays a button to trigger it.

- `message` (optional): A message to display instead of the default one.

You can see a small example of these functions in `hold_and_resume/hold_and_resume.py`, and a screenshot in *Figure 11.3*.

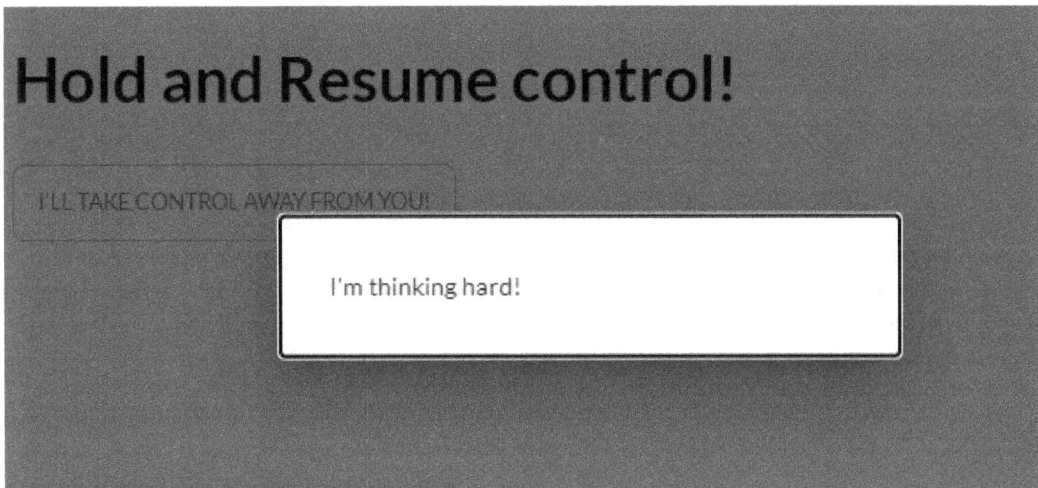

Figure 11.3: Application on hold

As you can see in *Figure 11.3*, holding the app's control disallows user interaction while notifying them of the state. In the next section, we'll discover a way to make your apps more modular: Partials!

Using Partials

Partials are components that you can use inside block elements (part, pane, and dialog) that run independently from the rest of the page. An intuitive way to think about them is as a page inside the page. Using Partials, we can have callbacks that update the content in the Partial and don't interact with the rest of the page. Partials are useful when you have content that's updated often and you can isolate it from the rest of the page, such as dynamic charts and tables, chatbots, or if you need to have repeated elements across your app.

Coding our first Partial

The code for this section is in `partials/first_partial.py`. We're going to code an app that has two variables, x and y. We'll display them in the UI, and we'll code a callback function that creates a Fibonacci-like update of x and y, like this:

```
def update_x(state):
    new_y = state.x
    new_x = state.y + state.x
    state.x = new_x
    state.y = new_y
```

Then, we'll create a `Page` element, which we'll use as a Partial. We can put any Taipy code in it, like for any other page. For example, we'll just put some text and include the bound variable, x, but not y (we'll add it later, from the Partial):

```
with tgb.Page() as a_partial:
    tgb.text("# I'm a text inside a Partial!", mode="md")
    tgb.text("#### x has a value of {x}", mode="md")
    tgb.text("#### I won't show y until it's more than 10!",
            mode="md")
```

Once we have our Partial, we create our "regular" `Page` element. In this case, we also stick to text, and bind the x variable and add a button to call the `update_x` function. We also add part block elements, with the `partial="{partial_variable}"` argument. The `partial_variable` variable is the Partial object itself.

First, we need to start our app, under the main guard, giving initial values to x and y, starting and running the GUI, and creating the `partial` bound variable, like this:

```
partial_variable = gui.add_partial(a_partial)
```

Next, we add the `partial` variable to the main `Page` element:

```
with tgb.Page() as main_page:
    tgb.text("# Hello from the main page!", mode="md")
    tgb.button("update x", on_action=update_x)
    tgb.part(partial="{partial_variable}") # First Partial here
    tgb.text("## This is also in the main page!", mode="md")
    tgb.text("#### x outside the partial has a value of {x}",
            mode="md")
    # reuse the partial:
    tgb.part(partial="{partial_variable}",
            class_name="color-primary")
    tgb.part(partial="{partial_variable}",
            class_name="color-secondary")
```

As you can see, `partial_variable` is the name of the bound variable that we use as an argument in the `Part` element. The `a_partial` variable is the `Page` element with the Partial's code. To create `partial_variable`, we need the `add_partial()` method from the `gui` object. We need to add the Partial in this way because it behaves as an independent `Page` element, even if it's embedded in other pages. This is similar to passing the `Page` element to the GUI with `Gui(page = page_name)`.

If you run your app, you should see your Partial code in several places. If you click on the button, the value of x should update everywhere, because it's used both in the main page and the Partial. But you can also update the Partial without updating the rest of the page, which we'll look at next!

Updating Partials

Let's code an `update_partial()` callback. This function is a normal callback that takes `state` as the first parameter (and all the other parameters from where it's triggered). Inside the function, we place the code to create a `Page` element (the Partial's page), and we end it using the `state.Partial.update_content` function, where `Partial` is the name of the Partial variable. This function takes `state` and the `Page` name as arguments. In our example, we add the bound variable, y (that we haven't added to the UI yet), to evidence the update, like this:

```
def update_partial(state):
    with tgb.Page() as a_partial:
        tgb.text("# I'm a text inside a Partial!", mode="md")
        tgb.text("#### x has a value of {x}", mode="md")
        tgb.text("#### y has a value of {y}", mode="md")
    state.partial_variable.update_content(state, a_partial)
```

This callback won't do anything if we don't call it from somewhere! For demonstration purposes, we'll add the call from the `update_x()` function, and we'll call it when y > 10, with this code:

```
if new_y > 10 :
    update_partial(state)
```

Now, the application should run the same as before until y goes over 10. At that point, your Partials should change and display the code in `update_partial()`.

To finish the presentation, it's important to know that you can initialize your Partials with the on_init(state) special function. You just need to call `update_partial` from it, but in that case, it will override the initial `a_partial` variable. You can use it like this:

```
def on_init(state):
    update_partial(state)
```

This should make your app render the Partial from the moment it loads. Now, let's discuss how Partials can help us improve our app's performance.

Partials and performance

The previous example illustrates how we can place Partials in different parts of the page, how we can update them, and how they are independent from the rest of the page. In a more realistic approach, you would probably not reuse the same partial inside the same page, although it may make sense in a multi-page application, and in that case, having a reusable block would be more efficient and more maintainable.

Putting your code in Partials can increase your app's efficiency by making your app more modular, only updating some parts (this requires some trial and error; see whether adding Partials to parts of your app makes it faster). Using Partials also allows different pieces of code to show in a block depending on certain factors (this, in fact, is what we did in our example), and that can be a terrific way to increase your app's performance by reducing the number of elements it displays at a time!

Improving the performance of Scenario Management

In the previous sections, we covered ways to improve our app's efficiency from the GUI side. In this section, we'll take a look at ways to improve speed and efficiency when working with Scenario Management pipelines. We'll start covering how to use events in Scenario Management, and we'll then see how to run them in parallel.

Event-driven architecture in Taipy

Taipy Scenario Management uses an event-driven model to track asynchronous changes in entities such as Scenarios, Data Nodes, Tasks, and jobs. You can see events as changes in the scenario flow, such as creations, updates, deletions, or submissions.

Since Taipy 4.1, the library incorporates an `EventProcessor` class that lets us declare the type of scenario events we want to track. Events trigger an event callback function; this function will be called every time a certain event happens in the Scenario Management side.

These event callbacks receive an `event` object as a parameter, with properties of the event that triggered it. We have two main event functions:

- `EventProcessor.on_event()`: Triggers a function inside the server, and does not propagate to the UI

- `EventProcessor.broadcast_on_event()`: This one triggers a callback with both an `event` object and a `state` object, which we can use to broadcast actions to all the UIs

On top of these generic functions, Taipy has specific processing functions for specific events. For example, `on_datanode_written` triggers an event callback when a Data Node is written, just like `broadcast_on_datanode_written`, but this one triggers an event callback with a `state` parameter. You can see more of these functions in the documentation (`https://docs.taipy.io/en/latest/refmans/reference/pkg_taipy/pkg_event/EventProcessor/`). To select the proper event, we can use a narrower function (such as `on_data_node_written`, which is more specific than `on_event`) or use a specific event attribute to filter them. Here are the two event attribute classes we can use:

- `EventOperation`: Describes the operation performed on a scenario entity (`https://docs.taipy.io/en/latest/refmans/reference/pkg_taipy/pkg_core/pkg_notification/EventOperation/`)

- `EventEntityType`: Describes the scenario entity type (`https://docs.taipy.io/en/latest/refmans/reference/pkg_taipy/pkg_core/pkg_notification/EventEntityType/`)

We can combine these elements to trigger callbacks at very specific moments, such as when a job is created, or when a cycle is deleted; we can also trigger functions to respond to less specific events, such as when anything happens in a scenario, or for every single event (for example, if we use `on_event` with no filter parameters). All these combinations are called a **topic**. We can register events for different topics.

We wrote a lot of theory; let's take a close look at event processing! We created a minimal example to showcase this concept; you can see it in `job_execution_mode/add_1_2.py`. The code in this "app" is straightforward. We have two functions, one that adds 1 to a number and another that adds 2. Both functions wait for 5 seconds before returning (we use `time.sleep(5)`). We added two scenarios to add and wait sequentially. *Figure 11.4* shows the pipeline.

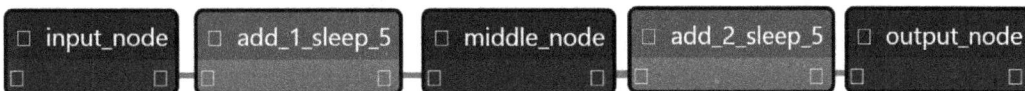

Figure 11.4: Adding and waiting sequentially

The GUI has two input buttons, where users can select a number between 0 and 10, and a button that triggers the submission of both scenarios, one after the other.

In this application (see *Figure 11.5*), we're going to add a notification when a middle node is completed, and we'll also update the application's visual element for the middle node. We'll add a different notification when the output node is updated, and update the visual element accordingly.

Adding numbers

SCENARIO	enter number	Add 1	Add 2
Scenario 1	Input number 1 — 1	2.0	4.0
Scenario 2	Input number 2 — 6	7.0	9.0

ADD NUMER FOR BOTH SCENARIOS

Added 2 successfully!   ×

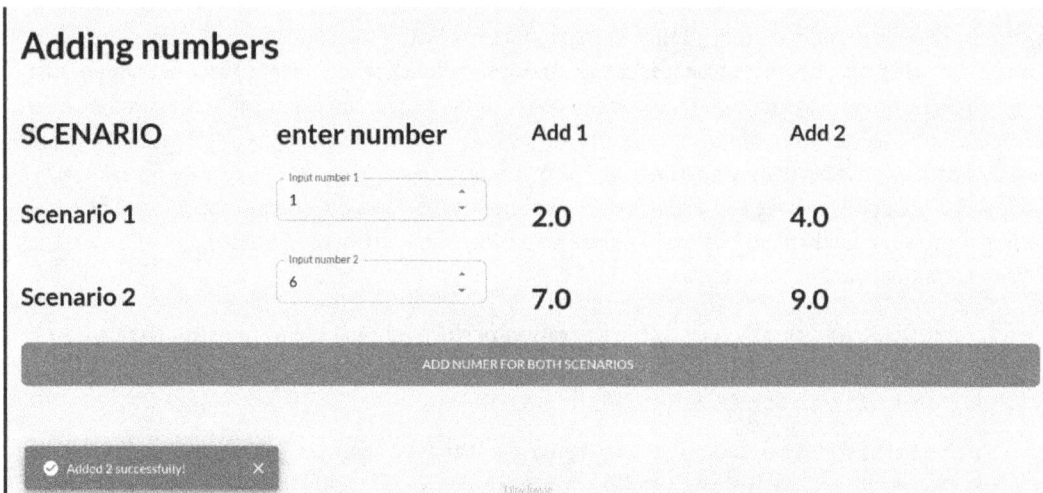

Figure 11.5: Application that adds 1 and then 2

We start importing EventProcessor and the event attribute classes. We can also start an event_ processor instance under the main guard. We can pass gui as an optional parameter (we need this to call broadcasting event processors). This is how we import and start event processing:

```
from taipy.event.event_processor import (
    EventEntityType, EventOperation, EventProcessor)
# after declaring the gui!!
event_processor = EventProcessor(gui)
```

After we create the event_processor instance, we can define some event processing functions. In our example, we register on_event and broadcast_on_datanode_written. Look how they both take a mandatory callback argument (we discuss them right after), and how we can narrow the scope with the operation and entity_type arguments:

```
event_processor.on_event(
    callback=track_output_data_node,
    operation=EventOperation.UPDATE,
    entity_type=EventEntityType.DATA_NODE,
    attribute_name="edit_in_progress",
)
event_processor.broadcast_on_datanode_written(
    callback=notify_add,
)
```

In the preceding example, all the Data Node updates (with `"edit in progress"`) will trigger the `track_output_data_node` event callback, and all the Data Node write-ins will trigger the `notify_add` event callback. Both callbacks are executed in the server, and they can interact with scenario elements. `notify_add` receives a `state` parameter and can interact with all the GUI states running.

After we register all our event processors, we need to start the service like this:

```
event_processor.start()
```

This is how we define the `track_output_data_node` event callback:

```
def track_output_data_node(event, gui):
    _print_event_properties(event)
    data_node = tp.get(event.entity_id)
    if data_node.config_id == "output_node":
        _read_data_node_and_print_stuff(data_node)
```

This event callback has an `event` parameter. It calls `_print_event_properties()`, so you can see some of its attributes. An important attribute is `entity_id`, because we can use it to select a scenario element (in this case, a Data Node) and interact with the scenario. In this case, we check whether `config_id` is `output_node`, since the event callback is called for each Data Node update, and then we perform a basic `print` operation.

We can imagine several use cases for this type of event:

- To interact with Scenario Management, such as trigger scenario submissions, update Data Node values, or add scenario tags
- Alert via email depending on a threshold
- Generate logs

Let's now take a look at the `notify_add` event callback. As you can see, the `state` parameter comes before the `event` parameter. The way you use `event` is exactly the same for all event callbacks. In this case, we use it to select the Data Node and the parent scenario:

```
def notify_add(state, event, gui):
    data_node_config_id = event.metadata.get("config_id")
    data_node = tp.get(event.entity_id)
    # get_parents return scenarios in a set,
    # we see next(iter()) to the value
    scenario = next(iter(data_node.get_parents().get("scenario")))
    with state as s:
        if data_node_config_id == "middle_node":
            if scenario.name == "scenario_1":
```

```
            s.middle_number_1 = scenario.middle_node.read()
        elif scenario.name == "scenario_2":
            s.middle_number_2 = scenario.middle_node.read()
    notify(s, "w", "Added 1 successfully!")
elif data_node_config_id == "output_node":
    if scenario.name == "scenario_1":
        s.output_number_1 = scenario.middle_node.read()
    elif scenario.name == "scenario_2":
        s.output_number_2 = scenario.middle_node.read()
    notify(s, "s", "Added 2 successfully!")
```

What's really different in the preceding callback is how we use `state` to update the UI and call the `notify` function. We update the numbers by reading in the selected Data Node, and we use different notification types depending on the Data Node configuration ID.

In this section, we saw how to use events generated by Taipy's Scenario Management pipelines to trigger precise callbacks depending on the specific event, once the event takes place. Let's now see how to run the Scenario Management pipeline asynchronously, to increase our app's efficiency!

Changing job execution mode

Taipy's Orchestrator's configuration also has settings to increase your app's efficiency. You can set your application with two different running modes: `development` and `standalone`. By default, all scenario configurations are in `development` mode. In `development` mode, all the tasks within a scenario and all the scenarios get executed sequentially, one after the other. In standalone mode, the application runs in an asynchronous way. When you set `standalone` mode, you can also choose the maximum number of workers that will run in parallel.

The default `development` mode owes its name to the fact that it's easier to understand and debug an execution flow when it runs sequentially. There may also be reasons to run your app synchronously, such as if it runs in an environment with limited resources or with lots of other processes and apps, and you don't want your app to drain the server. Your app may also do simple calculations, and it may just not be worth it to increase its efficiency with asynchronous programs.

If your app does heavy operations and you're not (very) limited by resources, setting `standalone` mode could help with your app's efficiency. Taking advantage of this mode also requires you to think about how you architect your application. For example, if you want to compare two scenarios, you could create a callback that triggers two scenario submissions at once, so they can run in parallel. If you wait for users to launch one and then the other one with two button clicks, you won't be exploiting asynchronous capabilities. Let's now see how to configure execution mode!

Configuring job execution mode

You can configure execution mode with one line of code. You just need to add the following line at the beginning of your configuration section (in your `config.py` file, or wherever you create your scenario configuration objects):

```
Config.configure_job_executions(
    mode="standalone", max_nb_of_workers=2)
```

Here, `configure_job_executions` takes two arguments:

- `mode`: The default is `development`, and the other option is `standalone`.
- `max_nb_of_workers`: The default is 2. If you add more workers, your app takes more resources but also runs more tasks concurrently.

Since the default is `development` mode and there is no reason to add workers to this (because it works sequentially), you don't need to add this line if you don't set `standalone` mode. When setting the number of workers, keep in mind that the "sweet spot" exists. Increasing them beyond a certain point can lead to diminishing performance. Let's now compare both execution modes!

Running several scenarios in parallel

In this section, we'll discover how to run scenarios in parallel. For our first example, let's come back to the previous example, with our app that adds 1 and then 2 (`job_execution_mode/add_1_2.py`).

The app has an input Data Node with a value of 1, an intermediate Data Node, an output Data Node, and two tasks that point to the adding functions, to build a sequential pipeline, as shown in *Figure 11.4*. The application runs two scenarios of the `on_init()` special callback.

In the code, we added a commented line with the `Config.configure_job_executions()` function. Run it and see what happens. Then, uncomment the line and run the app again. You'll see that when you uncomment the line, both scenarios run at the same time, the numbers in the UI are updated in parallel, and therefore, the callback that launches both scenarios takes about half the time!

Running tasks in parallel

In the preceding example, we run two "linear" scenarios in parallel, but we could also have single scenarios with tasks that can run asynchronously. For this example (see the code in `job_execution_mode/generate_random_image.py`), we code a small app that creates 3 NumPy 2D arrays of random integer numbers between 0 and 255 (using `numpy.random.randint`), and then it takes those 3 arrays to create one single 3D array using `numpy.stack....` In other words, we're creating an RGB image with random color pixels! *Figure 11.6* shows a representation of the tasks. As you can see, this scenario really looks like it could use some parallel processing!

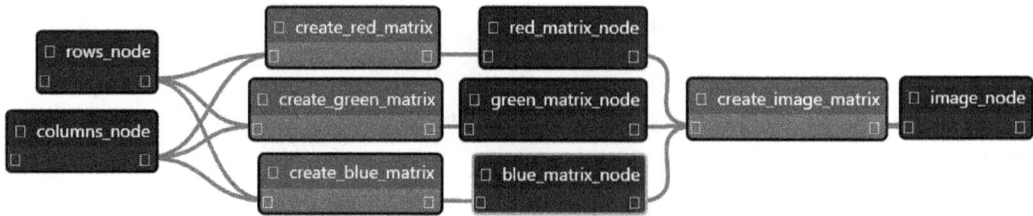

Figure 11.6: Parallel tasks

We add some `time.sleep(5)` statements in the `generate_random_matrix` function, as well as some prints to help understand what's going on. We code a minimal page with a button that triggers a callback that submits the scenario, and a `chart` element that displays an image as a `plotly.express.imshow()` figure. We also code a function to generate it and call it from the callback.

Before running the app in `standalone` mode, we test it using `developer` mode: this creates the red, green, and blue matrices one after the other (taking the extra 5 seconds each), then creates the image matrix.

Now, we can test our app using `standalone` mode. Since there are three parallel tasks, let's add `max_nb_of_workers=3`, as it seems reasonable. Let's launch the app, click the button, and... Boom! There is an error! If you wait a little and press the button again, an image may show in the `chart` element... But what's going on? We didn't use event consumers (see the previous *Event-driven architecture in Taipy* section).

To make the asynchronous jobs work properly, we need to create events. In this class, the `notify_color_matrix` function reads the output `scenario_image` Data Node before creating the Plotly image figure. Here is the function:

```
def notify_color_matrix(state, id_name):
    color = id_name.split("_")[1]   # example id_name:
                                     # "create_blue_matrix"
    if color == "image":
        notify(state, "s", f"Created Image!")
        image_matrix = scenario_image.image_node.read()
        state.image = create_imshow_fig_rgb(image_matrix)
    else:  # red, green, blue
        notify(state, "i", f"Created {color} matrix!")
```

We call this function from an `event` callback, like this:

```
def process_event(state, event):
    if (
        event.operation == EventOperation.UPDATE
        and event.entity_type == EventEntityType.JOB
```

```
            and event.attribute_value == Status.COMPLETED
    ):
        print(event)
        id_name = event.metadata.get("task_config_id")
        notify_color_matrix(state, id_name)
```

The preceding function is triggered from the event processor. We add it under the main guard using a broadcasting event processor:

```
 event_processor.broadcast_on_event(callback=process_event)
```

In this section, we discovered how to run your scenarios in standalone mode, which can greatly improve your app's performance if your server is running tasks that can run in parallel and that are computationally intensive, since standalone mode leverages multiprocessing.

Summary

In this chapter, we covered techniques to help you make faster applications. You already knew how to create complete applications; you should now have the elements to polish them. Throughout the chapter, we showed how to manage your GUI's performance in several ways: by leveraging state context management to increase your app's speed, by using threads to deal with long running callbacks, by learning how to hold your app's control from users, and by using Partials to have less crowded apps and less elements to load in the browser at once. We also covered how to use Scenario Management's events and how to exploit parallelism with standalone mode to increase your app's performance.

In this chapter, we also saw that performance is highly context-dependent; it depends on your specific use case, algorithms, data, infrastructure, and the user experience you are looking for. It requires trial and error, testing, and measuring, but you now know various techniques to address these issues. And of course, don't forget to check Taipy's documentation, as there might be more ways to create even more efficient applications!

In the next chapter, we'll cover how Taipy apps can handle large data, which will address performance challenges such as file I/O operations, handling large data volumes, and displaying large amounts of data.

Questions

1. Create a Taipy application that runs 50 iterations assigning random values to *n* different variables (from 1 to 10 variables), twice: once using a `with` block and once without. The result will be used to generate a bar chart that compares the running time in milliseconds using `with` vs. not using it (we want a result similar to *Figure 11.2* in this chapter). The running times may differ depending on your hardware. It would be interesting for you to look at how different the numbers are! Tip: you can inspire yourself from the `/state/state.py` app.

2. Create an application that lets users select a mathematical operation (addition, multiplication, subtraction, or division) and select an integer between 0 and 10. The app performs the selected operation between the selected value and a result value that has an initial value of 1; it also waits for `input_factor` number of seconds before returning (use `time.sleep(input_factor)`). Use a long callback, and notify success and error (such as a 0 division error), as well as waiting time (try to do something original with the `status` value).

3. (Difficult) Code an application that returns the text from several URLs using requests when the user presses a button (bind all the text from all the URLs in a single bound `str` variable). Create two distinct callbacks: one that uses one thread per URL and one that uses classic callbacks, and measure how long each takes. What do you notice?

4. Create an app with a single block element displaying a partial (you can add other stuff outside the `partial` block, such as a title). The application will have three different `Page` elements for the `partial` block, and users can navigate from one to the next one (or the previous one) using buttons. The first partial updates two bound variables, a and b, and the second partial displays, in a table, the result for x = a.x + b, in two columns, x and y (you can use `numpy.linspace` and about 100 values). The third partial displays the DataFrame as a scatter plot.

5. Develop an app that lets users enter a certain amount (of money) and 2 different interest rates (between 0 and 30) and creates a DataFrame with the compound interest values for both rates for the same amount of investment. Consider the case of an initial invested amount of money, without periodic investments over time (you can get that with `amount * (1 + interest_rate) ** year`, where `year` goes from 1 to 30). Use scenarios to run the calculations and `standalone` mode with two workers. Let users display data in a table or a comparative chart, using a partial. Use `hold_control()` and `resume_control()` in your callback.

Answers

1. We coded an app that does this in /answers/answer1.py. The important part here is how we loop three times to calculate these numbers.

    First, we launch the calculation for each amount of simulated variables, from 1 to 10 (for number_of_variables in range(1, 11)).

    For each number of variables, we loop 50 times to later calculate an average.

    The third loop assigns values (in range(number_of_variables)). It happens inside the with statement in the example that uses it.

    It's also important to notice that we multiply seconds by 1,000 to convert to milliseconds and that we divide the execution times by the number of iterations (50) to calculate an average:

    ```
    time_with_with = time_with_with.total_seconds() * 1_000
    ...
    df_performance_builder["time_with_with"] = (
        df_performance_builder["time_with_with"] / 50
    )
    ```

2. You can find an answer in exercises/answer_2.py. We use a drop-down selector for the type of operation, and a number selector for the factor. We also display the target value with a text element. The algorithm function used by invoke_long_callback has three arguments, and we pass them all in the list. The update_status function has a conditional execution to update the result value (0 if the operation returns a negative value, and the result otherwise), and it returns an error message if it fails. When the algorithm runs, it notifies that the work is in progress and prints a joke from a list of 10 terrible jokes, using status as an index.

3. A possible answer to this question is in exercises/answer_3.py. In this application, users can select a list of websites from the UI. We use a function to request URLs and return their HTML content as text (fetch_url), which is called by the "normal" callback (scrape_websites_no_threads) in a loop, and by the callback using threads (scrape_websites_threads), which starts the threads in a loop as well. Both callbacks update a bound variable that displays the time for the function execution. You should see that using threads, the returned time values should be lower (20 to 50% lower – in our example, we didn't retrieve data from slow websites, in that case, the difference should be higher).

4. You can find an answer in exercises/answer_4.py. We did the page navigation by creating a partial_page variable that starts at 1 (for the first page) and gets a value of 1, 2 from 3 callbacks (go_to_page_1...) that call another callback that updates the partial from a conditional branch. The DataFrame comes from a function called create_linear_df.

5. You can find an answer in `exercises/answer_5.py`. Notice how we also used the `with` statement to update `State` when possible. The `generate_results` function updates the Partial based on a Boolean bound variable, `display_chart`; users can change its value from a toggle button, and the function is called from the toggle button change, or when users run the scenario comparison.

Join our community on Discord

Join our community's Discord space for discussions with the authors and other readers:

`https://packt.link/taipybook`

12
Handling Large Data in Taipy Applications

The term **big data** gained prominence in the 2010s as companies collected data that was too large for traditional methods. It's defined by the **3 Vs**: **volume** (large amounts), **velocity** (high-speed generation), and **variety** (diverse formats such as images and videos). Not all three Vs must be present for a problem to be considered big data; for example, other scenarios include large-scale sensor networks generating continuous streams of uniform readings, clickstream analysis from millions of web users, or scientific simulations producing petabytes of homogeneous results. High-frequency trading involves massive, fast-processed structured data but lacks variety. These challenges led to specialized solutions such as NoSQL databases (e.g., MongoDB) and parallel computing frameworks such as Hadoop and Spark.

This chapter explores how applications handle large data, which is a relative term. For instance, in one case, plotting 100,000 points can overwhelm a chart, but it isn't too large for pandas. In other cases, large data may refer to DataFrames exceeding even pandas' capacity, benefiting from lazy evaluation tools such as Polars or DuckDB, which aren't traditional big data tools. Large data can also relate to the *volume* "V" of big data or files and data structures too large to process efficiently. Not all large data is big data, and big data is not just about large data.

In this chapter, we'll explore how you can adapt your Taipy applications to deal with different large data problems with a focus on large volumes of tabular data.

In this chapter, we will cover the following topics:

- Connecting to large data with Taipy
- Caching with Taipy
- Processing large data with Taipy
- Displaying large data in Taipy applications

Technical requirements

You can find the complete code used in this chapter on the GitHub repository: `https://github.com/PacktPublishing/Getting-Started-with-Taipy/tree/main/chapter_12` In this chapter, we'll use Amazon S3 storage to store Parquet files. We won't cover how to set it up, but we made sure that you can follow most of the chapter even if you don't do that part. We also use Spark, Dask, Polars, and DuckDB.

The data for our application comes from this page: `https://www.nyc.gov/site/tlc/about/tlc-trip-record-data.page`. We'll use 2023 data. We'll discuss how to retrieve it in the *Connecting to large data with Taipy* section. You can find the documentation here: `https://www.nyc.gov/assets/tlc/downloads/pdf/data_dictionary_trip_records_yellow.pdf`.

We created a README file with information to help you set up Spark and an Amazon S3 bucket. You can find it in the GitHub repo, in `/how_to_help`.

Connecting to large data with Taipy

In this section, we focus on tools and techniques that help us handle large tabular data with our Taipy applications. We'll start looking at the I/O of our applications and how to use file formats for large tabular data. We'll also see ways to use Taipy with technologies that handle large data, such as Apache Spark or Dask. We'll also cover some specific Taipy functions that let us visualize large data efficiently.

Big volumes of data are challenging to deal with, at least at the following four levels:

- They take up a lot of space to store
- They take up a lot of space in memory
- They take a lot of resources to process
- They are hard to visualize in charts (dots can overlay in scatter plots)

For a more hands-on understanding, we'll develop a small Taipy application that analyzes NYC's yellow taxi trip data. We'll be looking at factors that influence tipping (see link in *Technical requirements*). Let's start with a discussion about the file and filesystems we can use for our app.

Choosing the right storage

Choosing the storage format for your data is an important decision when you create your application, and it becomes crucial when you deal with large volumes of data.

Before we dive into ways to handle large data, we'd like to remind you that you can leverage external tools to process your data before passing it to your application. While we won't explore this in depth, classic examples include the following:

- Using your enterprise database to preprocess data before importing it to your application

- Offloading heavy calculations to external servers

- Leveraging any kind of external service using an API

Sometimes, the best approach is to avoid processing large data directly within your application (see *Chapter 7*).

Sometimes we have to deal with large data in our app, so here are some important things to consider with tabular data sources:

- **Avoid Excel files**: They're slow, prone to formatting errors, and files are larger.

- **CSVs are human-readable but impractical**: They are hard to open for large datasets, and they don't hold metadata about data types. Use Parquet files (a columnar storage format optimized for fast queries and compact storage) for efficiency:

  - They are 2x to 10x smaller than CSVs and have faster read/write speeds, especially when retrieving a few columns out of many (due to the column indexing, vs. CSV's row-based index, which needs to read all the rows completely, no matter how many columns you need)

  - They retain data types and don't require reprocessing

  - They integrate well with big data tools (Spark, Hadoop, etc.)

- **Databases are better for real-time updates**: Use them if you need live data. You can export them to Parquet periodically to reduce database load (batch processing). They also log changes and allow data versioning.

- **Check legal/compliance rules**: Storing files (e.g., Parquet/CSV) with personal data may violate policies or laws. In this case, you could use secure services such as Amazon S3 or opt for database connections.

In our example, the NYC yellow taxi dataset uses Parquet files, which are perfect for analyzing big batches of data. Let's now see how to add them to our app!

Adding Parquet Data Nodes

To create our application, we can start downloading the 12 Parquet files with 2023 data from the NYC trip record data. We want to get the files called `Yellow Taxi Trip Records` (refer to *Figure 12.1*).

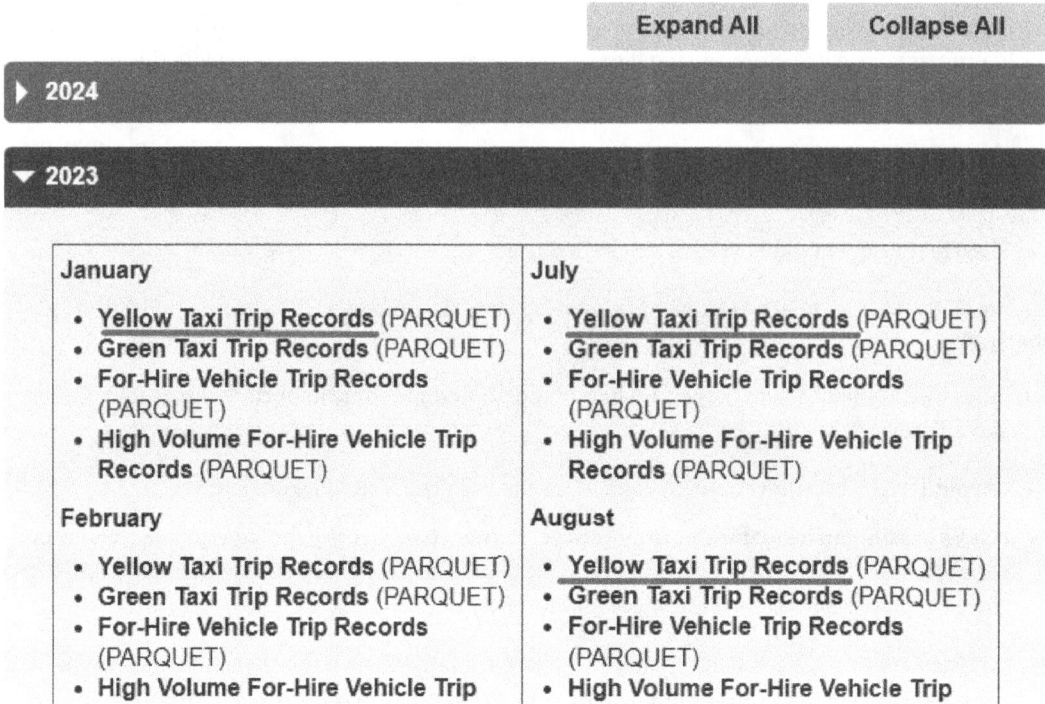

Figure 12.1: Data sources to download

Before we add our source data to our final application, let's code a simple app that reads these files from Data Nodes. You can see the code in `/reading_data/main.py`. For this application to work, you need to add the Parquet files to `/reading_data/data/raw_data`.

We start by creating a set of 12 GLOBAL Data Node configuration objects, like this (refer to *Chapter 3*):

```
month_1_node_config = Config.configure_parquet_data_node(
    id="month_1",
    scope=Scope.GLOBAL,
    default_path = "./data/raw_data/yellow_tripdata_2023-01.parquet"
)
```

Under the `main` guard, we create a `month_data` dictionary to reference all the Data Nodes, and we set initial values for our mini-app:

```
if __name__=="__main__":
    selected_month = 1
    month_data={
        1 : tp.create_global_data_node(month_1_node_config),
        ...
```

```
    }
    def select_node(selected_month):
        selected_month_node = month_data.get(selected_month)
        return selected_month_node
    selected_month_node = select_node(selected_month)
```

On the application's Page, we can add a `data_node` object and a selector with a lambda function to get the right month, like this:

```
tgb.selector(
    value="{selected_month}",
    lov = list(range(1, 13)),
    on_change=lambda state: state.assign(
        "selected_month_node",
        select_node(int(state.selected_month))
    ),
    dropdown=True
)
```

Figure 12.2 shows how our application looks. It displays a Data Node with around three million rows.

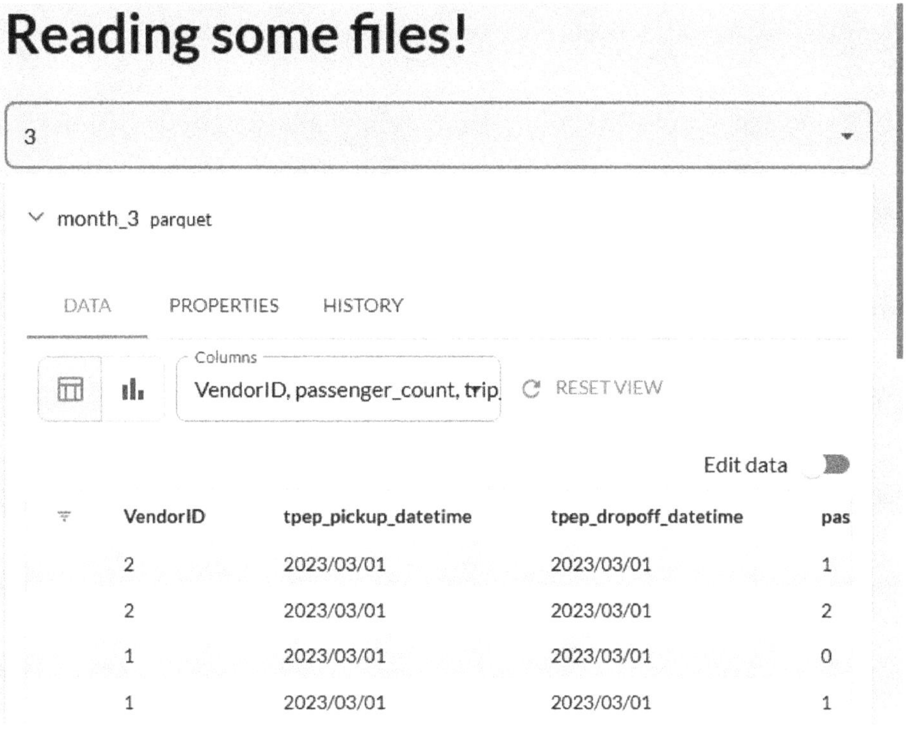

Figure 12.2: A Parquet global Data Node

Figure 12.2 shows a selector to select a month, and the Data Node visual element below; if you launch it, you'll see how each month has around three million lines. This dataset is *kind of big*, both for the human analyst (would you go through a table that has three million rows?) and for the client (tables this big can render, but they make the application slow). Before we deal with these issues, let's see how we can open files from Amazon S3 storage!

Using Amazon S3 buckets

In this section, we'll read files from an Amazon S3 bucket. In our case, we named the bucket `taipy-nyc-tlc-trip-data`. If you know how to create an Amazon S3 bucket, you can retrieve all the TLC yellow taxi files from 2023 and add them there. If you're unfamiliar with this, we created a step-by-step guide to help you set it all up. You can find it in `/how_to_help`.

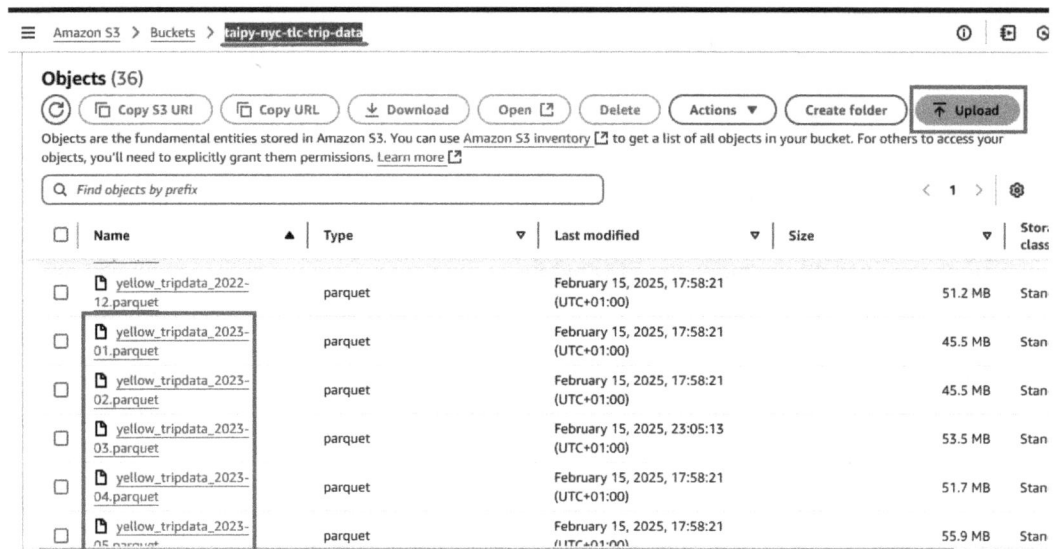

Figure 12.3: An Amazon S3 bucket with Parquet files in it

We added code to retrieve the S3 data with Data Nodes in `/reading_data/main.py`. We commented the code in the file; you can uncomment (and comment the Parquet Data Nodes) to test them. This is how we can set our Data Node configuration objects:

```
aws_access_key_id= os.environ.get("AWS_ACCESS_KEY_ID")
aws_secret_access_key = os.environ.get("AWS_SECRET_ACCESS_KEY")
region_name=''us-east-1''

month_1_node_config = Config.configure_s3_object_data_node(
    id="month_1",
```

```
        aws_access_key=aws_access_key_id,
        aws_secret_access_key=aws_secret_access_key,
        aws_region = region_name,
        aws_s3_bucket_name="taipy-nyc-tlc-trip-data",
        aws_s3_object_key="yellow_tripdata_2023-01.parquet",
        scope=Scope.GLOBAL,
)
```

In this case, the Data Nodes point to S3 objects that contain the Parquet files. S3 buckets retrieve the data as binaries, so if we wanted to replace our previous Parquet Data Nodes with these, we would have to convert the binary data to a pandas DataFrame using `BytesIO` and also change the selector's lambda function. Here is how to create a DataFrame with `BytesIO`:

```
from io import BytesIO
import pandas as pd
...

parquet_file = BytesIO(selected_month_node.read())
df_month = pd.read_parquet(parquet_file)
```

If you try the code, you'll notice that it's extremely slow! This is because we're retrieving all the data from the bucket each time! On top of this, we have all the problems linked to the dataset size on the client side (we're creating a huge table). Before we see how to deal with these problems, let's also put them in perspective:

- If we had used CSV files, our application would be even slower

- Retrieving data from S3 buckets takes time, but it's a secure environment (important when working with enterprise data), and it's faster than downloading the Parquet files from the website

We've seen how to use S3 and Parquet Data Nodes for large files, and we've seen that there are some challenges to solve. Let's see how we can deal with them.

Caching with Taipy

One downside of Taipy Data Nodes and Taipy visual components is that they rely on pandas DataFrames (and other non-DataFrame structures), which can lead to performance problems with large data. We could imagine a system where we read the S3 files as an S3 Data Node and use a task to store them as a Parquet Data Node, but we'd be creating pandas DataFrames all along. An alternative could be to use generic Data Nodes with different types of structure, such as a Polars LazyFrame, which doesn't load all the data in memory (we ask this in *Question 1*!). That still requires reading the stream at some point, so we're going to create a downloader instead.

> **Note**
>
> Taipy Enterprise edition offers the option to use Polars as an alternative to pandas.

The code for this section is in `caching_data/main.py`. The goal is to create a function that retrieves the data from the S3 bucket and stores it locally (in `data/raw_data`), and to do this, we'll implement two forms of caching. **Caching** allows us to sidestep repetitive, heavy tasks, ensuring applications run faster by reusing what exists.

> **Note**
>
> One of the goals of this chapter is to test different ways to work with large files. Downloading large files from a website, uploading them to an S3 bucket, and then downloading them to use them locally isn't a great workflow! If you take a look at the `/how_to_help` section in the chapter's repo, you'll find instructions to retrieve the files to your Amazon S3 bucket without downloading them locally. As for the files from the S3 bucket, you can use Spark (or Dask or other frameworks) to read directly from the bucket, without downloading them directly (which is fine in some cases). We created an alternative app in `/ analyze_data_direct_ read_version`. You can take a look at it to see how to work solely with an S3 bucket, without local downloads.

In our application, we create a `read_s3` function with no inputs that returns the current date and downloads the files. We also create a scenario with one task and one Data Node (`check_download_ data_node`). For now, the application just shows a table with the data read from the Parquet files directly. A selector calls the `update_month` function, which triggers `download_scenario` each time, to check whether we have all the data before loading it.

For demonstration, we use two types of caching. You would typically choose one:

- **File caching**: Our `read_s3` function loops through all 12 months to get the S3 files. As a previous step, it creates a download path. We just check whether the file already exists, and skip this download:

    ```python
    if local_path.exists():
        print(f"File already exists, skipping: {local_path}")
        continue  # Skip to the next file
    ```

- **Skippable tasks**: Taipy has a setting to cache tasks for a certain period. To do this, we need to set the `skippable` parameter to `True` in the task configuration object, and we also need to add the `validity_period` value as a `timedelta` class. This way, the task will run once and never again for the validity period:

    ```python
    current_date_data_node = Config.configure_data_node(
        id="current_date",
        validity_period=dt.timedelta(days=1) # Set this for caching
    ```

```
)
download_task = Config.configure_task(
    ...
    skippable=True,
)
```

Our file caching implementation resembles an **incremental pipeline** (or **delta pipeline**). One of its key advantages is resilience: if a previous execution encountered an issue and only partially downloaded the files, the pipeline can resume from where it left off. This approach supports batch processing, allowing for the integration of new files as they arrive in batches.

On the other hand, skippable tasks are closer to "real" caching. They are practical if we know that our file's content evolves. They're also adapted to any kind of task; they don't require checking files with physical addresses to work.

> **Note**
>
> You can leverage caching to make faster applications, but you can also use it during development to avoid repeating tasks you're not focusing on at the moment.

We can now access our raw data, but we want to process it to clean it and create some extra features. Let's see how Taipy can interact with tools to process large amounts of data!

Processing large data with Taipy

Now, we'll explore how to process large datasets using two popular parallel computing tools: Spark and Dask. Both enable efficient data processing through parallel execution. This section will demonstrate how to integrate these tools into your applications to optimize performance, and hopefully, we'll show that you can adapt your applications to any tool or library to process your data efficiently.

Processing data with Spark

Our data is raw and it has mistakes, so we need to clean it. We also need to adapt our data and create some new synthetic features for our analytic needs or data science tasks.

Spark is beneficial in this example because it enables efficient distributed processing of large-scale datasets (such as NYC TLC's millions of taxi trips) by leveraging parallel computation across multiple cores or nodes. Spark optimizes memory usage, handles out-of-core computations to avoid crashes with massive data, and automates task scheduling for operations such as filtering, feature engineering, and aggregations. In this example, our data is not *that* big, but Spark is a tool that can scale to compute terabytes of data while maintaining performance.

The code for this section is in the `/data_processing` directory and is an extension of `caching_data`. To use Spark to process our raw data, we create a new directory, `/data_processing/data/processed`, and two different Python files:

- `/algorithms/spark_process_nyc_tlc.py`: This has the Spark application. We explain this in the *Spark application* section.
- `/algorithms/process_nyc_tlc.py`: This has the `run_spark_processing` function that triggers the Spark application and which we reference in the scenario (we explain it in the *Calling the Spark application from a subprocess* section).

Let's see how we create a Spark application to process our data.

Spark application

Our Spark application (`/algorithms/spark_process_nyc_tlc.py`) cleans and transforms the raw NYC TLC trip data to focus on understanding tipping behavior for credit card payments. The application has four functions:

- `read_nyc_tlc_df`: Reads a Parquet file into a PySpark DataFrame (there is no pandas intermediate DataFrame)
- `process_nyc_tlc_df`: Holds the functional logic; it does all the transformations, using three helper functions:

  - `_wrangle_nyc_tlc`: Casts pickup and drop-off time as a timestamp and fills NaN values with zeros for airport fees and congestion surcharge
  - `_filter_rows`:

    - **Filters credit card payments**: Keeps trips paid with credit cards (`payment_type = 1`) since cash payments do not record tips
    - **Removes invalid transactions**: Drops trips where `total_amount = $0` to avoid corrupted or refunded transactions, and trips where the pickup data is not in 2023

  - `_create_features`:
    - Removes negative `airport_fee` and `congestion_surcharge` values (reimbursements)
    - Converts `airport_fee` to a binary feature (1 if charged, 0 otherwise)
    - Replaces missing fee values (NaN) with 0 (we assume there was no fee here)
    - **Trip duration**: Calculates trip time in minutes
    - **Trip speed**: Derived average speed (miles per hour)
    - **Time features**: Adds `hour_of_day`, `is_weekend`, `is_peak_hour`, and `is_night` to analyze temporal trends

- `process_month`: Processes a single month of data and does the following:

  - Constructs the file path for the input Parquet file using the provided `dataset_name`, `year`, and `month` values

  - Reads the data using `read_nyc_tlc_df`

  - Applies transformations using `process_nyc_tlc_df`

  - Saves the processed data to the specified `output_folder`

- `process_all_data`: Orchestrates the processing of all 12 months of data by calling `process_month` for each month and collecting the results

If you go through the Spark code, here are the important functions we used, and what they do:

- `filter`: This filters rows based on conditions

- `col`: This selects a column for transformations (such as filtering)

- `withColumn`: This adds or replaces a column in the DataFrame (to create new features or to cast columns)

- `cast`: This changes the column's data type

- `fillna`: This replaces null values with a specified value, like in pandas

- `when`: This uses a condition to create new values

- `unix_timestamp`: This converts a timestamp to Unix time (number of seconds since epoch)

- `hour/year`: These extract the hour and year from a timestamp, respectively

- `dayofweek`: This extracts the day of the week (1 = Sunday, 7 = Saturday)

The file is then transformed into a CLI application, using `argparse`. The reason for this is that we must start and end the Spark session properly. By using the CLI, the Spark session is created at execution. If we imported the script as a Python module, the Spark session might persist if it's not closed explicitly, leading to resource leaks or conflicts.

To create the app, we create a `SparkSession` object, indicating the application name as `"NYC TLC Processing"` and configuring Spark to use `400` shuffle partitions and a default parallelism of 8, which optimizes how data is distributed and processed. We then set the session time zone to UTC to ensure consistent handling of timestamps across all data operations:

```
if __name__ == "__main__":
    # Initialize Spark session when run as script
    spark = (
        SparkSession.builder.appName("NYC TLC Processing")
        .config("spark.sql.shuffle.partitions", "400")
```

```
        .config("spark.default.parallelism", "8")
        .getOrCreate()
    )
    spark.conf.set("spark.sql.session.timeZone", "UTC")
```

Since we created a CLI app, we need to create a Python function to launch it. You can find it in `run_spark_processing`. Notice how we added a `check_download` argument, which is a trick to ensure that the linked Taipy Task takes the output Data Node of the previous task: We do this because we're not persisting the processed files as Data Nodes for now (to avoid having to read them with pandas, since they're kind of big). We also add plenty of optional arguments, so we can configure it with ease.

> **Note**
>
> You can leverage the subprocess built-in library to run any CLI tool from your Taipy applications!

Inserting the Spark process in a Scenario

Since we don't persist our processed files as Data Nodes, we can create a new task that references the `run_spark_processing` function and create an output Data Node to have an input for the next function and use caching, like this:

```
check_spark_data_node = Config.configure_data_node(
    id="cache_spark",
    validity_period=dt.timedelta(days=1) # Set this for caching
)
pre_process_task = Config.configure_task(
    "pre_process",
    function = run_spark_processing,
    skippable=True,
    input= check_download_data_node,
    output = check_spark_data_node)
```

This section was intense! Now, let's process our clean and preprocessed data to create some analytical variables. We could also use Spark for this, but since we want to show different tools, we'll use Dask for the next task!

Using Dask to handle large data

Our data is preprocessed, so we can now process it! Our application will create aggregated statistics for the complete year 2023. We'll use Dask to do all this. You can find the code for our application in `/analyze_data`. We keep all the previous code, but we rename the scenario to `analyze_scenario` and we remove the selector. The application will submit the scenario at execution, and it will generate all the data for our application.

> **Important**
>
> The application in `/analyze_data` extends the previous examples and uses Spark for preprocessing. The goal of this app is demonstrative; in a real project, you'd stick to one solution. In case you weren't able (or didn't want to) run the Spark application, we created an alternative app in `/analyze_data_dask_version`. This way, you'll be able to follow the example of this section. Take a look at it if you used Spark too!

Dask is a great library for processing medium to large datasets. Here are some key features:

- **Lazy evaluation**: Dask optimizes the computation graph before executing

- **Parallel processing**: It handles large datasets efficiently across cores

- **Memory efficiency**: It just computes the necessary aggregations

To process our data, we use `analyze_tipping_patterns check_preprocess`, which should be `True` if the preprocessing from the Spark application was successful (refer to the previous section). This variable comes from a Data Node that stores a Boolean value returned by the `run_spark_processing` function.

Our function uses Dask to process all the data from the 12 months as a single Dask DataFrame. Since Dask uses lazy evaluation, it knows how to process it efficiently, and the data from all 12 months is not loaded in memory at once (nor when it's created). We use a helper function to retrieve all the Parquet files (we select the subset of columns we need for the analysis, and discard the rest):

```python
def _concat_dask_year(address, columns):
    entries = [
        os.path.join(address, d) for d in os.listdir(address)
    ]
    parquet_paths = [
        f for f in entries
        if f.endswith(".parquet") or os.path.isdir(f)
    ]

    if not parquet_paths:
        raise FileNotFoundError(
            f"No parquet files or directories found in {address}"
        )
    return dd.concat([
        dd.read_parquet(p, columns=columns)
        for p in parquet_paths
    ])
```

Dask is a framework that allows lazy evaluation, which means that we can define all our transformation steps and run them at once, all together! We create a dedicated task (we call it `analyze`), we add it to the scenario, and we also create all the output Data Nodes. We cache the process, like for the other tasks. *Figure 12.3* shows the pipeline. We create a `tasks` dictionary with the computations we want to carry out. We start creating the functions to count the tips, and to calculate the sum and the average:

```
tasks = {
    "avg_tip": ddf_year["tip_amount"].mean(),
    "total_trips": ddf_year.shape[0],
    "no_tip_count": ddf_year[ddf_year["tip_amount"] == 0].shape[0],
    "total_tips": ddf_year["tip_amount"].sum(),
}
```

After defining the basic metrics, we extend the `tasks` dictionary with grouped aggregations that will allow us to analyze tipping behavior by specific categories, such as weekend versus weekday, day versus night, each hour of the day, and trips starting from the airport. For this, we call the `_calculate_group_stats` helper, which takes the Dask DataFrame, the column to group by, and an optional mapping to rename the group values into more meaningful labels:

```
aggregations = {
    "df_weekend": ("is_weekend", {0: "Weekday", 1: "Weekend"}),
    "df_night": ("is_night", {0: "Day", 1: "Night"}),
    "df_hour": ("hour_of_day", None),
    "df_from_airport": ("airport_fee_binary", {0: "No", 1: "Yes"}),
}
for key, (col, mapping) in aggregations.items():
    tasks[key] = _calculate_group_stats(ddf_year, col, mapping)
```

We also prepare a filtered subset containing only trips with a tip between 20 and 100 dollars, keeping only the tip amount and the pickup datetime. This subset is stored in the `tasks` dictionary as well, so it is computed along with the other results:

```
tip_and_pickup_ddf = ddf_year[
    ["tip_amount", "tpep_pickup_datetime"]
].loc[
    (ddf_year["tip_amount"] >= 20)
    & (ddf_year["tip_amount"] < 100)
]
tasks["tip_and_pickup"] = tip_and_pickup_ddf
```

Once all the tasks are defined, we execute them in a single `dd.compute(*tasks.values())` call. This triggers Dask to run all the pending transformations in an optimized way, minimizing the number of passes over the data. The results are then zipped back into a dictionary using the same keys from the `tasks` definition.

After computing the metrics, we calculate the percentage of trips without tips, and for the filtered subset, we replace the `pickup_datetime` column with an integer timestamp for more efficient storage and easier plotting. Grouped results are reset to have a flat index.

Finally, the function returns a tuple containing the total tip amount, the average tip, the percentage of no-tip trips, the grouped results, and the filtered subset. This design ensures that all computations are done lazily until the very end, allowing Dask to optimize execution across the entire pipeline.

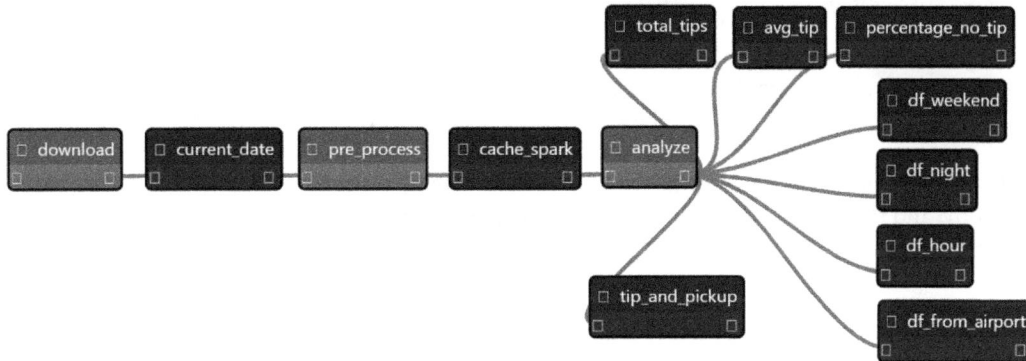

Figure 12.4: Download and processing pipeline

As you can see in *Figure 12.4*, `analyze` is a single Task with lots of outputs; all these outputs are calculated at once, efficiently, using Dask, thanks to its lazy evaluation and multiprocessing.

For the GUI part, we add some cards and some basic charts. In this case, once the processing is over, the application is not heavy because we removed the big tables with all the data in them. The code for the GUI is nothing we haven't seen yet. *Figure 12.5* shows how the application looks (the GUI is not this section's focus).

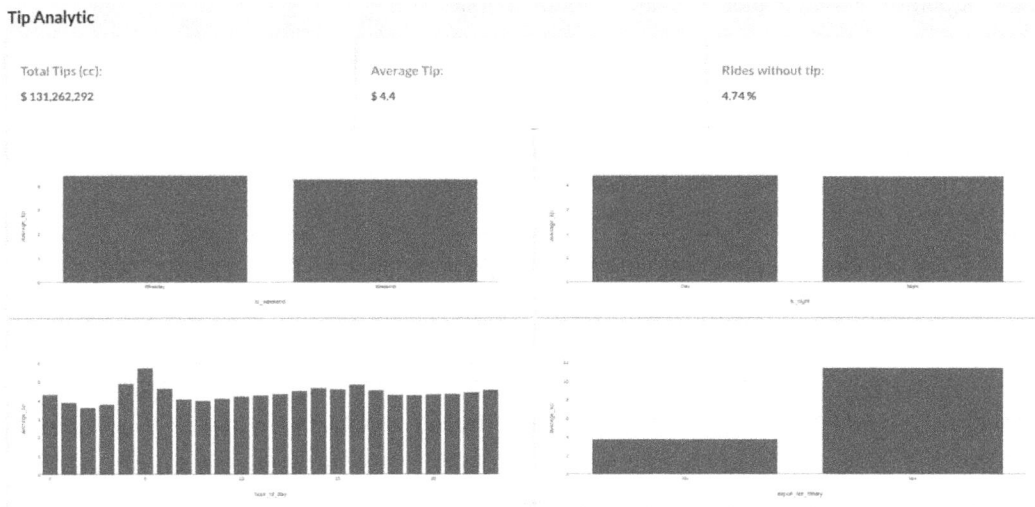

Figure 12.5: Tip analytics for 2023

Our application also returns a pandas DataFrame called `tip_and_pickup`, containing over 200K rows. This is the computed result of the Dask subset we defined earlier (with `tip_amount` between 20 and 100, and the pickup `datetime`).:

```
tip_and_pickup = tip_and_pickup.loc[
    (tip_and_pickup["tip_amount"] >= 20)
    & (tip_and_pickup["tip_amount"] < 100)
]
```

The DataFrame is huge for plotting; it would require too many resources to compute such a chart using Plotly, and there would be so many data points that we wouldn't see anything relevant. In the next section, we'll see how Taipy helps us plot this type of big DataFrame!

Displaying large data in Taipy applications

Plotting large amounts of tabular data in a scatter plot is a mess, for the following reasons:

- The resulting object is heavy, so it takes a lot of bandwidth to send to the frontend, where it also consumes lots of user resources in the client computer, making the application slow

- Charts with too many points are hard (or impossible) to read

Taipy offers three **decimator** functions; decimators process the DataFrame, using a downsampling algorithm to reduce the number of points to plot while preserving the visual shape. All three functions come from `taipy.gui.data.decimator`, and they all take an `n_out` parameter, which is the number of points we want to plot. The functions are as follows:

- `MinMaxDecimator`: This divides a dimension into `n_out` number of segments, and for each segment, it keeps the min and max values. It's the fastest one, but the least precise.

- `LTTB`: **Largest Triangle Three Buckets** (**LTTB**) is an algorithm used in cartography that selects key points based on the largest triangular area. It's about 10 times slower than the `MinMax` algorithm, but gives better visual results.

- `RDP`: The **Ramer-Douglas-Peucker** (**RDP**) algorithm simplifies a curve by removing points while preserving its shape, using a threshold-based approach to keep key points. It's way more compute-intensive, but it's the algorithm that shows the best results.

The `tip_and_pickup` DataFrame has over 200K lines, with tips of $20 or more and under $100. Including all tips (over 30 million rows) would likely crash the application, as these algorithms are computationally intensive—they help solve data problems but aren't a magical solution!

To use a decimator, we start an object using the function and pass a **number of points (NOP)** to the n_out variable (see main.py). In the following code, we show how to create the three functions. The initialization process is the same for all decimators:

```
NOP = 5000
min_max_decimator = MinMaxDecimator(n_out=NOP)
# rdp_decimator = RDP(n_out=NOP)
# lttb_decimator = LTTB(n_out=NOP)
```

Then we just need to pass the decimator object name (as a string) to the decimator argument, like this:

```
tgb.chart("{tip_and_pickup}",
    ...
    decimator=rdp_decimator)
```

Figure 12.6 shows how the chart looks: going from over 200,000 points to 500 points makes the chart visible. An important aspect of decimator algorithms is that they allow for resampling. Try to zoom in on the chart, and you'll see that it will show 500 points (if they exist) in the zoomed area as well!

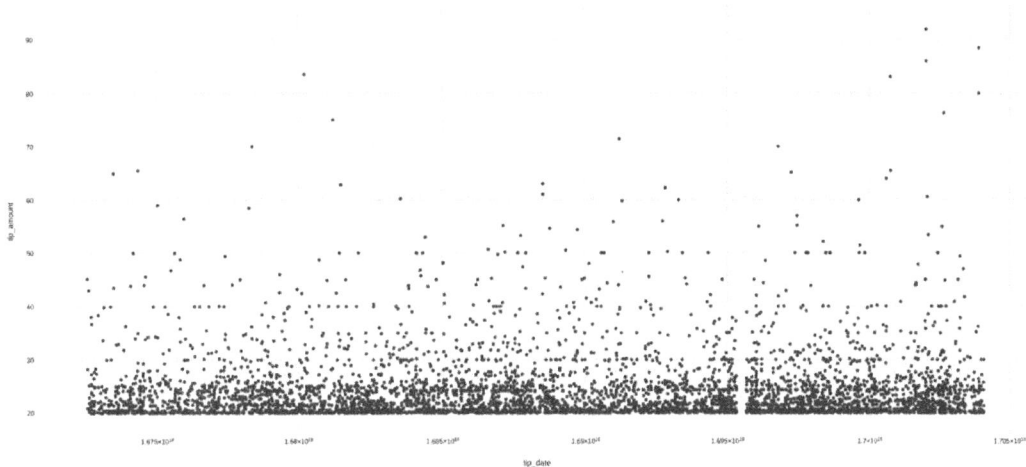

Figure 12.6: Tips between $20 and $100 over time; chart using rdp_decimator

In this section, we saw how to handle large amounts of data in Taipy applications, at different levels: big files for I/O operations, large DataFrames to process from the application, and functions to display large amounts of data.

Summary

In this chapter, we discovered how Taipy can interact with big data thanks to dedicated components (Data Nodes and visual restitutions), but also thanks to its integration with other tools and Python libraries. To handle big files, Taipy has dedicated Data Nodes, and we saw how it can leverage Spark and Dask. For medium-sized data, you could use Polars or DuckDB, which outperform pandas in memory efficiency and speed, making it perfect for datasets that are too large for pandas but don't require distributed computing. We also saw in this chapter how the use of `subprocess` can help us add CLI tools to our applications.

In the next chapter, we'll go one step further, showing how we can add HTML and JavaScript components to our Taipy applications.

Additional reading

The 3 Vs of Big Data: `https://subscription.packtpub.com/book/data/9781839219535/23/ch23lvl1sec19/the-three-vs-of-big-data`

Questions

1. Create a scenario with a generic Data Node that reads files from an S3 bucket and returns a Polars LazyFrame (a deferred execution DataFrame enabling optimized computations on large datasets). The scenario has a function that returns the rows with the 20 biggest tips for January 2023. It returns a pandas DataFrame so we can display it on the GUI. Here are some tips:

   - All LazyFrame methods: `https://docs.pola.rs/api/python/stable/reference/lazyframe/index.html#`.

   - Specifically, you'll need `https://docs.pola.rs/api/python/stable/reference/api/polars.scan_parquet.html`. You'll need to pass storage options with AWS credentials (you can also read directly from a Parquet file).

   - You can try this exercise with Dask DataFrames or other data formats!! Also, if you don't want to use Amazon S3 storage, you can try reading local Parquet files with Polars.

2. Can you change the Spark application and/or the function that calls it to add file caching (make it detect whether the data exists, then do not download it)?

3. Can you change the `analyze_tipping_patterns` function to return an extra DataFrame (`df_location_trips`) that has four columns: two that have the pick-up and drop-off locations (`'PULocationID'` and `'DOLocationID'`), the average tip for each `from-to` couple, and the number of trips for each combination, and keep the rows with 10 or more tips. Add the new DataFrame to your scenario, and bring it to the app as a table.

4. Create a pandas DataFrame with a sinus signal and 100,000 points (use numpy arrays to build it like this: `x = np.linspace(0, 10, 100000)` and `y = np.sin(x) + 0.1 * np.random.randn(100000)` and plot it using 200 points with the three decimator functions Taipy offers.

5. DuckDB (`https://duckdb.org/docs/clients/python/overview.html`) is a library that allows querying large datasets using SQL. We created a notebook with some examples of how to use it in `/answer_5/discover_duckdb.ipynb`. Create a small application that uses DuckDB. For example, allow users to create a table with two columns: one that users can select from a dropdown, and all tips between a minimum and maximum value.

Answers

1. The answer is in `/answers/answer_1`. We need to create a function that scans the file in the bucket to return the LazyFrame, like this:

```
s3_url = f"s3://{bucket}/{key}"
    storage_options = {
    "aws_access_key_id": aws_access_key_id,
    "aws_secret_access_key": aws_secret_access_key,
    "aws_region": region_name
    }
    lazy_df = pl.scan_parquet(
        s3_url, storage_options=storage_options)
    return lazy_df
```

And we create the Data Node configuration object, which uses the preceding function for reading:

```
read_s3_as_polars_config = Config.configure_generic_data_node(
    id="s3_as_polars",
    read_fct=read_parquet_from_s3_lazy,
    read_fct_args=[s3_file],
)
```

We also need to create a function to process the data with Polars and return a pandas DataFrame, like this:

```
def sort_and_get_top20_lazy_input(
    lazy_df: pl.LazyFrame,
    sort_column: str = "tip_amount"
) -> pl.LazyFrame:
    result_lazy = lazy_df.sort(
        sort_column, descending=True).limit(20)
    result_polars = result_lazy.collect()
    result_pandas = result_polars.to_pandas()
    return result_pandas
```

Despite using Polars, we still need to retrieve the data from the S3 bucket, which takes time. Also, keep in mind that this is not equivalent to Taipy Enterprise's Polars support, since we need to create a pandas DataFrame to create charts and tables.

2. This is a non-trivial task; we changed the `process_nyc_tlc.py` and `spark_process_nyc_tlc.py` files, which you can find in /answer_2. We create a first function, called `all_data_is_processed`, that checks whether all the files are generated from a previous processing.:

```
def all_data_is_processed(
    output_folder: Path,
    year: int,
    expected_count: int = 12
) -> bool:
    search_pattern = (
        f"processed_yellow_tripdata_{year}_.parquet"
    )
    matching_folders = list(output_folder.glob(search_pattern))

    if len(matching_folders) == expected_count:
        print("skipping Spark Task - All files exist")
        return True
    else:
        return False
```

This function would cover most of the cases; however, if some files were processed but not all of them, we would process them all again. We create a second function that returns a list of months to process (all of them if we process for the first time). Look at how we transform the list to return it as a string. The reason is that this will be passed as an argument to the Spark CLI command:

```
def get_months_to_process(output_folder, year):
    months_to_process = []

    for month in range(1, 13):
        month_str = str(month).zfill(2)
        file_name = (
            f"processed_yellow_tripdata_{year}_"
            f"{month_ str}.parquet"
        )
        local_path = Path(output_folder) / file_name

        if not local_path.exists():
            months_to_process.append(month)
    months_str = ",".join(map(str, months_to_process))
    return months_str
```

And then we pass the list as a CLI argument:

```
cmd = [...
    "--months", months_str,
]
```

In `spark_process_nyc_tlc.py`, we need to add the new received arguments to `argparse` and then convert the input strings back to a list:

```
parser.add_argument(
    "--months",
    # Default to all months:
    default="1,2,3,4,5,6,7,8,9,10,11,12",
    help="Comma-separated list of months to process (e.g.,
1,2,3)"
)
...
months_to_process = list(map(
    int, args.months.split(",")))
```

Finally, we add `months_to_process` as a new argument to the `process_all_data` function, both in the call, at the end of the file, and at the definition level, where we also remove the hardcoded month list (since we're now passing it as an argument!):

```
months = list(range(1, 13))
```

3. The answer is in `/answers/answer_3`. We need to create the DataFrame using Dask to calculate the aggregates, filter, and sort the DataFrame, before transforming it to pandas with compute. We create a helper function for this:

```
def _create_location_trips(ddf_year):
    df_location_trips = ddf_year.groupby(
        ["pulocationid", "dolocationid"]
    ).agg(
        {"tip_amount": ["mean", "count"]}
    )
    df_location_trips.columns = [
        "average_tip", "trip_count"]
    df_location_trips = df_location_trips[
        df_location_trips["trip_count"] > 9]
    df_location_trips = df_location_trips.sort_values(
        by="average_tip", ascending=False)
    df_location_trips = df_location_trips.reset_index()
    return df_location_trips
```

We compute the Dask DataFrame and get the pandas DataFrame from the `results` dictionary, before returning it in the function:

```
df_location_trips = results["df_location_trips"]
```

We also need to create a Data Node configuration object, add it to the scenario configuration, and create the Data Node in `main.py`. We can then read it.

4.   The answer is in `/answers/answer_4`. It's interesting to compare different decimator algorithms together.

5.   The answer is in `/answers/answer_5.py`. The key here is to create the SQL query dynamically, using an f-string; that's what `query_dataframe` does. Users can select the parameters from a drop-down selector (the `dimension` column) as well as the minimum and maximum tips.

Unlock this book's exclusive benefits now

Scan this QR code or go to `packtpub.com/unlock`, then search this book by name.

Note: Keep your purchase invoice ready before you start.

13

Creating Real-Time Apps with Taipy

In this chapter, we'll discover how to create real-time (or near-real-time) applications with Taipy. The demand for applications and dashboards that display or interact with data in real time is increasing. Imagine a stock trading platform that reflects price fluctuations instantaneously or a live sports dashboard updating scores and statistics with every play. Real-time data can also come from IoT sensors; in this case, we can monitor environmental data or scientific experiments instantly. Or, consider real-time **Business Intelligence** (**BI**), where companies can automatically adjust pricing, promotions, or product availability based on external factors such as weather, time of day, or local events. For instance, a retailer might trigger an on-the-spot discount or send a promotional message if customer interactions suddenly drop. We'll explore techniques for updating data periodically through polling or in real time using WebSocket. We'll also look at how to design UIs for real-time dashboards.

To build applications like these, we'll cover two different approaches and discuss their pros and cons. We'll start by showing how to create an app that polls data periodically. This is the easiest approach, but it's not truly real time; you can use this technique to consume data at periodic, not-so-often intervals, which also makes it suitable for batch processing. The second approach uses sockets and allows for real-time data consumption.

In this chapter, we'll cover the following topics:

- Polling data with Taipy
- Making a real-time UI
- Creating real-time apps with WebSocket

Technical requirements

The second part of this chapter uses Python websockets (`https://pypi.org/project/websockets/`) to connect to WebSocket servers (`https://developer.mozilla.org/en-US/docs/Web/API/WebSockets_API`). Familiarity with it and async will help you understand that part of the chapter.

You can find the complete code used in this chapter in the GitHub repository: `https://github.com/PacktPublishing/Getting-Started-with-Taipy/tree/main/chapter_13`.

Polling data with Taipy

In this section, we'll create an application that shows data from recent earthquakes; *Figure 13.1* shows how it looks. This example demonstrates how to use polling within a Taipy application to get periodic updates of your data. You can find the code for this example in the `/earthquake_app/main.py` file.

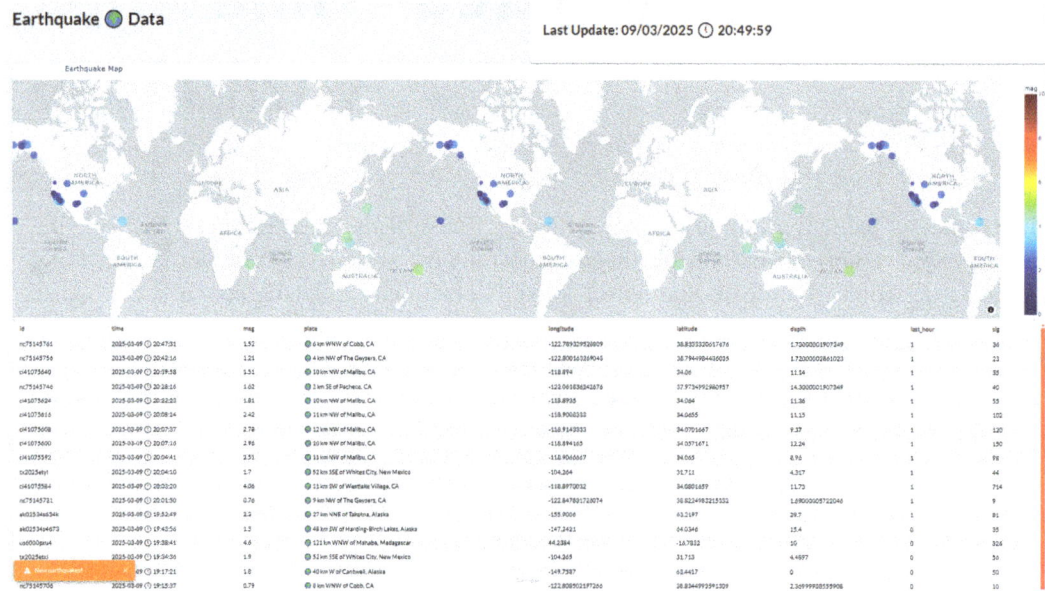

Figure 13.1: Earthquake data app

The earthquake data for this application comes from a **United States Geological Survey** (**USGS**) website (`https://earthquake.usgs.gov`). This site delivers data in JSON format, similar to an API, and doesn't require any authentication. The website doesn't provide true real-time updates; it reports earthquakes of magnitude 5 or higher within about 30 minutes. Still, our app can fetch the latest available data directly from their service. To do this, we'll use **polling**—a technique where the app repeatedly makes API calls at regular intervals to check for new data. In our case, we poll once every minute. Let's briefly look at the pros and cons of polling before we show how to create our app.

Advantages and disadvantages of polling

The main advantage of polling is its simplicity. Since it's a classic API call that happens in an infinite loop, it's easy to set up, either for testing or for basic needs; it's also easy to understand and debug. Another reason to choose polling over other true real-time techniques is that it works with APIs that provide data via HTTP, so your choice could come from the data availability rather than the application side.

On the other hand, polling is inefficient with large amounts of data since it makes requests even when the data hasn't changed; it also puts a significant load on the API server. Most servers limit the number of calls or have a price based on the number of API calls, which may also limit how frequently we update the data. Depending on the data you're getting, polling can miss updates, especially if an update occurs and goes away between poll requests. And, of course, polling is "near real time" at best, which can be fine in some cases but not so much in others. This is particularly true in the context of real-time results in sports or emergency alerts.

Let's now see how we can create an app that polls data!

Requesting data

We're going to see how we can create an app that retrieves data from an API periodically. To poll data with a Taipy application, we start by creating a function called get_earthquakes that retrieves the data from the API, like this:

```
def get_earthquakes(limit=10):
    earthquake_url = (
        f"https://earthquake.usgs.gov/fdsnws/event/1/"
        f"query?format=geojson&limit={limit}"
    )
    response = requests.get(earthquake_url)
    earthquakes = response.json()["features"]
    return earthquakes
```

> **Quick tip**: Enhance your coding experience with the **AI Code Explainer** and **Quick Copy** features. Open this book in the next-gen Packt Reader. Click the **Copy** button (**1**) to quickly copy code into your coding environment, or click the **Explain** button (**2**) to get the AI assistant to explain a block of code to you.

```
                                              Copy      Explain
function calculate(a, b) {                     1          2
  return {sum: a + b};
};
```

> **The next-gen Packt Reader** is included for free with the purchase of this book. Scan the QR code OR go to packtpub.com/unlock, then use the search bar to find this book by name. Double-check the edition shown to make sure you get the right one.

We call this function from the `update_earthquake` callback. The callback uses another function, `update_dataframe`, to update `df_earthquakes`, the DataFrame we use to visualize earthquake data:

```
def update_earthquake(state):
    print("Updating Earthquake")
    earthquakes = get_earthquakes()

    state.df_earthquakes = update_dataframe(
        earthquakes, state.df_earthquakes, state)
```

There isn't much to say about the `update_dataframe` function. We created some helper functions to separate the code a little:

`_process_and_update_quake` checks whether the earthquake's ID already exists in our data. If so, it updates the row; if not, it adds it. It calls `_process_quake`.

`_process_quake` returns data for a single earthquake as a dictionary.

If we have new rows, that means we have new earthquakes, so we notify it using the `_notify_new_rows` function.

Finally, we clear the DataFrame using the `_get_last_hour` function, which removes rows older than 60 minutes (refer to the *Making a real-time UI* section).

So far, we have a callback function that updates a DataFrame from an API call. Let's see how to trigger this callback.

Using long callbacks for polling

Polling data implies making a function call every fixed amount of time, in an infinite loop. If we used a regular callback function, our UI app would be blocked by this never-ending process. The trick to making this happen is using long-running callbacks, as explained in *Chapter 11*. Long-running callbacks are functions that run in a separate thread and can update the state periodically. These are the components we need:

- `invoke_long_callback`: We covered this function in *Chapter 11*. It allows us to trigger a long-running function in a separate thread and trigger a different callback every fixed amount of time.

- An `idle` function: This function is just an infinite loop; it never ends.

- `on_init`: This is a special Taipy callback (a reserved function) that triggers any callback when we launch the app.

In the following example, the on_init function triggers the idle function using a long callback with invoke_long_callback. While the function runs (and it does so *forever*), it triggers the update_earthquake function every 60,000 milliseconds (that is, 60 seconds or 1 minute):

```
def idle():
    """
    An infinite loop
    """
    while True:
        time.sleep(100)
        print("Listening...")

def on_init(state):
    """
    Start the update loop
    """
    invoke_long_callback(
        state, idle, [], update_earthquake, [], 60_000)
```

This approach lets us work with frequent updates and near-real-time data, but it has efficiency issues, especially in the context of multiple user applications. Let's see how we can deal with that!

Working with shared variables

In the earthquake application we just developed, invoke_long_callback is called every time a client connects to the application (in other words, every time a new browser requests the app). This approach is fine if you're just prototyping or using the app with a single client, but it's highly inefficient in the case of a shared application, because the earthquake data is the same, no matter what. Yet each client is triggering an infinite running thread, with periodic API calls. The code for this section can be found in /earthquake_app/main_with_broadcast.py and is a variation of the previous app.

To deal with this situation, we can use **shared variables** and **callback broadcasting**. Shared variables are variables that we can update across all clients of the same application, and callback broadcasting is a special way of triggering callbacks that affect all the clients running the application. The trick here will be to launch the long-running callback from the first client connection and make that long-running callback update the values for all of the next clients.

The first step in using shared variables is to declare them, after creating our Gui() object. To do so, we use the add_shared_variable method. Note how we pass the variable name as a string:

```
gui.add_shared_variable("df_earthquakes")
```

When a variable is bound to the client's state (and shared variables are also bound to their client state!), we update their value from a callback using a `state.variable_name = x` formulation. In the case of a shared variable, if we want the variable to change across all clients, we should use `gui.broadcast_changes`, for example, in the `update_earthquake` function:

```
updated_df_earthquakes = update_dataframe(
    earthquakes, state.df_earthquakes, state)
gui.broadcast_change("df_earthquakes", updated_df_earthquakes)
gui.broadcast_change("last_update", get_now())
```

Now, so far, this change doesn't make things better: we still need to figure out a way to launch the long callback once. To achieve this, we can create another shared variable, called `is_update_running`, with an initial value of 0. We change the `on_init` function to launch the callback when the value of our variable is 0 (which it is for the first client connection), and we also change it to 1 for all future clients. This way, the future clients won't trigger the callback at launch!

```
if state.is_update_running == 0:
    gui.broadcast_change("is_update_running", 1)
    invoke_long_callback(
        state, idle, [], update_earthquake, [], 60_000)
```

This solution creates a new problem. The `update_earthquake` function updates the values (for all clients now), but it also notifies of changes (using `notify` and `chime`). These functions are run from the first client, so they won't notify users from other clients! To fix this, we can leverage the `broadcast_callback` function (we need to import it: `from taipy.gui import broadcast_callback`). This function triggers a callback for all the clients using the app. To use it properly, we create a function called `notify_update`, like this:

```
def notify_update(state):
    chime.info()  # Sound notification: we have new row
    notify(state, "w", "New earthquakes!")
```

We can trigger it from the `update_dataframe` callback like this:

```
broadcast_callback(state.get_gui(), notify_update)
```

> **Note**
> Taipy Enterprise includes a built-in scheduler that enables reliable data polling and supports robust batch processing.

We now have an app that polls data and shares it with all the users! We'll now comment on some aspects of the app's UI regarding time and updates before moving on to real-time app creation.

Making a real-time UI

Making a real-time application involves more than just retrieving the data in real time; it requires thinking about a UI that's adapted to this workflow and also to user requirements. In this section, we discuss some aspects of the app's UI and how we adapted it for real-time use.

Working with time in the UI

When we work with real-time (or near-real-time, or frequently updated) data, it can be a good idea to let users know when the last update happened. This will make them more confident about the data they're using, and it can show them if there is a problem with the app. In our application, we create a get_now function that gets the current time, and we call it from the update_earthquake callback:

```
def get_now():
    now = datetime.now(timezone.utc)
    formatted_date_time = now.strftime("%d/%m/%Y  %H:%M:%S")
    return formatted_date_time


def update_earthquake(state):
    ...
    state.last_update = get_now()
```

Notice that we get the current time specifying the time zone (timezone.utc) to match the one from the API calls. *It's important to use consistent time zones in your app!* We can insert the last-updated date like this:

```
with tgb.part(class_name="card"):
    tgb.text("## Last Update: {last_update}", mode="md")
```

Another way to use relative time in our application is by showing whether an event happened in the last hour. Every time the app calls update_dataframe, it recalculates a last_hour column using the _get_latest_minutes and _get_last_hour functions and compares it to the time column, like this:

```
def _get_latest_minutes(minutes):
    now = datetime.now(timezone.utc)
    return now - timedelta(minutes=minutes)


def _get_last_hour(df):
    cutoff = _get_latest_minutes(60)
    df["last_hour"] = (df["time"] >= cutoff).astype(int)
    return df.sort_values(
        by="time", ascending=False, ignore_index=True)
```

Another important aspect of data visualization in real time is distinguishing what parts need to change over time and which don't. For example, you probably want to have fixed scales in your charts. This is because if you get data with values over the maximum or under the minimum (for example, a new earthquake with a bigger magnitude than any other in your records), the color scale will re-adjust, and all the data points will change color, leading to a poor visual experience. For instance, look inside /earthquake_apps/charts.py; we created a fixed color scale with the following line:

```
range_color=[0, 10],  # Force consistent scale
```

We have seen a couple of examples of how to deal with time evolution in our application. Next, we'll discuss some ways to notify users of changes.

Notifying of changes

Notifying of changes in real-time applications can be important because users may not see the changes otherwise (since the changes aren't coming from user-triggered callbacks). Also, if users want a real-time app, it can be important to signal major changes as they come.

There are several ways to notify users of changes. In our app, we added three notification types when new rows are inserted. We use the notify function to create a visual notification, we print a statement in the terminal, and we create a sound notification using the Chime library (https://pypi.org/project/chime/), like this:

```
if new_rows:
    ...
    if state:  # No state when called from the __main__
        notify(state, "w", "New earthquakes!")
        print(f"""inserting...\n{new_rows}""")
        chime.info()
```

We have covered how to create near-real-time apps and how to think about UIs that update their data in real or near-real time. In the next section, we'll see how to create real-time applications using sockets.

Creating real-time apps with Taipy

In this section, we'll cover how to create a real-time app using the websockets library (https://pypi.org/project/websockets/). This Python library allows handling **WebSocket**, or **bidirectional communication**. While we use websockets in particular, there are other Python libraries you can use to work with WebSocket. For all such alternate libraries, you can apply the same principles as we use in this section.

WebSocket is a communication protocol that enables a persistent, two-way connection between a client (such as a web browser) and a server. Unlike HTTP, which follows a request-response model, WebSocket allows both sides to send and receive data at any time. This technique has pros and cons; let's briefly discuss them. The biggest advantage of this approach is that it allows for **true real-time connections** and is more efficient than polling since it transmits changes when they happen. Using sockets also allows for bidirectional communication (sending data back to the API server), although we won't be covering this in this chapter. This technique is great for displaying data from sensors or captors, such as for educational or IoT projects.

The drawback of using real-time servers is that they're more complex to implement and they require the implementation of strategies for maintaining a persistent connection. Also, if you don't own the data source, using WebSocket just may not be an option. Let's get to work and set up a server to create our first real-time app with Taipy!

Creating real-time apps with WebSocket

For our example, we'll be coding a sender and a receiver that communicate with each other using WebSocket. This example will simulate a captor that sends a wave signal that is more or less sinusoidal. The code for this section can be found in `/sinus_wave`. *Figure 13.2* shows the application.

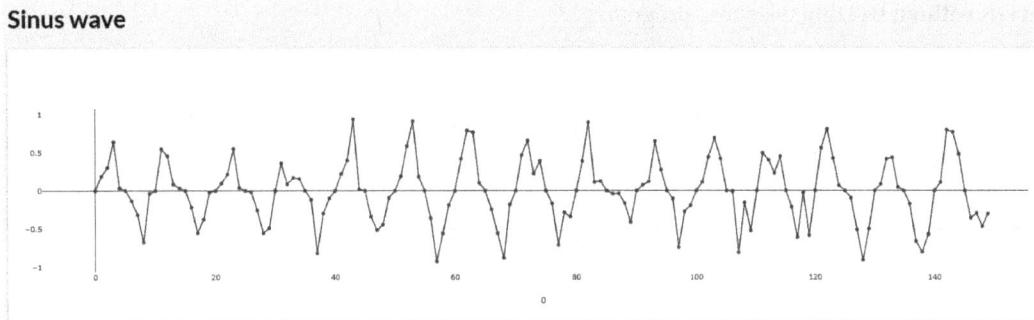

Figure 13.2: An app showing a wave that evolves in real time

You'll find three files in the directory:

- `sender.py`: Emulates a continuous, distorted sine wave sender.
- `receiver.py`: Establishes a WebSocket server and listens to the sender. It employs a circular buffer strategy to handle continuous data streams efficiently (it gets the latest data and overwrites older data past a certain time). This prints the results in a terminal.
- `taipy_receiver.py`: This is a Taipy app that incorporates the receiver and displays the results in a Taipy app.

The WebSocket server is in the receiver, which means we have to run the receiver before the sender. Our advice would be to test `receiver.py` before you see how it's implemented in the Taipy app (unless you have experience running websockets, in which case you may start the Taipy app right away). We start the server with the following line of code:

```
server = await websockets.serve(handler, "localhost", 8765)
```

Since this function is asynchronous, it does not block execution, allowing the event loop to handle other tasks while waiting for client connections.

The sender establishes a persistent WebSocket connection to `ws://localhost:8765`. It then generates a continuous sine wave using the following:

```
y = A * math.sin(2 * math.pi * f * t)
y = y * random.random()  # to add variability
```

The asynchronous design (using `async with` and `await`) enables non-blocking data transmission.

`async with websockets.connect(uri) as websocket` sets up the connection and `await websocket.send(str(y))` allows sending messages without halting execution. Also, `await asyncio.sleep(sampling_interval)` ensures that the loop continues at controlled intervals without freezing the entire program.

The receiver uses a buffer initialized with 200 zeros (`buffer_size = 200`), which corresponds to 20 seconds of data (2 cycles for a 1 Hz signal at 100 ms intervals). The `current_index` variable implements ring buffer logic, `(current_index + 1) % buffer_size`, creating an overwrite mechanism that preserves memory efficiency for infinite-duration streams. As new values arrive via WebSocket messages, the buffer updates in real time while maintaining a fixed-size window of recent history.

Now that we have our sender and receiver, we can bring the data to the UI. We'll explore two methods, but you can figure out other ways to do it! The first method is a hybrid approach between polling and real time, and then we'll see true real-time connections.

Bringing the stream to the UI periodically

The way we bring real-time data to the UI is similar to how we bring the data when we do periodic updates (see *Polling data with Taipy*). The `taipy_receiver.py` program has a `Page` block with a `chart` element that displays the `sinus_series` variable (a pandas Series version of the `sinus_buffer` variable).

We move the receiver from the previous section to the Taipy app. The first big difference is that we rename the main function to `listen`, and we run it from another function instead of running it as an app (in this case, our app is the Taipy app!):

```
def start_listening():
    asyncio.run(listen())
```

The second change between the simple receiver and the one in `taipy_receiver.py` is that we bring the `sinus_buffer` (the NumPy array with the sinus wave values) and `buffer_size` variables outside the `handler` function. We declare them under `__name__ == "__main__"` and we call them as global variables:

```
async def handler(websocket):
    global buffer_size
    global sinus_buffer
```

To update the app, we can use the `invoke_long_callback` function. We trigger the `start_listening` function, which updates the global `sinus_buffer` variable, and we periodically call the function that updates the UI, `update_sinus`, like this:

```
def update_sinus(state):
    print("updating")
    global sinus_buffer
    state.sinus_series = pd.Series(sinus_buffer)

def on_init(state):
    invoke_long_callback(
        state, start_listening, [],
        update_sinus, [], 500
    )
```

`invoke_long_callback` can trigger the update callback every 500 ms (twice a second) at most. When you launch the app and the server, you'll notice that every update plots around five points. This is because the sender emits a signal every 0.1 seconds (five every 500 ms).

In this application, we're closer to real time than pure polling. We get the data as a stream in real time, but the UI updates periodically. This kind of setup can be interesting if you only need real time in the backend as it prevents data loss if you process the data properly, and the app could process some data before sending it to the UI. This approach reduces frontend load if you have lots of data. In our example, we update the frontend once for every five inputs. Let's now see an example of real-time updates in the frontend.

Bringing the stream to the UI in real time

This example builds on the sinus wave application from the previous section (*Bringing the stream to the UI periodically*) and dives deep into the steps to update the frontend in real time. The code for this example can be found in the `/sinus_wave_real_time` file.

Here is how this example differs from our previous one. First, the app still uses the `listen` function that calls a handler function, but we have removed the part that creates the buffer—the NumPy array that previously held the data for plotting. Instead, we now create a data queue in the main guard, and as new data is received in real time, it is pushed into this queue by the receiver:

```
async def handler(websocket):
    try:
        async for message in websocket:
            new_value = float(message)

            await data_queue.put(new_value)
(...)

if __name__ == "__main__":
    (...)
    data_queue = asyncio.Queue()
```

We have a data queue, so now we can create a callback that creates the buffer (which is still a global variable) using the data from the queue (which comes from the sender), using `get_nowait()`, like this:

```
def update_real_time(state):
    global sinus_buffer
    current_index = 0
    while True:
        try:
            new_value = data_queue.get_nowait()
            sinus_buffer[current_index] = new_value
            current_index = (current_index + 1) % buffer_size
            update_sinus(state)
            print("update")
        except asyncio.QueueEmpty:
            pass
        except Exception as e:
            print(f"Error in main loop: {e}")
        import time
        time.sleep(0.001)
```

Note how we add `time.sleep(0.001)` to not overload the CPU. A 1 ms pause is more than acceptable to consider the app to be in real time. The last step is to launch our updating functions. We use `invoke_long_callback` to trigger the `start_listening` listening function, which runs in a separate thread, but we don't trigger the `update_real_time` function periodically from `invoke_long_callback`; we initiate it directly from `on_init`, like this:

```
def on_init(state):
    invoke_long_callback(state, start_listening, [])
    update_real_time(state)
```

This application is way more CPU-intensive than previous ones because it updates the frontend frequently. If you run it, you'll notice the "real-time effect," which is cool and you could need in some situations; most likely, though, you won't.

However, there is at least one case where this approach is more efficient—if you need to retrieve real-time data that happens infrequently. For example, if your app monitors earthquakes in real time, you may want the app to notify users of any earthquake over a certain magnitude. If this is an event that happens once a week on average (let's imagine), updating your frontend every few seconds would be absurd, but if you wait too long between updates, it may be too late to respond to the earthquake emergency. For these types of events, triggering the update callbacks in real time is way more efficient. Other examples of this could be monitoring sports events (notify when teams score goals), monitoring markets (notify when an asset's value goes over or under a certain threshold), or security monitoring (notify of catastrophic or dangerous events).

Summary

In this chapter, we discussed two techniques for retrieving data in near-real time and real time and how to achieve them within a Taipy application using long callbacks and global variables. We also discussed some ideas for displaying real-time data in the UI.

We discussed how to decide on which technique to use. The first constraint is data availability; if you can't access the data in real time, you'll have to choose polling. Polling is often less efficient than true real time, and it can induce problems with the API server. As for real-time WebSocket connections, we saw that we can separate the real-time data collection from the real-time UI display. We also saw that updating the UI frequently is CPU-intensive and shouldn't be a default choice, except if really needed or if we need real-time data that doesn't update frequently.

You should now be able to create real-time applications for your real-time BI dashboards or your IoT projects. Congratulations! In the next chapter, we'll go one step further, showing how we can add HTML and JavaScript components to our Taipy applications.

Additional readings

- Adrian Bridgwater. *MIT: The rise of real-time IT creates the real-time business*. Computer Weekly. Published: 21 August 2024. `https://www.computerweekly.com/blog/CW-Developer-Network/MIT-The-rise-of-real-time-IT-creates-the-real-time-business`

- Taipy's documentation: An example of how to use threads and the websockets library to get real-time data: `https://docs.taipy.io/en/latest/tutorials/articles/multithreading/`

Questions

1. The earthquake app we created notifies the user of changes using `notify`, printing a statement in the terminal and making a ring sound. Can you display recent earthquakes (less than 15 minutes, for example) in the UI in a noticeable way? Can you think of other ways to notify users of updates?

2. For the earthquake app, create a sender that gets the data from the URL and a receiver that updates the data for the application.

3. (Difficult) Create an app that streams in data from Wikipedia using WikiMon (documentation: `https://github.com/hatnote/wikimon/`; listen to `wss://wikimon.hatnote.com/`). You can retrieve data and place it in a table. Please note: You won't need to create a server; instead, your app will connect to the server, like the senders in our examples.

Answers

1. The files for this answer are in `/answers/answer_1`. One way to display earthquakes from the last 15 minutes is to create a separate DataFrame that filters out older events and keeps only the most relevant columns. We create a `get_last_15_minutes` function, and we call it from the `update_earthquake` function:

```
def get_last_15_minutes(df_earthquakes):
    now = datetime.now(timezone.utc)
    fiteen_minutes_ago = now - timedelta(minutes=15)
    df_last_15 = df_earthquakes[
        df_earthquakes["time"] >= fiteen_minutes_ago
    ]
    df_last_15 = df_last_15[["time", "mag", "place"]]
    return df_last_15
```

We can then display this table within a card to make it stand out, like this:

```
with tgb.part(class_name="card"):
    with tgb.layout("1 3"):
        tgb.text(
            "### Earthquakes in Last 15 minutes:",
            mode="md"
        )
        tgb.table(
            "{df_last_15}",
            date_format="yyyy-MM-dd 🕐 HH:mm:ss",
            rebuild=True
        )
```

To make some data stand out in a table, we can apply CSS style to rows based on a time condition or other relevant information. For example, the `row_class` callback assigns an HTML class to rows that satisfy some condition, such as a magnitude over 4 and happening in the last 15 minutes:

```
def row_class(state, row_number, row):
    class_name = ""
    if row["mag"] > 4:
        class_name += "red-row "
    if row["time"] > get_latest_minutes(15):
        class_name += " recent-row"
    return class_name
(...)
tgb.table(
    "{df_earthquakes}",
    (...)
    row_class_name=row_class,)
```

Once we have our HTML classes, we need to add the CSS code (in `main.css`):

```
.red-row>td {
    color: yellow;
    background-color: red;
}
.recent-row>td {
    font-weight: bold;
}
```

We can imagine all sorts of notifications. For example, we could send an email or an SMS when an event occurs or push a notification to another app. It's possible to trigger any Python function that performs any of those actions. Just as an example, here's a function that logs the events as they occur:

```python
def log_notification(message, log_file="app_log.txt"):
    timestamp = get_now()
    log_entry = f"[{timestamp}] {message}\n"
    try:
        with open(log_file, "a", encoding="utf-8") as f:
            f.write(log_entry)
    except Exception as e:
        print(f"Error writing to log file: {e}")
```

2. The answer is in /answers/answer_2. The charts.py file is the same as in the book's example. We add sender.py, and we move the get_earthquakes function there. We also create a send_earthquake_data function that connects to ws://localhost:8765 and sends the raw data to the receiver.

In main.py, we add the async WebSocket functions to create the server and listen to the sender (handler, listen, and start_listening). The functions that build the DataFrame and the UI remain almost unchanged, except for update_earthquake(state, earthquakes):, which now takes the earthquakes parameter. This function is called from update_real_time, which creates the earthquakes object by getting the data from the queue:

```python
def update_real_time(state):
    while True:
        try:
            earthquake_data = data_queue.get_nowait()
            earthquakes = json.loads(
                earthquake_data.decode("utf-8")
            )["features"]
            update_earthquake(state, earthquakes)
        except asyncio.QueueEmpty:
            pass  # No new data, continue looping.
        except Exception as e:
            print(f"Error in main loop: {e}")
        import time

        time.sleep(0.001)
```

The last step is to change the on_init function:

```python
def on_init(state):
    invoke_long_callback(state, start_listening, [])
```

3. The answer is in `/answers/answer_3`. The `wikipedia_edits` function connects to the server and gets the data in real time. It also generates a Python dictionary with some of the message's data and puts it in a queue. Then, the `process_data` function consumes the data from `data_queue` and appends it to a global DataFrame (`df_wikipedia_edits`). The `listen_wiki()` function creates a `data_queue` asynchronous queue object and two tasks, `wikipedia_edits` and `process_data`. It runs them both concurrently using `asyncio.gather`. The `start_listening()` function starts the `listen_wiki()` coroutine using `asyncio.run`. This is the function we trigger from the long callback.

While the async functions run in a separate thread, the `invoke_long_callback` function triggers the `update_wikipedia_df` function every second (1,000 ms), which updates `df_wiki` using `state`, to display in the UI.

Join our community on Discord

Join our community's Discord space for discussions with the authors and other readers:

`https://packt.link/taipybook`

14

Embedding Iframes in Taipy Applications

You now have all the tools to create complete, efficient data applications with Taipy. In this chapter, we'll see how to enrich our applications with external frontend content, such as HTML pages, PDF documents, or small JavaScript-based widgets (little programs that execute solely in the application's frontend).

This external content can be static, which means the application loads the content and never changes, or it can be dynamic when it is JavaScript frontend code.

The application can also generate dynamic content from the backend. For example, users can interact with selectors to display certain HTML or JavaScript-based elements, or this code can come from a callback function. To show external content, we need a single element: the part block element. Let's see how we use it!

In this chapter, we'll cover the following:

- Embedding HTML content and widgets in Taipy applications
- Adding content dynamically

Technical requirements

You can find the complete code used in this chapter in the GitHub repository:

`https://github.com/PacktPublishing/Getting-Started-with-Taipy/tree/main/chapter_14`. Having a basic knowledge of frontend web development is recommended. The last section of this chapter, *Adding JavaScript-based charts*, requires some knowledge of JavaScript.

For this chapter, we'll use the following Python libraries: GeoPandas, Folium, Matplotlib, FPDF (to create PDF files with Python), and pydeck (to create 3D maps).

Embedding HTML content and widgets

In this section, we'll see how to add static HTML components and widgets to your application.

Classic frontend web development combines the following three main technologies:

- HTML code to create the page's structure
- CSS code to add the page's style
- JavaScript to create programs that run in the browser (on the user's computer)

When you create Taipy applications, you declare visual elements and other components, and Taipy transforms all that into frontend code that's sent to the browser, but you can also add some HTML, CSS, and/or JavaScript code directly and place it in your application, inside a part component. Let's see some examples of this and how you can supercharge your apps with them!

To show how to use these components, we'll code a small mock application, called *Andorra App*, with information about Andorra, one of Europe's smallest countries! It's a multi-page app, with a footer showing some useful resources about Folium (a Python library we'll use later on).

> **Important**
> To add a footer to a Taipy application, add the code to the `root` page, as you would for the header, after a `tgb.content()` statement.

Adding static content

By static content, we mean code—or other elements—that you declare once and doesn't require any work in the backend (but it can be dynamic in the frontend). *Figure 14.1* shows the GENERAL_INFO part of the application, as well as the footer. We numbered all the elements, and they're all static; we will discuss them in all the following subsections. The code for the footer is `/src`; we add it to `root` `Page` element. The code for the GENERAL_INFO tab is in `/src/general_info.py`.

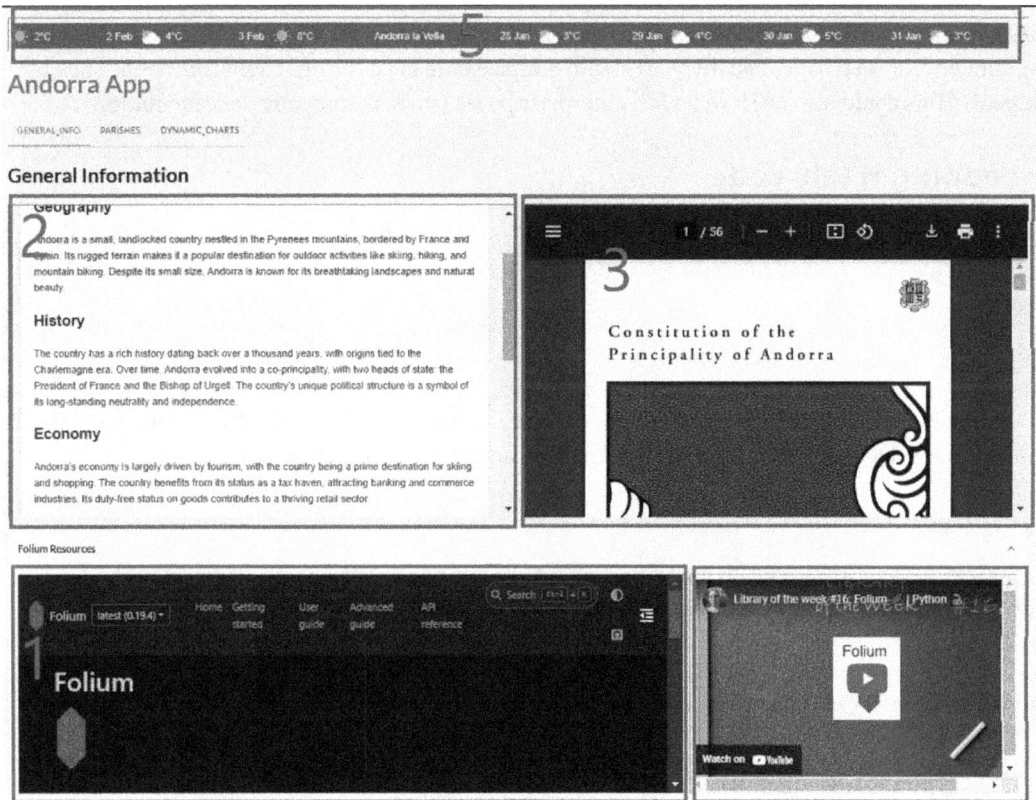

Figure 14.1: Andorra App's GENERAL_INFO tab with static elements

Embedding web pages

You can embed web pages in `part` elements using the `page` argument. To have a big enough frame, it's important to use the `height` parameter and see what works well.

Figure 14.1-1 shows Folium's documentation in the left part of the page's footer. Here's the code to create the element:

```
tgb.part(
    page="https://python-visualization.github.io/folium/latest/",
    height="350px",
)
```

Most of the time, you'd probably want to provide users with a link to open a page in a new browser tab. However, embedding web pages can be handy if you want users to compare two pages side by side (such as to display A/B testing choices), or if you want the content to be next to other elements (maybe you have a chatbot showing you this content).

It's important to notice that embedding web pages is often restricted (for example, YouTube will block this). Embedding web pages usually works with simple static pages or open environments, such as Wikipedia. This could also work well with enterprise pages (such as company documentation).

Embedding HTML code

You can also use the `part` element to reference a local HTML file; this is what you see in *Figure 14.1-2*. The HTML file is in `/src/iframes/andorra_presentation.html`. Here is the code to embed it:

```
tgb.part(page="./iframes/andorra_presentation.html", height="500px")
```

Embedding HTML files this way can be a good choice when we need big chunks of static text. This can be ideal for documentation, contact information and references, or legal disclaimers.

> **Note**
> This text could also be semi-dynamic and updated periodically (daily, weekly, or monthly) by an external batch. In this case, we could also provide periodic reports.

Embedding PDF files or other media

The `page` element accepts other media types and generates either an `<iframe>` or `<embed>` HTML tag. *Figure 14.1-3* shows a PDF document (Andorra's constitution—check who the co-princes are; it might surprise you!).

Browsers recognize these special tags, so they display elements in a proper *wrap*. For example, the PDF renders inside a PDF reader, with a **download and print** button, a page navigator, or a zoom button. PDF offers an alternative to plain HTML if you want to present reports or documentation to your users. You can also embed other media (see *Question 1* at the end of the chapter), such as sound, which can be nice if you're creating an app that analyzes sound data or SVG images.

Embedding iframes

Some websites provide specific iframes to embed their content. We discussed earlier how big pages, such as YouTube, don't allow you to directly embed their websites, but they provide iframe URLs to get specific content. *Figure 14.1-4* shows a YouTube video about Folium (by this book's author; like and subscribe if you like it 😊!).

To add this video, we copied the iframe code from YouTube and pasted it in `/src/iframes/yt_video.html`, then we just added the path to the `part` element:

```
tgb.part(page="./iframes/yt_video.html", height="350px")
```

Plenty of websites offer iframes. You can use them for documentation or education purposes, or they may be a primary source of data (maybe you're analyzing social media data and want to embed some social media feeds).

It's important to note that iframes can also move and show dynamic content. *Figure 14.1-5* shows a weather widget that displays the weather in Andorra la Vella, Andorra's capital. The code for this widget is copy-pasted from `https://weatherwidget.org/` to `/src/iframes/andorra_weather.html` (we selected **Ticker** and **Andorra la Vella** for the location). The `part` element is just like the others; you'll find it in the header section (the one at the top of the application, shared by all pages) in `/src/main.py`. Let's now see how we can dynamically generate external content!

Adding iframes dynamically

All the content we've seen so far (and any other thing you can embed) can be updated dynamically using buttons and selectors, either with simple binding or using callbacks.

The code for this part is in `/src/parishes.py`. This page uses data from *Open Street Maps* with information about accommodation in Andorra. It divides data by *parishes*, which are the country's main administrative divisions (like states or provinces in other countries). The source data is in `/src/data`, in GeoJSON format. You can see the notebook we used to create these datasets in `/create_geojsons/hotels.ipynb`.

Figure 14.2 shows the **Parishes** tab, with numbers that identify the main components. In this section, we'll focus on elements *1* and *2* (we will cover element *3* in the *Adding Folium maps* section).

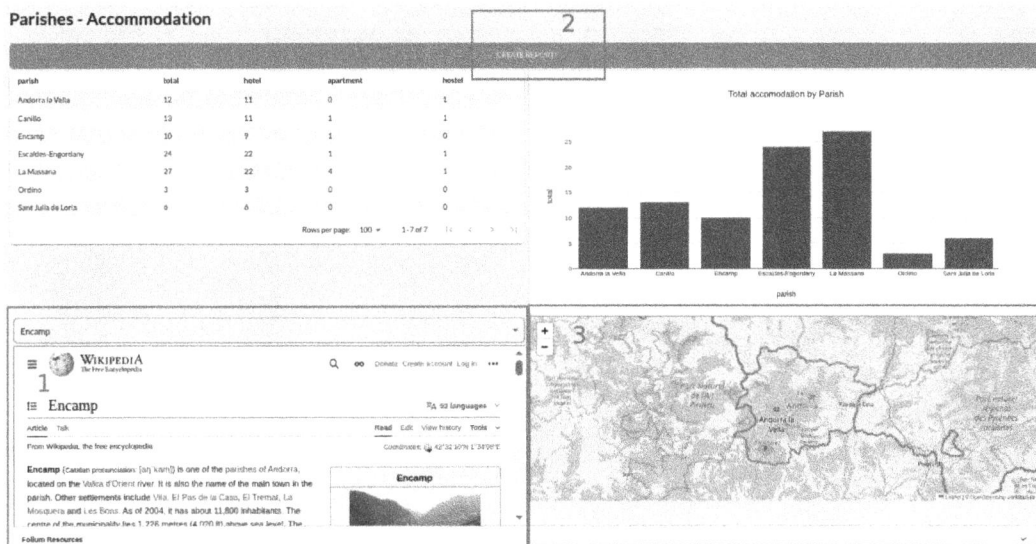

Figure 14.2: Information by parish, with dynamically added components and a Folium map

Selecting iframes dynamically

Figure 14.2-1 shows a drop-down selector with the names of the nine Andorran parishes and the Wikipedia page for the selected parish. We created this in a *classic* Taipy way. This is how we created the selector and `part` element:

```
tgb.selector(
    value="{parish}",
    lov="{parishes}",
    dropdown=True,
)
tgb.part(page="{parishes_dict.get(parish)}", height="350px")
```

Here, `parishes_dict` is defined in `main.py` and links each parish name to its URL. You could use this approach for other types of widgets and also leverage other selector types. The only limit is your imagination!

Creating files from a callback

Another dynamic approach is to create the pages from a callback function. In our example, the **CREATE REPORT!** button in *Figure 14.2-2* creates—and displays—a PDF report when users click on it (see *Figure 14.3*). The application shows a table and a chart, which are usual Taipy elements, so you can compare them with the generated report, which uses the FPDF library and Matplotlib for the chart.

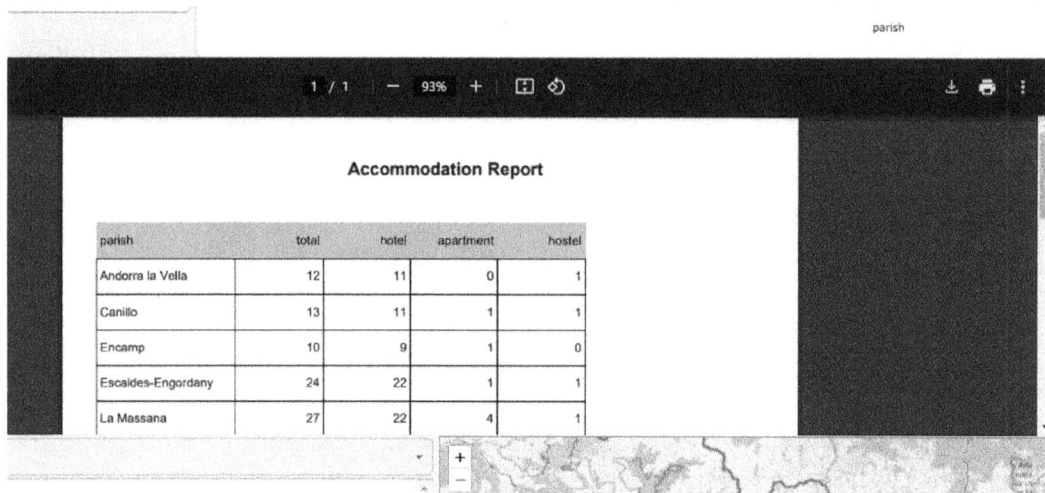

Figure 14.3: A PDF report generated by our app

The button triggers a long-running callback (refer to *Chapter 12*), which we code like this:

```
def create_report(state):
    invoke_long_callback(
        state, create_pdf_report,
        [state.df_parish_info], update_pdf_part)
```

The function that creates the report is in `/src/algorithms/create_report.py`. It uses FPDF, which has a descriptive syntax to place elements around the PDF report file. Here is what the function does:

- It creates one page and sets the main variables (font, cell size, etc.)
- It creates a table from the DataFrame, in an iterative way
- It creates a Matplotlib figure object and adds it to the report

To update the `part` element, we use an `update_pdf_part` function, as a **user status function**, so the PDF renders after the long callback is done running (as said previously, we explained this in *Chapter 12*):

```
def update_pdf_part(state, is_finished):
    if is_finished:
        state.show_report = True
        notify(state, "i", "The pdf report is ready!")
```

The `update_pdf_part` function updates the `show_report` variable to show the report and sends a success notification when completed.

Important

`create_report.py` uses the following setting to set Matplotlib's backend to `Agg`, which is a non-GUI backend that renders plots to files instead of displaying them on the screen. It avoids conflicts with Taipy's GUI: `matplotlib.use("Agg")`.

Creating reports this way allows end users to visualize them directly in the application and download them if they're satisfied with them! You could also use this approach to create dynamic HTML, CSS, or JavaScript code.

Important

You should be careful when you create documents from multi-user applications: if all users create a file called `report.pdf`, they'll be overridden. Depending on your case, you can add elements to your file's naming, such as the user's ID, a timestamp, or a universally unique identifier (uuid - `https://docs.python.org/3/library/uuid.html`).

In this section, you learned how to add HTML content and widgets to your Taipy applications and how you can leverage this to add different types of media, such as videos or PDF files. You learned how to add JavaScript-based widgets to extend your application with client-side widgets, and how to use Taipy to update the HTML widgets. In the next section, we'll see how to add client-side code to our applications without creating files!

Adding content dynamically

In this section, we'll see how to create content dynamically for applications. The big difference between this approach and what we saw in the previous part of this chapter is that we're going to create the content from functions. We won't create files and links to internal or external URLs. To add our content dynamically, we also use the `part` element, but we use the `content` argument instead of `page`. Let's see a couple of use cases!

Adding Folium maps

In this section, we'll see how to add Folium maps to our app. *Figure 14.2-3* shows the map in the **Parishes** tab. It displays all the accommodation locations from *Open Street Maps* in Andorra. The code is in `/src/algorithms/folium_map.py`. Let's explain it!

We start by creating a class called `FoliumMap`, and we define the `__init__` constructor with input attributes (in this case, a GeoPandas `GeoDataFrame`) and outputs (in this case, a Folium map object that's returned from `create_accommodations_map`—see the next point):

```
def __init__(self, gdf):
    self.gdf = gdf
    self.map = self.create_accommodations_map()
```

The `FoliumMap` class has a `create_accommodations_map` function that returns a Folium map. You can check the function in the repo. Here are the main steps:

- It calculates the average location of all accommodations to set the map's central point

- It adds a feature that groups markers together when zoomed out for better visibility (with the `MarkerCluster` extension)

- It sets different colors for each accommodation type's marker

- It places the markers in the map using an `add_marker()` function (we define it inside the function itself so we can apply it to all rows in a vectorized way)

To bring our Folium map to our application, we need to register the *content provider*. This is a four-step process:

1. First, we define the class that produces the frontend element (we just did it).

2. We then create a function that reads the content from the class and returns it in a binary format. Folium requires us to save maps in a file, so we create a temporary file, read it as binary, and return it as a string:

```python
def expose_folium_map(folium_map: FoliumMap):
    with tempfile.NamedTemporaryFile(
        delete=False, suffix=".html"
    ) as temp_file:
        folium_map.map.save(temp_file.name)
        with open(temp_file.name, "rb") as f:
            return f.read()
```

3. Once we have a class that creates the output and a function that returns it as a string, we need to register the provider with Gui.register_content_provider(), like this:

```python
Gui.register_content_provider(FoliumMap, expose_folium_map)
```

4. The last step is to create the part element using the content parameter and the class name of the object we're creating as a bound value, with all the parameters it needs to return the desired output. Taipy will know what to do with this specific object because of the preceding step. Here is how the element looks:

```python
tgb.part(content="{FoliumMap(gdf_accommodations)}",
         height="350px")
```

And that's it! You can now display Folium maps in your UI! We're almost done here, but we'd like to show an example of how to use JavaScript elements in your Taipy applications.

Adding JavaScript-based charts

Taipy is a pure Python builder, and by no means do you need to know how to code with JavaScript (as you should know if you followed the previous chapters!), but if you or your team know JavaScript, this technique unlocks access to lots of useful libraries.

Figure 14.4 shows a dynamic chart that we created using the chart.js library (https://www.chartjs.org/). Creating a JavaScript element involves the same steps as we saw in the previous section: we need to create a class and register the content provider before using the class in a part element.

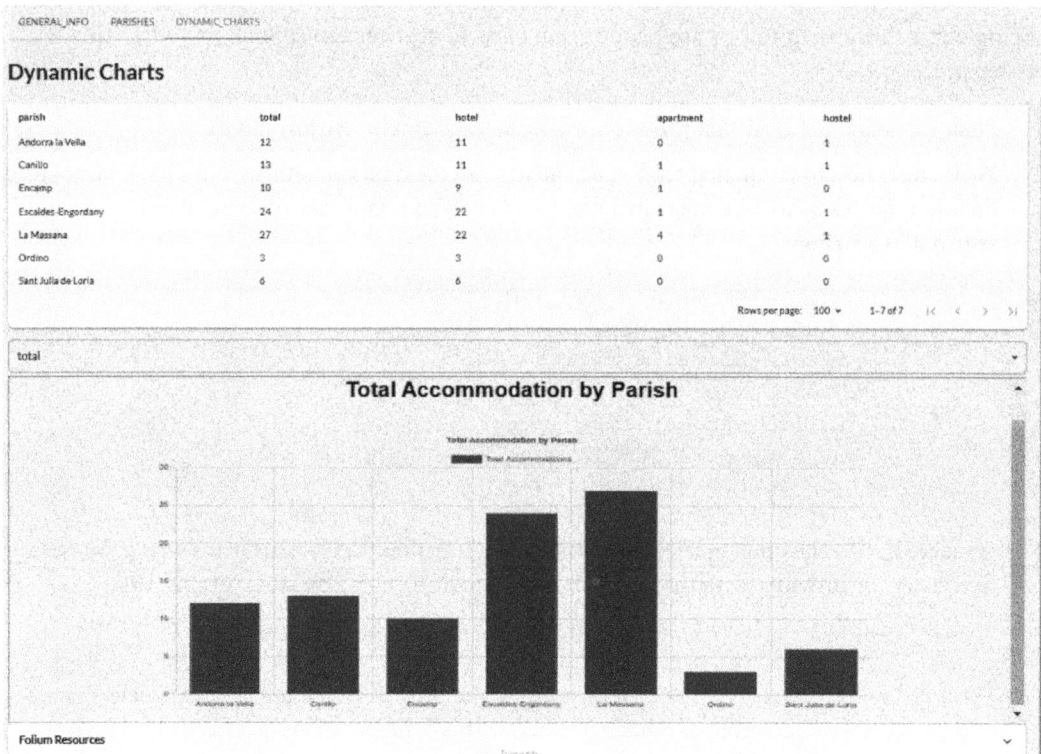

Figure 14.4: A `chart.js` dynamic chart

The code to create the element is in `/src/algorithms/js_charts.py`. We're not going to comment on the JavaScript code in depth, but here are some important remarks:

- We use `io.StringIo` to create an in-memory file object. The `_generate_chart_page` function creates this in-memory file object, and it's accessed from `JsChartClass.content`.

- The `_generate_chart_page` function creates a complete HTML file. It includes a `<style>` section for styling, an `<h1>` header for the title, and a `<script>` that contains the code to generate the chart.

- We add variable content using Python—`dict_data` is a dictionary that we build from the `accommodation` DataFrame. We add it as a string to `const parishData` (this "simulates" JSON data):

```
s.write("""<!DOCTYPE html>
# HTML content
...
    const parishData = """
)
s.write(str(dict_data))
```

- We also add the accommodation type, with the `accommodation` Python variable, to the JavaScript data object to create the `parishData.accommodation_type` array (where `accommodation_type` can be `total`, `hotel`, `apartment`, or `hostel`).

Once we have our class, we create our registration function, which just needs to return the input, since it's already a file object (unlike the Folium map object). Here is how the function looks:

```
def expose_js_chart(chart_element: JsChartClass) -> str:
    return chart_element.content
```

The way we register it in the `main.py` page is the same as for the Folium map example. We use this component in `/src/pages/dynamic_chart.py`. Our chart is a dynamic component that accepts two variables, the `df_parish_info` DataFrame, and the `accommodation` variable. We also add a drop-down selector to change the accommodation type and update the `chart.js` chart accordingly, like this:

```
tgb.selector(
    "{accommodation}",
    lov="{accommodation_type}",
    dropdown=True
)
tgb.part(
    content="{JsChartClass(
        df_parish_info, accommodation
    )}",
    height="500px"
)
```

Summary

In this chapter, you learned how to enhance your Taipy application with frontend elements, ranging from simple static pages and widgets to advanced components powered by the backend. While Taipy's core elements meet most of a data specialist's needs, the ability to add external or custom elements provides an extra touch—like the perfect seasoning that elevates a dish!

All the external elements we covered allow for the backend to update the frontend. These updates can come from user interaction with Taipy components (buttons, selectors, etc.), but users won't be able to interact with the backend using these custom elements. Taipy has an extension mechanism (https://docs.taipy.io/en/release-4.1/userman/gui/extension/) that allows you to create custom visual elements using React JS, so you can interact both ways with the app via sockets. While this is a powerful capability, it requires a good knowledge of React and it's out of this book's scope.

You are now able to create complete data applications using Taipy! Congratulations!

In the next chapter, we'll discover Taipy Designer, a drag-and-drop GUI builder that's part of Taipy's Enterprise version.

Questions

1. Can you add Andorra's anthem (`https://nationalanthems.info/ad.htm`) to the `general_info` page? Can you find other widgets and content to explore? (The goal of this exercise is to look for widgets to see what's "out there" and how it renders in your app.)

2. Improve the app's map. Show the accommodation within the selected parish (same selector as for the Wikipedia pages), and add some widgets to the Folium map (check Folium's documentation!), maybe a Geocoder and a fullscreen button, and remove the marker cluster.

3. Embed a pydeck map (`https://deckgl.readthedocs.io/en/latest/index.html`) showing the total accommodation by parish. We provide a notebook that creates the pydeck map in `/create_geojsons/pydeck_map.ipynb`.

Answers

1. You'll find an answer in `/src/answers/answer_1`. To add Andorra's anthem to the `general_info` page, download the MP3 file in the `iframes` directory, and add the following line of code:

   ```
   tgb.part(page="./iframes/ad.mp3", height="350px")
   ```

   Your browser should display a media player. You can now listen to Andorra's anthem anytime you want!

2. You'll find a file with the changed Folium map object in `/src/answers/answer_2`. Since the class now has an extra input variable, you'll need to add it to the `part` element as well, like this:

   ```
   tgb.part(content="{FoliumMap(gdf_accommodations, parish)}",
            height="350px")
   ```

3. The `pydeck_map.py` file in `/src/answers/answer_3` shows how we create the class and the `expose_deck_map` functions. They look like the Folium map one. Note how we use `deck_map.map.to_html(temp_file.name)` in the `expose_deck_map()` function, because pydeck's method to create files is `to_html()` (instead of `save()` for Folium).

Then, you just need to import it in `main.py` and register it:

```
from answers.answer_3 import DeckMap, expose_deck_map
...
Gui.register_content_provider(DeckMap, expose_deck_map)
```

You can add your pydeck map anywhere you want using the part element:

```
tgb.part(content="{DeckMap(gdf_parish_info)}", height="800px")
```

Unlock this book's exclusive benefits now

Scan this QR code or go to packtpub.com/unlock, then search this book by name.

Note: Keep your purchase invoice ready before you start.

15

Exploring Taipy Designer (Enterprise Version)

In earlier chapters, we explored how to build applications using the free and open source Taipy library. This version is ideal for a wide range of use cases, from personal and educational projects to prototypes, lightweight applications, and research tools. Behind Taipy is a dedicated team and company that also offers a commercial version: **Taipy Enterprise**. In this chapter, we'll look at what the Enterprise edition offers and introduce one of its key components: **Taipy Designer**. This tool is available for on-demand testing (one-month free trial), and this chapter will guide you through installing the trial version and give you a quick tour of its capabilities.

Adopting new technology in mid-to-large organizations is no simple task. These companies often have complex ecosystems of existing systems, strict internal policies, regulatory constraints, and the need for scalable, high-performance solutions. Their workforce has a variety of technical skills, which can make onboarding new tools challenging. Having a drag-and-drop application builder enables new team members to collaborate in the construction of new apps (without taking the Python GUI builders away from more experienced developers!)

In this chapter, we'll cover the following:

- Discovering Taipy Enterprise
- First steps with Taipy Designer
- Creating a demo application using Taipy Designer

Technical requirements

You can find the complete code used in this chapter in the GitHub repository: `https://github.com/PacktPublishing/Getting-Started-with-Taipy/tree/main/chapter_15`. We'll use GeoPandas to create leaflet maps, but you don't need to have a deep understanding of the library.

Discovering Taipy Enterprise

In this section, we'll provide a brief overview of the features and components included in Taipy Enterprise, specifically designed to meet the needs of corporate environments. Let's see some of them!

- **Taipy Designer**: This is a no-code drag-and-drop app builder, which we will present in the following sections of this chapter. This is an extra UI builder; you can also create apps with the Python API, as we covered throughout the book!

- **Charts and UI components**: The Enterprise edition offers extra visual elements, such as Excel-like tables, dynamic visualizations, and e-charts. It also includes a 2D graphical editor.

- **Improved scenario capabilities**: The Enterprise version supports scheduling and job queuing and has scenario history features that can take your analytical pipelines way farther in complex business environments.

- **Notification between users**: This is an extra feature that allows users to collaborate in multiple-user apps.

- **Authentication and authorization**: The Enterprise edition includes native authentication, Active Directory integration, and **single sign-on** (**SSO**), along with robust role-based access control. This allows you to display different pages to different users and customize or restrict visual elements based on user roles.

- **Deployment and integration**: You'll get support to deploy your apps in different infrastructures, such as Azure, AWS, Heroku, and Kubernetes. Enterprise also supports integrations with Databricks, Snowflake, Dataiku, and Amazon Sagemaker. Taipy is also a validated Databricks Technology Partner (`https://taipy.io/blog/taipy-a-validated-databricks-technology-partner`).

- **Dedicated support**: Getting the Enterprise version means you'll get full dedicated support from Taipy's team.

- **Distributed computing**: Enterprise supports both horizontal and vertical scaling, thanks to clustering capabilities for performance and scalability. You can define clusters to use to run your heavy jobs and distribute the load.

- **Observability**: The Enterprise edition offers OpenTelemetry-based telemetry to monitor your apps.

- **Version control**: Taipy Enterprise offers tools for versioning the application's logic, the data pipelines, and also for migrating from one version to another.

- **Collaboration**: Taipy Enterprise allows unlimited developer seats and unlimited end user access with Taipy support.

It's important to know that you can deploy the free version of Taipy in production environments as well, and you can extend it to incorporate custom visual elements (we saw this in *Chapter 14*), integrate your schedulers (we saw this in *Chapter 13*), and other custom systems! Partnering with the Taipy team and offloading parts of the infrastructure, such as deployment or observability, can often be more cost-effective than handling everything in-house, especially if your team lacks the time or expertise to set and maintain complex custom solutions. You have the information, now it's up to you to decide!

In the next sections, we'll cover how to test and use Taipy Designer, the no-code application builder. Let's look at it!

First steps with Taipy Designer

Taipy Designer provides a UI for users to build applications, adding components manually (by "drag and drop"). The tool targets an audience of analysts with no (Python) code experience, who want the freedom and flexibility offered by Taipy and the Python ecosystem to create dashboards and decision support applications using their domain knowledge.

Taipy Designer gives an extra option to your team to build UIs with a drag and drop interface; it doesn't provide extra Scenario Management tools, but you can make apps that run `Orchestrator()` for scenario manager. In this section, we'll cover how to install and how to start using Taipy Designer. Let's go!

Installing Taipy Designer

In this section, we'll install Taipy Designer. First, you'll need to request a free trial from Taipy's team. Go to the designer page (`https://taipy.io/designer`) and look for the **Request a Demo** button. You'll need to book a call with the team, and they can then send you a free trial of Taipy Designer.

You'll receive Taipy Designer in a compressed file (`.tar.gz`). In this chapter, we are using the `taipy_designer-1.2.2` version. To install it, we recommend that you start by creating a new environment. Then, go to the directory containing the file and install it without decompressing the file, like this (replace `<version>` with yours, but you're just passing the filename to the `pip install` command):

```
pip install taipy_designer-<version>.tar.gz
```

Since Taipy Designer is an extension, you also need to install Taipy in your environment. Once it's installed, we'll create our first app. Let's look at that.

Launching Taipy Designer

Taipy designer uses a special `.xprjson` extension to keep the GUI (the Page element) definition. When we use Designer, we use the `Gui` class exactly like with the Python application builder, but we pass a different `Page` instance to it. The `taipy.designer` package has a dedicated `Page` class, which takes the name of an `.xprjson` file as an argument.

Let's launch our first app builder. The code for this example is in `/hello_designer`. In the following example, the application will automatically create the file using `Page("hello_designer.xprjson")`:

```python
from taipy import Gui
from taipy.designer import Page

if __name__ == "__main__":
    page = Page("hello_designer.xprjson")
    Gui(page).run(design=True)
```

We run this app with `taipy run hello_designer.py` (or any other method that remains the same when using Designer), and we get a display like the one in *Figure 15.1*. The `run` method gets a `design=True` parameter to activate the drag-and-drop Designer mode. Once you finish building the app, you can remove this argument, and the app will render.

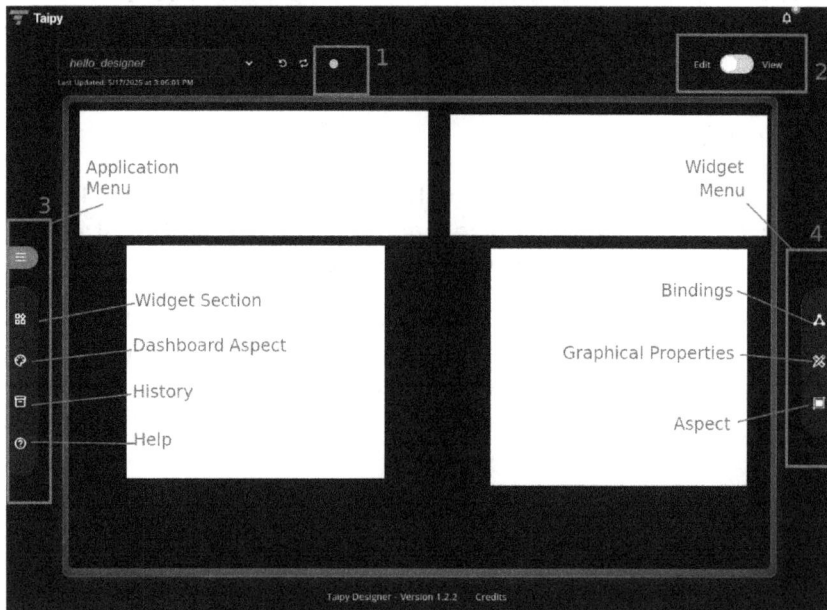

Figure 15.1: Application builder (1: Server status, 2: Edit/View
switch, 3: Application menu, 4: Variables menu)

Figure 15.1 shows the builder. At the top left, you'll see a green (or red) dot, which indicates whether our server is running. In the top-right part of the application builder, there is a toggle button to test your app as you build it. The left side menu has all the sections to build your application: you can add widgets (visual elements) to your application and change its style and layout. The right menu has sections to edit widgets (you need to add widgets to your app first and select them). This section allows us to bind variables, customize widget properties, and adjust their visual appearance.

Before we move forward, we suggest you look at the widgets, try to add them to the app, and explore all the menus. We also suggest you look at the .xprjson file; you won't ever need to directly interact with it, but this will help you understand how the builder works. In the next section, we'll build a small converter app and discover all the menu sections.

Creating a small app with Taipy Designer

In this section, we'll discover the main components of Taipy Designer by creating a small currency converter application. We'll discover how to add visual elements to our UI and how to bind them to variables; we'll also see how to style the pages with the designer.

The first thing is to create the Taipy application. We create two variables, with the conversion rate of US dollars to Euros, and Euros to US dollars (which we calculate as 1 / usd_to_eur_rate). We also create an on_change callback that transforms the eur_to_usd_rate value if usd_to_eur_rate changes:

```
## Callback ##
def on_change(state, var, val):
    if var == "usd_to_eur_rate":
        state.eur_to_usd_rate = 1 / state.usd_to_eur_rate


if __name__ == "__main__":
    usd_to_eur_rate = 0.9
    eur_to_usd_rate = 1 / usd_to_eur_rate
    page = Page("converter_page.xprjson")
    Gui(page).run(
        design=True,
        title="converter_app",
        use_reloader=True
    )
```

Notice how we pass the use_reloader=True argument to the run() method; while design=True allows you to change the app's GUI, you won't be able to change the backend code if you don't set it up. Let's now see how we build a page around this!

Changing page style

We launch the application, and the GUI builder appears. First, let's look at our general styling options. In the left menu, click on the **Dashboard** aspect, as shown in *Figure 15.2*. We prefer apps with lighter colors, so we choose an appropriate theme (see *Figure 15.2, 2*).

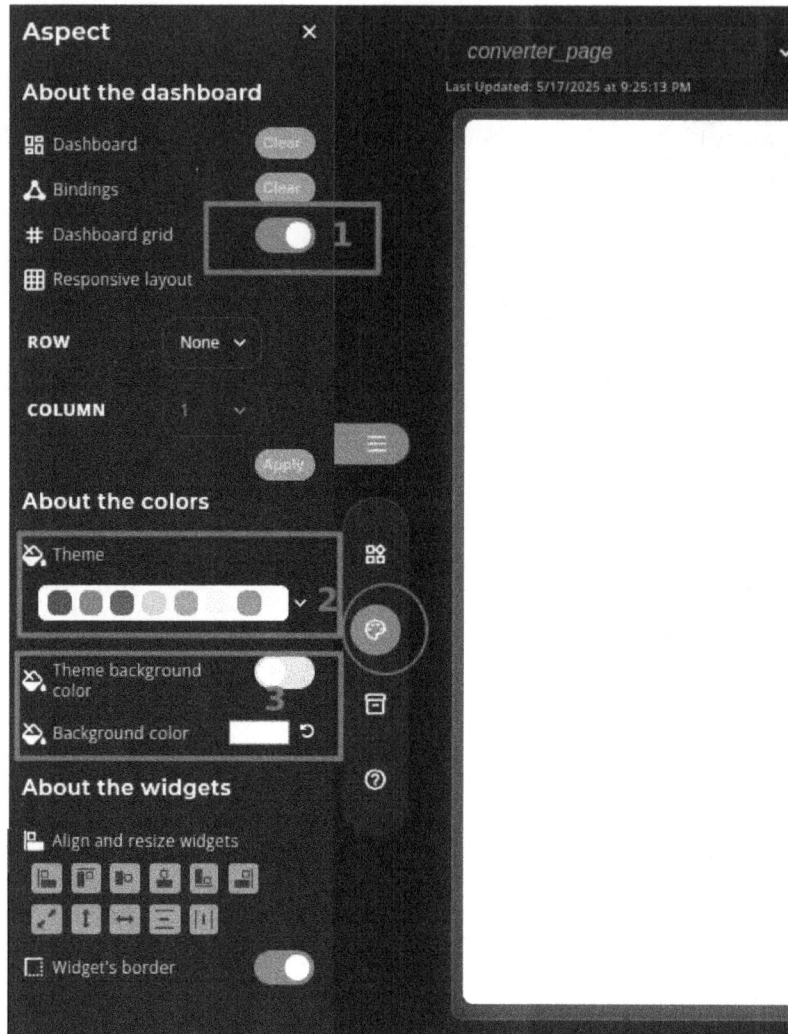

Figure 15.2: Styling menu (1: Show a grid for development; 2: Choose a theme; 3: Enable and choose a different background color)

As you can see in *Figure 15.2*, we can add a grid to help us organize the app's widgets. We can also set a background color, different from the theme's default (in our case, we'll stick to the default). Let's now add some widgets to our app!

Adding widgets to the app

The first widget we'll add to the app is a label. This is a text-based widget that doesn't bind to any variable and just displays some text. In our case, it will be the app's title. To add a widget, go to the left panel and click on **Widget**; within the **Widget** panel, go to the **Annotation & Video** section, and drag and drop a **Label** element in your app (as shown in *Figure 15.3*).

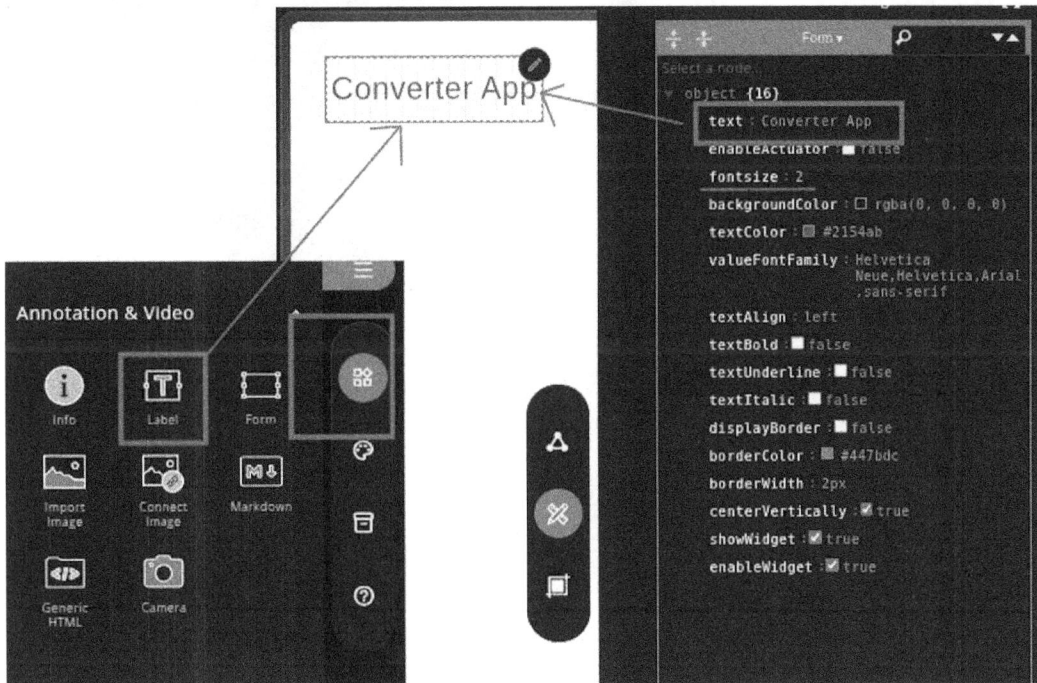

Figure 15.3: Adding a label widget (left pane) and changing its graphical properties (right pane)

To change the element's properties, click **Graphical Properties** in the right pane. You'll see a list of properties you can edit; this would be like the arguments of Taipy's visual element and their default values (excluding callback arguments). We add `Converter App` to the `text` property, and we increase the font size to 2, as you can see in *Figure 15.3*.

You now know how to add a widget to the app and how to style it; that's great! Let's add two more widgets:

- Add a **Horizontal Slider** widget; you'll find it in the **Basic Inputs & Controls** section of the **Widgets** panel (just like visual elements that let you change the values of bound variables)

- Add a **Value Display** widget; you'll find it under the **Basic Display** section (just like visual elements that let you display the values of bound variables)

Then, we can bind the variables. Select the widget and click on **Binding** in the right panel. You'll see a drop-down menu with all the variables that come from the app (you need to define them in your Python file).

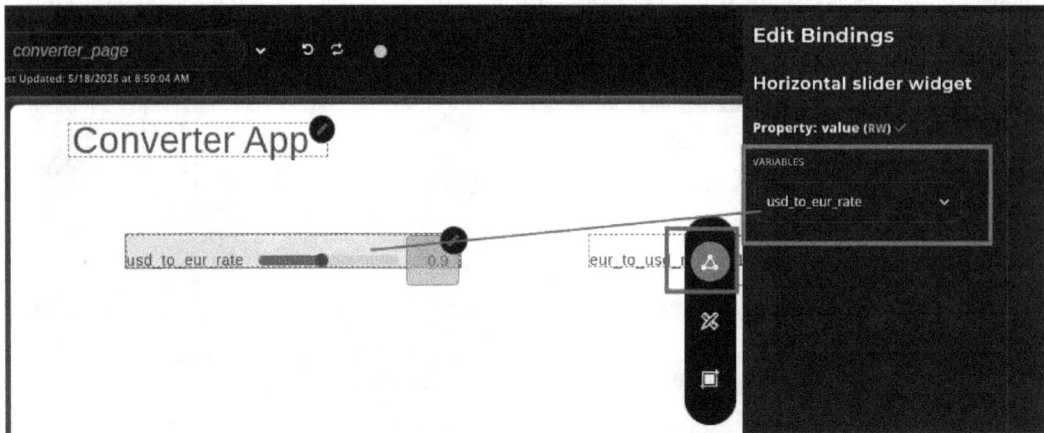

Figure 15.4: Binding variables with Taipy Designer

As you can see in *Figure 15.4*, we bind the slider to usd_to_eur_rate, and we bind the **Value Display** widget to eur_to_usd_rate. This is because our on_change callback calculates the Euro to USD rate from the USD to Euro rate. Save both values and click on the **Edit/View** toggle button. You'll see a display of your app. Move the slider around; the value in the display widget should now update as you move it!

> **Important**
>
> When we bind variables with Taipy Designer, we don't select a particular on_change callback function like with the Python application builder. You need to name your callback on_change and use the var argument to know where the call comes from to change other values (buttons bind to a callback function instead!)

If you play with the app for a little while, you'll see that setting the USD/EUR rate to 0 will raise a 0 division error. Let's now select our widget and edit its graphical properties:

For the horizontal slider, make the following edits:

- Rename the label to USD/EUR and set labelFontSize to 1 to improve display for end users.

- Change the min value to 0.001, to avoid 0 division values.

- Change the max value to 2 (or another value that you think makes sense, but maybe not the default 100). This will create a better range for end users.

- Change the step to `0.001` so users can select a realistic conversion rate.

- For **Value Display**, change the label to `EUR/USD` and set `labelFontSize` to 1.

You should now have a working app (look at the chapter's `README` file to see the result). We could add input fields to convert any value based on these rates, which is what we asked in *Question 1* (at the end of this chapter)! Now, let's explore Taipy Designer a bit more.

Creating a demo application using Taipy Designer

To keep exploring Taipy Designer, we'll create a small application that lets users select a country (or all countries, or capitals) and displays the top 10 most populated cities for the selection. All the files are in the chapter's repo, in `/cities_app`. The data used in this chapter comes from the Basic (free) plan of the World Cities Database provided by SimpleMaps (`https://simplemaps.com/data/world-cities`). For reproducibility, a copy of the CSV file is included in the `/data` directory. You can see how the app looks in *Figure 15.5*.

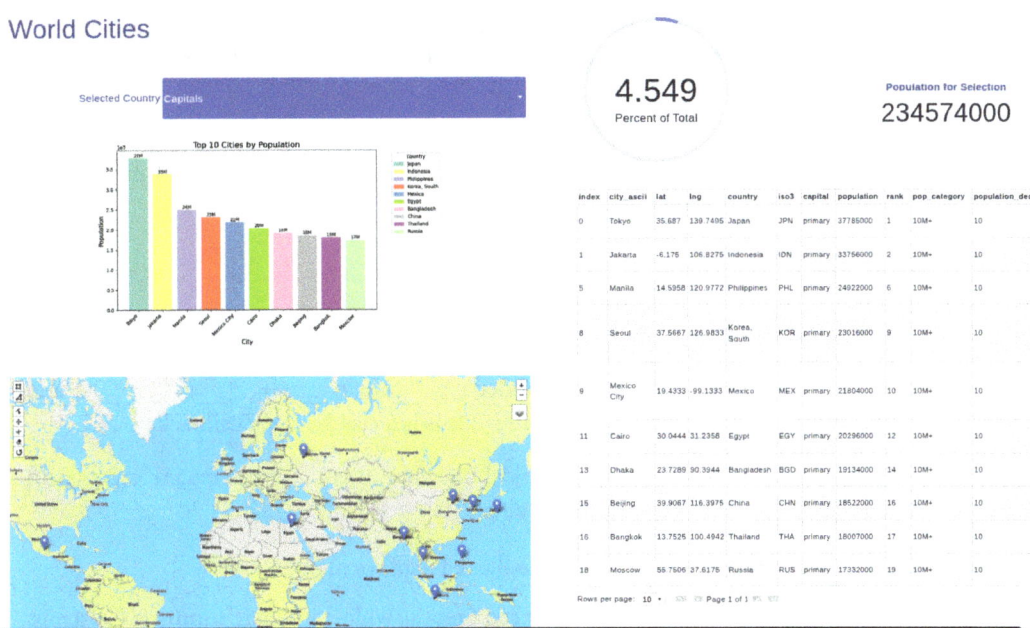

Figure 15.5: World cities app

The figure shows a selector at the top left, to let users choose a country to display the top 10 most populous cities (or fewer if there are not at least 10 cities). The display uses two metric cards on top (to display KPIs), a chart and a map on the left, and a detailed table to the right.

The Python code to arrange the data and to create the Matplotlib chart is in `algorithms/algos.py`; we won't explain in detail, but here is what the functions do:

- `clean_arrange_data` reads the data from the CSV file and removes cities with no population filled in or with less than 1,000 people. It categorizes cities in bins (<100K, 100K–500K, 500K–1M, 1M–2M, 2M–3M, 3M–4M, 4M–5M, and >5M) and orders them by deciles (we didn't use them, but maybe you can experiment and add more features to the dashboard).

- `plot_top_10_cities` creates a Matplotlib `fig` object, so we can add it to our GUI.

- `get_top_10` filters a DataFrame to keep the top 10 cities.

- `make_map` transforms the `cities` DataFrame and returns `__geo_interface__` (a GeoPandas object that describes geographic data in GeoJSON).

- `json string` means we can pass that string to the leaflet widget in our app.

> **Important**
>
> To add Matplotlib to a GUI, you need to add `matplotlib.use("Agg")` in your code before importing `matplotlib.pyplot`, so that it uses a non-interactive backend compatible with GUI frameworks such as Taipy.

The code in `main.py` has an `on_change` callback that triggers a `filter_by_country` function when the `selected_country` value changes:

```
def on_change(state, var, val):
    if var == "selected_country":
        filter_by_country(state)
```

The app defines all the variables for the application under `if __name__ == "__main__":` and updates them using `state` in `filter_by_country`; this is a classic Taipy callback.

The rest of the app is built from the Designer graphical interface. If you remove `main.xprjson` and want to rebuild the app, here are the important elements:

- **App title**: The **Value Display** widget from the **Basic Displays** menu.

- **Selector at the top left**: Select the widget; you can find the widget in **Basic Inputs & Controls**. We bind it to `list_country_selection`.

- **Bar chart on the left**: The Matplotlib generic widget from the **Plots** section. We bind it to `top_10_fig`.

- **Map at the bottom left**: Leaflet JSON maps in the **Geo & Time** section. We bind the `Property: geojson` field to the `leaflet` variable.

- **Percentage of total card**: Full-circular gauge in **Basic Displays**. We bind it to `percent_world_cities`.

- **Population of selection card:** The KPI value in **Basic Displays**. We bind it to `selected_cities_pop`.

- **Table**: The **Table** widget in **Basic Displays**. We bind it to `df_cities_display`.

You should now have an idea of how to use Taipy Designer and the value it can bring to a team with domain experts and non-developer business analysts. Feel free to add components and change the element's properties to explore Designer's full potential!

Summary

In this chapter, we provided an overview of Taipy Enterprise and the range of services it offers to businesses. You should now have a clear, high-level understanding of the company and the solutions they provide for scaling Taipy in corporate environments. We also introduced Taipy Designer, a no-code GUI builder that makes Taipy more accessible to team members with little or no coding experience. Taipy's goal is to bring applications to production, and Designer is a valuable tool for domain experts and business analysts. Taipy's Enterprise version extends the collaboration capabilities of teams by providing an extra no-code builder; it also provides tools (scheduler, secure authentication, server deployment solutions, or version management) that reduce the interactions that a BI department, a data science, or a data and statistics team would need with external departments, such as server administration departments. These extra tools, as well as the dedicated customer support, let Enterprise users create applications that are not only useful but also compliant with company policies and regulations (by managing user access, for example).

This is the final hands-on chapter of the book. In the next chapter, you'll find three insightful interviews with real Taipy users!

Questions

1. Can you add a numerical input widget to the converter app, as well as a drop-down menu and a value display, and a button so users can enter a value and a currency and convert it to another currency? Tip: check the documentation for the select element, to properly add the bindings: `https://docs.taipy.io/en/latest/userman/ecosystem/designer/wdg/wdg-basic-inputs/#select`.

2. Can you create an app that lets users select an item type from a drop-down list (say, technology items such as computers or smartphones), add a price and a description, and update a pandas DataFrame when they click on a button? Display the DataFrame in a table. Important: the button widget is bound to a callback function (don't use `on_action`; name your callback as you wish!).

3. Can you make a minimal app that uses the camera widget (`https://docs.taipy.io/en/latest/userman/ecosystem/designer/wdg/wdg-annotation-video/#camera`) and displays the screenshot it takes next to it (in an image widget)?

Answers

1. The answer is in /answers/answer_1. We added a GIF image to show how the app looks. First, we need to add variables to our app, so we can bind them to our visual elements:

    ```
    value_to_convert = 0
    converted_value = 0
    units = ["usd", "eur"]
    unit = units[0]
    ```

    Then, we need to add conditions to our callback. The goal is to calculate the converted value by multiplying the rate by the input value, and the rate is also user-selected, so we place it in a conditional statement:

    ```
    if state.unit == "usd":
        state.converted_value = (
            state.value_to_convert * state.usd_to_eur_rate
        )
    elif state.unit == "eur":
        state.converted_value = (
            state.value_to_convert * state.eur_to_usd_rate
        )
    ```

    Now, we just have to add the widgets and bind the variables. You can open the app and take a look at it.

2. The answer is in /answers/answer_2. We create variables to bind to different form items: a drop-down selector to display a list so users can select `selected_item`, a description variable to bind to a text input widget, and a price variable with a default 0 value to bind to a numeric Input. We also create an empty DataFrame, `df_items`, with columns but empty rows. We create a button and we bind it to an `add_to_dataframe` callback, which does the following:

    - Checks whether the input is correct, and returns otherwise
    - Creates a pandas DataFrame (a row) from the input values, and appends it to the existing `df_items`
    - Clears the input variables (to reset them)

    Reloads the bound variables to make sure the UI synchronizes.

    This small example could have used database connections to create a form to input data into tables!

3. The answer is in /answers/answer_3. We create a picture variable under main.py, which will hold a base64 string with a picture representation. We can bind the variable to both the camera (in Property: ImageData) and connect image widgets (under **Annotation & Video**). If you want to save your image as a PNG file, you can import base64 and decode the object like this:

```
image_data = base64.b64decode(val)
with open("output_image.png", "wb") as f:
    f.write(image_data)
```

Join our community on Discord

Join our community's Discord space for discussions with the authors and other readers:

https://packt.link/taipybook

16
Who Uses Taipy?

A different way to discover a project such as Taipy is by learning about real use cases and learning from the experience of current users. I wanted to end this book by sharing some profiles of current users with you. My goal was to ask for useful tips and to ask about real projects that involved Taipy. I selected three profiles from historical users of Taipy: *Zaccheus Sia*, a data consultant who works in the restaurant industry in Asia (who has also written some articles about Taipy), *Irv Lustig*, a USA-based optimization consultant (who is also a member of pandas' board – the Python library), and a data science team from *Les Mousquetaires* (a big European retailer and Taipy's first customer). *Vincent Gosselin*, Taipy's CEO, participated in the interview with Les Mousquetaires; I found it interesting to have his view as well.

I hope you like reading the following interviews as much as I enjoyed conducting them:

- Interview with Zaccheus Sia, data consultant

- Interview with Irv Lustig, senior optimization consultant

- Interview with Groupe Les Mousquetaires, data science department

> **Note**
> All interview participants provided informed consent for their content to be shared and used in this chapter in accordance with the agreed-upon terms.

Interview with Zaccheus Sia

This interview took place on August 13th, 2024.

Hello, Zaccheus. Can you tell me about your background?

My background and interests are in data. I started working with my current company to work on forecasting for one of its products. We develop workforce scheduling software. Part of this involves having a good sales forecast. That's why I joined the company. I discovered Taipy through this company. They had good relations with Vincent [Taipy's CEO], and they started using it. I specifically used Taipy to quickly develop applications to show and deliver our products to clients.

You discovered Taipy at work. Is it part of your regular toolbox?

Yes.

When you talk about "clients," do you have outside clients? Is it consulting, or are they other departments of your company?

It's sort of both. Sometimes, I do a small visualization tool internally for our teams. Some of our products are specifically for forecasting, without the workforce element.

Have you used products other than Taipy for this?

I used Streamlit for web applications quite a long time ago.

That's interesting. Have you seen big differences between Streamlit and Taipy? Taipy introduced a Python syntax in version 3. What do you think about it?

I feel like Taipy is easier because sometimes Streamlit does unexpected things. When we do very simple things, I like Streamlit because it's very easy to get started, and it looks good. But I feel that I end up stuck pretty often, and don't know how certain things work. With Taipy, there is a bit of a steeper learning curve, but once you get over that learning curve, it's easier. It's more intuitive for me as a developer and more predictable. I feel Streamlit would be more suited for very basic things.

About the Python syntax – it's very useful. I know they are making some improvements there, such as changing the variable naming from within pages, which is a bit confusing and makes code harder to refactor as well.

Do you have some examples of applications you developed using Taipy?

Within my company, it's mainly sales forecasting applications. I have also developed some demo applications for Taipy's team, which were used to create articles (`https://medium.com/@zaccheussia/elegant-dashboards-for-python-ml-apps-using-taipy-gui-6e3c59d70a1f`).

Do you participate in deploying the applications?

No, I don't do that part. There is someone else who does the deployment.

Do you work for a big company? And how do you work with your clients once the application is launched? Do you follow up with them?

We are about 30 people. I don't directly interact with the clients.

If someone asked for advice on how to use Taipy, such as a new teammate, what would you tell them?

First, look at the documentation. I think it's much better today than it was before.

Maybe look at some applications I created and try to understand the essential concepts, such as variable binding and scoping. Those are the most important things for us. Also, understand callbacks. The way you call visual elements is pretty uniform. I think that's good – if you understand one, you can understand the rest.

Do you use Taipy's Orchestrator?

We stay more on the GUI side. We sometimes use the Orchestrator when it makes sense, but I want to go deeper into it.

I suppose it makes sense to use Scenario Management when you make modifications within an existing scenario, not as much when you create a scenario, execute it, and never modify it. In our case, we do more of the latter. When I use scenarios, it's more for their persistence, for loading that scenario later on in the future, and not so much for the orchestration part.

By persistence, I mean that with scenarios, when end users close the app and then re-open it, the scenario will still be there. I don't use the caching feature that much. I like that Taipy's nodes can "save" your CSV files and your Parquet files easily, and I can load them in the future.

What do you think could be improved? How do you see the future of Taipy?

I think that, right now, the big features are all present, at least for the last year. I've been using Taipy for a long time, and it's not always been like today; it was harder to use before.

I don't need big changes anymore. I think it's pretty complete. Of course, when new features are coming out, I like to try them and test them; it's always nice.

If I had to make a minor change, it would be cool to have more themes that you could select by changing a single line of code. Maybe "cherry" or "yellow" mode instead of just light or dark mode. This would be more for hobby projects because you would still have to customize your applications when you deliver them to clients.

Do you use the Enterprise edition?

I don't use the Enterprise version for now. Our company has Enterprise support, but I don't think we use Enterprise features.

Do you use Taipy Designer?

I have tested it, and I've played around with it. It was quite a while ago. The experience was very different. It was much better than I expected. I expected it to create a Taipy Markdown code, but it creates its own thing. I have not gone very far with it. I'm more comfortable with Markdown or Python syntax.

But I can say, I did not expect it to be that easy to use. I think Taipy Designer targets a different audience. Maybe it makes sense if you know that your client will want to make changes of their own, but I haven't used it in this context.

How do you see the future of decision support in your industry, and how do you see Taipy there?

I do workforce scheduling optimization for the restaurant industry (labor planning).

I think that when it comes to forecasting, there's always been a need for it. The new thing is that the methods of doing it are now more accurate and sophisticated, and that's why people like me have jobs! People need better forecasts. To achieve that, there will always be a need to bridge the gap and be able to present the data to users. Dashboards render better than PowerPoint slides.

I think there is a lot of value when I create an application for customers to use. This gives a larger scope to my job, other than just working on the data.

My team also develops applications in Java. Before having Taipy, we would have to create a REST API for them to consume our data. Taipy makes me more independent.

Especially in the early stages of a project, before you sell it as a product and want something to show, reducing the development time is critical.

Do you have more needs for real-time data or data streaming?

No.

Have you had problems switching from development to production amounts of data?

Not really.

If you had some advice to give to someone who is looking for a solution to manage their data, would you recommend Taipy? What advice would you give?

I'd say to check it out and see whether it works for you. It works for me. It doesn't take long to try it out. I think Python developers are usually excited to try new packages, and I'm sure they won't mind!

Have you had any problems with integrating Taipy with other libraries?

I had this problem, but it's been solved since. I use Plotly as a visualization library. When I used Streamlit, the thing I liked about it was how easy it was to just add a Plotly chart without having to add extra code. This was not the case in earlier versions of Taipy, but now it's a very similar experience. But maybe people who use other visualization libraries have this problem too.

Interview with Irv Lustig

This interview took place on August 13th, 2024.

Hello, Irv. Can you tell me about your background?

I have a BS and MS in applied math and computer science from Brown University in 1983, and a PhD in operations research from Stanford. My PhD advisor was George Dantzig, the father of linear programming.

Then, I was a professor at Princeton University for six years, and I became known for a fundamental contribution known as the primal-dual infeasible interior-point method for linear programming. I received an award for this.

I left Princeton because I got an opportunity to work for a small company called CPLEX, and I was employee 7 at the time. My task was to build a solver for optimization problems, written in C, that could be embedded and used on multiple platforms. Back in the 90s (this was 1993), PCs were getting better at computation, and there was a proliferation of scientific workstations from companies such as Sun, Digital Equipment, HP, Silicon Graphics, IBM, and so on. So, portability across all of these platforms was essential. I spent four years as a developer bringing everything I had learned at university into CPLEX.

After those four years, in 1997, ILOG, a French company, acquired CPLEX. ILOG is where some of the folks from Taipy worked at the time, such as Vincent Gosselin, the optimization expert of ILOG in Singapore, and Fabien Lelaquais. At ILOG, I moved into product marketing, and after four years, I moved into sales. In 2009, IBM acquired ILOG. I was the vice president of ILOG and responsible for all the sales and marketing of ILOG's optimization products, including CPLEX and visualization. Occasionally at that point, I was doing some consulting as well.

At IBM, for the first three years, I worked trying to integrate ILOG's optimization business into IBM, then I joined IBM Research and did some internal consulting there.

About 10 years ago, I joined Princeton Consultants because I wanted to experience the other side and do some "real" consulting. My role here is to head up most of our sales of optimization-related projects, and I also get involved in the architecture and implementation of those projects. So, I end up doing both technical things and business development. We have done optimization projects for a wide variety of industries, for big and small clients. We've used Taipy in two of them.

I found out about Taipy from people at Gurobi, which is an optimization software vendor with a lot of former CPLEX employees. I thought it was a great idea to just write my Python code and not need to code some Angular interface – do it all in Python, using pandas. I'm actually on the pandas Core Team. I discovered pandas in 2016, and it changed my life. It solved a big problem in optimization that dealt with data.

What did you like about Taipy?

Taipy recognized the value of pandas, and it was easy to create apps with it. I ended up doing a **Proof of Concept (POC)** for a client. During that time, I also contributed to Taipy and did a bunch of pull requests. The POC was eventually accepted; we won the contract, and we used Taipy for that application, which was a scheduling problem.

For the second project where we used Taipy, I had a junior consultant learn how to do a small app in less than a day. The application was just a bunch of tables on the screen, and a button that said **Optimize**, and it would show you the results on screen. All tabular, nothing fancy. Using Taipy here was very beneficial, because often in our projects, we need to know whether we read in the data correctly and also be able to show the client the data they gave us. With Taipy, this was quick and easy because we do everything with pandas. This is why I'd like to use Taipy in more projects shortly.

I have a background in computer science for 40+ years, and I understand a lot about software. I have experience developing CPLEX; we needed a robust piece of software that worked on multiple platforms. I also understand the big picture of analytics, I'm a Certified Analytics Professional, and I know what optimization and machine learning are, how to apply them, and how to be successful in a business context.

Would you say you have both technical and functional skills?

Yes, technical, and functional... And I would even add the application side. Tools such as Taipy or Gurobi are means to an end. You want to develop applications that add value to your customers, that are going to change how people work, that are going to make better decisions, such as saving money, increasing revenue, and saving time. There are all sorts of metrics people use. All that comes from the optimization area.

I read your article about one of the applications where you use Taipy (`https://www.princetonoptimization.com/blog/blog/accelerating-agile-optimization-solution-development-taipy`)**. Was it to do better project management?**

This project is subject to some confidentiality, but I can say that, in this firm, they had to plan a schedule for about 1,300 projects. In October and November, they plan all the things for the following year. Each of these tasks has a planned amount of time of resources that they will need. Each project has a manager who may have more than one project at once, but also has a limited number of projects at the same time. On top of all this, some workers need to be assigned to the project, so one project may require two people, another project six people, and so on. The people who are assigned also have a limit on how many projects they can do at one time. The goal is to take all these constraints and try to figure out a schedule that works for the following year. That's the optimization problem; it's a scheduling problem.

During this project, we used an Agile development methodology. For each sprint, we had to show that we were pulling the data correctly. We also had to make sure the data from our end was correct – for example, the limit of how many projects a manager or an employee could handle. These were integers that were in databases that we created; this data did not come from our client's databases. At each sprint, we had new information to show to our client, and we needed to put this on a screen, quickly. We did all this with Taipy. By using Taipy, we were able to show, during the development process, that we were accomplishing the various requirements that were in the sprints. The client could see the requirements on the various screens. We had a screen with all the imported data, screens for the data they could enter, and a screen with the outputs, such as Gantt charts or the workload by person.

Also, some of the projects from one year could be extended to the following year, so you had to take that into account. The other problem was that as the year developed, some projects were already in motion, some were finished, and some were about to start. And things may have deviated from the plan – maybe projects needed more people, maybe they took longer – so you need to be able to recalculate your schedules every so often, to add this updated information.

We built the UI with Taipy, but we also built the backend with Taipy to manage the Jobs.

The interesting thing that happened with the UI is that the client had UI standards. They could not use Taipy's UI, so they built their own Angular application, and we created a REST API for them to consume the data. On the backend, it was still using Taipy. It's worth noting that their UI application was always behind our version developed with Taipy; it always took them longer to develop. But thanks to Taipy, we were able to show during each sprint that everything was working, even if they ended up creating their own UI.

Did you use Taipy REST for this task?

We couldn't use Taipy REST; we had to build our own, which was more at a business level.

Taipy's API is a lower-level API. Its objects are Taipy objects. If you're building your UI, you need higher-level objects, such as the schedules. Everything in the backend was Taipy objects, but we had to build our API on top of them.

In the project you just explained, if I understand correctly, at each sprint, you were receiving new "logical conditions" to solve.

It would be like new requirements. There is a whole set of different constraints that affect the optimization, so at each sprint, we would implement a new set of constraints. This often included adding more data to our visualizations or building a new screen that allowed somebody to enter the data relative to the constraint.

Then, the business user (the Product Owner, in Agile terminology) could validate the sprint, which was important for us, as it allowed us to show that we were on time with our deliverables.

Can you tell me about the other project where you used Taipy?

The second project was for a paid POC; we were subcontractors. It was for a high-security environment where the primary contractor had access to the real information – we didn't. In this project, the primary contractor gave us proxies or analogies of the real data, and our goal was to create an application with that proxy data. Then, the primary contractor used this to create its application with the real data, but I don't even know what the end project was really about!

However, I can tell you the primary contractor told us the end client was very satisfied with the POC. We used Taipy to show that we were able to easily show the data and how it is ingested. It was very easy to deploy. We built a Docker image and put it on the cloud, showing that the display was all working. In this project, we only used the frontend part of Taipy, but it had a lot of value. The other valuable aspect was that I could get a junior consultant to do this very quickly. He went through the tutorials; we had our six or seven tables, and he built an app that displayed them pretty quickly.

To me, that is the biggest thing: being able to quickly build an application that gives you some understanding of the data. It doesn't need to be beautiful! I hope to use Taipy for a project soon, but one of the issues will be: how can we customize the application a bit more? Because, you know, the default tables are big, they use big fonts... I know you can customize them with CSS, but I wish this were easier on our end.

Do you think it would be useful to have a set of CSS templates that you can use for some specific projects?

Perhaps more guidance on customization would be helpful, especially when it comes to tables. For instance, how can we make large tables smaller to fit more information on the screen? A new client's existing application, for which we don't have access to the source code, is heavily reliant on dense tables with small fonts to display large amounts of data at once. Clear examples of how to achieve this would be valuable. The flexibility is there, but more practical demonstrations would make it easier to implement. Ideally, customizing the display should be as straightforward as writing the Python code.

So far, Taipy has proven to be an effective tool. What remains to be tested is its viability in a production setting for an optimization application. In a previous project, the UI was built in a way that made Taipy unsuitable. For another, we conducted a POC that wasn't intended for production. However, with this new project, visual presentation will be a key factor.

One of the claims of Taipy is that it is production-ready. What are your thoughts on that?

It is production-ready, as long as you're comfortable with the default look and feel. The question is, how many clients will actually find that acceptable? I honestly don't know.

Have you tried Streamlit or other libraries?

We have our own platform for building UIs, where we control both the frontend and backend, including Scenario Management and optimization. The reason I used Taipy was that it handles this aspect as well. All our optimization is now written in Python; we don't do Java anymore.

When you work with clients, they all have a database management system of their own. How do you deal with this diversity?

Generally, in optimization, there is some corporate database that is the source of truth. We pull information from that database, and we create our database for our application.

We started this project four years ago using MySQL, but a year later, the client requested a switch to SQL Server, requiring us to convert all SQL to the new dialect. Later, when they migrated their data to the cloud, they transitioned again – this time, to PostgreSQL.

For our optimization problems, we always need a separate database since optimization-specific data typically isn't stored in an enterprise database. For instance, if an optimization is set to run for a maximum of 10 minutes, that parameter needs to be stored separately. Managing this aspect becomes an integral part of the application's database structure.

When users use the application, they solve scenarios by changing parameters with the UI. For example, if a user solves the scheduling problem with five people instead of four, that makes the schedule because they have fewer resources for that task. The end user understands all these trade-offs; they can select a whole bunch of these parameters and generate many scenarios. Eventually, they will like a certain schedule. When they select it, the application will send that schedule to the client's database.

Do you keep a history of all the data?

We retain all data as an audit trail. Each time we extract data from the database, it captures a snapshot of the customer's system at that moment. However, since their data is continuously updated, any new information added after our pull won't be reflected unless we retrieve it again.

In the application I mentioned, tracking when schedules were updated was crucial. The company decided to re-optimize schedules every Friday, so employees were instructed to input all changes, such as staff availability or project delays, by Thursday. This ensured that, by Friday, the system could generate an updated schedule based on the latest data. Adopting this process required a shift in business practices; previously, changes were handled manually and communicated through messaging platforms such as Teams or Slack, making it nearly impossible to track updates systematically.

What other things, besides customizing the UI, do you think could be improved in Taipy?

I'd improve error handling. If one of the jobs fails and raises an exception, the app needs to handle that robustly.

One area where I'm uncertain about the best approach is handling frontend changes and sending them to the backend. I know they introduced long-running jobs, which have helped, but I'm not sure how robust it is. I need to test it further. That particular piece of code is already 10 months old, so there's a chance things have changed since then.

You said earlier that the learning curve is not very steep.

Yes, I like that I can get my junior consultants to code applications pretty quickly, mostly by looking at the documentation.

How do you like Taipy's documentation?

I think it's great. A few things are missing here and there, but overall, it's good. The walk-through tutorial is especially very good; it helps people get started!

And, you know, here is another thing to consider: If we have to code our applications from scratch, it takes longer. Taipy is a software company that provides documentation as part of the product; it's one of the reasons why you can code applications faster. On the other hand, we are a consulting firm, and we are paid for our time. If we create our own tools, we don't have the time to document them properly, so it means that if I make juniors work on the project, I have to do it with them because there is no documentation. If I make a junior work with Taipy, they go fast and on their own.

Once you deliver your projects to your clients, such as a Taipy application, for example, do you "give the keys" to your clients? How does the transfer happen?

There are different cases:

- Most often, the application ends in a support contract when it goes into production.
- In lots of cases, we also do knowledge transfer.

All of this depends on various factors, but it often relies on how the contract defines **Intellectual Property (IP)**. Sometimes, the IP stays at Princeton; for example, we have some proprietary applications that clients use. In those cases, it's almost always a support contract, because we keep the IP. Sometimes, clients request all the IP; in that case, there is usually a knowledge transfer. Then there is what we call "custom IP." It's usually some modules that we give to the client, but we reserve the right to reuse them for other projects.

Do you see Taipy (or other similar products) as a way to make it easier to transfer knowledge to your end clients?

It could be a way. For example, we use commercial solvers such as CPLEX or Gurobi. I always tell clients to go with commercial solvers, because they are better than open source ones. The reason is that commercial solvers have complete teams versus open source solvers that usually rely on one or two people... Also, commercial solvers have support, and they are well documented. Now, if you take Taipy, we could treat it similarly. They provide a service, they give support, their project is well documented, and they allow us to put our time where our core expertise is, rather than developing applications from scratch.

Do you have any other comments?

I want to use Taipy in a project soon. One of the challenges will be to develop a drag-and-drop menu, to be able to move elements across columns with just the mouse; I don't think you can do this with Taipy. We may need to develop our Angular plugin and embed it in the app. I guess we will figure this out as we go!

I know that if I need some help, I can raise an issue, and the team at Taipy will help; they are pretty reactive.

Interview with Groupe Les Mousquetaires

This interview took place on September 11th, 2024. I was invited to a meeting with the data science team of Groupe Les Mousquetaires, a major retailer in France, and Vincent Gosselin, Taipy's CEO.

Hi! Can you introduce yourselves?

Stéphane Leray: I'm the manager of the data science team at the Datalab. I'm here today with the part of my team that has been coding Taipy applications since the beginning of Taipy, about three years ago.

Théo Demessance: I've been a data scientist at Groupe les Mousquetaires for three years.

Sylvain Goulet: I'm also a data scientist. I work with end users, help them get familiar with the applications, and focus on the interaction of end users with the data science components of the applications.

Pierrick Perez: I'm a data engineer. I work a lot with Taipy, and I participated in the development of our first Taipy application.

Vincent Gosselin: I'm Taipy's CEO.

How did you discover Taipy? What was the starting point?

Stéphane: We developed a POC three years ago with our direction of finance. They needed an application that used AI algorithms. The POC was satisfactory, so we decided to bring the project to a production stage. The editor we were working with at the time wasn't able to adapt to our working environment, and there were some legal issues as well.

At the time, I knew Vincent, who told me he was working on this new tool [Taipy], but his company didn't exist yet (it was on the way). I believed in this project, and I advocated for it. My directors agreed to include Taipy as part of our technical stack, which wasn't easy because the project was just born and not mature. That's how it all began; we pioneered this technology.

Vincent: We saw this approach in other companies that started working with us in the early days. The common point was the migration toward Python, from Java and Scala patterns. I worked in that world for a long time, but I was tired of it; they're not very friendly languages. When we started working with Les Mousquetaires, they had some AI components written in Python, but they were also thinking about moving a big part of their data stack toward it.

At the time, you had two choices: either you opted for hard-to-maintain tools, written in Java, or you went toward lighter Python frameworks, which are good for prototyping but aren't designed for production. That's the global context in which we began our collaboration.

You were pioneers. Today, Taipy is a polished tool, but this wasn't the case at the beginning. How was that experience?

Stéphane: Yes, it was a bet we took. Data science was a new practice in our group, so we were building our stack. What Vincent showed us and the perspectives he offered went in the right direction. We took the bet. There were hard times, also on our part, as it was challenging to explain our management practices, but overall, the result is positive, and we're all satisfied with our choice of Taipy. Théo is a pioneer developer. He joined our team as an intern at the time; he was in the first wave of Taipy users, along with Florian, another intern who now works for Taipy.

Are end users satisfied with the feeling and the interactions they have with Taipy applications?

Sylvain: I've been in touch with one of the main end users for the last three years. These clients spent their time looking at Excel charts. They're very happy with the new application experience that Taipy delivers. Clients used to spend two to three weeks building forecasting scenarios; with Python, we are now able to automate part of this work, so there's been a big win there. As for the visual components, clients are happier each time we have new features. We benefited from features that the community demanded, such as the inclusion of dynamic Plotly charts. We also gained experience as Taipy developers, and we're able to create better apps for clients.

Vincent: Taipy's Scenario Management has also been an important improvement for end users. They're able to record the outcomes of the scenarios and compare them. It's brought a new way of working with forecasting models.

Is it easy to keep your applications up to date, or to introduce new features?

Théo: Yes, technically, it's easy. Our bottleneck is our internal procedures; all our apps go from development to QA, pre-production, and production stages. There are several teams involved, so it's not a fast process.

Sylvain: We also have dependencies, such as our data streams, and we don't always own this part of the process.

Pierrick: We also have an issue with the European GDPR, because as data scientists, we need to train our models on production data, which is harder to access and slows down our application development.

Vincent: Taipy Enterprise edition comes with version management features that make it easier to switch between development and production environments.

You said that your inner processes determine your production release schedules. I could see Taipy as a way to increase the team's control over the process, and therefore reduce the dependencies with other teams and the red tape. What do you think about this?

Sylvain: Yes, that's correct, we have more control over the application. The only dependency we still have is for deployment in production. With Taipy, we need to have fewer people involved in our projects, which highly reduces the cost of launching an application. Another important fact is that Taipy is a Python library, which makes it easy for new teammates and interns to understand the code, and it's easier to onboard people thanks to Taipy.

How do you carry on the observability of Taipy applications?

Théo: There are two parts to this question. First, you have all the logs and the information that comes from the inner work of the application: the results of the models and the jobs that the application runs. Our team takes care of all this information. Then, you have all the system logs. We run our applications in AKS containers.

Pierrick: Once our applications run in production, it's up to the DevOps team to make sure that the app is up and running; we don't access those types of logs.

Sylvain: The team is more independent thanks to Taipy, which also means that, when the clients see a problem, we need to be reactive, to see whether the problem is in the application, in the models, the data, the scenario... There is a higher feeling of ownership over the applications that we produce.

Vincent: Since the last version of Taipy [3.1.1], we have offered an observability module when the backend is run over clusters. For example, some customers need to run thousands of forecasts in parallel. They need to know what's going on, so Taipy generates logs. But it's restricted to the specific usage within clusters.

Do you have some examples of applications that you coded with Taipy? Why was Taipy a good choice?

Pierrick: The first application we coded, three years ago, was a cashflow predictor.

Vincent: This was an app for the direction of finance.

Sylvain: Now, Taipy has become a standard for our team, and we try to use a limited set of tools and technologies. We developed an electricity consumption forecasting application using Taipy. For a more recent project, an intern coded a Streamlit application, but we turned it into a Taipy app to limit the code base and increase maintainability.

You can watch Théo presenting the electricity forecast application here: `https://www.youtube.com/watch?v=Em7MtxCuvnY`.

You've been using Taipy for three years now. Was it easy to master the tool?

Pierrick: Yes, it was fast. Before we adopted Taipy, we had an app that was coded with Streamlit. We migrated it with the help of Taipy's team, and then we took ownership of the application. We also followed some courses with Taipy's team, and we're always in touch with them; they help us when a new version is published.

Sylvain: In my experience, I had to work with an intern, and there was no problem for them to adopt the technology. We started with adding some elements to an existing page, and then we moved toward deeper work with data science models. It's difficult to measure precisely how easy it was to adopt Taipy, because any application has a big part that's related to the data science models, not to Taipy itself. But overall, the whole process was quick. I think it's a good idea to start with the visual GUI part, and then move toward creating scenarios and optimizing models.

Théo: We had another intern who had to migrate an app from Streamlit to Taipy. He didn't know anything about Taipy. In three months, he was able to migrate it all. I'd say that in three months, you can master all the aspects of app creation with Taipy – this is the front and the back, including connecting to databases and working in an enterprise environment.

Pierrick: It's also important to keep in mind that all these projects include all the inner processes and the time we spend with the interns to go through them, as well as the time spent to ensure they write clean code and so on, which is what internships are about.

Sylvain: In the case of internships, which have limited timeframes, it's very practical to use Taipy to create POCs fast and show them to clients. Even in general, we're able to create applications quickly for our clients.

Vincent: This was an objective for us at Taipy, on the GUI side. Creating a simple low-code tool for simple POC apps isn't hard. But to have that for production-ready, scalable applications isn't a simple task. Les Mousquetaires is a typical case of a company that sometimes needs demo POC applications, where some of them won't satisfy the needs and will be abandoned, but others will become production applications. Our goal is to have the same stack to create both POCs and end-product apps.

You mentioned several times that you migrated Streamlit apps to Taipy. What's the reason? Was it a previous standard?

No, we chose Taipy because of the partnership we had with their team. Streamlit and Taipy are both good tools; each has pros and cons. Now that we have adopted Taipy, we start all our application projects with this technology, which we know well. We don't want to use two technologies for the same task. We used Streamlit shortly before discovering Taipy. We had a Java-based application builder that was heavy to use, and Streamlit helped us build prototypes. But today, we use a single tool, Taipy, which is Python-based. Streamlit was never a real company pattern, but a way for the team to start putting ideas together. And then we also had some interns who started a project with Streamlit, and we then moved it to Taipy to avoid multiplying the stack. In that case, students had learned Streamlit at school, so we let them start the project with a technology they were familiar with and then migrated it.

What advice would you give to a beginner who is starting to learn about Taipy?

Pierrick: Read the docs and start building projects. I think reading the documentation is the simplest way to get started.

Théo: Maybe it depends on the type of person. I prefer demos and tutorials; some others may prefer the documentation.

Pierrick: I think tutorials are great to get started, and maybe the docs are better to dive deeper into the technology.

Sylvain: Maybe it's a bit of a cliché, but I'd say data scientists may prefer to learn from tutorials and mess around, and data engineers may prefer to read the docs and be more structured.

Can you tell me how Taipy and Databricks work together?

Vincent: Les Mousquetaires used Databricks to store data before working with Taipy. They use Databricks both for data storage and to run jobs in notebooks or scripts. Taipy's Enterprise version has special Data Nodes that connect to Databricks. We also plan to create special tasks to run Databricks jobs (we're currently in development). All these developments reduce the data exchange between the Taipy application and Databricks for better performance. They also make it easier to interact with Databricks from a Taipy application.

Is there anything you want to add?

Vincent: I'd like to add that Les Mousquetaires was one of our first customers. There've been some challenges with the first versions, in terms of backward compatibility, things that broke with the version change... usual things with early projects. We now have a more mature product with better compatibility.

Sylvain: It's also true that we have good communication with Taipy's team. It was challenging at first because the documentation wasn't complete, and the community wasn't big; there were few resources. But their team was very reactive and helped a lot.

Vincent: In the years 2021 and 2022, we were happy with our community, but there was a big increase in mid-2023. Today, we have three types of people interested in Taipy (customers or open source users):

- The first type is Python developers – people who know Streamlit and want to try something else

- The second type is people who come from Java or Scala and want to move toward Python

- The third type is people who don't code or are just starting to learn Python – people who come from the BI world and use tools such as Power BI

In the case of Les Mousquetaires, it's the first two profiles, but we have seen more people come from the BI sector in recent months.

Unlock this book's exclusive benefits now

Scan this QR code or go to `packtpub.com/unlock`, then search this book by name.

Note: Keep your purchase invoice ready before you start.

Index

‹packt›

`packtpub.com`

Subscribe to our online digital library for full access to over 7,000 books and videos, as well as industry leading tools to help you plan your personal development and advance your career. For more information, please visit our website.

Why subscribe?

- Spend less time learning and more time coding with practical eBooks and Videos from over 4,000 industry professionals

- Improve your learning with Skill Plans built especially for you

- Get a free eBook or video every month

- Fully searchable for easy access to vital information

- Copy and paste, print, and bookmark content

Did you know that Packt offers eBook versions of every book published, with PDF and ePub files available? You can upgrade to the eBook version at `packtpub.com` and as a print book customer, you are entitled to a discount on the eBook copy. Get in touch with us at `customercare@packtpub.com` for more details.

At `www.packtpub.com`, you can also read a collection of free technical articles, sign up for a range of free newsletters, and receive exclusive discounts and offers on Packt books and eBooks.

Other Books You May Enjoy

If you enjoyed this book, you may be interested in these other books by Packt:

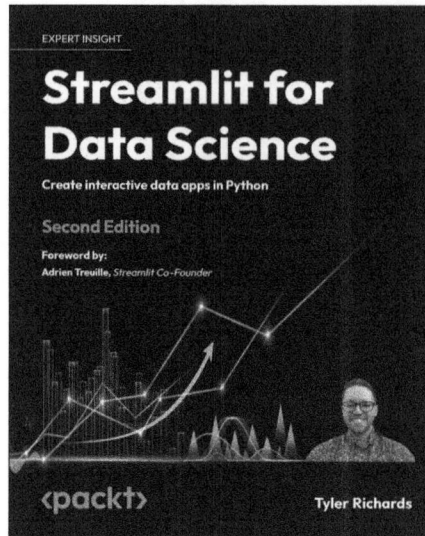

Streamlit for Data Science, Second Edition

Tyler Richards

ISBN: 978-1-80324-822-6

- Set up your first development environment and create a basic Streamlit app from scratch
- Create dynamic visualizations using built-in and imported Python libraries
- Discover strategies for creating and deploying machine learning models in Streamlit
- Deploy Streamlit apps with Streamlit Community Cloud, Hugging Face Spaces, and Heroku
- Integrate Streamlit with Hugging Face, OpenAI, and Snowflake
- Beautify Streamlit apps using themes and components
- Implement best practices for prototyping your data science work with Streamlit

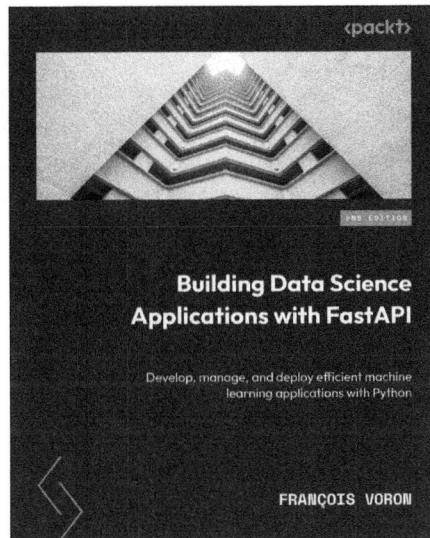

Building Data Science Applications with FastAPI, Second Edition

François Voron

ISBN: 978-1-83763-274-9

- Explore the basics of modern Python and async I/O programming
- Get to grips with basic and advanced concepts of the FastAPI framework
- Deploy a performant and reliable web backend for a data science application
- Integrate common Python data science libraries into a web backend
- Integrate an object detection algorithm into a FastAPI backend
- Build a distributed text-to-image AI system with Stable Diffusion
- Add metrics and logging and learn how to monitor them

Packt is searching for authors like you

If you're interested in becoming an author for Packt, please visit `authors.packtpub.com` and apply today. We have worked with thousands of developers and tech professionals, just like you, to help them share their insight with the global tech community. You can make a general application, apply for a specific hot topic that we are recruiting an author for, or submit your own idea.

Share Your Thoughts

Now you've finished *Getting Started with Taipy*, we'd love to hear your thoughts! Scan the QR code below to go straight to the Amazon review page for this book and share your feedback or leave a review on the site that you purchased it from.

`https://packt.link/r/1836203810`

Your review is important to us and the tech community and will help us make sure we're delivering excellent quality content.

www.ingramcontent.com/pod-product-compliance
Lightning Source LLC
Chambersburg PA
CBHW081045220326
41598CB00038B/6996